## ADVANCE PRAISE FOR THE REVISED EDITION
### *THE UNTOLD STORY OF MILK*

Dr. Ron Schmid chronicles the history of raw milk consumption throughout recorded time and gives us all a more clear perspective on what we have done to ourselves and precious raw milk in the last hundred years. In this most recent sliver of time, modern man has created superbugs, sterilized the food supply and suppressed the human immune system as never before. Diseases and human conditions never experienced on earth, with FDA-authorized drugs used to treat them, now kill hundreds of thousands each year and all of this after the onset of mandatory pasteurization. This book affirms that we are by nature "bacteriosapiens" that need a biodiversity of good bacteria, raw fats and essential enzymes to stay healthy. These essential elements are most easily consumed just by drinking raw milk.

This book will change your health and your life...guaranteed.

Mark McAfee, Founder
Organic Pastures Dairy Company

When we hear the words "conspiracy theory" related to governmental actions against a product, against consumer behavior and in this case against a food, in almost all cases they can be replaced with the words "controlling market share." When we use the right words, a clearer idea of what is really going on takes shape.

*The Untold Story of Milk* helps us understand how a product we value so much has become a commodity and an income base for an industry, which in turn has destroyed the very identity of milk as a wholesome food. Ron Schmid tells the story with accuracy and clarity.

Tim Wightman,
The Farm-to-Cc

D1131637

So many health problems are associated with the cheap, commerical, pasteurized, ultrapasteurized, homogenized, low-fat and no-fat milk products sold in supermarkets that milk itself has an image problem. The solution is "real milk," meaning raw, whole milk from clean, pastured, non-drugged and happy cows or goats. The problem is that the public has been warned repeatedly by medical authorities, dietitians and other "experts" that raw milk is dangerous, that milk fat promotes heart disease and that government regulations protect the safety of our milk supply. Ron Schmid not only thoroughly and responsibly addresses these controversial issues but also offers a fascinating history of milk, complete with a riveting exposé of government and corporate corruption.

Kaayla T. Daniel, PhD, author of
*The Whole Soy Story*

Raw milk is ultimately a freedom-of-choice issue. *The Untold Story of Milk* provides an in-depth look at the slanted science that political and economic forces have used to deny us our fundamental right to obtain the foods we choose to eat.

Pete Kennedy, Esq., President
The Farm-to-Consumer Legal Defense Fund

There are many stories that need to be told for the general well-being of individuals and of our society as a whole. The story of real milk—not the pasteurized, chemicalized, homogenized stuff for sale in supermarkets—is one of those stories. The story of real milk is the story of real agriculture, real food and real health. The story is ably told in these pages—read it, regain your health, get involved and become a voice for healing in our toxic world.

Thomas S. Cowan, MD, author of
*The Fourfold Path to Healing*

# The Untold Story
# of Milk

# The Untold Story of Milk

## REVISED AND UPDATED
The History, Politics and Science
of Nature's Perfect Food:
Raw Milk from Pasture-Fed Cows

## by Ron Schmid, ND
Foreword by Sally Fallon Morell

# The Untold Story of Milk

REVISED AND UPDATED
The History, Politics and Science
of Nature's Perfect Food:
Raw Milk from Pasture-Fed Cows

## Ron Schmid, ND
Foreword by Sally Fallon Morell

Cover Art:  Richard Morris

## NewTrends Publishing, Inc.
Washington, DC   20005

www.NewTrendsPublishing.com   newtrends@kconline.com
US and Canadian Orders (877) 707-1776
International Orders (574) 268-2601

Available to the trade through
National Book Network  (800) 462-6420

First Edition: 20,000
Second Edition: 10,000, 10,000

ISBN  978-0-9792095-2-9
0-9792095-2-8

PRINTED IN THE UNITED STATES OF AMERICA

To Elly

All truth passes through three stages.
    First, it is ridiculed.
    Second, it is violently opposed.
    Third, it is accepted as being self-evident.

                                        Arthur Schopenhauer

# Acknowledgements

My deep thanks go to the members of the Weston A. Price Foundation. The work of the Foundation—to restore nutrient dense foods to the American diet through research, education and activism—provided me with the inspiration to write this book. Without the effort and support of the Foundation's members, this untold story of milk would remain untold.

I'm particularly indebted to Sally Fallon Morell, founder and president of the Foundation. At her suggestion, I conceived and wrote this book, and her contributions—an idea here, a word there, a sentence here, a paragraph there—have been invaluable.

Three volunteers helped me discover obscure books and journal articles critical to my research, some available only at the National Library of Medicine or the Library of Congress. Thank you Diane Ducey, John DeRosa and Cory Mermer—you secured valuable material for me that would have been difficult for me to obtain without your help. Thanks also to Linda Forristal for her input on the milk industry, to Chris Masterjohn for his analyses of raw milk studies and research into Activator X, to Dr. Ron Hull for his invaluable professional expertise on raw milk, to Dr. Ted Beals for his expertise on milk testing, and to Katherine Czapp and Leonard Rosenbaum for their help in getting the manuscript to final form. My appreciation also goes to Dr. Mary Enig, who helped me sort out the science in the debate about homogenization.

I want to give special thanks to the farmers who produce raw milk and raw milk products from healthy, grass-fed animals. For those of us who understand the vital nature of these wonderful foods, you are central in our lives. Your courage and dedication inspire us all.

The five years since publication of the first edition have been especially difficult for many of these farmers as federal, state and local bureaucrats have attempted to restrict access to raw milk. It comes as no surprise that this crime is being perpetrated in a country where many of our national leaders daily demonstrate a blatant disregard for the rule of law and fundamental human rights. My heartfelt appreciation goes out to the men and women in government and the millions of concerned citizens who are committed to changing this situation and restoring democratic values in America. The survival of raw milk, as well as of prosperous small farms, depends on the success of their efforts.

The revisions and additions to this second edition of *The Untold Story of Milk*, particularly to Chapters 15, 16, 17 and 18, were the contribution of Sally Fallon Morell. Her tireless efforts leading the fight for raw milk are an inspiration to everyone involved in the movement.

Finally, I thank my partner in life, Ellen, for being the wonderful person she is, and the person whose love makes me whole.

Ron Schmid
January, 2009
Watertown, Connecticut

# Contents

# Foreword

Twenty years ago organic agriculture was a fringe movement, barely on the mainstream radar scope, a subject commentators treated with derision and politicians with scorn. Today organics is the fastest growing sector of the agricultural economy, a paradigm that garners tremendous public support, one that has proven a boon to many farmers.

Raw milk today is a fringe movement, a crusade of underdogs, a pesky mouse against the entrenched lions of medicine and industry. Who would be foolish enough to propose reinstating raw milk into the American diet? Or suggest that the agricultural model of the future will be the small farm with the dairy cow as its centerpiece?

In relating the untold story of milk, Ron Schmid takes us on a fascinating journey, one that starts with the beginning of recorded history and follows the cow as the economic unit upon which the wealth of nations—from Sumaria to America—was built. While those civilizations engaged in large-scale cultivation of grains became highly centralized, with great disparity between the ruling classes and the laborer, cultures that kept herds and drew sustenance from dairy animals fostered democratic ideals and a more equitable distribution of wealth. Dairy animals provided abundance and independence to Abraham and his descendants, and the dairy cow allowed the colonists of the New World to survive and prosper as independent yeoman farmers, freethinking agriculturists whom Thomas Jefferson recognized as the backbone of the newly emerging nation.

But milk is bad for us, say modern dietary gurus. It causes allergies and asthma, heart disease and cancer. No animal except humans drinks milk after infancy. Besides, we don't need it—many societies other than our own do without milk and are healthier than we are. Thus has the status of milk declined from Nature's perfect food to dietary anathema.

In the pages to come, Dr. Schmid describes the causes of milk's decline from a wholesome to a noxious food; confinement dairies, inappropriate feed, horrendous processing, removal of nutritious butterfat and addition of problematic compounds—all have taken their toll on milk's delicate nutritional balance. And these changes have occurred with the sanction of our highest governing agencies and the blessings of the medical establishment.

No one can read this book without realizing that the arguments against milk are specious; that raw milk and raw milk products have provided splendid nourishment for diverse peoples all over the globe; and that this once-vital food has been tarnished with the black brush of modern processing.

Yes, many cultures have prospered without milk. But these cultures obtain the nutrients concentrated in milk from edibles that rarely appeal to western palates, such as organ meats, blubber, raw sea food and insects; or that are time-consuming to prepare, such as bone broths. Non-milk-drinking peoples put a high value on guts and grease, foods that modern children often refuse to eat. But few youngsters need coaxing to drink delicious whole raw milk—which is rich in the very same critical nutrients that traditional peoples found in animal organs, animal fats and bones. Raw milk provides the welcome answer to modern parents, desperate to get quality nutrients into their finicky young eaters and mindful that children need extra protection against the junk food to which they are repeatedly exposed.

Only one force can reverse milk's decline and that is the educated consumer, the consumer who demands a quality product, a product that comes from cows on good pasture, that contains all the butterfat that nature put there and that has not been subjected to modern processing. As consumers are once again demanding pure and healthy milk, and have indicated a willingness to pay a fair price and even travel some distance to obtain such a product, farmers have responded by providing it—creating a groundswell that will eventually force regulators to abandon their unreasonable opposition.

The purpose of this book is to create millions of such consumers and by so doing revitalize family farms and local communities—because in the economics of raw milk lies the path to true prosperity, robust returns indeed compared to the dividends of stocks and bonds. No other investment promises such handsome income to the family willing to work. The cow on pasture produces approximately twelve hundred gallons of milk per year, for which farmers selling directly to the public receive five dollars per gallon—and this figure is conservative. On a farm of twenty cows, the gross income is about one hundred twenty thousand dollars per year. The farmer who starts a dairy by buying the cows outright will recoup the investment within two or three months. Farmers producing cream and butter make about the same amount per gallon as they do for fluid milk, but farm-produced yoghurt, kefir and cheese bring in four times as much, about twenty dollars per gallon. From the production of cheese, butter and cream, the farmer is left with a bonus of skim milk and whey, the perfect food for chickens and pigs, another source of income to add to the total. The major inputs to this tidy system are sunlight, which is free, and labor, which is the prerogative of the farmer.

Of course, the other side of this equation is customers willing to pay the farmer a fair price for his wonderful products. As our health crisis grows, and as the public becomes more desperate for answers, the demand for raw milk will increase. The despairing mother who gives raw milk to her autistic child and witnesses startling improvements, the laborer whose crippling arthritis clears up when he consumes raw butter and cream, the frustrated dieter who watches pounds melt away on an exclusive raw milk diet, parents who observe their children growing up robustly and easily on a diet bolstered by raw milk, asthma sufferers who finally get relief when they drink raw milk, vegetarians seeking a good source of the vital nutrients lacking in plant foods. . . all add to the growing body of consumers who refuse to be swayed by government admonitions and industry propaganda.

The day is fast approaching when no conscientious couple will dream of starting a family until they have found a source of pure and healthy raw milk for their children; when no town planner will proceed without first setting aside the most fertile land for the local dairy; when no doctor will omit raw milk as part of his or her treatment; and when no government official will dare to impede access in any way to raw milk and other pure foods.

Since the publication of the first edition of *The Untold Story of Milk* five years ago, we have moved from the first to the second state of Schopenhauer's timeline—from ridicule to violent opposition. As the raw milk movement has grown, so has the venom of government opposition—farm raids, sneak legislation, bogus reports of illness and arbitrary testing procedures define the latest tactics against Nature's perfect food. The official government position: raw milk is inherently dangerous and should be consumed by no one, especially not by pregnant women, children, the elderly and those with compromised immune systems.

Working in favor of this quintessential grass roots movement is new research showing the superior safety and health benefits of raw milk; the demise of the germ theory of medicine and the advent of probiotics; and increased consumer activism in the form of private milk clubs, cow-share and herd-share agreements and legal defense associations to defend consumer access to raw milk, especially for those who need it most—pregnant women, growing children, the elderly and those with compromised immune systems. This new edition includes expanded information on the science of raw milk and provides details on recent court cases and consumer activism.

Democratic ideals prospered among pastoral peoples and those democratic ideals can revive as we rediscover the value of pure, unprocessed milk. The roadblocks that have denied access to this life-giving food—government regulations and institutional prejudice—must give way to scrutiny as consumer consciousness expands. Are laws against raw milk fair and just? Are they even constitutional? Do they infringe on our right to freedom of religion and the pursuit of happiness? Or do they represent racketeering dressed up in the rhetoric of public good? The reclamation of our right to healthy food will lead to renewed awareness of our rights in other areas, rights that have been usurped by the steady accumulation of unnecessary laws. The ship of state needs to be careened and subjected to a good barnacle cleaning, and the raw milk movement can provide the first step in this purification process.

Raw milk is a movement whose time has come, one that will change our thinking and the shape of our society in a most beneficial way; already *The Untold Story of Milk* has served as a catalyst to this movement, and will continue to do so, providing consumers with the facts and inspiration they need to embrace Nature's perfect food.

Sally Fallon Morell, President
The Weston A. Price Foundation
January 2009, Washington, DC

# Introduction

*The cow is the foster Mother of the human race. From the day of the ancient Hindoo to this time have the thoughts of men turned to this kindly and beneficent creature as one of the chief forces of human life.*
William Dempster Hoard, 1885

In my early twenties, I moved to Martha's Vineyard. I was suffering from severe intestinal illness but holding on to the belief that I could find my own solutions to this intractable medical problem. I started buying raw milk at Fred Fisher's dairy farm in West Tisbury, drinking some fresh and using the rest to make yogurt or "clabbered milk." My intestinal problems mysteriously cleared up. Several years later I went on to medical school and became a naturopathic physician.

In the decades since, I've recommended raw milk and the foods you can make from it to most of my patients. I send them to Debra Tyler's Local Farm in rural Connecticut because she feeds her Jerseys only grass and hay, and I've found that makes for the best milk. I've never known one of my patients to have a problem with raw whole milk from grass-fed cows, though I've read accounts of people who have.

Over ninety-five percent of America's dairy farmers drink their milk raw. I've asked a number of them why, and the answers range from,

"Tastes better" to "Makes me feel good" to "Don't like store-bought food." Maybe they're on to something.

Did you know that raw milk and the products made from it shaped the cultures that founded western civilization? The earliest human artifacts include vessels containing residues of milk. Where people have traveled, the ox and the milk cow have followed. Rome was built on ground blessed by libations of milk. In America, the arrival of a shipload of cows saved the Jamestown colony from starvation. Cows went west with the settlers, hitched behind wagons pulled by their brothers the oxen, feeding families and calves alike. The bovine tribes have been our best animal friends for a long, long time.

Those contented cows fed on green pastures, and when the way cows were fed began to change in the 1800s, our relationship with bovines began to deteriorate. The decline began with distillery dairies and continued as cities grew. In those dairies, confined, diseased and abused cows were fed the acid waste products of the whiskey industry. The milk they produced often led to disease; the solution proposed was pasteurization. In recent years, we've seen the growth of modern confinement dairies, where cows never leave their stalls. Though conditions generally are not as bad as those of the distillery dairies, many of these cows are sick with mastitis and other chronic conditions. These facilities now produce something like seventy percent of our milk in the United States.

Many people want an alternative to modern commercial milk, and hundreds of thousands of Americans—perhaps millions—are drinking organic milk today. And a growing number are going to great lengths to obtain raw milk from healthy cows, while many more have grown curious about raw milk and want more information. Accurate information about raw milk can be hard to come by; advocates and detractors often appear at loggerheads and both sides are prone to erroneous and unsubstantiated claims.

The primary factor polarizing the climate, however, is the fact that many of the medical and public health officials who denigrate raw milk are tied to a system that demands compulsory pasteurization. As a result, in only a few states can consumers go to a store and purchase it; in just over half the states raw milk is available for purchase only at the farm. In a few states you can buy raw milk as pet food. In sixteen states all raw milk sales are outlawed. In Canada, it is against the law for a farmer to even give raw milk away—the penalty for breaking that law can be a two-hundred-fifty-thousand-dollar fine and three years in jail, although these measures are rarely enforced. In our final chapter, we'll examine the availability of raw milk and the legal situation in the various American states, Canada and Europe.

The very best milk comes from healthy animals that spend most of their time outdoors on fresh pasture eating lots of grass, supplemented seasonally by high quality hay, green chop, root vegetables and perhaps a little grain. Compared to milk from confinement cows fed mostly grains as well as various types of waste products, like leftover bakery goods and citrus peel, such milk is rich in a wide variety of nutrients. In fact, "summer milk," as it used to be called, is a completely different food from the milk generally available today. The differences will come into clear focus as we present our story.

The Eskimo languages are said to have over one hundred different terms to describe the many kinds of snow they experience in the Arctic environment. In similar fashion, we need more words for milk, for even if we consider only cow's milk, there are many, many kinds of milk besides the bland homogenized, pasteurized product available at the corner store or the supermarket. In fact, the milk from every cow is different, reflecting the genetics, feeding, environment and a host of other factors that affect the health and thus the milk of each animal. Raw milk aficionados appreciate these nuances, and taste the difference between summer milk from cows feeding on lush green pastures and winter milk from animals fed mostly hay.

The word milk itself has historically meant much more than the fluid beverage we drink today, whether pasteurized or raw. Until the middle of the 1800s, when the consumption of fresh, sweet, unfermented milk began to rise, most Americans, like Europeans, drank most of their milk fermented, soured into the yogurt-like food known as clabbered milk. But clabbered milk and similar drinks all were referred to as simply "milk," or sometimes "bonnie-clabber" milk. Even the "milk and honey" mentioned in the Bible is thought to be a reference to a form of fermented yogurt beverage. When we examine the importance of milk in earlier civilizations, including colonial America, it's important to realize that most of their milk was made into fermented drinks and concentrated products like cheese and butter; the drinking of fresh sweet milk was confined to children, milkmaids and farmers. According to many historical accounts of dairy food habits throughout Europe, "fresh milk was considered a luxury food. In fact, it seems that the drinking of fresh milk was the least important aspect of milk utilization overall." This was also true of traditional dairy-based cultures throughout the world that have survived into the twentieth century.

Fermented milk products, fresh cheese and butter were at the center of the traditional American diet as well. Americans consumed fermented buttermilk (equivalent to clabbered milk, with or without the milk fat), used it in cooking or fed it to hogs (four cows generally supported the feeding of one hog). "Buttermilk," that is soured whole milk, was particularly popular in the South. Although studies of milk's history often imply otherwise, drinking fresh milk did not begin to become popular in America until around 1850, when the need arose for a breast milk substitute and a food for weaned infants. Many of those demanding fresh milk were immigrants from Europe, where a similar transition was occurring.

There were many reasons why consumption of fresh milk became widespread. Many people had left farms and settled in cities, where poverty, poor sanitation and inadequate nutrition rendered more women unable to breast-feed successfully; others could not breastfeed because they worked long hours in factories. Poorly nourished toddlers who had been weaned also had a need for nutritious food. The problem was that the distillery dairies grew proportionally with the growth of the cities, and they supplied up to three-quarters of city milk. This meant that America's developing milk-drinking habit was beset with problems from the very start.

The rise in milk consumption was thus not inevitable, but rather the outcome of a complex set of social factors at play in nineteenth century America. By the 1880s, not just children in the cities but the population as a whole began to consume fresh milk, and by the 1940s it was a staple in the American diet. At the midpoint of that period, around 1910, many American cities had imposed a pasteurization requirement and by 1950, most milk was pasteurized.

Pasteurization had a great deal to do with the expansion of America's milk-drinking habit, and pasteurization provides the very foundation of the modern dairy industry. The manufacture and distribution of cheese and butter, accomplished in 1900 by tens of thousands of farms and small factories in every state, became, during the next fifty years, an industrialized process controlled by huge multinational corporations. Pasteurization made this possible and perhaps inevitable. We'll explore the history and implications of pasteurization in some detail; for now, suffice it to say that the reasons behind pasteurization were as much political and economic as they were scientific.

So the story of milk has many diverse elements, and like any story, this one reflects the particular viewpoint of the storyteller. My viewpoint is unabashedly in favor of free choice; I believe those who want to produce, sell and consume raw milk and raw milk products have a constitutional right to do so, and that the denial of that right by the government is a violation of our most basic freedoms. That viewpoint is shaped by elements of the history presented in these pages.

Ancient civilizations and the distillery dairies are part of that history, as are the stories of traditional dairy-based cultures that survived into the 20th century. The health enjoyed by the people of those cultures, their absence of chronic diseases, and the role milk played in their lives are subjects not widely understood. Yet they are highly relevant to a full understanding of the essential need for raw milk products in the diet today.

Also forgotten is "the milk cure," a highly successful method for treating chronic disease detailed in a 1929 article by one of the founders of the Mayo Clinic, John E. Crewe, MD. The article, entitled "Raw Milk Cures Many Diseases," is a fascinating account of how many physicians used natural foods, including raw milk, to tackle the problem of chronic illness in the years before the pharmaceutical industry persuaded doctors to use drug therapy instead.

History is one thing, and milk today is another. Confinement dairies, pasteurization, homogenization, bovine growth hormone—what do they do to modern milk? What made a renowned pediatrician write a book called *Don't Drink Your Milk*? What do dairy farmers think about dairy farming and milk production today? And what about those germs the public health authorities are worried about—how much of a threat are they? Isn't raw milk *dangerous*? What about pasteurized milk? Why does it cause so many health problems?

These are all good questions, worthy of considered and thoughtful answers. While I am an advocate for raw milk, I recognize that the public health authorities have valid concerns and a reasonable role to play. I also have some interesting details about how many "authorities" have abrogated their responsibilities to the public and acted dishonorably.

And what about cholesterol and saturated fat in dairy foods? You may quite naturally ask this question, given the generally accepted theory that animal fats cause heart disease. For many years I wondered too, and that kept me from fully appreciating fresh and fermented raw milk, butter, cream, eggs and meat. I finally made a thorough study of the cholesterol issue, and what I learned was very disconcerting, for the campaign against cholesterol has involved a betrayal of trust on the part of some of our most respected officials and institutions. I've written a chapter about that betrayal, and another to explain the information that convinced me that cholesterol and animal fats do *not* cause heart disease.

In fact, it's my belief that the best foods in the world are rich in cholesterol and animal fats. I call them vital foods—fresh and fermented unprocessed dairy foods, and eggs, meat and poultry from pasture-based farms. Pasture feeding is important because the nutrients just aren't the same when animals are confined and fed a lot of grains. The countryside isn't the same either.

When it comes to milk, fresh and unprocessed is important because raw milk contains enzymes. Enzymes are defined in medical textbooks as compounds essential to life; in milk they play numerous roles including protection from pathogens, support of the immune system, easy digestion and enhanced nutrient assimilation. Enzymes are vital, and they are destroyed by heat. Fresh and fermented raw milk is also important because it contains beneficial bacteria for our digestive tracts. Today we are witnessing an explosion of knowledge about the benefits of good bacteria. The six pounds of beneficial bacteria that inhabit the healthy digestive tract provide protection against toxins and disease, help digest our food, support nutrient assimilation and even produce feel-good chemicals.

While research scientists are busy revealing the benefits of enzymes and good bacteria, food engineers and medical personnel generally dismiss their importance. They will be the last to embrace the new paradigm, clinging to their phobias against live food while science leaves them in the dust.

In this book, we'll look at why the kinds of enzymes and bacteria found in raw milk are important to good health. We'll review Francis Pottenger's once-famous cat studies from the 1930s, Edward Howell's enzyme research, and recent studies on the myriad protective components in raw milk of all mammalian species. We'll find out why raw milk is not a health hazard but the safest food on the planet, and why for many its health benefits have been nothing short of magical.

A lot of people are fed up with the food situation today. My UPS deliveryman gets eggs from his cousin; he won't buy the ones in the store. Many people I talk to ask about where you can get a good, pasture-raised chicken. The local health-food store can't keep enough raw milk from Local Farm in stock. People everywhere seem to be looking for answers to questions about better and healthier foods.

For the past twenty-five years, I've tried to answer those questions for my patients. Many of the questions are addressed here, but the untold story of milk involves a lot more than just milk and health. It's also the story about why small farms in America have all but disappeared and why thirty million farmers have left the land since the end of World War II. You may wonder about that, and if you're like most post-Enron Americans, you may harbor a distrust of large corporations and perhaps suspect that the demise of small farms and the rise of corporations are somehow related. I'm particularly interested in the corporations involved in the agribusiness, food and pharmaceutical industries, and you may find your distrust growing as you read my story.

I think we're happiest when our sense of purpose is intact and when we feel that our place in the universe is secure and harmonious. Producing and using foods in traditional, time-honored ways is in tune with something that resides very deep in the souls of humankind. I like having top-quality raw milk in the refrigerator; I like to make my own yogurt, cheese and butter; and I like to grow vegetables and keep chickens. Going to farmers' markets and purchasing fresh cheeses, fruits and vegetables is a soul-nourishing activity.

Understanding what happened to milk, and knowing how to find good milk today, resonates with a surprising number of people. Perhaps as you peruse these pages, you'll find that you are one of them.

Part I
# Milk Yesterday

# 1
# Milk and Civilization

*And God said, let the earth bring forth grass. . . . And God made the beast of the earth after his kind, and cattle after their kind. . . . and God saw that it was good.*

Genesis 1:11, 1:25

*And the Lord said, I am come down to deliver my people out of the hand of the Egyptians and unto a good land, a land flowing with milk and honey.*

Exodus 3:8[1]

BEGINNINGS

At the mother's breast, the newborn tastes its first food, milk. The breastfeeding infant is a universal symbol of devotion and love. The food and the feeding, designed by nature as the perfect physical and spiritual nourishment for the young, rebinds the newly separated. Some of the earliest human artifacts tell us that the use of animal milk as an article of human sustenance has always carried with it the symbolic content of this primal maternal connection.

Historians usually link human consumption of animal milk with the cultivation of grain some ten thousand years ago.[2] Most treatises on the history of the human diet assume that animal husbandry began with the dawn of agriculture, making dairy products a relatively recent human food. But archeological evidence indicates that people in the High Sinai Peninsula at the north end of the Red Sea used fences for confining and breeding antelope for their milk as early as thirty thousand years ago.[3] They likely were one of many cultures that used milk long before the beginnings of agriculture.

H. G. Wells wrote that civilization began when huntsmen turned herdsmen, and it is probable that the earliest herdsmen, the Indo-Europeans of central Asia, were among the earliest consumers of animal milk.[4] These people consumed a sacred drink called *haoma*, made by crushing twigs of a sacred plant and mixing the juice with milk and sanctified water, a concoction said to produce "a fine condition of inebriation."[5] Antelope, reindeer, sheep, camels, goats, water buffalo, cattle—wherever people have controlled these animals, they have milked them. The earliest human artifacts include vessels containing residues of milk, and transhumance, the synchronous, seasonal movement of humans and semi-domesticated animals—a cultural fossil today—predates the agricultural revolution by many thousands of years.

The two great evolutionary periods in the history of humanity—first biological and then cultural—are very unequally divided. The steps of biological evolution that separate us, *Homo sapiens*, from a small stone-using creature in central Africa, *Australopithicus*, took millions of years, while cultural history is crowded into the last ten or twenty thousand. We might ask why cultural evolution began so recently. Twenty thousand years ago all humans were hunter-gatherers; the most advanced among them followed the herds and collected their milk. A marked change took place about twelve thousand years ago, a change upon which civilization was built. That change—the domestication of animals and the cultivation of plants—was precipitated by the ending of the last Ice Age.

Every spring, inhabitants of glacial mountains witness release from the seasonal ice age in an explosion of greenery, flowers and animal life emerging from a long winter sleep. In the same way, humans emerged from the age of snow and ice into a new life. Most anthropologists call this change the "Agricultural Revolution," but Jacob Bronowski, the mathematician turned historian and philosopher, calls it the "Biological Revolution."

"There was intertwined in it the cultivation of plants and the domestication of animals in a kind of leap-frog," writes Bronowski. "With that there comes an equally powerful social revolution. Because now it became possible—more than that, it became necessary—for man to settle. And this creature that had roamed and marched for a million years had to make the crucial decision: whether he would cease to be a nomad and become a villager. We have an anthropological record of the struggle of conscience among the people who made this decision: the record is the Bible, the Old Testament. I believe that civilization rests on that decision."[6]

Civilization may indeed rest figuratively upon that collective decision. Physically, civilization rests on the soil, because the soil produces the nutrients for the grasses that feed the animals, which in turn feed the people. Fertile soil ultimately provided the milk upon which civilization was quite literally built, as we shall see.

MILK IN THE ANCIENT WORLD

The word milk comes from the Latin *mulgeo*, which means to press out by softening with the hand. In the whole range of organic matter, milk is the only substance purposely designed and prepared by nature as food. Early humans did not hesitate to appropriate this gift of nature for their own use.

No state of civilization has ever arisen without the subjugation of animals and subsequent use of their milk; from the infancy of human society, the bovine species has taken its place as the aristocrat of grazing animals. Those species include the bison, buffalo, water buffalo, yak and domestic animals of the genus *Bos*, like cows and zebus, the humped cattle of India and Africa. Where people have gone, the cow and her kind have followed. Whether indigenous or naturalized, bovines grace the pasture lands of every country. In most, their milk has at one time or another served as an essential article of human sustenance—in many, as the chief.[7]

The Vedic religious songs of India, which are at least as old as the Old Testament, declare the cow as man's greatest benefactor. Milk is the symbol of nourishment. These ancient hymns described the consumption of milk and butter two thousand years or more before Christ. The most valuable offering to the gods was milk.

The high priest speaks to Indra, warrior-king of the heavens, god of war and storm:

> *With honey of the bees is the milk mixed,*
> *Come quick, run and drink.*

The religion of the Hindus considers the *brahminy* or bull so sacred that it grants cows and bulls free rein to roam the countryside, to be caressed and pampered, never slaughtered for meat. The Hindus believe that the cow was the first animal, created by their gods when the Supreme Lord told them to place animated beings on the earth.

The sea kings of Crete also consumed milk some two millenia before Christ, for at the Palace of Knossos anthropologists have uncovered "cups and vases with painted designs, and reliefs of cows and calves, wild goats and kids."[8] Zeus, king of the gods, took refuge on this island when his father Saturn sought to slay him; his mother Rhea hid him in a cavern on Crete, where legend tells us that he nourished himself on honey and goat's milk. There he gained the strength to take vengeance on his father. In even earlier times, in the fourth millenium BC, the Sumerians and the Babylonians worshipped the cow as a goddess. She was the "Mother of the Moon," while the milk goat was the "Mother of the god Ningirsu." The Babylonians depicted the mother-goddess with teats so full they needed support. Surviving Babylonian texts etched into stone and clay describe victory over the demon of sickness with the words, "Bring milk and laban [curdled milk] that man become as pure as laban; like that milk may he become pure."[9]

Many other cultures in the ancient world deified Taurus the bull. The ancient Egyptians placed the constellation of Taurus in the zodiac and often depicted the heavens as a cow with a full udder. They held the cow sacred and dedicated her to Isis, goddess of agriculture; moreover, the cow was a goddess in her own right, named Hathor, who guarded the fertility of the land and caused the Nile to overflow at regular intervals, bringing productive new soil.

The Egyptians depicted their god Apis as a bull, symbolizing fertility and strength. They kept a carefully chosen black bull, declared to be the incarnation of Apis, in a special enclosure; when it died they had it mummified and ceremonially placed in a tomb and installed a suitable living replacement. Throughout Egypt, the Zor Aster, or sacred bull, appears to have been worshipped in various ways. Eventually they recognized Apis as a manifestation of Osiris, a god originally connected with fertility and credited with the origin of agriculture.[10]

Perhaps from this practice the Greeks derived the Minotaur, a creature half man, half bull, and the Israelites the golden calf they worshipped in the wilderness.

## PASTORAL LIFE IN BIBLICAL TIMES

The ancient Hebrews, whose civilization co-existed with that of Crete, held milk in high favor; the earliest Hebrew scriptures contain abundant evidence of the widespread use of milk from very early times. The Old Testament refers to a "land which *floweth with milk and honey*" some twenty times. The phrase describes Palestine as a land of extraordinary fertility, providing all the comforts and necessities of life. In all, the Bible contains some fifty references to milk and milk products.[11] The word "milk" is often used metaphorically to signify privileges and spiritual blessings.

Moses, who led the Hebrews out of their bondage in Egypt, laid down numerous laws and regulations about flocks and herds, signifying the great importance attached to their milk, fleece, flesh and labors. By his time, pastoral tribes had begun to form connections, by compact or compulsion. This led to the adoption of the patriarchal form of government as some leaders came to the head of large groups of tribes. Thus originated the *Hycos*, or shepherd kings, a nomadic people who conquered and held most of Egypt for some two hundred years around 1700 BC. Similar tribes wielded influence throughout the civilized world.

The flocks and herds of these peoples were the foundation upon which their cultures were built. "The patriarchal shepherds," said one historian, "acknowledged no superior; they held rank and exercised the rights of sovereign princes; they concluded alliances with sovereign kings, in whose territories they tended their flocks; they made peace and war with surrounding states. They lived a plain and laborious life in perfect freedom and overflowing abundance. They lived in tents, and moved from place to place to find pasture for their cattle. They were conscious of their strength and jealous of their independence, with the skill and courage to vindicate their rights and avenge their wrongs.

"In the wealth, the power, and the splendor of patriarchal shepherds, we discover the rudiments of regal grandeur and authority. Hence the early custom so prevalent among the ancients of distinguishing the office and duties of their kings and princes by terms borrowed from the pastoral life: *Agamemnon, shepherd of the people*, is a phrase frequently used in the strains of Homer."[12]

The writers of the Psalms use the same allusions to celebrate the special care and goodness of God over his people: "The Lord is my shepherd; I shall not want." "Give ear, O Shepherd of Israel, thou that leadest Joseph like a flock." Many biblical passages compare the saints to a flock, and the church to a sheep's fold or enclosure; *fold* now also means a body of believers or the members of a church. Extending this metaphor, ministers are shepherds, responsible to the Great Shepherd who grants them their authority.

The Bible tells the story of Abraham, the emir or chief of a pastoral tribe some two thousand years before Christ. He receives a visit from three angels, and instructs his wife Sarah to prepare the bread, while he goes himself to select the finest calf. ". . . and he took *butter and milk*, and the calf which he had dressed, and set it before them" (*Genesis* 18: 8).[13] So important were the flocks and herds to the ancient patriarchs that their own sons and daughters tended the animals.

The Bible also reports that when Abraham led the Hebrews into Egypt, the Pharoah presented him with sheep and cattle. The Pharoah dreams of seven "well-favored and fat-fleshed" cows feeding on the succulent water-plants of the Nile. Later, when the Israelites depart, Moses proclaims that not a hoof belonging to them shall be left behind. Abraham's grandson Joseph was also a herdsman, and his countrymen were experts with cattle. A thousand years later, David, destined to be king of all Israel, carries ten cheeses as a gift to the captain of the army where his three brothers are serving against the armies of Goliath. His son Solomon admonishes his followers, "Thou shalt have goat's milk enough for thy food, for the food of thy household, and for the maintenance for thy maidens" (*Proverbs* 27:27).[14]

Two other Biblical passages provide strong evidence of the central role of milk and butter in the nourishment of ancient peoples.

> *Butter and honey shall he eat,*
> *that he may know to refuse the evil and choose the good.*
>
> Isaiah 7:15

> *And it shall come to pass, for the abundance of milk*
> *that they shall give he shall eat butter; for butter and honey*
> *shall everyone eat that is left in the land.*
>
> Isaiah 28:9[15]

In other parts of the world, ancient coins and medals offer mute testimony to the central role of domestic bovines during Biblical times. The Caucasus mountain range rises over eighteen thousand feet in the Republic of Georgia, between the Black and Caspian Seas. The medals of most of the ancient cities and countries around these mountains depict the bull as the prevailing theme. The eastern part of the Caucasus mountain range is called the Taurus Mountains. (*Taurus* is Latin for bull and the root word for bull in many other languages.) Nineteenth century historians conjectured that the reference to bulls celebrated the fact that after the flood, Noah sacrificed a young bull upon coming out of the ark when it was deposited on a Caucasus mountaintop.[16]

The management of flocks and herds marks humanity's earliest sign of civilization. Nomadic pastoralist societies dominated the transition from hunter-gatherer to early settled agricultural society. Skins and fleeces provided covering, while milk and flesh afforded sustenance.

Professor E. V. McCollum of Johns Hopkins University, one of the foremost nutritionists of the earlier part of the twentieth century, pointed out that from the dawn of history, the pastoral peoples of the world, whose diet consisted largely of the products of their animals, "without exception" have always displayed the finest physical development.[17] It would be difficult to overestimate the importance milk has played in the lives of these people and the rise of civilization.

## MILK FROM ANTIQUITY TO THE MIDDLE AGES

Early secular writers and poets testify as well to the antiquity and utility of cows and other domesticated animals. Hesiod is one of the oldest known Greek poets, contemporary with Homer. In his epics, written around 700 BC, he praises the pastoral life and speaks of the high honor in which it was held, even in times more ancient than his own. He himself may have been a shepherd.

Homer frequently mentions milk and cheese as common articles of food. Other Greek writers refer to milk and cheese over the ensuing centuries—Euripides in his nineteen surviving tragic plays and Theocritus, in his *Idylls*, which feature imaginary shepherds. Around this time, we find the first reference to butter in Greek literature, in the works of Herodotus, the "Father of History."

One group Herodotus describes are the Scythians, pastoral people who wandered with their animals in the country bordering the Black Sea, north of Greece. Now thought to be of central Asian origin, the Scythians were skillful horsemen and craftsmen, known for their distinctive stylized depictions of animals.

Hippocrates, the most famous of all physicians and a close contemporary of Herodotus, describes in great detail how the Scythians made butter, and he recommends milk and its products as wonderful foods. Hippocrates contended that nature has an innate power to heal; the quotation, "Let your food be your medicine, and your medicine be your food" is attributed to him.

Odes in honor of victories won by Greek athletes comprise the four surviving books of the poet Pindar. In one, he extolls milk with the words, "Rejoice, my friend! Lo, I send you, though at late hour, this honey mixed with white milk, fringed with the froth of blending, a draught of song conveyed in the breathings of Aeolian flutes." Could milk be described in lovelier or more enthusiastic terms?

Aristotle, a pupil of Plato and tutor of Alexander the Great, lived about one hundred years after Hippocrates, from 384 to 322 BC. As a scientific observer he had no rival in antiquity; historians have called him "The Father of Natural History." His surviving notes cover physical science, logic, psychology, metaphysics, ethics, politics, rhetoric and zoology. Biology is the science with which he was most at home. He correctly describes the multiple stomachs of ruminants and lists many of their characteristics with great judgment and accuracy. He details many observations about milk and cheese, affirming their importance in the diet of the Greeks during his time.

Four centuries later, the Greek philosopher Plutarch recorded a large body of vivid and memorable narratives about the ancient world. He praises cheese most highly and says that Zoroaster, the Persian prophet of the seventh century BC, lived for twenty years exclusively on cheese.

For the ancient Romans, the importance of milk as an article of sustenance reveals itself in many of their ceremonies, legends and religious offerings. According to legend, Romulus, the founder of Rome, and his brother Remus, twin sons of Mars by the vestal virgin Rhea Silvia, were left unprotected at birth, and were found and suckled by a she-wolf. When Romulus established Rome in 754 BC, he traced a furrow round a hill with a plough drawn by two milk-white cattle, enclosing the area with an earthen wall. He then poured out libations of milk to appease the gods. Eight hundred years later the devotional offering of milk in Rome continued, according to Pliny the Elder, statesman and scholar, and author of *Natural History*, a vast encyclopedia of the natural and human worlds. The Romans valued bovines so highly that they slaughtered them only on extraordinary occasions. Pliny records the tale of a citizen who killed one of his own cattle for the entertainment of a guest; for this he was banished from Rome by popular vote. Pliny also writes of several nations to the east that managed their herds so as to secure an abundant supply of milk throughout the year; the inhabitants nourished themselves on milk, its products and agricultural crops.

Strabo, Greek historian and geographer, presents a detailed physical and historical geography of the ancient world around the time of the birth of Christ. He describes the Ethiopians of northeast Africa, the

Lusitanians (inhabitants of an ancient province almost identical with modern Portugal), and several eastern peoples, all of whom used milk as their chief means of subsistence. The Roman poet Virgil wrote the greatest classics of Latin poetry. His first major work, the *Eclogues*, consists of ten poems that abound with allusions to shepherds and the pastoral life. His next work, the *Georgics*, is an instructive poem on farming, which also treats the wider theme of the relationship between man and nature; a part of that work covers the subject of breeding cattle.

At that time, the nomadic inhabitants living at the edges of the Roman Empire still lived on the produce of their flocks and herds. According to the Roman writers, this nomadic life also prevailed in the ancient German and other European states. In his description of military campaigns in Britain and Gaul (now northern Italy, France and Belgium), Julius Caesar tells us that the early Britons neglected the plough, undervalued farming and lived instead on the milk and flesh of cattle.

Two hundred years later, the Greek physician Galen became the court physician in Rome after a career tending gladiators in Asia Minor. His numerous works began the systematization of medical practice. Among his writings we find the curious tale of a man who lived more than one hundred years on milk alone. Galen's works reached Europe in the twelfth century as Latin translations from Arabic texts, and were widely influential.

Even before the spread of Roman influence, the traditions of the Celtic people, the pre-Roman inhabitants of Britain and Gaul, represented the cow as a kind of divinity.

The extension of Roman armies over much of the known world led to an increased cultivation of pasture in Italy, Greece, middle and southern Asia, Egypt, northwest Africa, Gaul and Spain, with subsequent increased abundance of the prime necessities of life.

Beyond the bounds of the Roman Empire, such benefits diffused gradually but extensively. The empire crumbled around 500 AD, and of the succeeding several hundred years we know but little. It was a time of predatory hordes and not a little anarchy, with most men trained to arms. We may assume that during these "Dark Ages," pasturage was preferred to tillage, for few would sow without the prospect of being able to reap. Herds could be concealed or driven away upon the approach of an enemy.

French laws from around the ninth century describe how cattle and sheep were pastured in the forests and commons, often with bells about their necks so they could be recovered easily. Britain abounded with flocks and herds when the Anglo-Saxons came to the island; many laws made by these conquerors described how the cattle they seized and pastured for their own use were to be cared for and protected from thieves and predators.

Even more than the Britons, the Welsh depended on their flocks and herds for support, while the inhabitants of Lombardy, a region of central northern Italy, were reputed to excel in the care and treatment of their cattle. In Switzerland, surviving documents show that the wealth and sustenance of the farmers was proportional to the number of their livestock.[18]

Do not these ancient documents provide considerable evidence that as civilization took root and grew, animal husbandry and dairying represented the very core of everyday life and that milk and milk products supported the well-being of human beings throughout the known world? This remained true throughout the Dark and Middle Ages, the period of European history from the fall of the Roman Empire in the West around the fifth century to the fall of Constantinople in 1453.

The thirty-seven plays of Shakespeare (1564-1616) contain about seventy-five references to milk, butter and cheese, many as figures of speech, some as metaphors, some similes. We have the celebrated "milk of human kindness" in *Macbeth* (I, 5-49), and in *Romeo and Juliet* (III, 3-55) we are told of "adversity's sweet milk, philosophy." In *King Lear*, the Fool entertains the King by telling him, "'Twas her brother that, in pure kindness to his horse, buttered his hay" (II, 4-127).

In the *Merry Wives of Windsor* Falstaff remarks "I'll have my brains ta'en out and butter'd, and give them to a dog for a new year's gift" (III, 5-8). In another passage in the same play, Ford states, "I will rather trust a Fleming with my butter than Parson Hugh the Welshman with my cheese, an Irishman with my aqua-vitae bottle, or a thief to walk my ambling gelding, than my wife with herself" (II, 2-318). Another character declares, "I will make an end to my dinner, there's pippins and cheese to come" (I, 2-13). And in *Love's Labour Lost*, the great bard makes his sole allusion to biblical milk and honey. "One sweet word of thee," he writes, "honey, and milk, and sugar" (V, 2-231).[19]

Butter receives plenty of mention in a number of Shakespeare's plays. Even dissolute and near penniless characters can fill up on eggs fried in butter as the cheapest item at a tavern or inn in *Henry IV*, and at one point Falstaff characterizes himself to Prince Henry as "vigilant as a cat to steal cream" (IV, 2-67).

All in all, Shakespeare's works confirm the widespread use of milk products in sixteenth century England and Europe.

A century earlier, Christopher Columbus landed in the Caribbean islands and set the stage for the colonization of the Americas by English and other settlers, settlers whose very survival would prove dependent on the bovines that accompanied them. We turn now to story of milk in early America.

# 2
# Bovine Friends
# in Early America

*A young fellow wantin' a start in life just needs three things: a piece of land, a cow and a wife. And he don't strictly need that last.*

Old Saying[1]

CATTLE COME TO THE NEW WORLD

Aurochs, the ancestors of domestic cattle, are not native to North and South America. Native Americans, many of whose lives centered on the buffalo or bison, were huntsmen who knew nothing of dairying. The North American bison, a species of ox, is an animal that cannot be tamed.

The first cattle to arrive in the New World landed in Vera Cruz, Mexico in 1525. Soon afterward, some made their way across the Rio Grande to proliferate in the wild. They became known as "Texas cattle."[2] Then some of the settlers transported cattle to South America from the Canary Islands and Europe. More followed, and cattle multiplied rapidly throughout New Spain, numbering in the thousands within a few years. By the mid 1700s, one D. G. Ordugna was reputed to own some two hundred thousand bulls and cows in Mexico.

Many animals ran wild, and in the lush country and mild climate of much of Central and South America, their numbers became immense. Herds of thirty or forty thousand ranged over the vast plains that extended from Buenos Aires towards the Andes. Settlers slaughtered them merely for the sake of their hides, as they did the bison in North America, leaving their carcasses in the field for vultures and wild dogs. In 1587, a fleet left Mexico for Spain with 64,360 hides, stopping at the West Indian island of Hispaniola (now divided into Haiti and the Dominican Republic) to pick up another 35,444. The trade continued to be a lucrative branch of commerce well into the 1800s. A Mexican historian observed that for every bovine transported from the old continent to the new, five million hides were returned to Spain.[3]

COWS SAVE THE COLONIES:
JAMESTOWN, PLYMOUTH AND NEW AMSTERDAM

During the 1500s, the Spaniards settled the southeast coast of the New World, bringing cows and bulls with them. But although some were expert farmers, as a group they failed to establish dairying, perhaps because the Conquistadors who ran the colonies were primarily interested in gold, silver and gems that could easily be shipped back to Spain. By 1570, the cattle that had come with the settlers, a gift of the Spanish monarchy, had largely been killed off by native peoples or eaten by the farmers themselves.

Life in the Jamestown colony, established in 1606, was very difficult in the early years. Despite several infusions of new settlers, by 1610 a pitiful remnant of sixty was all that remained. In that year, Lord Delaware arrived with a fleet of ships, relief provisions and three hundred people. Delaware observed that previous relief ships had carried a few cows, but it was Sir Thomas Dale's arrival with one hundred cows the following year that marks the beginning of dairying in America—and the beginning of some prosperity for the Jamestown settlers.

As deputy governor, Dale saw to it that cattle were provided with special grazing land, protected and, when necessary, fed. He directed colonists to grow and harvest hay during the summer and fall and store it for winter use. In addition, he built the first barn in the colony for the housing of dairy cattle. These were progressive ideas for a time when cattle were generally left to their own devices throughout the long winter. For a time, cattle multiplied and flourished in Virginia. By 1618, they numbered some three hundred, but when Dale returned to England in 1616 his ideas left with him, and the colonists by and large returned to their roughshod treatment of dairy cows. Many were fortune hunters who had come to the New World in search of the riches the Spaniards had found, and most had little or no experience in agriculture.

Poor treatment of cattle seems to have been a stubborn practice among the colonists. Disasters resulted from leaving livestock out all winter; thousands of cattle died of exposure and starvation during the winter of 1673, an unusually severe one in Virginia. As late as the early 1800s, winter dairying was practically unknown. According to an 1899 historical report by the U.S. Department of Agriculture, "As a rule, excepting the pasture season, cattle were insufficiently and unprofitably fed and poorly housed, if at all. It was a common thing for cows to die of starvation and exposure."[4] This *laissez-faire* attitude continued with the establishment and growth of the distillery dairies that flourished throughout the 1800s.

In his attempt to make the Jamestown colony self-sufficient, Dale even found it necessary to enforce strict martial law, making it a capital crime to wantonly kill cattle and other domestic animals. Another measure provided several goats and a cow, a house and twelve acres to English families that would agree to settle in Virginia. But many colonists became more interested in raising tobacco than in raising food crops and practicing animal husbandry. Only massive importation of cattle from Europe would lead to a sustained increase in dairying. This began in 1620 when the Virginia Company began supplying twenty heifers (mature young cows) per each one hundred new tenants emigrating to the colony. By 1629, the number of cattle in the colony exceeded two thousand, and a cottage industry in dairying had begun. Cows became valuable, bringing twice the price in Virginia that the same animal would bring in England. Food, especially milk, cheese and butter, became more plentiful, and the colony began to prosper.

So abundant did cattle become that in 1662, the settlers gave cows to various native chiefs in the hope of "civilizing" the tribes. The experiment failed, for the native peoples generally showed little interest in milking and caring for the animals. Then as now, a cow's cooperative temperament and natural gifts required an active partnership with a human if she was to become a primary producer of wealth.

No livestock accompanied the Pilgrims when they arrived in Plymouth on the Mayflower in 1620. They had set sail for Jamestown and landed instead hundreds of mile to the north. It was late November, with winter closing in; over half the settlers died by spring. Other ships subsequently arrived with provisions, but in 1623 one observer described the settlers as in "a very low condition, ragged and malnourished; something abated the freshness of their former complexion."[5]

The first cattle arrived the following March, three heifers and a bull aboard the ship *Charity*. Each successive ship brought more bovines; word had reached England of the important role cattle played in the survival of the Jamestown colony. Herds in Plymouth increased quickly; the Pilgrim farmers took care of their cattle. Milk, butter and cheese became plentiful, and by 1626 the Pilgrims were able to buy out the London men who had sponsored the colony. The final settlement of land and property included the allotment of one cow to each six persons; the settlers formed the Massachusetts Bay Company and considered cows essential for its well being. Cattle continued to arrive with each new shipload of settlers, and new communities soon sprang up, including settlements in the Boston area. In June of 1636, when the Pilgrim community in Cambridge decided to move, it took its cattle along. One hundred people traveled about ten miles a day, living mostly on the milk of their animals until reaching a fertile area some one hundred fifty miles to the southwest. There they founded the city of New Haven.

The arrival of one hundred ten people from the Netherlands on what is now Governor's Island in New York harbor, in March of 1624, marked the beginning of the New Amsterdam colony. With them came farming equipment, horses, sheep, swine—and cows. Unlike the Jamestown and Plymouth colonists, the Netherlanders did not suffer starvation. The Dutch founders of the West India Company realized that their settlements should be built on a firm foundation of agriculture and dairying. Only later did they establish trading posts, chiefly for fur.

The next year the colony received forty-two new Dutch immigrants. Their ship was accompanied by three others—the *Horse*, the *Sheep* and the *Cow*. Two ships carried one hundred three head of livestock, and the third carried supplies that might be needed should the voyage be unexpectedly long. Only two animals were lost during the passage.

With English colonies to the north and the south, the Dutch realized that they needed to increase the population of New Amsterdam in order to maintain any realistic chance of holding on to it. Holland was a prosperous land, with few people inclined to migrate. To encourage migration, the Dutch government promised religious freedom in the New World and also facilitated the migration of minorities throughout Europe. A program of free pasturage and livestock for immigrants, with a house, barn and farming implements, began in 1639; the farmer was required to pay back the number of cattle he had received within six years while "the entire increase" remained with him. By the time the British conquered New Netherlands twenty-five years later, the population had grown to ten thousand Dutchmen, Englishmen, Germans, Jews, Swedes, French Huguenots and other ethnic groups. Dairying thrived; for the next three hundred years, New York was the center of colonial cheese- and butter-making.[6] In fact, the consumption of cheese was seen as the distinguishing characteristic of the Dutch colonist. The moniker *Jan Kaas* (John Cheese) is the root of the word Yankee.

## THE FAMILY COW GOES WEST

Heavy imports of cattle to the East Coast continued throughout the seventeenth century, and dairying flourished as a cottage industry. As settlers began to move inland and west across the continent, they took their cows with them, hitched to the back of their covered wagons. Often the reason they moved westward was to find more room for their cattle. By the early 1700s, the Shenandoah Valley was dotted with barns and small dairy herds. By 1800, most New England land was claimed and pioneers poured into the Ohio Valley, looking for pastures for their herds. As early as 1707, cattle arrived in Detroit and then spread slowly throughout the region that would become Michigan and Wisconsin.[7]

The cow had a pervasive influence on America's history and culture, and no one has written of this more eloquently than Joann S. Grohman in her wonderful book *The Family Cow*:

"The cow very early in human history became the most prized dairy animal because of her cooperative temperament, the comparative ease with which she can be milked, the volume she is able to produce, and because of the versatility of cow's milk. The cream is easily skimmed and made into much prized butter in cold climates and ghee in hot climates. Ghee is butter that has been melted and strained.

"The cow is a primary producer of wealth. She can support a family. She not only turns grass into milk in quantities sufficient to feed a family but also provides extra to sell, *and* she contributes a yearly calf to rear or fatten. The byproducts from cheesemaking (whey) and from butter (buttermilk) will support a pig or two. Her manure improves her pasture and when dug into the garden, results in plant growth that cannot be surpassed by any other growth mediums. The family that takes good care of its cow is well off.

"Cattle are the original stock in stockmarket. Ownership of cattle has always been a mark of wealth. This is not just because the cow is a primary producer of wealth, adding enormous value to grass. In a 'which came first, chicken or egg' sort of way, it's also because only families possessed of a hardworking, cooperative spirit are able to keep a cow, let alone build a herd. Cows require humans for their survival. Huckleberry Finn's Pap might have had a pig or goat he could turn loose and still call his own but a cow requires consistent responsible care. If she doesn't get it she won't give milk and she won't start a new calf and she won't live through much cold or draught. Farmers in the north put up hay for the winter. African herdsmen walk their cattle to water and defend them against lions.

"The dairy cow doesn't ask for much but she asks every day. People who are creating wealth with a cow either are hard working and reliable or they get that way in a hurry. This is the way it has been for a very long time. The fine farms of Europe, England, New England and much of the United States were all established thanks to the wealth derived from cows. Wherever there is, or used to be, a big barn it was built to store winter hay for the cows which once dotted the pastures. The need to milk the cow twice a day determined the location of churches; people had to be able to walk there and back without disruption to the schedules of cows. Formerly, every district in Europe, England and the Eastern United States had a corn mill situated so that a farmer driving a horse and wagon could deliver his load and get home in time for milking. It is certainly no coincidence that such a large number of our finest American statesmen were born on farms. Important virtues are nurtured on the farm, including a graphic understanding of the relationship between working and eating. Over my farming life I have bred and raised all of the traditional farm animals and I love them all. But through association with the dairy cow I have come to understand and accept the words of that great 19th century agricultural essayist, William Cobbett: 'When you have the cow, you have it all.'"[8]

The introduction of cattle in the West occurred independently, and it isn't clear exactly when they first appeared. But the Franciscan fathers from Mexico who founded San Diego in 1769 and other missions along the Pacific Coast as far north as San Francisco brought cattle with them. The friars' dairying tradition helped them survive a difficult first few years, and they eventually built large herds of cattle.

NEW WEALTH IN THE NEW LAND

While the Spanish settlements in the west were establishing themselves, a home industry of butter- and cheese-making thrived in the East. By the early 1790s the new nation was exporting about one million pounds of butter and one hundred thousand pounds of cheese each year—a large amount relative to the population of about three million, ninety percent of which lived on farms and plantations. The largest city, New York, had thirty-three thousand people. The cattle population of the country had multiplied to an estimated eighteen million.[9]

Milk in America at the beginning of the nineteenth century was of the same character as the milk that had nurtured humanity for many thousands of years. Cows fed mostly or entirely on grass and hay, and milk and its products were pure and healthy. This was soon to change, as the growth of the cities would lead to changes in milk production, and this change would have devastating effects.

# 3
# Bad Milk:
# The Distillery Dairies

*Man is the only creature that consumes without producing. He does not give milk, he does not lay eggs, he is too weak to pull the plough. . . yet he is the lord of all the animals.*

George Orwell, *Animal Farm*, 1945

During the early 1800s, an accomplished zoologist remarked of domestic animals, "It is scarcely necessary to say that they supply us with the most truly precious of our earthly gifts. Without the cow, the horse and the sheep, how different would be the social, commercial and political condition of the most civilized of the human race!"[1] These were prophetic words. As New York and other cities grew rapidly in the first half of the nineteenth century, the cow as a species was not lost, but she was damaged in ways that would indeed forever change the "social, commercial and political condition" of humanity.

New York grew from a town of thirty-three thousand in 1790 to a crowded city of almost four hundred thousand in 1840, and six hundred fifty thousand in 1850. The masses of immigrants who came to the cities wanted milk, especially for their children. In colonial America bovines lived well in urban areas, as many town families had room to keep a

31

family cow. Others kept cows in common pastures, usually in the heart of town; Boston Commons is one of the most famous; cows grazed there as late as 1850.

But as the cities grew crowded, more and more grazing land was lost. As early as 1830, one man wrote that if you wanted really fresh milk, you had to send a messenger into the country to obtain it.[2] But a milk supply of sorts was in the works, one created by a new breed of dairymen, which would dominate the sale of milk in America's cities throughout the 1800s.

## THE WAR OF 1812 LEADS TO SWILL MILK DAIRIES

The War of 1812 with England resulted in the permanent severance of America's whiskey supply from the British West Indies. As a result, the domestic liquor industry was born, and by 1814, grain distilleries began to spring up in the cities as well as in the country.

Soon every major city had one or more distilleries, where grains were turned into whiskey. As the cities grew, readily available pasturage shrank, while the demand for milk—as well as for whiskey—rapidly increased. The processes of fermentation and distillation extracted the starch and the alcohol from the grains, and produced an acid refuse of grain and water known as distillery slop. This waste product was then fed to cows by individuals who cared nothing about the animals or the quality of the milk thus produced.

Distillery owners then began housing cows next to the distilleries and feeding the hot slop directly to the animals as it poured off the stills. Thus was born the slop or swill milk system. What began tentatively as an experiment became gradually ingrained, as the system proved to produce more milk at a lower cost than any other method. From small beginnings the slop milk business grew, especially during the 1830s, when distillery owners came under economic pressure from a contraction in the industry, which saw the number of distilleries in New York state shrink from over one thousand in 1829 to less than two hundred by about 1840. Lower profit margins meant increased pressure to garner whatever profits could be had from the milk side of the business, and slop milk became a huge industry.

Slop is of little value in fattening cattle; it is unnatural food for them and makes them diseased and emaciated. But when slop was plentifully supplied, cows yielded an abundance of milk. The milk was so defective in the properties essential to good milk that it could not be made into butter or cheese; it was good for nothing—except to sell. And sell it the owners did. Figures published in *Moore's Rural New York* in 1852 indicate that of the annual receipts from the sale of milk that year to New York City's seven hundred thousand people, three-quarters of the total was spent on slop milk, also known as swill milk.[3]

In the late 1830s, reformer Robert Hartley wrote a series of articles about the problems associated with distillery dairies. In 1842 he published his landmark book, *An Historical, Scientific and Practical Essay on Milk as an Article of Human Sustenance, with a Consideration Upon the Present Unnatural Methods of Producing It for the Supply of Large Cities*. Here Hartley describes the impressions an observer might have on visiting one of these establishments:

"If the wind is in the right quarter, he will smell the dairy a mile off. On reaching it, his visual and nasal organs will, without any affectation of squeamishness, be so offended at the filth and effluvia which abounds, that still-slop milk will probably become the object of his unutterable loathing the remainder of his life. His attention will probably be first drawn to a huge distillery, sending out its tartarian fumes, and blackened with age and smoke, casting a sombre air all around. Contiguous thereto, he will see numerous low, flat pens, in which many hundreds of cows, owned by different persons, are closely huddled together, amid confined air and the stench of their excrements. He will also see the various appendages and troughs to conduct and receive the hot slush from the still with which to gorge the stomachs of these unfortunate animals, and all within an area of a few hundred yards.

"The interior of the pens corresponds with the general bad arrangement and repulsive appearance of the exterior. Most of the cattle stand in rows of from seven to ten across the building, head to head and tail to tail alternately. There appears, however, no contrivance for washing the pens, or by which a circulation of air can be produced. But to survey the premises round about, and merely to look into the pens, will but inadequately convey an idea of the disgusting reality. Neither is it sufficient to enter into them while empty with the impression that the worst can be imagined. This is a delusion. Let the visitor go into the midst of the pens, when crowded with cattle, in summer, as the writer has done, and inhale but one breath of the polluted air, and an inexpressible impression of heart-sickening disgust will be produced, which time will never efface. The astonishment is, that animal life, with all its wonderful recuperative energies, and power of accommodation to circumstances, can exist in so fetid an atmosphere. Nor will the overpowering disgust produced be in any degree relieved by the spectacle of sick, dying and dead cattle, as was the case during a recent visit of the writer, and which, under this wretched management, cannot fail to be of frequent occurrence.

"Such is the barbarous and unnatural treatment of this docile, inoffensive and unfortunate animal, that is destined to supply us with nutriment, both when living and dead, and which is one of the most valuable gifts of Providence to ungrateful men. Here, in a stagnant and empoisoned atmosphere that is saturated with the hot steam of whiskey slop, and loaded with carbonic acid gas, and other impurities arising from the excrements of hundreds of sickly cattle, they are condemned to live, or rather to die on rum-slush. For the space of *nine months*, they are usually tied to the same spot, from which, if they live so long, they are not permitted to stir, excepting, indeed, they become so diseased as to be utterly useless for the dairy. They are, in a word, *never unloosed while they are retained as milkers*. In some few cases the cattle have stood in the same stalls for fifteen or eighteen months; but so rapid is the progress of disease under this barbarous treatment, that such instances are exceptions to the general rule, and of very rare occurrence. Facts show that all the conditions necessary to the maintenance of health and life, are recklessly violated to an extent which, if not well authenticated, might appear incredible in a Christian community. Of course, by a law of physical nature, the digestion of the animals becomes impaired, the secretions vitiated, loathsome and fatal diseases are engendered, and if not seasonably slaughtered, and eaten by our citizens, the abused creatures die, and their flayed carcasses are thrown into the river."[4]

Mortality in the swill dairies was high; in one ten-week period, out of over eighteen hundred cows kept at a dairy in Brooklyn, two hundred thirty died. Many cows died after yielding the usual quantity of milk for the day.

Hartley estimated that about eighteen thousand cows produced over five million gallons of slop milk each year for the consumption of New Yorkers—mostly New York's children. He called the slop milk industry "a curse and a scourge, as indicated by the Bills of Mortality." Infant mortality had risen sharply since around 1815 when the distillery dairies began to flourish, accounting for about half of all deaths in the city by 1839. Many deaths were caused by diarrhea, many others by tuberculosis. Hartley, as well as many medical men, laid the blame for many of these deaths squarely on slop milk. At that time, they knew little about the organisms involved in infectious disease but recognized that tuberculosis occurred in both cows and humans and believed there was a connection. It was not until 1882 that Robert Koch would announce his discovery of the tubercle bacillus as the organism involved with tuberculosis. In the same paper, he announced his famous postulates about the causes of infectious disease.[5] He was hailed as the greatest scientist of his day. A few years later, he announced that he had found exactly the same bacillus in the sores of tubercular cows and in their milk, and medical men assumed this to be the solution to the whole problem of tuberculosis.

But a few years later, Koch announced that a prolonged series of experiments had proved that the human and the bovine tubercle were neither identical nor transmissible, and that humans had nothing to fear from the bovine bacillus. This announcement shocked the world, and authorities in Europe and America soon declared that Koch was wrong. For many years, the advocates for compulsory pasteurization used the argument that pasteurization was the only way to make milk safe from tuberculosis. Eventually, however, it became apparent that only a small percentage of human tuberculosis cases was of bovine origin. Many scientists then and since have maintained that the only way the bovine tubercle may pass directly into the milk is if the disease in the animal has become generalized and tubercular lesions have formed on the udders. Another route is fecal contamination. And the human tubercle may contaminate the milk if a tubercular milker coughs into or otherwise mishandles the milk.

In the distillery dairies, the tubercle bacillus was probably passed by all of these routes. Diseased cows were milked in an unsanitary manner. Milkers were often dirty, sick or both. Milk pails and other equipment were usually dirty. Contamination with *Salmonella* and numerous other pathogenic organisms that may lead to diarrhea in susceptible individuals was undoubtedly common. Diarrhea was the most frequent cause of death in infants during those years, and many infants contracted tuberculosis, scarlet fever, diphtheria and other infectious diseases that were sometimes passed on in milk.

Most shameful of all is the fact that the distillery dairies continued to sell milk well into the 1900s; the last one in the New York City area was in Brooklyn, and it closed in 1930. For well over one hundred years, the citizens of the nation's most populous city were subjected to milk that was not suitable for human consumption.

Hartley's calls for reform did not go unheeded. In 1848, the New York Academy of Medicine appointed a committee to investigate slop milk. This and other committees made pronouncements about the harmful effects of the milk, but public authorities did nothing. Traditional dairymen, producers of clean, grass-fed, healthy milk, meanwhile did their best to produce milk for New York and other cities. They advertised "pure feed and pasture milk" and that "no swill or any other feed, which can in any manner, whatever, be deleterious for the human constitution or injurious to the milk, shall be used during the winter months for fodder." They shipped this "country milk," as it was called, into the cities by train—the so-called milk trains—using ice blocks to keep it cool and making a better profit selling whole milk to customers in the cities than they could making butter at home. Shipments direct from Goshen to downtown New York, seventy miles away, began in 1842. Hartley himself, never at a loss for words, wrote of the historic event, "What an exhaustless source of health and comfort is here brought to the doors of our citizens! We are gratified to learn that a company is already formed for the purpose of bringing milk to the city and that the specimen received is the first fruit of the enterprise."[6]

Shipments of country milk to New York grew to over thirteen million gallons in 1850. But compared to the output of the distillery dairies, this was just a trickle. The fight for pure milk would continue.

FEEDING AND THE HEALTH OF COWS:
THE EFFECT ON THEIR MILK

Three principles, each of which will be documented in the ensuing chapters, should underlie any discussions about the effects of milk on human health. First, the cow's diet largely determines the health of the cow. Second, the healthfulness of a cow's milk is largely determined by the health of the cow; therefore the cow's diet largely determines the healthfulness of the milk. Third, an individual's susceptibility to microbes often found in the milk of cows fed less-than-optimal diets greatly increases when his immune system has been compromised by immunosuppressive drugs, antibiotics, chronic disease or poor nutrition.

Hartley and certain of his contemporaries well understood the first two of those premises although even today, most modern medical and dairy scientists do not. But then as now, most medical doctors, dairy scientists and lay people largely ignored the connections. "Milk, being a natural secretion," Hartley wrote, "and not a manufactured article, it has been taken for granted, that in whatever way produced its nutrient and healthy properties are essentially the same; hence the ill-considered consumption of the milk of animals which are kept in confinement and upon unnatural food. The cow is an herbivorous and a ruminating animal; pasturage, of course, or grassy matter, is its natural and appropriate aliment. Unnatural food cannot fail to destroy the health of the animals that subsist upon it, and so deteriorate the quality of their milk, as to render it unfit for human sustenance."[7]

Throughout the nineteenth century, Hartley and other reformers found support from city health authorities and often the press, which mounted vigorous campaigns for pure milk. Adulteration of milk, particularly distillery milk, was rampant. Because slop milk was naturally very thin and pale bluish in color, dealers added a variety of substances to give it color and consistency, including starch, sugar, flour, plaster of Paris and chalk. Water was commonly used to dilute both distillery and country milk, thus increasing the dealer's profits. Called "the oldest food fraud" in 1860, dilution of milk with water is still a problem today. In Australia, the courts heard a case about the dilution of milk with water in 2007.[8]

The nation's first laws to curb some of these abuses were passed in the 1850s, in an attempt to control and oversee the supply and distribution of milk. Distillery dairy owners fought back by buying political influence. With a refrain that has become familiar in the ensuing years, politicians argued that a law against swill milk would keep individuals from the "peaceful possession and use of their property. How can we count upon any large outlay of capital in building or machinery unless men of enterprise, capitalists and others, have some assurance that their investments will not be made worthless?"[9]

Health workers found it difficult to estimate just how much disease was related to slop milk; Hartley and others in subsequent years pointed to infant mortality figures as an indication of the scope of the problem. "Milk sickness"—outbreaks of disease that were sometimes fatal in people drinking the milk of cows that fed on certain toxic plants—had been known for many years; people understood that bad milk could lead to disease. But microbes were yet to be discovered, as were the immune system and its functions. Observation and association were the chief means of reaching conclusions. In this regard, Hartley quotes from a letter he received by a man he described as an eminent New England physician:

"I live in the country, but occasionally go to the city. While there, I make a practice of securing, if possible, my accustomed glass of milk morning and evening. Three years ago last winter, I took lodgings at a respectable house near Broadway, and ordered my glass of milk. The taste of this milk was unnatural, unsavory, and I had no relish for it. In fact, it soon became loathsome, and at the end of one week I found myself greatly enfeebled, with loss of appetite, a feverish heat of the hands, and a slightly furred tongue, with other indications of disorder. The milk, I was informed, came from a dairy supplied with swill from a distillery. I left the boarding house, and took lodgings at the Clinton Hotel, where I found a well-flavored glass of milk morning and evening, and in three days I was well. The landlord assured me that he was supplied with milk from a farmer who fed his cows on wholesome food. Nothing can be more certain, than that the quality of the milk is greatly influenced by the state of the health of the animal producing it."[10]

Mr. Hartley's book was published over one hundred sixty years ago. I've nonetheless quoted him extensively because many of his points are as relevant today as they were in his day. Today in confinement dairies throughout America, cows are living in stalls they never leave, stalls literally welded shut, where they are fed "scientific" diets devoid of fresh grass, diets designed to maximize milk production. These diets include grains, soybeans, "bakery waste" (bread, cakes, pastries and even candy bars) and citrus peel cake loaded with pesticides. A recent addition to the diet of confinement dairy cows are pellets made from the swill of ethanol production![11] (More on this in Chapter 18.) Most will live only a quarter of their natural lives. While some of the grossest excesses of the distillery dairies have been eliminated, confinement cows today are not healthy animals, and they are not producing the kind of milk America's children and adults need and deserve.

## INFANT MORTALITY IN AMERICA EXCEEDS THAT IN EUROPE

From the early 1800s, America's largest cities kept thorough records of all deaths. Boards of health required physicians to give certificates designating the name, age and sex of all who died under their care, and no burial could take place without such a certificate. The certificates were then compiled into an annual publication, for example Boston's *A General Abstract of the Bill of Mortality*. "Heavy penalties are imposed for burying without permission," one Mr. Shattuck wrote in his *Vital Statistics* of the city of Boston. "All, or very nearly all the deaths that have taken place in the city are recorded. And the *Bills* contain a faithful abstract of the records."[12] Other authorities made similar statements attesting to the authenticity and accuracy of published records for New York City and Philadelphia.

Hartley examined the mortality records for these three cities for the years 1811 to 1839, especially deaths of children under five years old.[13] The city of Boston published totals for each decade. They showed that from 1811 to 1820, the percentage of deaths made up by children under five was 33.64 percent. It rose to 37.04 percent for the years 1821 to 1830, and to 43.09 percent for the years 1831 to 1839. The city of Philadelphia published yearly totals from 1814 through 1839. The percentage of deaths made up by children under five rose steadily from 25.28 percent in 1814 to 51.83 percent in 1839. For New York, yearly figures were available from 1814 through 1840. The percentage of deaths made up by children under five increased from 32.14 percent in 1814 to 50.02 percent in 1840.

Hartley's study of corresponding figures for European cities showed that despite conditions of extreme poverty, the percentage of deaths made up by children under five had been falling steadily for nearly one hundred years. In London, for example, the death rate had fallen from 74.5 percent in 1729 to 31.8 percent in 1829. This trend was typical of all large European cities for which records were available.

What is striking is the observation that while the percentage was falling in European cities, in American cities it was rising, to the point that over half of all deaths in New York and Philadelphia, and nearly half in Boston, were of children under five years of age. Hartley points out that the many causes of childhood deaths in European cities, particularly the extreme poverty and subsequent crowding and malnutrition, were at work to a much more limited degree in American cities. The necessities and even some of the comforts of life were in reach of most Americans. Why, then, the excessive infant mortality in American cities?[14]

Hartley found the explanation in swill milk. European cities too were afflicted with bad milk and its consequences, but their milk appears to have been not as bad as that of American cities, and the Europeans generally used less milk. Hartley quotes another writer: "The staple diet of the manufacturing population in England is potatoes and wheaten bread washed down with tea or coffee. Milk is but little used."[15] The same writer estimated that a family of five in London could only afford about a quart of milk per week. In New York, many families used almost a quart daily, and most two or three times as much. Hartley also points out that in London and many other European cities, as well as in Boston, the waste from brewer's grains used in beer making, rather than distillery slop, was used to feed cows in the city dairies. While still unhealthy, brewer's grains were comparatively less pernicious than slop, and he believed that the lower death rates of children in both Boston and the European cities reflected this fact.

The exact means by which poor foods undermine health are in many respects as little understood today as they were in Hartley's time. "But we may not doubt," he wrote, "that the sweeping mortality of infants amongst us is, to a great extent, the consequence of our ignorance or recklessness of the laws of life. Being still in pupilage in physiological science, we are incompetent to trace out with distinctness and specify all the causes that are inimical to existence, or to determine how largely the deteriorated quality of milk of which children so generally and freely partake may contribute to this melancholy result. But analogy, experience and observation, the testimony of facts, and the testimony of our most eminent medical men, fully justify the conclusion that slop milk's influences are not exaggerated, and that it should be classed among the most fruitful causes of suffering, disease, and death."[16]

## THE FIGHT FOR PURE MILK HEATS UP

The fight for pure milk would continue throughout the nineteenth century, as other writers continued Hartley's work and public health authorities and legislators became increasingly involved. Yet when Dr. Thomas Darlington became New York City's health commissioner in 1904, he learned that more than six thousand cows in Brooklyn were still receiving distillery slop.[17]

In 1907, over half of the milk used in Cincinnati was produced in distillery dairies. "Those of you unfortunate enough in your cities to have this same condition to fight know that wet distillery waste is one of the worst enemies of sanitary dairying," said Otto Geier, MD, at the First Annual Session of the American Association of Medical Milk Commissions. "The cow is made into a mere milking machine. The distilleries, in their long filthy pens, will furnish to any one desiring to enter the dairy business board and lodging for cows at ten cents a day. Here enters the large milk dealer of the city, who buys any kind of milk wherever he can. Competition forces others to haul slop to their dairies. These compete with decent clean dairies for business, with the natural result that the better farms have gradually dropped the production of milk. Bacterial counts made by the city chemist last summer ranged from two to fifteen millions per c.c. The milk cans were exposed to street dust stirred up by vehicles and street sweepers. The filling of bottles on streets presented another feature of contamination. Lack of ice regulations, another."[18]

Dr. Geier was Secretary of the Cincinnati Medical Milk Commission. The efforts of the members of the Medical Milk Commissions and other reformers to secure safe and healthy milk for America's cities are the subject of Chapter 5.

# 4

# Microbes versus Milieu: What Really Causes Disease?

*The doctor of the future will give no medicine, but rather will interest his patients in the care of the human frame through lifestyle and diet, and in the cause and prevention of disease.*

Thomas Edison

*We got it all!*

Anonymous surgeon

Because much of the modern and historical debate about raw versus pasteurized milk involves issues of safety in relation to infectious disease, it is important to take a look at the current paradigm, the belief that germs cause illness. Those who maintain that illnesses commonly associated with certain germs are caused simply by exposure to those germs will view raw milk as a threat and a danger. But for those who believe that illnesses are caused by a failure of the immune system to adequately cope with infectious agents, the issue shifts and focuses instead on the building of powerful immunity, mainly through nutritious food. The basic choice that lies before us is whether to choose foods that are nutrient-dense, or that have been rendered sterile.

Most people today believe that acute diseases are caused by infectious microbes—viruses, bacteria and parasites. The germ theory states that every infectious disease has a causative agent that attacks the individual and results in illness, with little consideration given to the reasons why some people are susceptible to attack while others are not. During the last thirty years, an explosion of knowledge about the immune system has contributed to a growing understanding that a strong immune system can protect us against infectious disease. Still, the generally accepted view is that pathogenic microbes are the cause of acute illness.

On the other hand, current medical thought posits chronic disease as lifestyle and environmental problems. Heart disease, for example, is blamed on sedentary habits and a diet high in animal fats. (The fact that middle-aged vegetarian runners sometimes drop dead of heart attacks is conveniently blamed on heredity.) Cancer is often attributed to a polluted environment or dietary fats. Although the mechanisms of immunity are now well understood, practitioners give little consideration to the role the immune system plays in preventing cancer and other chronic diseases, and even less to the important role of nutrients found only in animal foods, enzymes found only in raw foods and even beneficial bacteria in strengthening the immune system and preventing disease.

## CLAUDE BERNARD AND THE *MILIEU INTERIEUR*

What we now recognize as the immune system may be thought of as a component of the *milieu interieur*, a phrase coined in the 1860s by the great French physiologist Claude Bernard. The *milieu interieur* refers to the internal environment the individual brings to the battleground of infectious disease—that which creates resistance, inner strength and, for some, complete immunity. The great debate in science and medicine during the latter half of the nineteenth century was about microbes versus milieu in the etiology of infectious disease. At center stage stood Bernard and Louis Pasteur.

Scientists understood very little about the infectious diseases that caused most of the deaths during those years. By the 1880s, sophisticated microscopes and the bacteriological techniques developed by Robert Koch and his associates would allow discovery of the organisms associated with tuberculosis, cholera, diphtheria, scarlet fever and a host of other illnesses. Those discoveries led to a growing acceptance of Pasteur's germ theory. But in the years prior to Koch's discovery of the tubercle bacillus in 1882, the ideas of Claude Bernard held sway.

Born in 1813, Bernard became one of the most respected and influential scientists of his time. A professor of physiology at the Sorbonne, he had his own laboratory at France's famous Museum of Natural History in the Jardin des Plantes. He came to understand the fact that the blood and lymph that bathe the cells of the body make up the interior environment, the *milieu interieur*. Upon the self-regulating ability of that environment to maintain constancy or equilibrium rested the body's ability to function. A corollary that emerged derived from the observation that the balanced equilibrium in a fully healthy body was not easily upset by organisms that caused disease in a less healthy body. Thus did Bernard's work reinforce the ancient concept of empirical healers since Hippocrates, that the cause of all disease ultimately lies in the life and habits of the individual. *Vis medicatrix naturae,* "nature cures," is another corollary—when the body is ailing, it will cure itself if we provide the proper conditions.

## LOUIS PASTEUR AND THE GERM THEORY

Bernard's contemporary Louis Pasteur was born in 1822. The contrasting approaches the two men brought to medicine appear in sharp relief in the following quotes:

According to Pasteur, as quoted in Jacques Nicolle's 1920 biography, "If a man has committed himself to the pursuit of theoretical science, he should never, for the sake of his peace of mind and the success of his investigations, let himself be lured into the practical application of science." [1]

According to Claude Bernard, as quoted in Imago Galdston's 1951 book, *Beyond the Germ Theory*, "What we already know is a great hindrance into discovering the unknown." [2]

Pasteur was a chemist and bacteriologist, a prolific writer adept at self-promotion, who rose to become Director of Scientific Studies at the Sorbonne in Paris. Popularly remembered for his germ theory, his early work involved fermentation and wine. He discovered that by heating wine to a certain temperature, winemakers could partially sterilize it, killing the specific living microorganisms that caused spoilage. This was a great boon to the French wine industry, and Pasteur became a national hero, gaining admittance to France's prestigious Academy of Science in 1862.

Pasteur also studied the fermentation of milk and discovered that with milk, too, heat treatment (soon to be called pasteurization) destroyed the microorganisms that caused fermentation and souring. Pasteurization extended the time milk remained unfermented, but was not widely advocated until the discovery years later of specific pathogenic bacteria that were sometimes found in milk. (Ironically, milk is now pasteurized, but wine is not!) But long before that, Pasteur's discoveries met with widespread commercial success, for he worked primarily on problems of immediate economic, industrial and medical application. His methods for detecting the bacillus that caused disease in silkworms and preventing its spread saved the silk industry of France and several other countries. He isolated the bacillus responsible for anthrax, and he made a successful vaccine against rabies.[3]

But it was after Robert Koch's brilliant series of discoveries involving the isolation of the organisms causing tuberculosis and cholera in the 1880s that Pasteur's germ theory gained broad acceptance with both medical professionals and the public.

The ascendance and century-long domination of the germ theory in modern medical thinking is primarily a reflection of the political and economic scene that evolved after his discoveries. Pasteur's star began to rise when Emperor Napoleon III, an admirer of his work, created a laboratory of physiological science for him at the Sorbonne in 1867. Pasteur's mechanistic understanding of disease banished the individual's power to prevent it and placed the mandate to cure squarely in the hands of the medical professionals. In the years since, increasing control over the lives of individuals has also been the dominant theme of governments the world over. Professional medical associations have allied with the drug companies and with governments, contenting themselves with growing rich while ignoring the fundamental causes of disease. A neat arrangement that probably began without forethought or planning in nineteenth-century France perpetuates itself today in a labyrinth of ties between politicians, the drug and food processing industries, and the movers and shakers of the medical establishment. Proving an actual conspiracy would be difficult, but the undeniable result is gargantuan salaries, profits and privilege for the few, and today's health care crisis for the many.

It was not inevitable that science and medicine should go down the path of Pasteur's germ theory. The germ theory led to the assumption that disease germs could be overwhelmed and eliminated only by drugs. But ample evidence existed to support Bernard's alternative theory of the *milieu interieur*, or internal terrain, as the dominant element in determining the outcome of the interaction between humans and pathogenic microbes. Bernard contributed mightily to our understanding of human physiology, elucidating the complex interaction between the individual and the environment that regulates every aspect of metabolism. The French government held Bernard in such high regard that they honored him with a public funeral in 1878—an honor denied to Pasteur upon his death seventeen years later. Pasteur himself, by one account, declared on his deathbed, "Claude Bernard was right. . . the microbe is nothing, the terrain is everything."[4]

## WALTER BRADFORD CANNON AND HOMEOSTASIS

Bernard's concept of the *milieu interieur* found support in the work of the great American physiologist Walter Bradford Cannon (1871–1945). Cannon learned of Bernard's work from his mentor Henry Bowditch, chairman of the physiology department at Harvard in the late 1800s. Cannon described Bernard's work in his book *The Wisdom of the Body*, published in 1932. It was Cannon who coined the term *homeostasis*, the tendency to stability and the maintenance of a dynamic equilibrium in the normal internal environment of the body. Both his deep humanity and his understanding of Bernard's legacy are reflected in this brief quotation: "Only by understanding the wisdom of the body shall we attain the mastery of disease and pain that will enable us to relieve the burden of people."[5]

Cannon was universally regarded in his time as a man of great character and integrity. He served in World War I and afterward contributed much of his time providing aid and relief to refugees. He was a lifelong advocate for human rights and a lover of nature; Mount Cannon in Glacier National Park is named in his honor. But the medical profession—and the media and government that contribute to its hegemony—has largely ignored his work and that of Bernard and others, which contributed to the vast body of evidence that microbes are not the primary cause of infectious disease.

Cannon kept a framed photo of Bernard on his wall throughout his long career at Harvard.[6] Like Cannon, we would do well to remember those who have left us so much, and strive to understand what they taught.

## A NEW MEDICAL PARADIGM: PROBIOTICS

While the medical profession clings to the germ theory of disease, which is based on the assumption that the human body in a healthy state is sterile and that microbes make us sick by attacking it, medical researchers have discovered that the human body is in reality a "super-organism" composed of trillions of microorganisms inhabiting the digestive tract, the skin and every oriface of the body.

According to studies carried out by the Institute for Genomic Research in Rockville, Maryland, the human body consists of ten percent human cells and 90 percent bacterial cells.[7] In the healthy human being, approximately six pounds of beneficial bacteria inhabit the intestinal tract, carrying out a myriad of tasks including digestion, formation of nutrients, protection against environmental toxins, neutralization of natural carcinogens found in plant foods and even the production of feel-good chemicals. Use of antibiotics or overconsumption of certain foods such as refined carbohydrates create a condition called "dysbiosis," in which pathogens can take hold. But when the intestinal flora is robust and healthy, when it is composed of "probiotics," pathogens cannot gain a foothold—a perfect validation of Bernard's internal terrain. In fact, a few doctors and researchers are beginning to combat infections not with antibiotics but with probiotics that crowd out disease-causing organisms as part of treatment for digestive disorders and infection in the nasal cavities, in the bladder and even on wounds.[8]

## TWO SOLUTIONS TO THE MILK PROBLEM

The issues we've examined in this chapter provide a prism through which to view the next, as we focus on what became nationally known in the late 1800s as "the milk problem." How to save infants and children dwelling in large cities from dying by the thousands of infectious disease was one of the great national issues occupying health officials at the dawn of the twentieth century. Milk and the public water supply were at the epicenter of the debate about how to solve the problem, and rightly or wrongly, milk was blamed for many of the deaths. By 1890, the stage was set for the emergence of the two movements that would change milk forever in America.

One was led by medical doctors, mainly pediatricians, whose goal was safe and healthy raw milk for use in the treatment of disease. These physicians sought to make milk safe and healthy by controlling its production, and their efforts led to what became known as the certified milk movement. The other borrowed the name of Louis Pasteur to gain popular support. Led by a determined businessman and philanthropist, the backers of pasteurization were determined to produce milk that was first and foremost free of any potentially harmful bacteria, regardless of the effect the process itself had on the physical and chemical qualities of milk. Certification and pasteurization reflected the two fundamentally different philosophies about the cause of disease—philosophies at odds then and still so today. In the next chapter, we look at how early twentieth century America allowed both methods to provide solutions for different segments of our population in a democratic and pluralistic way.

# 5
# The Milk Problem, circa 1900:
# Certify or Pasteurize?

*Our motives are not personal, nor mercenary, nor commercial, but are expressed in the professional effort to obtain pure [raw] milk with which to save human life. We require approved and trustworthy dairymen, possessing honor, to conduct their dairies in conformity with a code of requirements, to establish a reliable safeguard against the common dangers of contaminated and impoverished milk.*

Henry Coit, MD, to the First Annual Session
of the American Medical Milk Commissions, 1908[1]

*The theorist says, 'Give us clean, raw milk.' But when you have made your milk microscopically clean, you want to go further and make it bacterially clean, and you can effect this only by pasteurization.*

Nathan Straus,
"The Practical Side of the Milk Problem," 1908[2]

By the last decade of the nineteenth century, a growing number of influential people throughout the country acknowledged the fact that American cities had a milk problem. Robert Hartley's articles and book exposing conditions in the distillery dairies inspired the work of other reformers. The yearly death rate of infants in the cities remained around

50 percent of the yearly birth rate, and officials believed that this was due at least in part to the poor quality of much of the milk available to the poorer people in the cities. The situation was known as "the milk problem." Politicians spoke about it, journalists wrote about it, and physicians complained about it. But no one did much about it until Henry Coit and Nathan Straus came along. The two men shared deep concerns about the high incidence of infant mortality and both promoted the goal of providing safe and healthy milk for the nation's cities.

Coit, a medical doctor, was founder of the first Medical Milk Commission and the certified milk movement, which resulted in the availability of safe raw milk from regulated dairies for physicians, their patients and the public. Straus, a businessman turned crusader-philanthropist, was the founder and subsidizer of New York City's milk depots, outlets that provided pasteurized milk at low cost for the city's poor; he became the chief advocate and spokesperson for the compulsory pasteurization of all milk. At first, Straus exempted certified raw milk from his demand for compulsory pasteurization, but by 1910 he was insisting that even certified milk must be pasteurized to be safe.

Initially, from around 1890 to 1910, the movements for certified raw milk and pasteurization coexisted and in many ways even complemented each other. From about 1910 until the 1940s, an uneasy truce existed. Certified raw milk, the legacy of Henry Coit, was available for those who wanted it, while the influence of Straus and his allies propelled most states and municipalities into the adoption of regulations that required all milk other than certified milk to be pasteurized. The end of this truce and the subsequent outlawing of all retail sales of raw milk in most states will be detailed in later chapters. Here we look at the lives of Dr. Coit and Mr. Straus, the men most responsible for conceiving and implementing the two alternative solutions to "the milk problem"— certification and pasteurization.

## HENRY COIT AND CERTIFIED RAW MILK

In 1889, Henry Coit, MD, of Newark, New Jersey, asked the Medical Society of New Jersey to formally investigate what was considered to be an urgent, fundamental question: how do we secure clean milk for our patients and the public? Coit's concern grew in part out of his own experience. For two years he had sought sources of good milk for his own infant son, whose mother had been unable to breastfeed successfully. His search culminated in a small suburban dairyman who kept four cows and delivered milk daily to the Coit household. "An honest and industrious man, but without knowledge of hygiene, he became unwittingly a dangerous element in my family life," Coit later said. "The factors of surety and safety for me were destroyed when, on visiting his farm, I found three cases of diphtheria in his house, and he was the patients' caretaker for the night and the dairyman of all work during the day."[3] (Coit did not report any cases of diphtheria in his family despite the exposure of his dairyman to the disease.)

The Society formed a committee of forty-two physicians, Coit recounted, to "inquire into the relations, if any existed, between the mortality among infants in large centers of population and the milk supply. After two years' work, in 1891, the Milk Committee discontinued their futile efforts, having demonstrated the helplessness of ordinary measures to accomplish for the cause of pure milk what physicians require. The State Dairy Commissioner wrote, 'Such a radical reform as you desire in the production and handling of milk may not be accomplished in our generation.' This aroused my indignation. I then devised a plan for a professional body composed of physicians, which should first educate, then encourage, and finally endorse, the work of dairymen who would bring to us milk designed for the most exacting needs of physicians." The plan included a legal contract between the dairyman and the committee, stipulating how the milk would be produced, inspected and certified.

Coit then enlisted several other physicians and together they formed the Essex County Medical Milk Commission in April, 1893. They selected professional dairy experts to act as consultants, and the group then chose the first dairyman to fulfill the requirements of the contract, Stephen Francisco, of Caldwell, New Jersey. Thus was born the first Medical Milk Commission and the certified milk movement.

Coit's plan included three general requirements. First, physicians in the local medical society selected members of a Medical Milk Commission and supported their efforts to bring to the city in which they lived a supply of milk produced under conditions that would assure purity. Second, "approved and trustworthy dairymen possessing honor" would be induced, by reason of promised medical support and an increased price of their milk, to produce and handle their milk in accord with the requirements imposed by legal contract with the Medical Milk Commission. Third, the Commission would set standards of purity for the milk and ensure that physicians made periodic inspections of the dairies, the animals and the employees. The Commission would conduct periodic chemical analyses and bacterial counts of the milk, so that it could be certified entirely free of pathogenic organisms. Coit coined the term "Certified Milk" to distinguish milk produced through the operation of his distinctive plan.

He had created a private organization of physicians to do what the local or state government had not. Other cities throughout the country began forming Commissions, and in 1906 the Medical Milk Commissions were federated into the American Association of Medical Milk Commissions. In 1909, the governor of New Jersey signed the Medical Milk Commission Law, passed unanimously by the New Jersey Senate and House, save one negative vote in the House. The law protected the professional interests of the Milk Commissions in the state and every feature of their activity.[4]

Certified raw milk, endorsed by a significant percentage of the medical profession and enjoying strong support from legislators and the public, was thus established as the standard to which all other milk was compared. Though more and more milk was being pasteurized, many saw pasteurization as a stopgap measure that would no longer be necessary once more careful regulation of the production and distribution of milk was in place. Certified milk became the model for the production of better milk everywhere. In writings about milk throughout the first half of the 1900s, time and again one finds references to the essential role the certified milk movement played in raising the standards of the entire dairy industry. This is reflected in the rules and regulations governing dairy production that have been codified in every state's laws, for both raw and pasteurized milk.

The physicians who led and supported the certified milk movement received no compensation for their efforts, testimony not only to how deeply these men and women believed in their cause, but also to the character of physicians of that era—leaders for whom service came before financial gain. "The Medical Commission wants clinical milk for the sick," Dr. Coit wrote. He and his colleagues understood the absolutely vital importance of having the best quality raw milk available for the ill—infants, children and adults alike. We'll explore the subject of milk as medicine in the next chapter.

NATHAN STRAUS, CRUSADER FOR PASTEURIZATION

The man most responsible for popularizing pasteurization at the turn of the century was Nathan Straus (1848-1931). Straus made his fortune in business as co-owner of Macy's department store, and then dedicated some thirty years of his life to championing the pasteurization of the milk supply in New York and other cities throughout America and Europe.

He had a powerful ally in Abraham Jacobi, MD, who served for many years as president of the American Medical Association. In 1917, Jacobi, Professor Emeritus of Diseases of Children at Columbia University, wrote of his experience during his first year in New York practice over fifty years earlier. He described visiting a tenement house on a scorching afternoon during the "excessively hot and fatal" summer of 1854, where he saw a baby dying of "summer cholera."

"In my despair I applied to two colleagues for consolation and advice. The first said, 'Give no milk'; the second added, 'Starve them for half a day or a day.' 'No milk' saved many of my babies."

Jacobi goes on to describe the milk available to New York's poor during the 1800s. "Part of New York was supplied by cows fed on brewer's swill in Long Island stables, which no cow had an opportunity to leave at any time after having been imprisoned there. There she was kept in foul air, standing or resting in her own manure, with no other food, sickening until her tail rotted off and her skin broke out in gangrenous ulcers, and she died.

"Such was a goodly part of the milk that reached our households. It was more or less white or bluish, more or less impure—or rather, dirty—half a day or a day old. When it was used for the baby it was rarely strained or boiled, often mixed with water which was more or less impure.

"The vast majority of households were those of working people in small dwellings, or even in tenement houses of four or five stories. What was done with the milk when it reached the household? Of present improvements none existed. Food stuffs would deteriorate rapidly and intensely. Ice could be obtained only by the better situated families. The tenement house people and the poor had none. The milk had to be kept in the coolest part of the dwelling, if there was such a place. I always advised boiling the milk for infants as soon as it arrived, and again once or twice in the course of a day. We knew nothing then of bacteria, but I felt sure that a minute's real boiling would accomplish all I could hope for. At all events, my order was, 'No raw milk.'"[5]

Conditions had only marginally improved by 1893 when Straus established the first of his "milk depots" for the distribution of low-priced pasteurized milk. At that time, the yearly death rate of infants and young children was about fifty percent of the birth rate. Children died from diarrhea and infectious diseases, including typhoid, cholera and diphtheria. Some died of tuberculosis, then the leading cause of death in the population at large. Straus, Jacobi and others were convinced that many of these diseases were spread by milk and that many deaths could be prevented if the milk supply to the cities were pasteurized. In the absence of official action, Straus began his own crusade to pasteurize the milk supply of New York City. He did not consider the premise that the poor quality of the milk itself, by failing to nourish, contributed to the problem.

For Straus and those officials who backed him, pasteurization was a matter of economics and practicality. Most recognized that fact that certified milk was safe and healthy, but it was expensive to produce and sold for two to four times the cost of ordinary milk. As a practical matter, the enforcement of strict rules of hygiene on the forty thousand independent dairy farms that supplied milk to New York City seemed impossible. Pasteurization promised a quick, technological fix that would make New York's milk safe to drink.

The popularity of Straus's milk depots grew rapidly, and several more were established in the city. Coincident with the increasing use of pasteurized milk, the death rate among infants and young children dropped dramatically, circumstantial evidence that milk contamination was indeed the cause of much illness. Infant mortality began dropping in the years immediately following the establishment of the first milk depots. With widespread pasteurization, it fell further, from a rate of one hundred sixty deaths under one year of age for every one thousand births in 1906 to ninety in 1916. Deaths from typhoid fever in New York fell as well, from fifteen per one hundred thousand in 1908 to four in 1916.[6] But chlorination of New York's water supply began during these years, eliminating a potential source of typhoid. Automobile use grew, and fewer horses and their excrement polluted city streets and water supplies. Other changes as well led to more sanitary conditions in New York and other cities, and it is impossible to know to what degree these factors affected the mortality figures.

The push for pasteurization in the late 1800s and the early 1900s is best understood by casting a light upon the conditions of that time. Some advocates for raw milk argue that the pasteurization of milk is an unmitigated evil, that all raw milk is safe, and that there was never any reason for public health authorities to advocate pasteurization. The authoritarian and often deceitful excesses that characterized the campaign for compulsory pasteurization of all milk began in the 1930s and continue to this day. Advocates for raw milk should understand, however, that sloppily produced and contaminated raw milk in America's circa 1900 cities contributed to considerable disease and death. Pasteurization began as an apparent solution to this acute problem.

PASTEURIZATION: STOPGAP MEASURE
OR PERMANENT SOLUTION?

Straus saw milk as a problem because "it is the only animal food taken in its raw state. When milk is used raw the germs are taken into the human system alive. The milk problem is to prevent this without cooking the milk."[7] It seemed logical for health officials to embrace pasteurization as the solution, but from the very beginning, proponents of pasteurization failed to understand fundamental nutritional principles. They did not grasp the fact that germs *per se* are not the problem, and that every traditional culture that has ever existed has emphasized the importance of raw animal foods in the maintenance of human health, resistance to disease and optimal reproductive capacity (more on this in Chapter 8). Proponents also failed to recognize the fact that the heat of pasteurization fundamentally alters the nutritional value of milk. And they failed to realize that only by creating conditions for healthy cows could we create a truly healthy milk supply.

Nevertheless, pasteurization appears to have provided some relief to a national problem of immense proportions. In 1910, President Howard Taft said, "It is not possible to overstate the far-reaching importance of the question of the reduction of infant mortality. Every man and every woman of every civilized country should feel a deep and personal interest in it."[8] The scope of the problem reveals itself in the fact that in 1914, twenty percent of all deaths were of babies under two years of age.

Contaminated raw milk was implicated in hundreds of outbreaks of scarlet fever, diphtheria and typhoid and many cases of tuberculosis in both children and adults were blamed on raw milk as was detailed in numerous official publications, including Bulletin Number 41 of the Hygienic Laboratory in Washington, "Milk and Its Relation to Public Health," published in 1914.[9]

We have no way of knowing today just how much of the problem really was caused by raw milk. But two conclusions seem clear. One, raw milk, particularly in the cities, frequently caused disease in infants and at least sometimes caused outbreaks of infectious disease. Two, the public health authorities perceived raw milk as a tremendous problem, leading them to push for compulsory pasteurization of all milk except certified raw milk.

Straus made it a point to sell his pasteurized milk at a cost well below the cost of production and distribution, absorbing the difference himself. His lifelong philanthropy in this and other causes made him a legend in his own time, hailed by statesmen and editorialists for his generosity. His own prose seems a curious mixture of preaching the necessity of pasteurization and self-aggrandizement, sprinkled with numerous allusions to his having saved the lives of tens of thousands of babies. By 1916, his milk stations had dispensed some forty-three million bottles of pasteurized milk over the course of twenty-five years.

In 1910, the Ontario Government Milk Commission published a report describing the work of Straus: "In visiting the Nathan Straus Laboratories in New York your Commission doubtless visited what might be described as the chief center of pasteurization influence on the continent. The milk is sold at actually what it costs on the farm, and so the cost of the expensive pasteurization plant, doctors and distribution machinery, must be borne by someone. It is borne by Nathan Straus and it is said to cost upwards of $100,000 a year. This is Mr. Straus' philanthropy."[10]

The control of the milk supply in New York City when Straus began his work in 1892 was largely in commercial hands. In 1873, New York City passed legislation prohibiting the production of swill or distillery milk, although distillery dairies continued to operate in nearby Brooklyn (then a separate city) and to ship their milk to New York. In 1894, a year after opening his first milk depot, Straus published his first article in a publication called *The Forum*. A year later the Health Department set chemical standards for milk and in 1897 began to require all milk shop dealers to take out a permit. In 1900 the Department required the cooling of milk in transit, and in 1906 the first systematic governmental inspection of dairies began.

Straus meanwhile demanded that New York require or provide for pasteurization of the city's milk supply. The Women's Municipal League supported this demand, and in a series of articles, the *New York Medical Record* also demanded pasteurization. In 1907, both the Academy of Medicine and the New York City Federation of Women's Clubs urged the adoption of pasteurization. An ordinance requiring the pasteurization of the city's milk supply was introduced, but was defeated by a coalition of milk distributors, physicians, social workers and Health Department officials who argued for clean raw milk and more inspection.

The mayor then appointed a special Milk Commission headed by Dr. Jacobi. The commission reported that "raw milk may be harmful on account of its containing the germs of tuberculosis, typhoid fever, scarlet fever, diphtheria and diarrhea diseases in infants." The members called for the Board of Health to "require pasteurization of all milk it finds un-safe for consumption as raw milk."[11]

All of these demands for pasteurization allowed for the continued production and sale of clean raw milk. No one was claiming that all milk should be pasteurized, as even the most zealous proponents of pas-teurization recognized that carefully produced raw milk from healthy animals was safe. They accepted the assumption that a sufficiently low bacterial count offered safety from milk-borne infection. Not until the 1930s did commercial dairy interests, segments of the medical commu-nity, politicians and public health agency officials and their allies in the media begin a campaign to smear *all* raw milk and then to eliminate its availability and sale.

Straus found an important ally in President Theodore Roosevelt, who ordered the Public Health Service to conduct a thorough study of the milk problem in 1907. Twenty government "experts" carried out the investigation and reported publicly in 1908 that raw milk posed a dan-ger. They further stated as fact that pasteurization does not change the chemical composition, taste, digestibility or nutritive qualities of milk. These "facts" have been repeated for over one hundred years and persist in government and medical literature about raw milk to this day, despite overwhelming evidence to the contrary, even evidence already available in the early part of the century.

The United States Surgeon General summed up the investigation with these words: "Pasteurization prevents much sickness and saves many lives."[12] This simple statement was true on its face, yet it epito-mizes the difficulty in understanding the meaning and implications of pasteurization and the milk problem. Given the sorry state of city milk supplies in early twentieth century America, pasteurization appears in-deed to have prevented much sickness and death. But with widespread pasteurization came the notion, fostered by the public health authorities and the media, that all milk must be pasteurized, the good with the bad, and that somehow pasteurization would take unhealthy milk and make it not only safe to drink but also healthy. The acceptance of this mantra led to compulsory pasteurization, confinement dairying, and the demise of milk and milk products as vital and health-sustaining foods—and it has played a significant role in the epidemic of cancer, heart disease and other chronic illnesses that ensued. The irony is that now, looking back, one can stand the Surgeon General's 1908 statement on end and accurately state that pasteurization has caused much sickness and cost many lives.

In 1911, the New York Milk Committee played an instrumental role in forming a National Commission on Milk Standards. That Commission then held that pasteurization should be compulsory, except for milk either certified or inspected according to the Commission's standards. The National Association for the Study and Prevention of Tuberculosis stated that milk from tuberculous cattle was "the medium through which transmission of bovine tuberculosis to human beings most commonly takes place," and recommended "the efficient pasteurization of milk as a safeguard against the transmission of bovine tuberculosis to mankind."[13] We'll look further at the issue of tuberculosis and milk later in this chapter and in Chapter 15.

Also in 1911, the American Medical Association warned that milk must come from tuberculin-tested cows or be pasteurized. That same year, New York City's Health Department commissioner announced that the Department would require the pasteurization of all milk except certified milk. Milk distributors selling raw milk not of certified quality managed to delay and modify this order to such a degree that a large proportion of the city's uncertified raw milk continued to be produced under insanitary conditions.

In 1912, the National Commission on Milk Standards issued another report stating that "Pasteurization is necessary for all milk at all times excepting certified milk or its equivalent. The majority of the Commissioners voted in favor of the pasteurization of all milk, including certified. Since this was not unanimous, the Commission recommends that the pasteurization of certified milk be optional."[14] Note that as early as 1912, powerful voices were already calling for compulsory pasteurization of all milk, including certified milk.

A 1913 epidemic of typhoid in New York City, allegedly caused by the milk of one dairy, involved over one thousand people. In 1914, raw milk took the blame for an outbreak of foot and mouth disease. The Commissioner of Health then ordered the pasteurization of the entire milk supply, with the exception of certified raw milk. At that time, there were only thirty-seven certified dairy farms supplying milk to New York City. The order affected an estimated one hundred thousand people involved in supplying New York with milk. The daily milk supply consisted of over two million quarts supplied by some four hundred thousand cows on forty-four thousand farms in seven states. There were sixty pasteurizing plants and fourteen thousand milk shops.

By this time, pasteurization was big business and getting bigger. Businessmen had invested large sums of money in plants and equipment for the new technique, and further implementation of the technology promised sizeable returns. The federal government had released Hygienic Report Number 41 and the Surgeon General had issued his statement about the desirability of pasteurization. Clearly, the public health and medical establishments were lining up behind efforts centered in the largest cities of every state to require pasteurization of most or all of the milk supply. The handwriting, so to speak, was on the wall, and physicians, newspaper writers and editors could read the message.

## THE VIEW FROM BRITAIN

A 1943 commentary from Great Britain has relevance here. Britain was about thirty years behind America in mandating pasteurization for a variety of reasons, so this depiction of conditions in 1943 Britain corresponds to those in America during the period when pasteurization first became mandatory. The author, James C. Thomson, was a nature cure practitioner, the director of the Kingston Clinic and the Edinburgh School of Natural Therapeutics. What follows is excerpted from his article "Pasteurized Milk, A National Menace: A Plea for Cleanliness," which appeared in *The Kingston Chronicle*.[15] Thomson's commentary may seem a bit Victorian, with his reference to "titled damsels and Society Doctors," but his observations lend valuable insight into the pasteurziation debate.

"When dealing with highly lucrative commercial enterprises, doctors are given a clear lead," Thomson wrote. "They know what is expected of them. For them, as for titled debutantes, there is a market for signatures. They have only to indicate a bias in the right direction and everything is made easy. Their investigations are tailor-made and tidy beyond description. Slides and specimens from the laboratories of the cartels are provided for them, meticulously labeled and annotated Petri dishes come to them teeming with unequivocal cultures of all the best microbes. In many cases even their opinions and observations are supplied; typed out all ready for signature.

"There is one infallible recipe for prosperity and peace of mind: conformity, conformity, conformity. Titled damsels and Society Doctors who are willing to pose in public, wearing their opinions at the fashionable angle can count upon substantial cheques for their complacent approbations.

"Not only so, but their carefully arranged portraits and opinions are publicized and broadcast for all to see and hear. The ladies are extolled for their 'Beautiful Skins'; the professional men are announced as 'Authorities' with unbounded and fulsome praise for this or that aspect of their investigations. The public reads and believes.

"Note the very different reception accorded the opinions of the genuine but non-conformist researcher. He travels any road free from all restraint or supervision. He can write letters and articles for scientific journals. He is even free to write the manuscript for a book.

"There are thousands of him. Why, then, do we so seldom learn anything about him? The answer is simple.

"There is no demand for his writings or for his services. Unlike his conforming opposite number, his portrait and his point of view remain unknown to the multitude. If—as sometimes happens—he does obtain notice he is sniped at and ridiculed by the company-owned 'Great Scientists' whose job it is to protect the profits.

"The average newspaper reader, subsisting upon headlines, advertisements and easily read editorials, receives a completely false impression of what the majority of investigators believe. So conformity is imposed upon less articulate investigators, but this does not mean that they approve. They keep silent because things are easier that way.

"The great blot upon our civilization is that in the professions, as in the commercial world and in the typical press, the profit-motive is all-embracing. Opinions that are profitable for the great vested interests are acceptable and saleable. Anything else is liable to censure and even to punishment."

Regarding pasteurization, Thomson is equally blunt: "The enthusiasm of the large milk distributors for pasteurization arises out of one economic fact: This modified sterilization prevents even dirty milk from going sour. After many days of travel and storage the milk is still sold as 'fresh.'"

Thomson comments on the preference of Liverpool physicians for raw versus pasteurized milk: "During the week ending January 23rd, 1943, 60,000 members of the National Federation of Milk Producers-Retailers held a conference. Their president said that out of 27 Liverpool doctors he supplied, by choice 26 took unpasteurized milk. Those who see the practical results of milk manipulation are not always so convinced by propaganda as might be thought by the casual onlooker. Their treasurer denounced pasteurization as a commercial ramp. 'The combines [milk industry cooperatives] could not live without it,' he said. Another member told of supplying a tuberculosis hospital with unpasteurized milk.

"Actually for such an institution, it would be criminal to do otherwise. Pasteurized milk is an unbalanced article of diet. Even in the healthiest of individuals it produces great vital strain. Due to their lessened margins of safety, it can be deadly for tubercular patients or for any one else whose health is below par. Here, as elsewhere, what may only be mildly hurtful for the healthy person can be lethal for the invalid."

Thomson's observations are consistent with my own professional experience; chronically ill individuals clearly do best when they stop consuming pasteurized milk. Even small amounts may retard their progress, and substantial amounts often cause great harm.

PASTEURIZATION MOVES FORWARD

Returning to New York, the order to pasteurize all but certified milk for use in the city created three grades of milk—A, B, and C. Grade A milk could be raw (certified) or pasteurized; all Grade B and Grade C milk had to be pasteurized. Certified raw milk was Grade A, and bacteria counts could not exceed sixty thousand per cubic centimeter. (By way of comparison, bacteria counts for licensed raw milk in the state of Connecticut today may not exceed ten thousand per cubic centimeter.) Grade A pasteurized milk could not contain more than thirty thousand bacteria per cubic centimeter once pasteurized, but up to two hundred thousand were allowed before pasteurization. Grade B milk, intended for adults only, could contain up to one and one-half million bacteria per cubic centimeter before and one hundred thousand bacteria after pasteurization. Grade C milk, intended for cooking and manufacturing purposes only, could contain up to three hundred thousand bacteria per cubic centimeters after pasteurization, and there was no limit on the number of bacteria allowed before pasteurization. Bacteria present before pasteurization did not disappear; they simply were killed in the process, and the residue of dead bacteria is not counted in bacteria assays. Then, as now, pasteurized milk obviously contained large amounts of dead bacteria.

During the early part of the century, the New York State Department of Health issued a weekly column, "Public Health Hints," which was published in several hundred newspapers throughout the state. In September, 1915, a column entitled "More Milk-Borne Disease" described epidemics of scarlet fever in Poughkeepsie and diphtheria in Rockland County that were traced to dairies where milkers were found to have mild, undetected cases.[16] Milkers were thought to have passed disease-causing bacteria into milk from their hands during the act of milking or by coughing over an open pail of milk. These were the days before closed-system milking machines eliminated these sources of contamination.

The column said that according to Professor M. J. Rosenau of Harvard University, between 1907 and 1911, over four thousand outbreaks of diphtheria, scarlet fever, typhoid fever and septic sore throat in Boston were "definitely traced to raw milk." A year after the 1914 institution of compulsory pasteurization of all milk except certified milk in New York City, the Bulletin of the New York City Department of Health reported that "No known milk epidemics of any kind have been discovered in New York City during the past year."[17]

How much of the disease attributed to raw milk was in fact caused by raw milk cannot be determined, but considerable controversy existed, even within the public health establishment, about the accuracy of the official figures. In 1929, William Dodge Frost, PhD and Doctor of Public Health, delivered a paper entitled "Some Bacteriological Problems of Milk Control." Frost analyzed a number of other papers that were critical of the official statistics. One paper concluded that while the official figures blamed anywhere from ten to forty percent of all typhoid fever cases in the years 1903-1907 on raw milk, the actual legitimate figure was only 0.19 of one percent. Another concluded that for the years 1906 to 1925 inclusive, only 0.221 percent of all the cases of typhoid fever, scarlet fever and diphtheria in the entire continental United States were milk-borne.

Frost summarized his findings as follows: "With any and all kinds of milk and extending over a long period, nearly half of which was before any particular or concerted attention was given to the hygienic production of it, milk has been far less a factor in the actual spread of disease than many of the current statements would lead us to believe. That there is an important danger that milk may serve as a vehicle of infectious diseases cannot be denied. But they accuse milk in every case and you have to prove that it is not milk. That milk is considered guilty until it is proved to be innocent does not seem a fair proposition."[18]

Wherever the truth may lie, "the milk problem" was real and pasteurization offered a quick fix to the most acute aspects of the problem. Compulsory pasteurization evaded the difficulty of making milk supplies safe through strict enforcement of higher standards. Powerful commercial interests applied further pressure on politicians and newspapers to extol the virtues of pasteurization and downplay the disadvantages. The push for compulsory pasteurization of all milk and the prohibition of raw milk retail sales in most states would eventually become unstoppable.

Other cities throughout America followed the lead of New York. By 1917, pasteurization of all milk except milk from cows proven to be free of tuberculosis was either required or officially encouraged in forty-six of the country's fifty-two largest cities. The proportion of milk pasteurized in these cities ranged from ten to ninety-seven percent; in most it was well over fifty percent.

Meanwhile, Nathan Straus became a virtual folk hero. There is no doubt that he was generous and had a genuine concern for the lives of children. He was zealous in his belief that his solution to the milk problem was the only one, and he shouted it from the rooftops. He gained great influence with the movers and shakers of society and in the media. From 1890 to 1915 he did more than any other person to promulgate the proposition that pasteurization was a boon to humanity. His corollary that all raw milk was dangerous was well on its way to acceptance by the majority of Americans, particularly those in positions of authority.

On January 31, 1911, some five hundred politicians, diplomats, bankers, businessmen, newspaper people, leaders in humanitarian, educational and philanthropic movements, and society people gathered to honor Straus. President Taft sent a congratulatory telegram. The Governor of New York attended and said, "Mr. Straus has devoted a large portion of his life, means, thought and fidelity to the care of the younger children, and through his tender mercies many thousands of them are living today who might otherwise have perished."

Many other dignitaries paid tribute to Straus, including newspaper magnate William Randolph Hearst who declared, "Mr. Straus' charity is as genuine as it is generous. It flows freely from an upright mind, a kindly heart, an open purse. It blesses the one who gives and the one who receives. It sets a noble example to us all."

The diners received a review of Straus's work which stated in part, "The name of Nathan Straus is identified the world over with the systematic saving of the lives of babies, for it was he who was the world pioneer in efforts to prevent the slaughter of the innocents by infected milk. He found a condition perilous to the public health and with unerring instinct chose a remedy. Today the pasteurization of milk is accepted with singular unanimity by all unbiased scientists. This demonstration of a scientific fact in advance of the researches of science is so dramatic that it gives Mr. Straus a title to fame apart from his philanthropies."[19]

Such is humanitarianism and science according to the publicists and the media. "World pioneer" Straus was neither the first nor the only individual concerned about the effects of bad milk. In reality, the "scientific facts" are complex and often in conflict with those that the press serves up. Pasteurization may have accomplished some good, but as a compromise alternative to broad and far-reaching steps that would ensure the production and widespread availability of truly healthy milk, it also caused great harm; pasteurization clearly does significantly alter the fundamental nature and nutritional value of milk. Raw milk from healthy animals, carefully produced and handled, does not cause disease. Such milk was available in Straus's time, and it continues to be produced today. In their headstrong rush to "save the babies" with a short-term technological solution, Straus and his supporters ignored the fundamental relationships between animals, food and human health. As zealots and politicians often do, they repeated a mixture of platitudes, truths, half-truths, buzz words and falsehoods often and loud, making it impossible for most people to separate fact from fiction. They set the stage for the epidemic of chronic disease, which ironically but significantly had its start during the very years they convinced Americans to accept universal pasteurization.

## PASTEURIZATION AND THE PUBLIC HEALTH AUTHORITIES

In 1917, the Registrar of Records for the Department of Health for New York City published tables showing the death rates for children under five years of age for the years 1891, when Straus began his work, to 1916. The death rate per thousand children per year fell from almost ninety-seven in 1891 to thirty-four in 1916. Public health officials and the newspapers (and thus much of the public) attributed the decline to the introduction of pasteurization but it is impossible to determine to what degree pasteurization contributed to the decline.

Similar reports came from cities in Europe where Straus introduced pasteurization as well. In early 1908, Straus convinced government officials in Sandhausen, Germany to pasteurize the milk supply of the city. On August 27 he received a telegram from the burgermeister (mayor) of the city: "Since February 1, 1908, there died in Sandhausen eleven children under two years of age, against twenty-five for the corresponding months in 1907, and against thirty-two for the five preceding years. We use the same milk as before, only pasteurized."[20]

These accounts have influenced professionals working in the public health and medical fields today. In general, these men and women have not even heard of the work of Henry Coit and the history of the certified milk movement; nor are they familiar with the work of Francis Pottenger and others who demonstrated the nutritional superiority of raw milk. This one-sided education may be responsible for the unwillingness of most public health workers to consider evidence of raw milk's benefits and to explore the premise that carefully produced raw milk is a healthy food that should be available to those who desire it. It is impossible for public health officials to see both sides of the issue fairly without accurate and unbiased information.

A blind prejudice against all raw milk—to the point of legislation banning not only retail sales of certified and inspected raw milk but even the sale or giving away of raw milk on the farm—is largely a product of recent times. In Straus's day, even his staunch medical ally M.J. Rosenau favored keeping raw milk certified as "fresh, pure and clean" available to those who wanted it, many of whom were his medical colleagues. The notion that an authoritarian and paternalistic government could strip this right from the American people is a phenomenon of more recent vintage.

Straus himself, however, made contradictory statements. He often said that raw milk from healthy, tuberculin-tested animals was safe. But he also made this statement: "There can be no question but that the entire milk supply everywhere ought to be pasteurized, not only that intended for infants, since the use of raw milk for adults is almost equally fraught with danger. Does it seem possible that anyone should ever use it in its raw state? Why ever trust it without due precaution?"[21]

This attitude became pervasive. The oft-repeated fallacies that pasteurization did no harm and guaranteed safety, while raw milk was never really safe, were to become an integral part of the belief system held by most Americans. A series of media campaigns using deliberate lies and distortions would eventually lead to legislation in most states that turned this belief system into law.

## WHEN PASTEURIZATION WOULD NOT BE NECESSARY

For all his diatribes against raw milk, Straus also wrote, "If it were possible to secure pure, fresh milk direct from absolutely healthy cows there would be no necessity for pasteurization. If it were possible by legislation to obtain a milk supply from clean stables after a careful process of milking, to have transportation to the city in perfectly clean and close vessels, then pasteurization would be unnecessary."[22] This is a statement with which any proponent of raw milk would agree. The advent of the modern milking machine in the 1920s has indeed made it possible to produce such milk not only for the few, but on a wide and general scale.

In April of 1908, Rosenau wrote in *The Milk Reporter*: "We prefer pure milk, but so long as we cannot obtain it we must purify what we get. Theoretically, pasteurization should not be necessary; practically we find it forced upon us. Special cases may require raw milk. The heating of milk has certain disadvantages which must be given consideration." Surgeon General Walter Wyman made a similar point in summing up the results of the federal government's milk investigation: "Pasteurization is forced upon us by present conditions." It is obvious that even among its most ardent supporters, pasteurization was seen as a necessary evil to render contaminated milk from improperly fed and unhealthy cows safe to drink. Many prominent public health officials saw pasteurization as a temporary fix for the tuberculosis problem, which was incorrectly attributed to milk from tuberculous cows. "Tuberculosis is so common among dairy cows," one wrote, "that many years must pass before we can reasonably hope to eradicate it, and *in the meantime* pasteurization is necessary for the protection of public health [Emphasis added.]."[23]

In a 1908 address at the University of Heidelberg, Straus referred to statistics on bottle-feeding versus breast-feeding. He referred to a French study indicating that of twenty thousand infants who died of intestinal disease, four-fifths were bottle-fed. Official German statistics he quoted showed that the mortality in the first year among bottle-fed infants was over fifty percent, compared to only eight percent among those exclusively breast-fed. It appears that like America, Europe had a milk problem; bacteria counts in various German cities at this time ranged from a few hundred thousand per cubic centimeter to many million. Straus did not point out, however—proponents of pasteurization as the solution to the milk problem never did—that breast milk is not pasteurized. Instead he endorsed a statement made in an American government *Milk Bulletin*, "Pasteurized milk is now claimed to be even more easily digested than raw milk."[24] I would venture to guess that anyone suffering from irritable bowel syndrome, colitis or any of a host of other gastrointestinal complaints who has ever tried raw milk from healthy grass-fed animals over the course of the eighty-six years since that claim was made would vigorously dispute its accuracy. We'll look at this subject in greater detail in the next chapter.

Official statistics do indicate that Straus's efforts in Germany resulted in dramatic declines in infant mortality, and his work was hailed in Europe as it was in America. Although pasteurization became the norm, European officialdom maintained a sense of tolerance for dissidents who chose to take their milk raw, and today raw milk continues to be available throughout Europe.

## THE CLOSED-SYSTEM AUTOMATIC MILKING MACHINE

Straus cites several examples of milk infected by the people handling it and causing epidemics of typhoid, scarlet fever and diphtheria. Sixty-six people came down with typhoid in Dublin in 1899, all of them supplied with milk from the same dairy farm. Several cases of typhoid fever received nursing care at the farm, and officials surmised that one of the persons providing care also handled the milk and passed the infection on.

A similar incident had occurred three years previous in Dublin, when the two children of a milk-shop merchant came down with typhoid; it was thought that the children's nurse infected the milk in the shop. Fourteen cases resulted.

In Liverpool in 1904, fifty-nine cases of scarlet fever occurred among people consuming milk from a dairy where a child was recovering from the disease. As for diphtheria, in Edinburgh in 1900 over fifty people contracted the disease after consuming milk from a dairy farm where milkers and others were found on bacteriological examination to be carriers.[25]

The problem of contamination of good milk by milkers and handlers who unknowingly carried disease was eliminated when closed-system automatic milking machines were installed, after their invention in the 1920s. Vacuum hoses fit snugly over the cows' teats, which are thoroughly cleaned with an iodine solution just before milking. Milk passes through the hoses, which are thoroughly cleaned after each milking, into a covered milk pail or directly into the holding tank where it is cooled. When milking is done according to standard procedures with this method, there is no way for contamination from the milker to occur. The milk can be subsequently bottled directly from the holding tank.

But the prevalence of serious infectious diseases such as diphtheria and scarlet fever in the early 1900s and the capacity of even good raw milk carelessly handled to occasionally spread these diseases were important reasons why many people feared raw milk and why public health authorities wanted pasteurization. Heating milk to kill whatever bacteria might be present was a simple and relatively inexpensive way to prevent the spread of infectious disease in milk.

The superior alternative, namely widespread enforcement of strict regulations governing the production and distribution of milk from thousands of small farms supplying the large cities, was simply not practical.

## TUBERCULOSIS AND MILK

Perhaps the most contentious subject related to raw milk in the years around 1900 was tuberculosis. TB was the major cause of death throughout the world, including America, throughout the 1800s and until about 1940. In 1882, Robert Koch had discovered the specific germ associated with the disease. At first he announced that the same organism caused TB in both animals and humans. But in 1901 he stated that the animal and human organisms were different, and that bovine TB was not transmitted to human beings. Great controversy ensued, and by 1915 various governments claimed that their researchers had proven Koch wrong, that TB, whether in animals or humans, was essentially the same disease and communicable from animals to humans in milk.

Many people, including Straus, claimed that raw milk was a major cause of TB. Because pasteurization was known to kill the tubercle bacilli, speculation and publicity about the scientific controversy surrounding TB played a major role in the move to pasteurize all the milk supplies of the large cities.

The tuberculin test, invented by Koch, both clarified and confused the issue. Tuberculin, a product of the growth of tubercle bacilli in the laboratory, causes a measurable immune reaction (swelling at the site of injection) when injected into a person or animal previously exposed to TB. The problem is that it is impossible to tell from the test alone whether the animal or individual has active TB or is simply showing immunity to TB due to the previous exposure, without active disease.

During the early 1900s, veterinarians began to use the test to screen cows throughout the world, and significant numbers were found to be reactive. For example, health officials tested more than fifteen hundred of the cows supplying milk to the city of Washington, DC, in 1916, and pronounced seventeen percent tuberculous. Reactive cows were eliminated, as a government-sponsored program in the United States sought to establish tuberculosis-free herds. In the early years of pasteurization, many cities required that milk be either pasteurized or come from cows that had been tested for TB and found non-reactive. Most states no longer test for bovine TB because it is nearly unknown in America today. However, most states that license the retail sale of raw milk do require testing the cows used for milk production.

Many scientists in the early 1900s reported finding the tubercle bacillus in milk, and it was widely believed that this was a cause of bovine tuberculosis in humans; others, however believed that milk's ability to protect against TB was compromised by pasteurization. A letter published in *The Pharmaceutical Journal and Pharmacist*, 1914, argues that the heating of milk did not prevent TB but actually contributed to the disease: "In a letter to the *Times* on April 15, Dr. Ralph Vincent combated the thesis that tuberculous meningitis in children was of bovine origin and came from drinking cows' milk. The immediate cause of the disease, Dr. Vincent maintained, was the tubercle bacillus which was derived from the inhalation of dust containing it. In a healthy and properly nourished child the tissues would rapidly destroy the bacilli. But in an improperly nourished child they would be unable to do so. And this condition would arise in the case of a child fed entirely on cooked, boiled, and sterilised food. Dr. Vincent stated that since 1904 he had been searching for a case of tuberculous meningitis in a child fed on raw milk but had never found one, whereas since the beginning of this year he had seen three cases in children fed on cooked milk."[26]

We'll look at some of the components of raw milk that protect against TB in Chapter 15. But now, let's move on to explore the unsung counterpart to "the milk problem"—the remarkable history of raw milk used as medicine.

# 6
# Good Medicine:
# The History of the Milk Cure

*"Raw milk cures many diseases."*[1]
J.E. Crewe, MD, The Mayo Foundation, January, 1929

MILK AND HEALING

Fresh milk has a long and rich history as a healing agent and build-er of health. Hippocrates advised tuberculosis sufferers to drink large quantities of asses' milk; Arabian physicians prescribed camel's milk. Homer called the robust horsemen and warriors of Scythia *Galactopha-gi*, or feeders on milk; Herodotus chronicled the varied ways these peo-ple used mares' milk. Many writers from cultures throughout the world and over the centuries have praised milk as a food that builds strong bodies and cures disease.

During the nineteenth century, Russian and German physicians popularized the raw milk cure. One Dr. Inozemtseff wrote a work en-titled *The Milk Cure*, published in Moscow in 1857; he reported treating over one thousand cases with an exclusive diet of raw milk. Dr. G. L. Carrick, physician to the British embassy at St. Petersburg, translated *On the Milk Cure*, by Philip Karell, MD, into English and published an article on the subject in the *Edinburgh Medical Journal*, August, 1866. Karell claimed to have successfully treated hundreds of cases of asthma, neuralgia (pain extending along one or more nerves), fluid retention, liver diseases and "conditions of faulty nutrition." He insisted that milk be taken at regular intervals in doses of two to six ounces, and that the best results were obtained when the diet contained only milk and no other food. A number of other physicians in Germany, said to be eminent medical authorities, advocated the milk diet in the treatment of various chronic diseases.[2]

In our discussion of raw milk as medicine, we should bear in mind the several meanings of the word "cure," derived from the Latin *cura* for "care." Today we tend to think of "cure" as something that completely solves a problem. But Dorland's *Medical Dictionary* defines "cure" as either the course of treatment of a disease, or the successful treatment of a disease, or a system of treating diseases. The literature of the nineteenth and early twentieth centuries uses the word "cure" in all three ways, and often in a context in which the meaning is not completely clear. But usually it refers to a course of treatment or a system. Thus "the milk cure" referred to a method and was not a claim that all of the diseases successfully *treated* were *"cured"* in the modern sense of the word. Even when referring to a successful treatment, we should not think of "cure" as something that allows a patient to walk away after the course of treatment, freed forever of his disease. Rather, think of the "cure" as the beginning of a healing process that may continue after the initial treatment if the individual maintains a proper diet and lifestyle. Though symptoms frequently disappear during the "cure," I have noted that they often return with a vengeance when the individual "cured" returns to old habits.

In 1876, the American physician A. S. Donkin wrote an article entitled "The Curative Influence of an Exclusive Milk Diet" for a medical journal called the *London Lancet*. Donkin claimed that diabetes could be cured by large quantities of milk, some cases needing up to seven quarts per day. In the same volume appeared an article by an English physician making the case for greater use of the exclusive milk diet in certain diseases. He noted particularly that in many cases of Bright's disease, a term formerly used to describe a broad range of kidney diseases involving protein in the urine, the protein disappeared "under the influence of rest in bed, a few warm baths and copious libations of milk."

He also described cures of bladder inflammation using the same treatment.[3]

According to Weir Mitchell, MD, the American physician said to have had the greatest experience with chronic disease during the late nineteenth and early twentieth centuries, "It is difficult to treat any of these cases without a resort at some time more or less to the use of milk." Mitchell reported of laboring men who lived for long periods on milk alone, sometimes two and one-half to three gallons daily. One of his patients was a diabetic who had lived on milk alone for over fifteen years while managing a large and prosperous business.[4]

The milk diet was recommended for diabetes, Bright's disease, gastric disturbances and obesity by a Professor James Tyson writing in the June, 1884 *Journal of the American Medical Association*. He noted that uric acid in the urine disappeared and that consistent use of milk cured kidney stones. No other food than milk should be permitted in the treatment of gastric ulcers, he said, and no treatment for obesity is so effective as the milk diet.

In 1905, Charles Sanford Porter, MD published *Milk Diet as a Remedy for Chronic Disease*. The book went through eleven editions, the last published in 1923. "At least 18,000 patients have taken the treatment under my direction in the last 37 years," Sanford wrote. "A good food is a good remedy, and, as disease is only a disturbance of the mechanism of nutrition, it is only natural that the use of milk in ill health should be almost as old as its use as a food in health."[5]

Porter believed that many of the constituents of milk are absorbed directly into the lymphatic circulation, whence they pass into the blood. Milk is secreted from the animal's blood, he claimed, and the fluid portion of milk is similar to blood serum. The enzymes in milk may be identical with those elaborated by the various tissues of the human body, he claimed. According to Porter, as milk is full of living elements of vital character, it is obvious that the application of heat will have a serious detrimental effect on its value.

During Porter's day, all the principal medical textbooks advocated the use of milk in the diet of patients with chronic diseases. Porter stated that most of his thousands of patients with chronic disease who took the treatment in the manner he recommended were either cured or greatly helped. The popularity of the treatment grew during those years, extending to physicians and a few sanitariums around the country.

Porter emphasized that the milk must be raw, writing "What is required is good, clean milk as it comes from the cow, without the removal or addition of any substance whatsoever. Boiled, sterilized or pasteurized milk, or milk artificially preserved in any way, can not be used for this treatment. Pasteurizing milk renders it unsuitable for human use. Dogs fed on pasteurized milk only, are liable to have the mange and other disorders, while others of the same litter thrive on raw, sweet and sour milk."[6]

Porter wrote that in his thirty-nine years of experience with this treatment, he had obtained uniformly good results. His cases included patients suffering from heart and kidney disease, brain and nerve disorders, blood clots, paralysis, colitis and irritable bowel syndrome, ulcerative processes in various parts of the body, gastritis and chronic poisoning due to lead, mercury, arsenic and various other toxic medicines used at the time. He had never seen any injury or bad results from the milk diet, but advised against giving the diet to any patient who had recently had an operation for fear that the increase in blood volume caused by the milk might increase bleeding tendencies. He strongly advised complete rest with the diet.

Porter also wrote that a number of experienced dentists concurred with him, finding the diet of great benefit to the teeth and especially beneficial for periodontal disease.[7] He found that the average adult needed two to four quarts a day of four percent butterfat milk to maintain weight. He believed strongly that the diet should be exclusive. "It is wrong, if not positively dangerous, to attempt the exclusive milk diet on any amount of milk less than that required to noticeably stimulate the circulation and promote body growth. There is no halfway method of taking the milk diet for people who have much the matter with them. Enough milk must be taken to create new circulation, new cells, and new tissue growth, and cause prompt elimination of the waste and dead matter that may be poisoning the system." The use of other foods was prohibited. "With milk alone, digestion and assimilation may go on throughout practically the whole length of the alimentary canal. The addition of even a cracker to the milk seems to cause the stomach to hold all its contents for hours without discharging much into the intestine." The minimum time for his treatment was four weeks.

At the time Porter published his book, an Austrian physician, Herman Schwartz, had lived exclusively on milk for twenty-three years, using about three quarts daily. He was by all accounts in the best of health.[8]

In 1913, a Burlington, Iowa man, Mr. W. F. Kitzele, sent a letter to Porter. "I have lived on a strictly milk diet for the past forty-two years, not as a matter of choice, but from the fact that I am unable to take solid food of any kind, even a crumb of bread. At the age of two years I took a dose of concentrated lye, which caused a stricture of the food pipe and since then have lived on a milk diet. I believe I have gotten along better than the man who eats. I am five feet, six inches tall, weigh one hundred and forty pounds, and am married and have four strong, healthy children. I take one quart at each mealtime and none between meals. My health is good, in fact I have never been ill in bed in forty-two years."

In 1921, Porter wrote to Mr. Kitzele, a city official in Burlington, and asked him for more information. Kitzele reported that he was still living on an exclusive milk diet, and would do so for the rest of his life. It had been fifty years since he had tasted solid food of any kind. In the fifty years he had never been sick in bed with an illness and physically he was as strong as any man doing office work. He reported knowing another man in Chicago who had suffered the same injury, from the same cause, who also lived exclusively on milk.

The writer Ella Wheeler Wilcox wrote Porter in 1905 of her personal experience with the milk diet and that of many of her acquaintances. One man who destroyed his digestion by wrong habits had for the last five years lived in perfect health and strength on milk alone. "He is able to work more hours with less fatigue," she wrote, "than any of his friends. He possesses a marvelous complexion and is never ill. Another friend who had been a hopeless invalid for ten years, through complications of diseases, has lived on milk for three years, and finds herself perfectly well unless she attempts to return to solid foods. A dozen skilled physicians failed to give her even three days of health, until she gave up foods for milk. Seventeen other personal friends restored their health, and the ability to digest a natural, varied diet, by taking the milk treatment for a few weeks."

From such accounts—all of which are consistent with my own experience in over twenty years of naturopathic practice—can we doubt that raw milk from healthy, grass-fed animals is a wonderful, health-building food? Porter states that a course of four weeks on the milk diet should be sufficient to cure the following conditions: fatigue, skin troubles, poor digestion, pleurisy, ringing in the ears, constipation, asthma, allergies, hemorrhoids, insomnia, ulcers, colitis, goiter, malaria, arteriosclerosis, neuralgia, arthritis, hives, cystitis, dysentery or chronic diarrhea, impotence, gout, sciatica, migraine, enlargement of the prostate, gallstones and liver disorders, kidney disease and the first stage of tuberculosis. More advanced stages of tuberculosis or chronic diseases took longer. In the preface to the last edition of his book, Porter wrote, "Diabetes can now definitely be added to the list of diseases cured by the milk diet."

A striking thing about the milk cure, according to Porter, is normalization of either high or low blood pressure. Milk greatly benefits the heart, according to Porter, building up the strength of a weak heart by building the blood, but in all cardiac problems complete rest was to be combined with the diet. The diet was also safe for invalids with badly diseased kidneys, in spite of the increased work for the kidneys. Some of these patients experienced slight pains in the kidneys the first few days, "probably due to a rapid growth of the organs as they increased their function and became stronger." One patient came to Porter to be strengthened up for an operation to remove a tubercular kidney; a well-known specialist had made the diagnosis and prescribed surgery. After four weeks on milk and rest, a re-examination found no trace of the disease. She never had the operation and subsequently became pregnant and gave birth to a healthy baby.

According to late 19th century proponents, the "secret" of the milk cure lies in the fact good raw milk is a food the body easily turns into good blood. In illness, according to this theory, there is one or both of two blood conditions: insufficient quantity or abnormal quality. The milk diet corrects both and, acting through the blood and the circulation, heals the cells and thus the tissues and organs. The muscles of those on a milk diet harden, almost like an athlete's, because they are pumped full of blood, as are the organs.

Just as blood pressure normalizes, so too does weight; those who are too thin gain, while the overweight lose. Excess fluids are lost by the natural diuretic effect of the milk; lots of good milk, or an exclusive milk diet, has a wonderfully beneficial effect on edema.

## RAW MILK AND FERMENTED MILK FOODS
## FOR SPECIFIC MEDICAL PROBLEMS

Nearly every medical problem is accompanied by stomach trouble of one sort or another. The symptoms usually include indigestion but may be quite varied. In my experience, a primary cause is too much cooked or processed foods. Indigestion is easily solved in most people by a diet based on lots of raw and fermented foods, rich in enzymes and beneficial bacteria. Those with digestive problems usually tolerate good quality raw milk, both fresh and fermented into yogurt or kefir. In years past when high quality raw milk was more available, the milk diet readily solved the problem of indigestion.

Constipation frequently accompanies poor digestion. When properly practiced with the full ration of milk, Porter claimed that the milk diet is a natural cure for most cases of constipation. I have found that sometimes when milk is used in conjunction with other foods, there is a tendency to constipation. The inclusion of homemade yogurt, soured milk, soured milk cheese and other fermented foods usually solves this problem. The sea vegetable dulse is also very helpful, as may be fresh fruit, if constipation persists.

Porter reported that most of his practice prior to 1905 was for patients suffering with tuberculosis, and that the milk diet was the most successful treatment he knew of for the disease. In 1905 he moved to Long Beach, California, where the hot and dry coastal climate was less suitable for consumptives than that of more elevated localities. He reported that the sanitarium of J. E. Crewe, MD, at the Mayo Clinic in Minnesota, successfully treated tuberculosis by using "three to nine quarts daily, taken at half hour intervals, of fresh, raw, warm milk, and fruit if the patient is constipated." Bed rest was required along with the diet.

While I have not prescribed an exclusive milk diet for extended periods of time as Porter did, I have found that asthma, allergies and hay fever have all responded well for patients using liberal quantities of good raw milk and raw milk products. Porter wrote that a four-week course of the milk diet followed by a reasonable diet often resulted in a complete cure for these problems.[9] I have also found that lactic acid products—soured milk, clabbered milk, koumiss, kefir, soured cheese and yogurt—made from fresh raw milk from grass-fed animals are invaluable in the treatment of the sick, including those with various arthritic diseases. (We'll talk more about fermented milk products in Chapter 17.) All chronic disease, if not too far advanced and if the patient has not been poisoned by drugs, may respond well to a diet containing liberal amounts of these foods (as well as raw butter and cream). Even severe forms of heart and kidney disease may be treated successfully, as well as kidney stones and fibroid tumors of the uterus.

Diabetics are benefited, and in some instances the disease is permanently reversed; soured milk is most effective in diabetes, and this remedy is also beneficial in the treatment of cancer. Cancer patients do improve on the raw milk diet, though neither Porter nor I claim cures with raw milk alone.

Porter found that the exclusive milk diet was extremely successful for high blood pressure. Many of my patients with high blood pressure have used quantities of good quality raw milk with great benefit and often a return to normal blood pressure. And low blood pressure, which frequently accompanies chronic fatigue and the weakened nutritional status so common today—often the result of vegan or near vegan diets—also responds well to quantities of good raw milk and raw milk products.

Bernarr MacFadden was another practitioner who had extensive experience with the milk cure. In his 1923 book *The Miracle of Milk*, MacFadden wrote, "Milk is the greatest of all diet cures. I have personally come in contact with thousands of people who have been amazingly benefited by adhering to the exclusive milk diet. I have personally secured benefits at different times in my own life that could not be measured in money value. There are times in the life of every human unit when the milk diet can be of extraordinary value. I am convinced that the milk diet properly adjusted to the individual case is of tremendous value in practically any functional or organic disturbance that may affect the human body. The best milk, either for the milk cure or for general uses, is good, clean milk, unaltered in any way since coming from the cow."[10]

## THE MAYO FOUNDATION EMBRACES THE RAW MILK CURE

In 1929, J. E. Crewe, MD, one of the founders of the Mayo Foundation (forerunner of the Mayo Clinic) in Rochester, Minnesota, published an article entitled "Raw Milk Cures Many Diseases." Here are excerpts from Dr. Crewe's account of his experience with raw milk:

"For fifteen years the writer has employed the certified milk treatment in various diseases and during the past ten he had a small sanitarium devoted principally to this treatment. The results obtained in various types of disease have been so uniformly excellent that one's conception of disease and its alleviation is necessarily changed. The method itself is so simple that it does not greatly interest most doctors. . . . The fact that many diseases are treated and successful results claimed, leads almost to disrespect.

"To cure disease we should seek to improve elimination, to make better blood and more blood. . . . to build up resistance. The method used tends to accomplish these things. Blood conditions rapidly improve and the general condition and resistance is built up and recovery follows.

"In several instances Osler [an eminent physician at that time[11]] speaks of milk as being nothing more than white blood. . . . Milk resembles blood closely and is a useful agent for improving and making new and better blood. . . . blood is the chief agent of metabolism. Milk is recognized in medical literature almost exclusively as a useful food and is admitted to be a complete food. . . .

"The patients are put at rest in bed and are given at half-hour intervals from five to ten quarts of milk a day. . . . Most patients are started on three or four quarts of milk a day and this is usually increased a pint a day. Very rich, raw milk is used. . . . Diaphoresis [intense sweating] is stimulated with hot baths and hot packs. A daily enema is given.

"The treatment is used in many chronic conditions but chiefly in tuberculosis, diseases of the nervous system, cardiovascular and renal conditions, hypertension, and in patients who are underweight, run-down, etc. . . . striking results are seen in diseases of the heart and kidneys and high blood pressure. . . . In cases in which there is marked edema, the results obtained are surprisingly marked. This is especially striking because so-called dropsy has never been treated with large quantities of fluid. With all medication withdrawn, one case lost twenty-six pounds in six days, huge edema disappearing from the abdomen and legs, with great relief to the patient. No cathartics or diuretics were given. This property of [raw] milk in edema has been noted in both cardiac and renal cases.

"Patients with cardiac disease respond splendidly without medication. With patients who have been taking digitalis and other stimulants, the drugs are withdrawn. . . . High blood pressure patients respond splendidly and the results in most instances are quite lasting. . . . The treatment has been used successfully in obesity without under-alimentation. One patient reduced from 325 pounds to 284 in two weeks, on four quarts of milk a day, while her blood pressure was reduced from 220 to 170. . . . Some extremely satisfying results have been obtained in a few cases of diabetes...

"When sick people are limited to a diet containing an excess of vitamins and all the elements necessary to growth and maintenance, they recover rapidly without the use of drugs and without bringing to bear all the complicated weapons of modern medicine. The treatment of various diseases over a period of eighteen years with a practically exclusive milk diet has convinced me personally that the most important single factor in the cause of disease and in the resistance to disease is food. I have seen so many instances of the rapid and marked response to this form of treatment that nothing could make me believe this is not so."[12]

THE IMPORTANCE OF GRASS FEEDING AND ENZYMES
During the time the above accounts were written, ruminant an-

imals in rural America were largely kept at pasture most of the year. Even then, observers recognized that milk from pasture-fed animals has qualities that are lacking when the animals are confined and fed grains. MacFadden wrote, "The best time of the year for the milk diet is spring and early summer. At this time of the year the cows are eating new grass, which seems to give the milk a greater curative value, probably on account of the better health of the cattle when outdoors and eating their natural diet."[13]

A 1928 article published in the *American Journal of Public Health* states, "Milk varies with the season and with the feeding of the cow, especially in regard to vitamin content. . . the public deserves to have the information that there is a great difference between the milk derived from pasture-fed cattle and that obtained in winter from stall-fed animals, unless particular attention is paid to their diet. . ."[14] These observations were later confirmed by the famous cat studies of Dr. Francis Pottenger, described in Chapter 7.

In my own practice, I have seen time and again that raw milk from animals fed only or mostly grass and hay often has a profoundly superior effect on my patients compared to raw milk from animals fed quantities of grain. We'll explore these issues further in other chapters. The point here is that the exclusive milk diet, or any diet using substantial amounts of milk and milk products, should emphasize the use of milk from grass-fed animals.

Dr. Edward Howell brings this point home in his 1985 book *Enzyme Nutrition*. Born in 1898, Howell had a lifelong interest in the health benefits of enzymes—richly supplied only in certain raw or fermented foods (not all raw foods are good sources of enzymes)—and considerable familiarity with the use of raw milk in therapy. In the section of the book entitled "Raw Milk Diet," he is highly critical of the methods used to produce some certified raw milk:

"In producing commercial raw certified milk, the cows spend their day standing in barns stuffing themselves with an abundance of dry fodder and milk-producing additives. They are denied the right to go on pasture to feed on fresh green vegetation. They are allowed to walk around outside an hour or two in a barren plot for daily exercise. This is a typical factory operation designed for top milk production; the antithesis of milk with full value. The interests of mass production have led to the selection of cows with abnormally large udders. The so-called 'scrub' cows of former times, with their smaller udders and less milk secretion, had less strain on their metabolism and could produce milk of higher health value."

Howell then points out the detrimental effect of pasteurization: "To ignore the health intangibles is inexcusable for anyone concerned with human well-being. The full impact of these intangibles can only be appreciated when a comparison is made between the favorable health benefits of raw milk noted by Dr. Sanford and his predecessors dating back to the time of Hippocrates, and the negative values of today's pasteurized milk. No one would expect health benefits from an exclusive pasteurized milk diet. It has no medical sponsors or curative value. Medical enthusiasm for milk as a therapeutic agent suffered an abrupt ending with the advent of pasteurization, and its killing of milk enzymes. An important conclusion emerges from studying the long history of milk as food and medicine: When one takes enzymes away from milk, it loses some of its health value and most of its curative properties. The virtue of effective foods resides in their possession of all of the nutritional factors nature gave them. The status raw milk gained as a remedy for chronic diseases throughout hundreds of years vanished with the coming of pasteurized milk."[15]

Most people—and certainly most medical practitioners—have little understanding of the value of raw milk from grass-fed animals, though most inherently sense its power when the value is explained. But such milk is difficult for most of us to procure; the industrialization and politicization of the food supply has seen to that. With the loss of raw milk and other sources of food enzymes, the people of the modern world have lost much of their strength and health. Dr. Howell's work on food enzymes and raw foods is the focus of our next chapter.

# 7
# Enzymes:
# Essential to Life

*In living cells, the dynamic, driving power, which apparently in-troduces the* spark of life, *is found in their* enzyme contents.

Dr. Laird, *Medical Record*, 1922

Medical textbooks tell us that enzymes are large molecules com-posed mostly or entirely of protein; they are found in all cells and are essential to life. Enzymes act as catalysts for biochemical reactions both inside and outside the cell. Every enzyme has a unique shape that en-ables it to catalyze only a specific type of reaction. Without enzymes, there is no life; kill the enzymes and you kill the organism.[1,2]

Scientists have discovered over five thousand enzymes, group-ing them into three major classifications. The largest class is that of the metabolic enzymes, which play a role in all bodily processes including breathing, talking, moving, thinking, behavior and maintenance of the immune system. The second category is the digestive enzymes, most of which are manufactured by the pancreas (a more apt description is that they are assembled there) and a few by the salivary glands. The third cat-egory is the food enzymes, present in large amounts in certain raw foods. When present in the diet in sufficient quantity, food enzymes initiate the process of digestion in the mouth and stomach.

Such is the conventional definition of enzymes, and even this dry statement of facts convinces us that enzymes are vital. But it is a mistake to think of enzymes as mere catalysts, proteins that speed up biochemical reactions, for enzymes are matter impregnated with energy. In 1921 Professor Moore of Oxford University published *Biochemistry—A Study of the Origin, Reactions and Equilibria of Living Matter*,[3] in which he describes enzymes as "biotic energy."

Professor Troland of Harvard University expressed a similar understanding five years earlier, writing in the *Cleveland Medical Journal*: "The conception that constitutes the secret of life, in my belief, is that the peculiarly vital properties of living beings depend directly upon catalytic action. The essence of life is catalysis [building up], and this is but a plain physico-chemical process. *Life*, according to this conception, is something which has been built up about the enzyme; it is a corollary of *enzyme activity*."[4]

Another medical man, a Dr. Laird, writing in the *Medical Record* in 1922, expressed similar ideas: "In living cells, the dynamic, driving power, which apparently introduces the *spark of life*, is found in their *enzyme contents*. The metaphysical explanations of life are scarcely needed since the discovery of the enzymes and their functions."[5]

A wet temperature of about 118 degrees F (the temperature at which substances feel too hot to the touch) kills many enzymes, including those in food; dry or oven heat kills enzymes at about 150 degrees F. Thoroughly cooked food contains no enzymes. Pasteurization kills all the enzymes in milk. In fact, the test for successful pasteurization is the complete destruction of the enzyme phosphatase.

Not all raw foods are rich sources of enzymes; common fruits and vegetables such as peaches, peas, apples and salad greens, for example, have a low enzyme content. Animal foods are generally much richer in enzymes than foods from the vegetable kingdom.

The role of food enzymes in health and disease has received little interest from the food and pharmaceutical industries that sponsor much of today's scientific research. In fact, they claim that enzymes in food are broken down during digestion and therefore serve no purpose. The wheels of the modern industrial state are greased by processed foods, completely devoid of enzymes, and food companies have little incentive to invest money for research into areas that would demonstrate the importance and benefits of enzyme-rich foods.

But in the first half of the twentieth century, a great deal of effort went into research on enzymes. The work of two physicians in particular provides important understanding of the role of food enzymes and thus certain raw or fermented foods in human metabolism. One was Francis Pottenger, a well-known clinician and researcher whose work was widely published in the professional literature; the other was Edward Howell. While Pottenger conducted many now-classic experiments himself, Howell assimilated and expounded on the enzyme research of others in a remarkable book first published in 1946, *The Status of Food Enzymes in Digestion and Metabolism*. We'll look first at Pottenger's work.

## FRANCIS POTTENGER ON THE VITAL NATURE OF RAW FOODS

The impact of quoted work is often influenced by the reputation of the person quoted. But what makes a reputation, in particular the reputation of a person who died many years ago? Certainly the accuracy and importance of the written work left behind plays a part. But when most of society ignores or maligns a person's life and work, reputation suffers. Which yardstick may we use then to evaluate the import of the life? We may be left with only our judgment of the work itself. If the work is complex and perhaps not readily available, as is Dr. Pottenger's, making that judgment may be difficult.

In explaining Pottenger's work, I'll quote key passages from several of his papers, allowing his words to speak for themselves. To help the reader assess the importance of those words, I first present some details of the man's life so you may form your own opinion of what Pottenger's reputation should be.

Thomas Hotchkiss knew Francis M. Pottenger, MD, from the time Thomas was eleven years old in 1912. His "Personal Memoir" of Francis, written after the doctor's death in 1967, is the source for many of the following details about Pottenger's life.[6]

Two years before his death, Francis received the Distinguished Alumnus Award at Otterbein College in Ohio. In presenting the citation, the Chairman of the Board of Trustees praised Francis's exemplary career in medicine and public service.

Service indeed. By the time he received that award, Francis M. Pottenger had published over fifty peer reviewed articles in the scientific literature, mainly in the fields of medicine, chronic disease and nutrition. He had served as president of the Los Angeles County Medical Association, the American Therapeutic Society and the American Academy of Applied Nutrition. "Francis was among the first in his profession to recognize the hazard to health caused by air pollution in Los Angeles County," Hotchkiss wrote. "He worked indefatigably over a period of many years to mitigate its deleterious effects upon human health. His efforts were widely recognized and as a result he became a member of the Los Angeles County Air Pollution Control District's Scientific Committee on Air Pollution."

In 1951, the Texas State Dental Association honored Pottenger with an award for the Advancement of the Science of Dentistry, a rather unusual accolade for a medical doctor. He had written a number of brilliant articles about the effect of raw versus cooked foods, including pasteurized milk, on the dental and facial structures of animals and human beings. The articles had a powerful and lasting impact on the many American physicians and dentists who were actively interested in the effect of nutrition on human health and disease.

In 1940, Francis founded the Francis M. Pottenger, Jr. Hospital at Monrovia, California for the treatment of asthma and other non-tubercular diseases of the respiratory system. And beginning in 1945, he served as Assistant Clinical Professor of Experimental Medicine at the University of Southern California.

Dr. Pottenger also served as volunteer Medical Service Chief for the Civil Defense Area surrounding his home during World War II. Japanese invasion of the West Coast of America was considered a real threat in the dark days just after the 1941 attack on Pearl Harbor. The project to set up the first portable hospital in Los Angeles County under simulated disaster conditions was directed by Pottenger.

In 1940 he began the Pottenger Cat Study, the groundbreaking research for which he is best known. There's no money these days in promoting the fame of a man who proves the value of raw foods; in the last forty years or so, Pottenger's fame in the conventional medical and nutritional establishment has faded as surely as the stocks of processed food companies have risen. Yet he remains an icon to those who understand his work and its importance.

Pottenger kept a large colony of cats at his sanatorium. As part of the nutritional regime, his patients received extracts from the adrenal glands of cows and steers. During the 1930s, no laboratory was able to determine the hormone content of biological extracts so Pottenger tested the potency of various adrenal extract batches by removing the adrenal glands from cats and then measuring the amount of extract required for their survival. Despite careful surgical technique, however, and a seemingly adequate diet of raw milk, cod liver oil and meat scraps from the sanatorium kitchen, many cats died after the surgery to remove their adrenal glands.

The cats that did not survive exhibited signs of nutritional deficiencies, skeletal malformations, internal malfunctions and reproductive problems. The inspiration for the study came when the cat population grew to the point that it became necessary to secure raw meat scraps from a local butcher. Before long, Pottenger observed that the cats receiving the raw meat scraps were plainly in better health than those on the cooked meat scraps. Their post-op mortality decreased, they reproduced more easily and their kittens were healthier.

Because pathological problems in cats eating cooked meats were similar to those Pottenger observed in his patients, he believed a controlled feeding experiment with the cats would isolate variables of importance in human nutrition. His experiments met the most rigorous scientific standards. All pathological and chemical findings were co-supervised by a physician who was a professor of pathology at the University of Southern California, as well as by a pathologist at Huntington Memorial Hospital in Pasadena.

Modern science has largely ignored the nutritive value of heat-labile elements in food, including enzymes, destroyed by heat and available only in raw or undercooked foods. This was precisely the area on which Pottenger focused. The initial experiment, begun in 1932, compared the effects of raw versus cooked meat; it went on for over ten years, involving hundreds of cats over many generations. Pottenger found that a diet of one-third raw milk did not compensate for the deficiency-induced diseases that occurred in the cats fed cooked meat for the balance of the diet. Also significant was the fact that the medical problems occurring in the cats fed cooked meat were the same ones he repeatedly saw in his patients. Many details of the study, which strongly confirmed Pottenger's initial observations, are given later in this chapter when I discuss how this work was deliberately distorted in a 1982 medical journal article.

Another important Pottenger study, also involving hundreds of cats over the course of more than ten years, compared the effects of raw milk versus pasteurized milk on four groups. All received raw meat for one-third of the diet. The other two-thirds of the diet consisted of various forms of milk: raw milk, pasteurized milk, evaporated milk or condensed milk sweetened with sugar.

The raw-milk group thrived with virtually no illness, producing generation after generation of healthy cats. The other groups became diseased and eventually unable to reproduce. They were highly susceptible to infectious and chronic illness and exhibited degenerative skeletal changes. The most rapid and severe changes took place in the animals fed sweetened condensed milk.

Another of Pottenger's experiments, which compared the effect of fresh greens versus dried greens, demonstrated both the vital nature and the heat-sensitive factors in food, including enzymes. One group of guinea pigs was fed grains, cod liver oil and field-dried alfalfa. Deficiency symptoms appeared—loss of hair, diarrhea, pneumonia, paralysis and high infant mortality. Fresh-cut greens were then introduced, with the grass cut after sundown, sacked and delivered before sunrise. The animals gained weight, infant deaths decreased, loss of hair decreased and no new cases of paralysis developed.

Some guinea pigs that had developed severe symptoms initially and had not fully recovered were then allowed to feed on grass and weeds growing outside the pens. Within a few weeks, all diarrhea and loss of hair stopped, and their hair became soft, shiny and velvety; the animals appeared even healthier than those kept inside the pens on fresh-cut greens.

Pottenger got similar results with cats on raw milk from cows fed dry feed, which developed some of the same health problems as cats fed pasteurized milk.

In a July, 1938 article published in *Certified Milk Magazine*, Pottenger explained the superiority of the live, growing grass and weeds over fresh-cut green feed that was twelve hours old. "What takes place?" he wrote. "Unstable and probably thermo-labile substances whatever they may be have probably been destroyed in the short time between that when the feed is cut and the time that it is fed. As my animal caretaker says, 'It is burned.' If you put your arm into one of the bags of feed, the temperature is from 5 to 20 degrees above atmospheric temperature."[7] There is little doubt now that the major thermo-labile factors (destroyed by heat) of which he wrote are food enzymes. In the same article, Pottenger described the importance of these factors in raw milk in relation to children's health:

"Some of the factors which are transmitted by milk are thermolabile. Though their destruction may not produce death, their deficiency may prevent proper development of the child. This may show in the development of an inadequate skeleton or a decrease in resistance." Pottenger demonstrated this finding in papers described in this chapter and others detailing his clinical work.[8,9] Pottenger's research so convinced him of the importance of raw millk that he recommended one quart of raw milk per day to pregnant and nursing women. According to Pottenger, women who did not have access to raw milk, or who refused to drink it, put the development of their babies in jeopardy and should not breast feed.[10]

Many other workers maintaining animals for extended periods on natural foods had findings similar to those of Pottenger. Of particular note are the experiments of Robert McCarrison, a British physician in the Indian Medical Service and the founder of the Nutrition Research Laboratories at Coonoor, India. From 1902 to 1935, McCarrison studied goiter and other health problems of the Indian people. He carried out extensive experiments with large populations of laboratory animals and in 1933 published a report containing statistics about several studies. In conjunction with those studies, McCarrison kept a control colony of about one thousand white rats for more than three years. These animals were fed whole-wheat flour cakes of unleavened bread lightly smeared with raw butter, sprouts, raw carrots, raw cabbage and raw milk, plus raw meat and bones once a week. The animals were killed and autopsied when two years old. In more than fifteen hundred autopsies, he found no sign of disease, with no deaths from natural causes and no infant mortality.[11]

## DR. POTTENGER'S HEALTH FETISH

For years, advocates for raw milk have pointed to Pottenger's research as confirmation of raw milk's benefits. Those who would outlaw all sales of raw milk have meanwhile disparaged and distorted his work. An example of such misrepresentation is found in an article entitled "Unpasteurized Milk, The Hazards of a Health Fetish" which appeared in the *Journal of the American Medical Association (JAMA)* on October 19, 1984.[12] The choice of the word *fetish* is interesting; one meaning of the word is "a thing evoking irrational devotion or respect." Let us see whether Pottenger's respect for unpasteurized milk can be classified as irrational.

The *JAMA* authors refer to a 1946 Pottenger article from the *American Journal of Orthodontics and Oral Surgery,* "The Effect of Heat-Processed and Metabolized Vitamin D Milk on the Dentofacial Structures of Experimental Animals."[13] The authors of the "Health Fetish" article comment as follows:

"Numerous studies of the relative nutritional merits of raw and pasteurized milk have been conducted in animals and humans, and no differences were detectable. One animal study deserves particular attention because a misrepresentation of the results has become prominent in the raw milk folklore. In 1946, Pottenger published a report about his observations on cats fed varying combinations of raw and heat-treated milk and raw and cooked meat. In his first and largest series of experiments, Pottenger observed many diseases in cats fed raw milk and cooked meat. Raw milk advocates have erroneously cited this article as having reported that disease occurred in cats fed *pasteurized* milk. Smaller experiments in the same article showed that a diet of one-third raw meat and two-thirds milk (pasteurized or not) did not provide adequate nutrition for the cats."

Based on this quote, one might reasonably wonder whether the diseases Pottenger observed in the first series of experiments were caused by raw milk, and whether the smaller experiments showed that raw milk was not superior nutritionally to pasteurized milk. Publication in so prestigious a journal by two medical doctors and two veterinarians lends further weight to the pronouncements.

Let us examine what Pottenger actually had to say in his article:

"In the first series of experiments, one group of cats was fed a diet of two-thirds raw meat, one-third raw milk and cod-liver oil. The second group was fed a diet of two-thirds cooked meat, one-third raw milk, and cod-liver oil. Within the ten-year period, approximately nine hundred cats were studied. The amount of data accumulated is large.

"The cats receiving raw meat and raw milk reproduced in homogeneity from one generation to the next. Abortion was uncommon and the mother cats nursed their young in a normal manner. The cats had good resistance to vermin, infections and parasites. They behaved in a predictable manner. Their organic development was complete and functioned normally.

"Cats receiving the cooked-meat scraps reproduced a heterogeneous strain of kittens, each kitten of the litter being different in skeletal pattern. Abortion in these cats was common, running about 25 per cent in the first generation to about 70 per cent in the second generation. Deliveries were in general difficult, many cats dying in labor. Mortality rates of the kittens were high, frequently due to the failure of the mother to lactate. The kittens were often too frail to nurse."

Based on this quote, one might reasonably conclude that the problems observed were due to differences in the nutrition provided by raw versus cooked meats. We see here how a true statement in the "Health Fetish" article ("Pottenger observed many diseases in cats fed raw milk and cooked meat") may be placed in a context designed to lead the reader into making false conclusions. The next half-truth is even more subtle:

"Smaller experiments in the same article showed that a diet of one-third raw meat and two-thirds milk (pasteurized or not) did not provide adequate nutrition for the cats." Further examination of Pottenger's article is required to understand the subterfuge involved.

Again quoting Pottenger: "We did three other series of feeding experiments. In these series we used the following kinds of milk: raw milk, raw metabolized vitamin D milk, pasteurized milk, evaporated milk, and sweetened condensed milk. Roughly, our results corresponded with those of the previous experiments; animals on raw milk and raw meat reproduced a homogenous strain, the usual causes of natural death being old age or injuries from fighting.

"The male cats fed on [raw] metabolized vitamin D milk (from cattle fed irradiated yeast) and raw meat showed osseous disturbances very like those on pasteurized milk. . . . Young males did not live beyond the second month, and adult males died within ten months. . . . The cats fed pasteurized milk as their principal item of diet, and raw meat as a partial diet, showed lessened reproductive efficiency in the females, and some skeletal changes, while the kittens presented deficiencies in development. . . . Later, we made a comparative study of several types of milk on white rats, the general results of which coincided with those found in the cats."

We see that Pottenger's own words describe clearly the superior value of raw versus pasteurized milk for the animals. Yet the "Health Fetish" authors statement that "a diet of one-third raw meat and two-thirds milk (pasteurized or not) did not provide adequate nutrition for the cats" is strictly speaking true, because of the use of the phrase "pasteurized or not." One experiment used raw metabolized vitamin D milk, and like the pasteurized, evaporated, and sweetened condensed milks, this resulted in diseased animals. The metabolized vitamin D (a synthetic form of the vitamin present in the milk because the cows had been fed irradiated yeast) proved to be so toxic that it overrode the benefits of the otherwise optimal all-raw diet that were obtained in the animals fed plain raw milk. Thus one type of milk that was *not* pasteurized had indeed not provided adequate nutrition. Had the "Health Fetish" authors used the phrase "pasteurized or raw," the statement would have been false, because the word raw would be referring to *both* raw milks tested—the raw, metabolized-vitamin D milk that did not provide adequate nutrition and the plain raw milk that did. The choice of the word "not" makes the distortion possible without actually making a false statement. Very clever indeed. The "Health Fetish" authors avoid discussion of synthetic vitamin D toxicity and make no mention of the sparkling health seen in generation after generation of cats fed raw meat and raw milk free of synthetic vitamin D.

The authors make one other statement that may not be called an untruth, yet is obviously designed to elicit false conclusions: "Raw milk advocates have erroneously cited this article as having reported that disease occurred in cats fed *pasteurized* milk." I'll repeat what Pottenger reported: "The cats fed pasteurized milk as their principal item of diet, and raw meat as a partial diet, showed lessened reproductive efficiency in the females, and some skeletal changes, while the kittens presented deficiencies in development." Pottenger indeed does not use the word "disease" here or anywhere else in this article in reference to animals fed pasteurized milk (the article is about effects on the dental and facial structures of the animals). Yet his findings on the superiority of raw milk are clear. In fact, in one experiment, described briefly, thirteen cats fed pasteurized milk all died within several months.

The "Health Fetish" authors make no mention of a number of other relevant findings published in the Pottenger article. For example, an autopsy photograph shows the internal organs of a cat that had received a diet of one-third raw meat and two-thirds pasteurized milk for eight months before sacrifice. The caption reads, "Note poor tone of skin and inferior quality of fur. Fair heart. Slight fatty atrophy of the liver. Lack of intestinal tone: moderated distension of uterus. Note the disturbance of the skin with a shift from the creamy color of the raw-milk fed cat to the purplish discoloration of congestion."

In contrast, another photograph shows the internal organs of a cat fed a diet of one-third raw meat and two-thirds raw milk all its life. The caption reads, "Note excellent condition of fur and creamy yellow subcutaneous tissue with high vascularity. Moderate heart size. Good liver, firm intestines, and resting uterus. Note the muscle of the raw-milk-fed animal has a deeper red color and appears more vascular than that of the animals receiving the heat-processed milks."

Another experiment began with thirteen cats in excellent health that had been raised on raw meat and raw milk. A table is used to show how long these cats lived after placement on a diet of one-third raw meat and two-thirds pasteurized milk. The average length of life for the males is four months eleven days, for the females three months twenty-seven days. The calcium-to-phosphorous ratio of each cat's femur (thigh bone) is shown, and all are abnormal.

Two x-ray photographs depict the results of another experiment involving two rats, one fed raw milk (rat A) and the other pasteurized (rat B). The caption for the raw milk animal reads, "Note advanced maturity, greater diameter and length of the olecranon process [part of the elbow] of the ulna [the long bone in the foreleg]." The caption for the pasteurized milk animal reads, "Note smaller olecranon process and delayed maturity when compared with rat A."

Another photograph shows a number of bones from one of the cats, previously healthy, that died four months after beginning the one-third-raw-meat and two-thirds-pasteurized-milk diet. The caption reads, "Note missing teeth, chalky appearance of bone, squaring of the bases of teeth and marked root resorption. Osteoporosis. Lack of completion of orbital arches [the orbit is the eye socket]. Malar bones [the cheek bones] have become separated at suture lines [where the bones come together]."

The article includes an x-ray of the jaw of a living cat fed the raw-meat, raw-milk diet all of its life. The caption reads, "Normal jaw structure, good distribution of trabeculae [part of the bony structure], well developed condyle [a knob at the end of the bone], and well developed pterygoid process [a little outgrowth of bone] of the mandible [jaw bone]. Alveolar crest [the alveolus is the bony socket for the root of a tooth] of normal height; even distribution of teeth."

My object here is not to give a lesson in anatomy, but rather to make accessible to the reader some of the details that Pottenger described. In this article he focused primarily on the effects of heat-processed foods, including pasteurized milk, on the bones and jaws of his experimental animals because the article was written for a dental journal. In many other articles published over the course of some fifteen years, he emphasizes the diseases that result in cats and other animals when fed diets that include pasteurized milk.

Another statement by the "Health Fetish" authors deserves further comment: "Numerous studies of the relative nutritional merits of raw and pasteurized milk have been conducted in animals and humans, and no differences were detectable." This appears to be a simple statement of fact. Since in reality numerous studies of the relative nutritional merits of raw and pasteurized milk conducted in animals and humans *have* shown clearly the nutritional superiority of raw milk, one is tempted to declare the "Health Fetish" statement to be untrue. But in fact it is a true statement! Now how can that be? To answer this question, we must do a little exercise in logic. Examine these two statements:

1. Numerous studies of the relative nutritional merits of raw and pasteurized milk have been conducted in animals and humans, and *no* differences were detectable.

2. Numerous studies of the relative nutritional merits of raw and pasteurized milk have been conducted in animals and humans, and *vast* differences were detectable.

It appears that if one statement is true, the other must be false, right? Wrong! *Both* statements may be true—it all depends on which "numerous studies" the writer is referring to. Even if the writer is aware of numerous studies that favor both sides of the argument, statements 1 and 2 may both be defended as true statements (in a court of law, for example, or in a subsequent article). Understanding this element of logic is necessary when writers employ logical tricks. Young people who go on to medical school usually study logic as undergraduates.

Notice that although the authors refer to Pottenger's animal study in the very next sentence, they carefully do not say it is one of the "numerous studies" to which they have just referred. We get the impression that it is, of course. But they do not say this, for to do so would be false;

as we have seen, Pottenger's study undeniably shows the nutritional superiority of raw milk compared to pasteurized.

But it is almost as though someone played a game of perverse (dare
I say fetishistic?) logic, devising technically true statements that would
disguise Pottenger's findings, distort the meaning of his words and trick
the reader into false conclusions. I've studied Pottenger's work for over
twenty years, and it took me hours to untangle the web I've described.

It is indeed a fact that a number of researchers supported by grants
from the dairy industry have published research claiming to find no significant differences between raw and pasteurized milk. In other parts of
this book I detail reasons to question the validity of research funded by
corporate money or conducted by individuals funded by corporations.
The "Health Fetish" authors give no references for the "numerous studies" mentioned above, so it is not possible to examine them.

The "Health Fetish" authors carefully avoid any simple, straightforward statement to the effect of, "None of the reasonable studies in
animals or humans of which we are aware have shown that there is a
significant difference in the relative nutritional merits of raw and pasteurized milk." They also avoided words to the effect of "The Pottenger
study under discussion showed no significant difference in the relative
nutritional merits of raw and pasteurized milk." Either statement would
have been patently false, because scores of reasonable studies, obviously
including this Pottenger study, and many others examined in this book,
demonstrate the nutritional superiority of raw versus pasteurized milk.

We've seen that the "Health Fetish" authors used statements that
are technically (and logically) true to completely distort Dr. Pottenger's
findings. Only careful study of Pottenger's article would allow the choice
of precisely the right words to accomplish this distortion while avoiding false statements. We may hope that the authors gained considerable
understanding of Pottenger's work and its implications for the health of
people everywhere. Perhaps they may someday use that knowledge in
the way Dr. Pottenger intended.

Pottenger concludes his article with possible explanations for his
findings, referencing his words to physiology textbooks and articles by
other scientists: "What vital elements were destroyed in the heat pro-

cessing of the foods fed the cats? The precise factors are not known. Ordinary cooking precipitates proteins, rendering them less easily digested. All tissue enzymes are heat labile and would be materially reduced or destroyed. Vitamin C and some members of the B complex are injured by the process of cooking. Minerals are rendered less soluble by altering their physicochemical state. It is possible that the alteration of the physicochemical state of the foods may be all that is necessary to render them imperfect foods for the maintenance of health. *It is our impression that the denaturing of proteins by heat is one factor responsible.* The principles of growth and development are easily altered by heat and oxidation, which kill living cells at every stage of the life process, from the soil through the plant, and through the animal."

## DR. EDWARD HOWELL AND THE FOOD ENZYME CONCEPT

Edward Howell was born in 1898 and held a limited medical license from the state of Illinois throughout his professional life. He joined the staff of the Lindlahr Sanitarium after his medical training and remained there until 1930 when he established his own practice for the nutritional treatment of chronic disease. Throughout his life, Dr. Howell researched the scientific literature on the subject of enzymes, refining his understanding of what they are and their role in health and disease. Many people knowledgeable in the field of nutrition and natural foods consider him to have been the world's leading expert on enzymes until his death in 2000.

His pioneering book, *The Status of Food Enzymes in Digestion and Metabolism* was reprinted in 1980 under the title *Food Enzymes for Health and Longevity*, complete with a list of over four hundred references cited in the original book. Those references came from among the seven hundred scientific papers Howell accumulated over the years of his research. Howell collectively called his enzyme theories "the food enzyme concept."

Howell saw enzymes as essential nutrients. "Enzymes are substances which make life possible. They are needed for every chemical reaction that occurs in our body. Without enzymes, no activity at all would take place. Neither vitamins, minerals nor hormones can do any work without enzymes. Enzymes are much more than catalysts. Catalysts are only inert substances. They possess none of the life energy we find in enzymes."[14]

Years of study into the biological and chemical facts about enzymes convinced Howell that they must be considered more than simply chemical substances. "It becomes mandatory to consider enzymes vital substances—matter impregnated with energy values. At first thought, this might suggest a departure from the sphere of science to that of philosophy. But I fail to see why it should be more difficult to form such a conception of enzymes than it is to conceive of a flashlight battery as possessed of energy. In neither case is it necessary to leave anything to assumption since the energy values may be measured in both instances. *When a battery is "dead," the energy value has vanished; similarly, when enzymes are destroyed by heat, the energy value disappears, leaving behind only its vehicle.*

"Although enzymes contain proteins—and some contain vitamins—the activity factor of enzymes has never been synthesized. Moreover, there is no combination of amino acids or any other substance that will give enzyme activity. There are proteins present in enzymes. However, they serve only as carriers of the enzyme activity factors. Therefore, we can say that enzymes consist of protein carriers charged with energy factors just as a battery consists of metallic plates charged with electrical energy.

"It seems that we inherit a certain enzyme potential at birth. This limited supply of activity factors of the life force must last us a lifetime. The faster you use up your supply of enzyme activity, the quicker you will run out. Experiments at various universities have shown that, regardless of the species, the faster the metabolic rate, the shorter the life-span. Other things being equal, *you live as long as your body has enzyme activity factors to make enzymes from.* When it gets to the point that you can't make certain enzymes, then your life ends.

"When a food is heated at 212 degrees, the enzymes in it are 100% destroyed. If enzymes were in the food we eat, they would do some or even a considerable part of the work of digestion by themselves. However, when you eat cooked, enzyme-free food, this forces the body itself to make the enzymes needed for digestion. This depletes the body's limited enzyme capacity. I believe diets of cooked food are one of the paramount causes of premature aging and early death. I also believe this is the underlying cause of almost all degenerative disease. This state of enzyme deficiency stress exists in the majority of persons on the civilized, enzyme-free diet."[15]

Howell theorized that disease in humans began when our ancestors began to use fire extensively in cooking, pointing to findings of arthritis in Ice Age Neanderthal man as evidence. But his theory ignores the fact that Weston Price (whose studies of nonindustrialized peoples will be discussed in the next chapter) found many societies that were free of arthritis and other chronic diseases and all cooked some or even a large portion of their food. Both Native Americans and South Seas Islanders, for example, ate large quantities of meat or fish, much of it cooked, and enjoyed marvelous bone structure and freedom from arthritis. However, all of these cultures consumed fermented foods, which might be called "super-raw foods" because they are very rich in enzymes.

It remains a matter of conjecture why some primitive cultures had problems with arthritis while others did not. We cannot simply blame cold weather. Primitive Eskimos lived in an environment as frigid as that of the Neanderthals, yet the Eskimos never suffered from arthritis and other chronic diseases until the introduction of refined foods into their culture.[16] The Eskimos did eat much of their meat and fish diet raw and fermented, and much of the food that was cooked was boiled and left pink in the middle. The word *Eskimo* comes from an Indian expression that means, "He who eats it raw," yet the Eskimos did, in fact, cook some of their food. Howell pointed out that the Eskimos had no tradition of medicine men; many anthropologists described them as the healthiest and the happiest of all aboriginal people. But among other North American aboriginal people, medicine men played significant roles.[17] Howell attributed their need for medical attention to the fact that they cooked much of their food; others blame the effects on corn and other carbohydrate foods, often consumed in large amounts.

Howell studied thousands of scientific documents to substantiate his theory that humans eating cooked and refined foods suffer from food enzyme deficiency. He wrote, "Human beings have the lowest levels of starch-digesting enzymes in their blood of any creature. We also have the highest level of these enzymes in the urine, meaning that they are being used up faster. These low enzyme levels are not due to a peculiarity of our species. Instead, they are due to the large amounts of cooked starch we eat. Incriminating evidence indicates that cooked, enzyme-free diets contribute to a pathological over-enlargement of the pituitary gland, which regulates the other glands. There is documented research showing that almost one hundred percent of the people over fifty, dying from accidental causes were found to have defective pituitary glands.

"Incidentally, another defect associated with food enzyme deficiency is that the size of the brain decreases. In addition, the thyroid enlarges, even in the presence of adequate iodine. This has been shown in a number of species. Of course, you can't prove it on human beings. The evidence, however, is very suggestive. . .

"Although most nutritionists claim that enzymes in food are destroyed in the stomach, they overlook two important facts. First of all, when you eat food, acid secretion is minimal for at least thirty minutes. The food drops into the top portion of the stomach, called the cardiac section, since it's closer to the heart. The rest of the stomach remains flat and closed while the cardiac section opens up to accommodate the food.

"During the time the food sits in the upper section, the body secretes little acid or enzymes. The enzymes in the food go about digesting the food. The more of this self-digestion, the less work the body has to do later. When this thirty- to forty-five-minute period is over, the bottom section of the stomach opens up and the body starts secreting acid and enzymes. Even at this point, the food enzymes are not inactivated until the acid level becomes prohibitive. You see, food enzymes can tolerate chemical environments many times more acid than neutral. . .

"Some raw foods, seeds and nuts, contain what are called enzyme inhibitors. Nature doesn't want the seed to germinate prematurely and lose its life. When you eat raw seeds or raw nuts, you are swallowing enzyme inhibitors that will neutralize some of the enzymes your body produces. In fact, eating foods with enzyme inhibitors causes a swelling of the pancreas. All nuts and seeds contain these inhibitors. Raw peanuts contain an especially large amount.

"There are two ways to destroy enzyme inhibitors. The first is cooking; however, this also destroys the enzymes. The second and preferable way is sprouting, which destroys the enzyme inhibitors and also increases the enzyme content by a factor of three to six.

"As we pass our prime, the amount of enzymes in our bodies and excreted in our urine continues to decline until we die. In fact, low enzyme levels are associated with old age and chronic disease. There's not much hard evidence on whether taking additional enzymes will extend the life-span. However, we do know that laboratory rats that eat raw foods will live about three years. Rats eating enzymeless chow diets will live only two years. Thus, we see that diets deficient in enzymes cause a thirty percent reduction in life-span. If this held true for human beings, it may mean that people could extend their life-spans by twenty or more years—just by maintaining proper enzyme levels."[18]

Howell had little to say about the importance of enzyme-enriched fermented foods, a significant oversight given the emphasis he placed on the Eskimo diet. (And he was not aware of the fact that the process of soaking grains in an acid medium, and raw nuts in a salted medium, will neutralize enzyme inhibitors while also increasing enzymes.)[19] Because the process of fermentation greatly increases enzyme content, fermented foods can make up for the enzymes lost in foods that are cooked. Virtually all healthy traditional cultures consume fermented foods, and because few people today would choose to consume only raw foods, fermented foods provide a vital addition to the modern diet.

Howell, however, emphasized the importance of large amounts of raw foods in the diet and promoted the use of enzyme supplements—and lived to the ripe old age of one hundred two.

## ENZYMES IN MILK AND PASTEURIZATION

Enzymes are destroyed by heat and pasteurization in a heat-intensive process. Normal pasteurization involves heating milk to 161 degrees F for fifteen to twenty seconds (called the high-temperature short-time or HTST method) by forcing it between metal plates or through pipes heated on the outside by hot water; increasingly modern milk is subject to the ultra-heat treatment (UHT) method, which heats the milk to a temperature of about 230 degrees F (above the boiling point) for a fraction of a second. The following are the principal enzymes in milk:[21]

**Lactase:** Milk contains lactose, a sugar about fifteen percent as sweet as sucrose and found only in milk. The enzyme lactase splits lactose into the simple sugars galactose and glucose. In raw milk, lactase is produced by certain naturally occurring lactic-acid producing bacteria. Pasteurization inactivates these bacteria and also the lactase they produce. The enzyme also occurs naturally in the lining of the intestines in all normal human infants, and decreases after the age of about three or four. Many people who do not digest pasteurized milk well and are thought to be lactose-intolerant digest raw milk without problems, in part because of the lactase content in raw milk. (More on lactose intolerance in Chapter 13.)

**Galactase:** The enzyme galactase then breaks down galactose, a sugar that plays a vital role in the development of the nervous system. It is completely inactivated by heat at 165 to 175 degrees F. As with all enzymes, destruction begins at about 118 degrees F.

**Lactoperoxidase:** A temperature of 158 degrees F completely inactivates this enzyme, which is a protein-derived enzyme from the hemoglobin in the cow's blood. It works with hydrogen peroxide to catalyze the oxidation of organic substances in the milk. The lactoperoxidase enzymes also seek out and destroy bad bacteria in milk.[22]

**Lactoferrin:** This enzyme performs many functions. It kills a wide range of iron-loving pathogens (most pathogens have an affinity to iron) such as the TB bacillus and *Candida albicans* by binding to iron and facilitating its absorption.[23] At the same time, it supports the assimilation of iron in milk, thus preventing anemia. Research indicates that lactoferrin strengthens the immune system and supports growth in children. [24] In fact, this beneficial compound found in raw milk is sold as a dietary supplement and weight loss product. Ironically, the FDA has approved lactoferrin for use as an anti-microbial spray to combat virulent *E. coli* contamination in the meat industry.[25] Lactoferrin activity is greatly reduced by pasteurization and destroyed by UHT pasteurization.[26]

**Catalase:** This enzyme, found in almost all animal cells, catalyzes the conversion of hydrogen peroxide into water and oxygen, thus protecting the cells. A temperature of 150 to 158 degrees F inactivates this enzyme.

**Amylase:** Pasteurization inactivates amylase, a starch-splitting enzyme, in milk. All mammals secrete amylase from the salivary glands and the pancreas, but when they consume raw milk, these glands are spared the need to do so.

**Lipase:** Lipase is a fat-splitting enzyme secreted by the pancreas; when activated by the proper pH in the gut, it functions to split individual fatty acids away from triglyceride molecules. Some critics of modern milk processing claim that once fats are homogenized, lipase may easily act on them and cause them to become rancid; immediate pasteurization, which renders the lipase in milk inactive, is necessary in order for milk to be homogenized without subsequent development of rancidity.[27] In a study on human milk, premature babies had lower weight gain when fed pasteurized human milk compared to babies fed raw human milk. The researchers attributed the poor results to the destruction of lipase by pasteurization.[28]

**Phosphatase:** The role of phosphatase in raw milk is unclear, but in the body it plays many roles. Because pathogenic bacteria are said to be killed at temperatures lower than those that inactivate phosphatase, a post-pasteurization test for the complete absence of phosphatase has become the standard for testing the adequacy of the pasteurization process.[29]

We see that pasteurized milk is largely devoid of enzyme activity; nearly all of the enzymes have been killed. The dairy industry claims that the only nutrient significantly affected by pasteurization is vitamin C. Pasteurization destroys anywhere from ten to fifty percent of the vitamin C content in milk, and lesser amounts of several other important vitamins, including vitamins $B_6$ and $B_{12}$. But research has also shown that changes occur in the physical and chemical state of calcium and other minerals that affect absorption. Defenders of pasteurization minimize the impact of pasteurization on vitamins and minerals, maintaining that most are well absorbed, and claim that people receive adequate vitamin C from other foods. Meanwhile advocates for raw milk have pointed out that the quantity of vitamin C destroyed in milk is greater than the amount in the entire U.S. citrus crop. Many studies on milk and mineral metabolism have demonstrated the superior absorption of the minerals in raw milk. We'll discuss some of these studies in Chapter 16.

The debate on nutrient destruction pales in comparison to the issue of enzymes. Here there can be no debate about the physical fact: pasteurization destroys the enzymes in milk. What the industry has minimized is the implication of this fact. These enzymes play a vital role in the assimilation of the vitamins and minerals in milk, support the immune system and provide powerful protection against pathogens. They are what make raw milk a living food.

Yet the pasteurization proponents assert that the enzymes in food are unimportant and have no health effects; furthermore, they claim that food enzymes are not absorbed but are destroyed during the digestive process. The secretion of digestive enzymes by the salivary glands, the pancreas, and other glands is said to be adequate for digestion, and the enzymes in food are not needed.

This argument fails in a number of ways. To begin, considerable evidence proves that enzymes are indeed absorbed:

- Bacteria and yeast cells, both of which contain enzymes, can be absorbed, as are many large, intact proteins.
- Enzymes administered orally are subsequently found in the urine.
- While large amounts of enzymes are secreted into the gastrointestinal tract, only a small amount is recovered in the feces.[30]

‣ Enzyme extracts given to cancer patients often results in improvements, as demonstrated recently in clinical trials with pancreatic cancer patients conducted by Nicholas Gonzalez, MD.[31]

In addition, it is a physiological fact that the enzymes in food take priority in digestion over secreted enzymes. The moment the cell walls of the foods are broken down in chewing or by contact with saliva or stomach acids, the food enzymes become active, before secreted enzymes have even begun to appear.[32] Experiments in both test tubes and living animals have shown that enzymes in foods do a measurable amount of digestive work.[33]

Howell points out that cows and other herbivorous animals have a pancreas gland that is about one-half the size of the human pancreas, relative to body weight, and that their salivary glands do not secrete enzymes. Herbivores nevertheless digest huge amounts of raw carbohydrate food in grass and other plants, while humans eating cooked foods devoid of enzymes require a large pancreas and enzyme-filled saliva to accomplish digestion.

The only reasonable explanation for this disparity is that the animals efficiently utilize the enzymes in their raw foods during digestion, or they have lots of microorganisms to produce enzymes for them in the gut. In countless feeding experiments, animals fed cooked foods have done poorly compared to animals fed raw foods. Every zookeeper in the world now feeds zoo animals only raw foods; it took many years, but zookeepers finally learned that animals eating cooked foods fail to reproduce, become diseased and die prematurely, a fact that provides further evidence for the critical importance of food enzymes found only in raw foods.

Howell believed that the relatively large size of the human pancreas and salivary glands was an aberration caused by the consumption of excessive amounts of cooked foods; others argue that the relatively large pancreas and salivary glands in humans are indications that we are well adapted to eating cooked food. While the amount of raw versus cooked food in an idealized "optimal" human diet is subject to debate, the vast body of animal research on diets devoid of enzymes provides ample proof that human diets consisting *only* of cooked food lead to disease.

A final piece of evidence proving the importance of food enzymes comes from reports on the exclusive milk diet, described in Chapter 6. Critics generally are unwilling to dismiss as lies the testimony of men such as John E. Crewe, MD, a founder of the Mayo Clinic, discussed in the last chapter. Rather, when confronted with such evidence, they simply ignore it, perhaps hoping that it will go away. Men and women die; truth does not. We have powerful evidence of the efficacy of the milk cure—Crewe wrote that four weeks on nothing but raw milk reversed most chronic disease. On the other hand, no one has ever claimed that pasteurized milk heals anything; the milk cure disappeared from the annals of medicine with the advent of widespread pasteurization.

Countless physicians, healers and other individuals who have studied the matter carefully have testified to the power of enzyme-rich foods as healing agents. We have considerable evidence that a large part of the therapeutic value of raw milk lies in its enzyme content. Food enzymes from raw and fermented foods are vital; my personal experience is that without them there can be no lasting healing and no true health.

TRADITIONAL ESKIMO DIETS

In his pioneering work on nutrition and human health, *Nutrition and Physical Degeneration*, Weston Price told a simple but stirring story of primitive Eskimos at a time, during the long winter night north of the Arctic Circle, when food had run short. An Eskimo man takes his kayak to stormy seas to hunt seal with a harpoon. In darkness, bitter cold, high winds and rough seas, he searches the dark waters for food. A wave crashing over a kayak can snap a strong man's back; as breakers approach, the kayaker rolls the vessel, submerging himself. The tight fit of seal skins between the upper edge of the kayak and his waist keeps water from entering the vessel. When the white water passes, he flips upright and continues the hunt, finally killing a seal and returning home with food for his family.

Price described the impressive physical strength of primitive Eskimos, but he was even more impressed with their character—their courage, honesty, openness, dedication to family and community, and ability to survive and thrive in the harsh northern environment. In village after village, he found among Eskimos subsisting entirely upon the native diet of meat, fat and fish, much of it raw, fine characters and virtually no decayed teeth, and no evidence of chronic disease.

In 1933, Dr. Price interviewed Dr. Josef Romig, a surgeon beloved among the Eskimos. For 36 years, Romig had provided medical care to primitive and modernized Eskimos and Indians in Alaska. Cancer was unknown among the truly primitive natives, he stated; in them, he had never seen a case, though when they began eating refined foods, it frequently occurred. Other acute surgical problems common among modernized Eskimos and Indians were similarly rare among primitives. Price attributed this to the large amount of fat-soluble activators—such as vitamins A and D—provided in the diet. Other investigators have credited the high enzyme content of fermented raw meat and fish.

Whenever possible Romig sent modernized natives, eating refined foods and afflicted with tuberculosis, back to native conditions and the native nutrient-dense diet. He reported that although tuberculosis was generally progressive and eventually fatal when patients remained on refined foods, the disease often resolved when patients returned to their traditional foods.[34,35]

Other qualified observers have provided equally impressive reports. In 1927, the physician for the Macmillan Arctic Expedition reported in the *Journal of the American Medical Association* that the carnivorous Greenland Eskimos showed no tendency toward heart or kidney disease, scurvy or rickets. Their foods included the meat of whale, caribou, musk ox, Arctic hare, fox, ptarmigan, walrus, seal, polar bear, sea gulls, geese, duck, auks and fish, all often (but not always) eaten raw and fermented. But he found that the Labrador Eskimos had adopted the white man's ways, overcooking their meat and eating various prepared, dried and canned foods; they were very much subject to the aforementioned problems.[36]

Eskimos living in the traditional manner almost always positioned their homes near deep water where salmon was abundant. They dried the salmon eggs and used them in quantity; the dried roe, rich in iodine, important fatty acids and fat-soluble vitamins, formed an important part of the diet for small children after weaning and for women of childbearing age, to ensure fertility. The men ate the milt of wild salmon for the same purpose. They consumed the organs of large land mammals and dipped their fish in seal oil, rich in nutrients. They also used seal oil to preserve sorrel grass and flower blossoms. The diet was rich in animal fats; some were partially or completely cooked, such as the marrow of certain bones and other fats considered delicacies. Others were eaten raw, often fermented. They gathered kelp in season and stored it for winter use.[37] The stomach contents of caribou were often fermented and consumed as a special treat.

Studies on the metabolism of primitive Eskimos have revealed fascinating information about differences between raw and cooked fats. Ketone bodies are compounds produced in the body during the metabolism of fats. Elevated amounts found in the blood (ketosis) and urine are typical in human subjects eating diets restricted to proteins and fats, or in abnormal states such as diabetes. Ketosis occurs on the Atkins diet, for example, with its large quantities of cooked protein and fat, and Atkins states that the passage of ketone bodies in the urine helps in the weight loss that typically results from the diet.

Remarkably, according to a study published in the *Journal of Biological Chemistry*, primitive Eskimos studied during the Putnam Baffin Island Expedition in 1928, by doctors from the Departments of Biological Chemistry and Physiology at the Washington University School of Medicine, showed no ketosis.[38] These native people completely metabolized the fats in their high-protein, high-fat diet because many of the fats were raw.[39] This is not surprising, since lipase is found in concentrated amounts in raw, natural fats, including the butterfat of raw milk. According to another study published in the same journal, when the same foods were cooked and fed to humans in a civilized area, ketosis occurred. Yet another experiment with animals showed that after several months of feeding on seal fat, the lipase content in the blood and organs was definitely increased.[40]

These accounts highlight the importance of the fact that the native Eskimos ate much of their food not only raw but "super-raw," that is, fermented. Another published account by a man who lived for several years among them provides the following fascinating details:

"Fish are put into a hole and covered with grass and earth and the mass is allowed to ferment and decay. I learned, to my utter astonishment, that they would eat those rotten, poisonous foods and thrive on them. Lest the reader might think that the cooking process would destroy the poisons in their vitiated foods, I wish to say that in only a few instances did they cook their food. The usual and customary method was to devour it raw."[41] Other experienced observers have confirmed that "high," that is, gamey and smelly, meat and fish were always eaten raw.

"The excellent health of the primitive Eskimo is stated by a number of qualified observers to be surpassed by no other race of people on this earth and equaled by few if any," wrote Howell, who emphasized the fact that meat and fish are consumed "usually and preferably raw. The Eskimo, like the wild animal, partakes of much of his food in the natural state, with all of the original enzymes intact."[42] Present-day advocates of all-raw-foods diets sometimes cite Howell as evidence for their theories.

Howell, however, never lived with the Eskimos. Vilhjamur Stefansson, a famous Arctic explorer who led many expeditions, did—he spent the winter of 1906-1907 as the guest of an Eskimo clan on the coast in the Mackenzie River District and spent much of the next ten years living with and among these people. Stefansson wrote that they enjoyed perfect health and had no dental caries, scurvy, rickets or cancer. He said that when meat or fish was cooked, as it customarily was for the evening meal, chunks were heated in water over a small flame until the water began to boil, and custom ordained that the inside of each piece should be "pink." This was called "northern style, which was also the style of the heavily meat-eating Plains Indians," he wrote. "Fish heads and fish livers were always eaten boiled," but the Eskimos never fried anything and rarely roasted their food. Game on the Mackenzie River coast was scarce because of depredations for many years by white hunters supplying a whaling camp on a nearby island, so most meals besides the evening meal consisted of fermented raw fish.[43] Stefansson's account makes it abundantly clear that native Eskimo people cooked some of their foods—but made up for the enzyme loss with raw foods that had been fermented.

A medical doctor who practiced among the Eskimos of Northern Canada near Aklavik also commented on the use of raw fish in a 1935 article published in the *Canadian Medical Association Journal.* The article is important in that it provides independent verification of Price's reports on the health of primitive Eskimos. Howell describes this physician's report as follows:

"He has never seen a single case of malignancy during seven years of practice in the region. Gastric or duodenal ulcer, acute or chronic nephritis, or scurvy, are extremely rare. Teeth are in excellent condition. Rheumatic fever, asthma, and the common cold are rare. In the performance of urinalyses running well into the thousands during seven years, not a single case of glycosuria [glucose, or sugar, in the urine, a sign of diabetes] was seen. Fish fills a large part of their menu and they eat the entire fish raw and very 'high.'"[44]

Two other published journal articles confirmed reports that Eskimos eating their native diet were not subject to tuberculosis, the leading cause of death throughout the civilized world at this time. The author, a Dr. Rabinowitch, was a physician from the Department of Metabolism, Montreal General Hospital and a member of the Canadian Government Eastern Arctic Patrol to Baffin Island, Devon, and Ellesmere Islands on the R.M.S. Nascopie. The stated purpose of the expedition was to prevent extinction of the Eskimo race.

The physician examined hundreds of Eskimos and provided a fascinating report: "The use of flour was found to be determined by the availability of meat," he wrote. "Where seal hunting is good, flour was found in only one of eight tents visited. Where hunting is poor, flour was found in all of the tents visited." Tuberculosis was common where flour was used, while no evidence of the disease was found in the far northern areas where the Eskimos ate only animal foods.

Likewise, high blood pressure and evidence of arteriosclerosis occurred only in the areas where flour was consumed. "When food is abundant, a healthy Eskimo, living under primitive conditions, will eat five to ten pounds of meat or more a day and the greatest meat eaters are in the northerly regions. The Eskimo disturbs our ideas about the high-protein [and high-fat] diet. There were no signs of any heart disease except an apical murmur in one case. All of the tonsils had healthy pink surfaces and no pus was found upon pressure. No case of cancer or diabetes was seen." (Actually, according to Stefansson, protein provided only about 20 percent of the calories in the primitive Eskimo diet, with the remaining 80 percent supplied by fat.[45])

Dr. Rabinowitch found no ketone bodies in urine samples taken from those eating the primitive diet, confirming the findings of other investigators that traditional Eskimos completely metabolize fats in a manner not seen in people eating large amounts of cooked animal protein and fats.[46,47]

Thus, many reports establish the fact that the primitive Eskimo diet of meat and fish, rich in fat-soluble vitamins and enzymes, much of it eaten in a raw and fermented state, produces splendidly healthy people. These reports prove the vital nature of enzymes and fat-soluble vitamins supplied in the traditional western diet by raw whole milk, butter, cream and cheese. Most Westerners would prefer to consume their raw animal food as raw milk and raw milk products rather than raw meat and fish, and obtain their fat-soluble vitamins from butter rather than organ meats. This western food preference makes access to raw, unprocessed dairy products a necessity if we are to reverse the tide of chronic disease that has engulfed our culture.

ESSENTIAL FOR LIFE

Many people understand the importance of enzymes and of including some raw and fermented food in the diet. But many mistakenly believe that some fruit daily and an occasional green salad will provide an adequate supply of enzymes. Many people go further and include larger amounts of raw vegetables and fruits in their daily routine. But very few understand the vital role of raw and fermented proteins and fats from healthy animals.

The level of enzymes present in a food is proportional to its calorie content. Vegetables and fruits are thus poor sources of enzymes relative to raw milk, cheese, butter, meat and other animal products. Some plant foods are richer in enzymes than others; mangoes, papayas, bananas, pineapples and avocados are good sources. Enzymes in fruit are largely responsible for the ripening process, and some go back into the stem and seeds after that process is complete. Unprocessed, unheated honey is another good source of enzymes.

The use of fermented foods and drinks among indigenous peoples enhanced the enzyme content of their diets. A number of traditional cultures, particularly in Asia, have used these foods to complement diets that consist largely of cooked foods.

Even though our agricultural forefathers and primitive peoples cooked some (and in some cases, most) of their food, they got far more enzymes in their diets than modern people because they always ate at least some animal foods raw and because they fermented so many of their foods. Dairy foods were usually consumed raw and often fermented, and cooked foods were accompanied by condiments pickled by old-fashioned methods that increased enzyme content. Beer and wine were raw and unpasteurized, and rich in enzymes.[48]

Traditional European diets provide good models for many people wishing to make a transition to a diet that contains more raw and fermented foods. In life-threatening situations, radical and abrupt change may be desirable. For most people, though, change should not be forced. It's usually best to give the body and the mind time to adjust, and to gradually become used to more raw and fermented foods. Including raw milk and raw milk products in the diet is a powerful and effective way to make that change.

The rewards of using large amounts of carefully selected raw foods from healthy animals far outweigh the risks, which are quite minimal when certain precautions are observed. In fact, as we shall see in Chapter 15, the risk from consuming raw milk is very low compared to the risk of consuming other foods.

An indication of how great those rewards can be is given in our next chapter as we explore how milk was used in several of the last traditional cultures.

# 8
# Milk in the
# Last Traditional Cultures

*People have forgotten what the savage instinctively knows—that a perfect body is the supreme instrument of life.*
　　　　Havelock Ellis, physician and psychologist

*Primitive men are more intelligent in dietary matters than we are.*
　　　　Earnest A. Hooton, Professor of Anthropology,
　　　　Harvard University, 1938[1]

THE WAY OF THE WANDERER: PROTEIN ON THE HOOF

Civilization cannot occur on the move; it was mankind's decision to settle that led to the rise of cities. Of the nomadic people who never made that decision, few survived into the twentieth century, and even fewer into the twenty-first.

Until about 10,000 BC, all nomadic groups followed the seasonal movement of their herds of wild or semi-wild animals, a way of life that came to be known as transhumance (from *trans*, "over," plus *humus*, "ground"). Transhumance began as an extension of the hunter-gatherer way of life. For example, many of the indigenous tribes of North

117

America's central plains timed their movements seasonally to coincide with the movements of the buffalo. In many places, this kind of activity led to the beginnings of animal husbandry and the semi-domestication of animals. The Lapps of northern Scandinavia, who milked semi-wild reindeer, exemplified this transition. Their way of life has survived well into the twentieth century.

Life on the move with semi-domesticated animals represents a peculiar adaptation. In some ways it is like hunting; it is a pursuit, and the animals set the pace. Yet the intimate association of a people with a mobile reservoir of food is a step between the hunter-gatherer way of life and the agricultural revolution, with its domestication of animals for milk and meat.[2]

With the domestication of sheep and goats—animals that have no natural migration patterns—around ten or twelve thousand years ago, some nomadic peoples took on the responsibility of nature and began leading their flocks and herds. These people lived as pastoralists—keepers of sheep, goats and cattle—most of whom sooner or later settled down. When they did, they thrived and prospered, at least until the recent industrialization of agriculture.

A few groups of nomadic pastoralists never settled. These wanderers specialized in making their living on the fringes of civilization or far from it, in land areas with enough space to meet the needs of their herds—protein on the hoof, as one anthropologist team has described their way of life. Often they occupied areas receiving insufficient rainfall for crops.[3]

At times the nomadic peoples gathered and even grew some of their plant foods, or depended partially on plant foods grown by their sedentary neighbors. But always the demands of the animals came first, and the animals provided the foods upon which the lives of the people depended.

NOMADS, SETTLERS AND THE BEGINNINGS OF AGRICULTURE

The way of life of one nomadic tribe, the Bakhtiari of Persia (now Iran), was depicted by Jacob Bronowski in his 1975 BBC television series, "The Ascent of Man," and described in his book based on the series.

Bronowski lived and traveled with the Bakhtiari for a brief period and poignantly recorded the lives of these modern-day wanderers. Taking their name from a legendary herdsman of Mongol times, Bakhtyar, all the Bakhtiari considered themselves a family, the sons and daughters of this single founding father.

The staple of their diet was a clabbered milk yogurt they made by churning their milk in a goatskin bag on a simple wooden frame. They spun wool on simple, ancient devices. Their technology was light enough to be carried on the daily journeys as they followed their animals to fresh pasture.

The Bakhtiari had neither time nor skill for specialization; they bartered for stirrups, toys and metal pots. "The only habits that survive are the old habits," according to Bronowski's narration. "The only ambition of the son is to be like the father. It is a life without features. When the day breaks, there is one question in everyone's mind: Can the flock be got over the next high pass? The tribe must move on, the herdsman must find new pastures every day, because at these heights grazing is exhausted in a single day."

In *The Ascent of Man*, Bronowski celebrates the domestication of wild wheat and the cultivation of grains as the foundation upon which civilization was built. But it is accurate to say that civilization also rests on the domestication of animals, with the attendant local production of milk and meat. It was the domestication of animals that allowed people to create settled villages, and people kept animals for milk for thousands of years before the advent of grain farming. In addition, the nutrient-dense milk products of grass-fed animals provided optimal nutrition consistently, without subjecting people to the dangers and uncertainties of the hunt.

The ending of the last Ice Age meant more grass and more animals, animals that people gradually tamed. At first people followed the animals, but by Biblical times they largely led the animals. And gradually, various cultures learned enough about pasture and fences in relation to their animals to settle down in one place. As they had as nomads, they lived largely on milk and its fermented products, killing some animals for meat, skins and bones. They learned to grow crops, and most importantly, they cultivated pasture, and from green pastures, civilization grew, fed by the animals that ate the grasses. Cultivated pastures were most important because the core of every culture was always the animals. We know this from the writings and artifacts that people of ancient cultures left to us; animals were held sacred. We know it from the work of scores of anthropologists who investigated traditional cultures, and from a multitude of historical accounts.

The fact is that most people alive today in Europe, North and South America, and large parts of Africa and Asia are the descendants of indigenous people who depended on raw milk, its fermented products, and meat from pasture-fed animals, for the most important part of their sustenance. And in most of the western world, processed foods and the products of industrialized agriculture have replaced or eliminated such traditional foods. These modern foods all are ultimately based on the monocropping of huge quantities of grain and soybeans.

Joann Grohman, author of *Keeping a Family Cow*, again provides some useful insights. Her analysis of the beginnings of grain farming offers eerie parallels with the way our modern industrial state feeds itself:

"To produce grain in useful quantities requires rich flat land such as flood plains. It requires a huge amount of energy, available in antiquity only where complex cultures developed. This energy was provided by slaves. The more slaves you had, the more grain you could grow. And the more grain you could grow, the more slaves you could afford, thus giving rise to a wealthy class able to afford monumental tombs and other durable artifacts of civilization. Grazing animals have been around for millions of years thriving on grass. They are not dependent on grain. For many thousands of years they were herded and milked, tasks which require neither slaves nor even permanent dwellings."[4]

Traditional grass-based dairy farming was a highly egalitarian enterprise; anyone with initiative and a few acres could herd animals on any kind of land, and sell or barter the products to his neighbors. Societies that consume the products of pastured animals are much less likely to exhibit huge disparities in wealth compared to societies where the economics of food are based on grain.

The few nomadic cultures with remnants surviving today include the Maasai, Barabaig and Kalenjin cattle herders of East Africa and the high-mountain nomads of Tibet. Another, the Lapps of northern Scandinavia, became fully settled only during the last few decades.

EAST AFRICA

The nomadic cattle herders of East Africa once roamed over vast areas. As recently as the 1970s, some one hundred thousand Maasai still followed their traditional ways in an area of about ten thousand square miles in southern Kenya and northern Tanzania. Anthropologists think the Maasai originated somewhere in the upper Sudan and migrated about two thousand years ago through the Rift Valley to their present location. They have intermarried little with other tribes and maintain striking physical characteristics—very tall and slender.

For several centuries, Maasai warriors dominated much of eastern Africa by force of arms. It was their pride and duty to protect their herds and to capture those of other peoples, for they believed God had given all the cattle in the world to the Maasai. They disdained permanent settlements and dominated their agricultural neighbors.

Their courage was legendary. Protection of their animals from predators called for great skill and bravery. One or two men—often boys by western standards—frequently guarded entire herds using only spears. One writer in the 1930s called the skill of the Maasai in killing a lion "one of the most superb of human achievements."[5]

Perceived as stubborn and arrogant, the Maasai refused to adapt to western ways. Even today, almost within sight of Nairobi's office towers and traffic jams, the Maasai have continued to practice certain of their ancient rituals and ceremonies and to maintain their warrior caste of moran, sometimes called the commandos of the tribal world. Until recently, many Maasai followed all of the old ways, which the government has now supressed in many areas. When a teenage boy passed through ritual circumcision with the members of his age-set, they became comrades, a band of brothers. Each was entitled to marry and become a junior elder, and was permitted to sleep with the wife of any of his comrades if he so desired. A Maasai woman did not marry just one man, she married a whole age-set.

The African governments who took over from colonial rule have as their avowed aim the abolition of tribal distinctions and the blending of all tribes into one united people. The suppression of tribal conflicts, the enforcement of western law-and-order values and land ownership, and the removal of tribal elder power by the western legal system have all worked to suppress the foundations of tribal mores. Ten years ago, a government program imposed on the Maasai in Kenya conferred individual land ownership to groups living together. This resulted in most of the land passing into individual ownership for maize cultivation. In Tanzania, many Maasai were evacuated from the Serengeti Plains when much of the region was declared a nature protection area and wildlife park. Traditional Maasai culture is rapidly becoming a cultural anachronism.

Maasai still living under primitive conditions in more remote areas center their lives on their goats, sheep and zebu cattle. Milk is the staple food, usually fermented. In the dry season when the milk supply dwindles, they consume fresh cow's blood instead, taken from a wound made in the neck and then allowed to heal; each animal may be bled about once a month. Occasionally, they eat large amounts of meat, usually from goats or sheep (rarely from the beloved cattle). I found no reference to any plant foods in the traditional Maasai diet.

Cattle are milked directly into a gourd that is specially prepared to encourage quick fermentation. When enough milk is available, the average Maasai will consume up to a gallon or more daily. The milk contains more total fat and cholesterol than standard milk in the United States, but the traditional Maasai have low blood cholesterol and are free of cardiovascular and other chronic disease. For years, academics, researchers, physicians and nutritionists have debated the "Maasai paradox," a flagrant contradiction to the conventional wisdom about cholesterol, animal fats and heart disease.[6]

Some seventy-five thousand Barabaig live on a similar diet in a semiarid area of about sixteen hundred square miles in Tanzania, in the northern volcanic highlands dominated by Mount Hanang. The sacred nature of the mountain is an important theme in Barabaig myth and song. Their attire is the color of the reddish brown soil, with leather dresses, bead work and brass bracelets and necklaces. A prominent decoration consists of circular patterns of tatoos around the eyes. Their culture is polygamous, and they practice divination, rainmaking, witchcraft and sorcery. These people were part of the broad Nilotic migration from the Sudan along the Nile River some two to three thousand years ago.

The Barabaig speak a dialect of the Datooga language, which is very different from Swahili, the national language of Tanzania. This accentuates their isolation even though modern political developments have had a profound effect on their lives. Formerly nomadic, in recent years many have been forced to farm plots of maize, beans and millet.

All over the world, former pastoral grazing grounds are giving way to crop cultivation. In the early 1990s, the Barabaig lost some four million acres to a wheat-growing project funded by the Canadian government. Along with many Maasai, thousands of Barabaig were driven out of their homesteads to make way for the project, which grows wheat and beans on huge fields for the export market. Their massive immigration with their cattle into Hadzaland caused great problems for the Hadzabe people.

The privatization of former communal lands provides fodder for the global agricultural machine but undermines the existence of pastoralists everywhere. According to a 1983 estimate, there were then about seventeen million pastoralists following their traditional lifestyles in Africa, three million in the Middle East, and two million in Central Asia. Those numbers are considerably smaller today. Many pastoralists have a history of strained relations with central authorities, sometimes leading to outright hostilities. Because they inhabit remote areas and are widely dispersed, they generally have little political influence. The formation of modern nation states has further contributed to their deteriorating situation, as borders interfere with their traditional migration patterns and government policies usually favor settled farming and crop production. Under the banner of socioeconomic improvement and modernization, governments often force nomadic peoples to settle by providing them with plots of land and houses—usually substandard houses. The similarities to the American government's policies toward American native tribes in the 1800s are obvious.

As with the Maasai, the Barabaig's zebu-type cattle provided their principal ritual and economic focus for thousands of years. The traditional diet is rich in raw dairy foods—milk, curdled milk and butter—as well as meat and a blood-milk mixture. They use a specially designed arrow to extract blood from the jugular vein of live cattle and consume meat only when they sacrifice cattle in rituals or when an animal dies. Hunting and gathering provide some additional foodstuffs and in recent years maize has played an increasingly important role in the diet. The Barabaig gather wild honey and use it for making enzyme-rich unpasteurized beer.

The Kalenjins are a much larger tribe than either the Maasai or the Barabaig. They live in Kenya where they number nearly three million, some ten percent of the population. Like the Maasai and the Barabaig, the Kalenjins are a Nilotic ethnic group, descendants of the same ancestors. The traditional diets of the three groups are similar, and all marry for the most part within their tribe.

While about one quarter of Kenya's population lives in comparatively sultry conditions at altitudes below four thousand feet, many Kalenjins live at altitudes of six thousand feet or higher, in the more remote areas of the Rift Valley highlands. In these areas, fermented milk remains a staple of the diet—over half the milk production is consumed as fermented milk, which is said to make one grow stronger and more resistant to disease. Indigenous methods of production for various regions and communities have long histories and form an integral part of the culture.

A Kalenjin community in the Kapsabet area of the Rift Valley obtains over half its calories from a soft cheese-like fermented milk product called *mursik*. With the aid of a cured wood stick known as a *sosiot*, obtained from palm branches, a gourd is washed with hot water and then left outside for a few hours to dry. Then it is rubbed inside with the burning ends of chopped sticks obtained from special trees. The charred ends of the sticks break off when they are rubbed inside the gourd, and the *sosiot* stick is then used again, this time to break the charcoal into finer particles that will color the *mursik* and enhance its flavor. The bigger charcoal particles are removed using a special instrument made from parts of a cow's tail attached to a small stick. Raw milk is then put into the gourd. For about one month, as the milk sours and whey forms, the whey is removed and more milk is added. Once whey formation stops, the *mursik* ripens in the same gourd at ambient temperatures for up to a year. Long fermentation times are said to produce the finest *mursik*. The various natural objects used in making this food clearly have a deliberate and planned influence on the flavor and ripening properties of the final product.

Traditionally the Kalenjins built round homes of sticks and mud plaster, covered with distinctive pointed thatch roofs attached to a center pole. Many now have abandoned their pastoral life, built modern wood and stone houses, and grow millet, corn, tea and sorghum. A Kalenjin became president of Kenya in the mid 1990s, which contributed to growing political power for the Kalenjin people. Beginning around 1985, a number of Kalenjins adapted to one aspect of the modern culture in a particularly spectacular fashion—the world of elite running.

In the mid 1980s, the Kenyan government began to sponsor contingents of the country's runners in top-level competitions throughout the world. The result has been a string of unparalleled successes. In the ten-year period from 1988 to 1998, athletes from this one tribe of three million people have won about forty percent of all the highest international honors available in men's distance running. Their success has cut across all three of the sport's disciplines—track, cross-country and road racing.

There are five major distance events in track—800, 1500, 5000, 10,000, and 30,000 meters. At the Olympics and World Championships during the ten-year period, Kalenjin runners won thirty-one medals, with twelve golds—of the available totals, thirty-four percent and forty percent respectively. If we take the best ten performances ever for each of the five events, anywhere, Kalenjin runners won nineteen of those fifty performances. If we take the best twenty performances ever for each of those five events, Kalenjin runners won thirty-seven of those one hundred performances.

These figures represent a geographical concentration of achievement that is unprecedented in the history of any sport. It is all the more remarkable in a sport in which success is a measure of pure speed, strength and endurance.

The annual rankings for the years 1992-1996 make Kalenjin dominance of track distance events even more clear. The rankings are based on race times. There are top ten ranked men in each of the five events, for a total of fifty per year. For those five years, Kalenjins occupied ninety-eight of the total of two hundred fifty spots. That's forty-four percent of the top ten rankings in the five events over the five-year period.

Kalenjin men have dominated the World Cross-Country Championships since 1986. In 1998, four of the first seven finishers were Kalenjins. Of the thirty-six individual medals awarded in the men's competition in the twelve years between 1986 (the year Kenya first started sending a contingent to the championships) and 1998, Kalenjins have won eighteen. As for the marathon, a Kalenjin runner had the second fastest time in history, and Kalenjin runners have won the Boston Marathon four times since 1988. In 1997, Kalenjin runners took the first two places in Boston, three of the top five, five of the top eight, and twelve of the top eighteen.[7]

You don't have to be a runner, or even a jogger, to appreciate those figures. They are an indication of profound natural forces at work. And the Kalenjins are related linguistically to other East African tribes that have produced world-class runners. All these tribes are pastoral cattle herders as opposed to agriculturists. A number of cattle-herding tribes in Kenya lead similar lives at comparable altitudes yet have produced no notable runners. What makes the Kalenjins so special? No one knows for sure, but we may assume that it is some combination of the physical and the psychological.

The Kalenjin are known to be hard working and enduring, and are generally regarded as a serious, quiet ascetic people inclined to remain in their traditional areas. One researcher found that Kalenjins showed the highest scores for "achievement orientation among Kenya's seventy ethnic groups."[8] Many of the records and medals were achieved by one particular Kalenjin clan, the Nandi, who take their name from one of the districts within a small part of the Rift Valley. In Kenya today, the Nandi have the strongest tradition of competitive individualism. According to the author of *The Nandi of Kenya*, ". . . even superficial observers of the Nandi have been struck by their haughtiness and arrogance. The Nandi considers himself the equal of any man, and superior to all who are not Nandi."[9]

Superficial observers make superficial observations; a sense of pride in one's cultural heritage and a determination to maintain that heritage may easily be misunderstood. Nandi warriors were the only native Kenyans to have engaged in prolonged resistance against the British when the colonialists tried to exert control over Nandiland in 1895, fighting until 1905 when their leader was murdered by a British officer at a meeting called to discuss peace. The Nandi have remained a proud and independent people, yet they and other Kalenjins now have a real voice in government and Kalenjin names are common in all areas of Kenyan life.

Kalenjin competitiveness was eventually channeled into sport, and a tradition of athletic prowess was established early on, well before the 1980s. During the 1968 Mexico City Olympics, the Nandi Kip Keino became the first famous Kenyan runner when he won the gold medal in the 1500 meter race. Many observers believe that his success gave rise to a tradition among the Kalenjins that led to early recruitment and well-organized training of young athletes.[10]

We'll never know how much of an influence the traditional Kalenjin diet had on the victories of Kip Keino and the many other Kalenjin champions who followed. That Mr. Keino continues to believe in the importance of traditional Kalenjin dairy foods becomes apparent in the following excerpt from a 2001 *Los Angeles Times* article. The story tells a little about milk and a lot about the character and integrity many observers have found to be typical of people from traditional indigenous cultures.

"Kip Keino, one of the greatest Olympic runners of all time, a living legend in the East African nation who could command the sort of classy ride befitting a man of distinction, drives himself around this high plateau town in a beat-up old four-door Nissan. 'The money is needed at home,' he says. 'I have people depending on me. I can get where I need to go.'

"Keino, 61, and his wife, Phyllis, make abundantly clear what the grace of selflessness and a heartfelt devotion to others can accomplish in life. Over the last 30 years, the Keinos have taken in more than 100 orphaned or abandoned children, and made them their own. A few months ago, the Keinos realized a long-held dream. They opened the Kip Keino School, funded by various donations. Now some 250 boys and girls line up in the school's quadrangle each Monday morning.

"'I am happy,' says Faraj Kiptarus Keino, 13. He lives on the Keino farm across the highway from the school, in a dormitory with two dozen other adoptive Keino kids. 'Mum and Dad care for us,' he says.

"Neither Phyllis nor Kip Keino see anything extraordinary about the path they pursued. 'We feel they need help,' Kip says of the extended family. 'They need shelter. They need a mother and a father.' He pauses, and then continues: 'I came into this world with nothing. I will leave with nothing. While I am here, I should be mindful of those people who need help. They need food. They need clothing. They need shelter. They need love.' Phyllis adds, 'There are other people who do like this. Or more.'

"Virtually everyone who comes to know the Keinos remarks not only on their sincerity but on their humility. Bob Keino, 24, the fifth of seven children born to Kip and Phyllis, says, 'He always taught us you can be the best in the world at your sport but you always have to be humble. . .

"If they are old enough to remember, Phyllis said, the children who come to the Keino house typically have a horrifying tale to tell: They were abandoned. Or one or both parents died of AIDS. Or they were born to a mentally disabled woman who was unable to care for children. The current Keino child count is 82, Phyllis said. Half are off at area boarding schools—essentially high school—or away at college. Of the others, 18 live at the first farm Phyllis and Kip bought. It is called 'Kazi Mingi,' Swahili for 'a lot of work.' About 200 acres, it is dominated by a ranch-style house.

"Twenty-three more live at the Keino's second farm, dubbed 'Baraka,' Swahili for 'blessing.' Five of these 23 kids are nursery school-aged. All 23 live in a dormitory-style building on the grounds. Baraka was bought in 1989 for the Children's Home through a Swiss priest stationed in Eldoret. The idea was Phyllis'. She wanted more land in order to grow food for children and to generate income for the Home.

"It took the better part of ten years to make the land productive. Now Baraka is ringed with trees and boasts a reservoir. It even looks like a farm, with a herd of 120 Holsteins as well as a barn, feedlots, a milking station, and the main house, a garden with fruits and vegetables.

"The farm now produces milk, yogurt and cheese under the name 'Tamu,' Swahili for 'delicious.' Demand is high; the farm is producing 300 liters a day of milk or milk-related products and it typically sells out. Wheeling into Baraka one day recently, Kip stopped by the milking station to pick up a few cartons of 'lala,' a fermented milk considered a local delicacy.

"At Kazi Mingi, meantime, Phyllis' day begins at 5:30 a.m. It ends late at night. A woman of strong and abiding religious faith, she said, 'My pleasure is this: When these kids are happy, I am happy.'

"'I look upon Phyllis as a saint,' observed Fred Hardy, who for 36 years was the track coach at the University of Richmond and has become a Keino family friend. 'She is a strong, strong woman. And of course Kip is what he is, a great guy.'"[11]


TIBET

The Tibetan Plateau and Himalayas stretch across parts of China, India, Nepal and Bhutan. In this vast rangeland, perhaps the harshest pastoral area on earth, the high-mountain nomads of Tibet still thrive, demonstrating the powerful effect that the relationship between animals and terrain can have on the lifestyle of a people. These Tibetans live at an altitude of twelve to seventeen thousand feet, where they keep yak, sheep, goats, cattle and horses. The yak are the most important of their animals, large and powerful cousins of cattle, with great agility for navigating steep mountains. Descendants of wild yaks, the animals make life possible for people across much of the Tibetan steppe, and they play essential roles in rituals and religious festivals. The Tibetan term for a family's group of yaks can be translated as "wealth."

Tibetan nomadic culture is unique. In most pastoral areas of the world, the major challenge is lack of water. Here, water is abundant; altitude and temperature are the challenges. The temperatures are too cold for crop cultivation, but the land provides excellent forage for the livestock.[12]

The tribes move with the animals up and down the high slopes, storing hay in the lower valleys to use in the winter and enjoying the higher pastures in the summer. They buy barley, dried fruit and tea from agricultural people whose lands they border, and they hunt for some of their food. But the staples are raw dairy foods from yak and cattle—milk, yogurt, butter and cheese—with some meat and blood.[13]

Movements of the people and their animals reflect a complex social organization. Topography and climatic factors influence the rotation of livestock between different pastures in order to maintain animal productivity and conserve the grass. Movements also take advantage of topography and climatic factors to make the best use of distant pastures at different seasons.

Many of these nomads have built comfortable houses across the Tibetan Plateau during the last twenty years. The traditional yak-hair tent is still in common use, but increasing numbers spend increasing amounts of time, especially in the winter, in their homes.

Some two million Tibetan nomads still roam the Tibetan steppe; because the region is so inhospitable to farming, there has been little agricultural encroachment into the nomadic areas. The vibrant nomadic culture the Tibetans have developed is a successful adaptation to one of the most inhospitable places on earth.

Daniel Miller is a range ecologist who first worked with Tibetan-speaking nomads in Nepal as a Peace Corps volunteer during the 1970s. He has published numerous articles and books about Tibetan pastoralism, and for seventeen years has been involved in pastoral development and wildlife conservation programs with nomads in Bhutan, Nepal and throughout the Tibetan areas of present-day China, Mongolia, and Pakistan. He reports that Chinese government programs to force nomads to privatize and fence the grasslands now threaten the nomadic culture; another threat is rangeland degradation caused by year-round grazing of livestock around the settlements.

But the Tibetan nomads have prevailed under forbidding circumstances for thousands of years—their pastoral system has proven to be surprisingly stable, aided by the fact that much of the Tibetan Plateau is suitable only for grazing. Miller believes that their way of life will survive if the governments involved allow it.[14]

These Tibetans are avid horsemen; sports and games center on their horses. They are the descendants of the armies of Genghis Khan, founder of the Mongol empire, which swept out of central Asia eight hundred years ago, conquering all in its path, from the shores of the Pacific in the east to the Black Sea in the west. One reason for the Mongol success was the use of stirrups, which freed both hands for fighting. Another was their ability to travel quickly with few supplies, because they could live on the milk of their mares. Their women traveled with them, milking the mares and drying much of the milk. The men would carry this dried milk on their horses into battle, first mixing a half a pound or so with water in a leather pouch.[15] Dinner—for those who survived— would be a tasty, fermented, yogurt-like food. The Mongol victory was the original blitzkrieg, powered by blood, guts and raw milk.

## LAPLAND

It may have been the desire to avoid war that led the Laplanders into the hinterlands of Scandinavian, where until recently they followed their semi-wild reindeer from the mountains to the coast and back again every year, just as they have since the last Ice Age. The Ice Ages forced a change in the way most humans lived, making them less dependent on plants and more on animals. In many parts of the earth, the rigors of the ice also forced a change in the hunting strategy, as stalking single animals became more difficult. Anticipating and adapting to the habits of herds, including their wandering migrations, became a new way of life for many population groups.[16]

For thousands of years the Lapps depended completely on the reindeer. They castrated some of the males to make them manageable as draught animals. They ate the meat, drank the milk, made cheese and butter, and used the bones and marrow in stews. They used the sinews, hides, bones and fur to make clothes and tools.

No fixed boundaries define Lapland, for it covers the Arctic regions of Norway, Sweden, Finland and western Russia. The ancestors of the remaining Lapps who live there today began roaming these lands some ten thousand years ago. Nominally under Norwegian and Swedish control since the Middle Ages, about half of today's Lapps live in permanent settlements with year-round pasture; small communities also reside in Finland and Russia. There are several mutually unintelligible dialects of the Lappish language, which is related to Finnish.[17]

Lapland's thirty thousand people fall into three distinct groups. Two, the forest and coastal groups, had joined the mainstream of modern life by the late 1960s, making their livelihood from fishing, hunting, trapping and farming. At that time, the third group, some fifteen hundred mountain Lapps, still depended on reindeer for their livelihood, making the month-long seasonal migration with the animals each spring in pursuit of pasture, across the hills and coastal mountains to islands off the northern Norwegian coast. It was a long, hard drive northward, and in the fall, they would return south to their winter homes in the rolling hills.[18]

Today, only a few Lapps continue this nomadic way of life. But over two hundred thousand reindeer still provide an essential source of livelihood for Lapland's people. Of the almost two hundred thousand people comprising Finnish Lapland's population, about seven thousand are Saami, the indigenous people of Lapland. Most of them own reindeer, which are semi-domesticated animals. Each reindeer bears the mark of its owner. They roam freely from late spring, until they are rounded-up in the late fall. Today the autumn reindeer roundup is a tourist highlight in Lapland, when members of the Reindeer Owners Association gather up the animals for return to their individual owners, some for slaughter but most for winter keeping. There is also a brief summer roundup using specially made corrals, where the fawns are marked with the same mark as their mothers, and the mothers are milked.

The Lapps have been able to preserve important aspects of their traditional way of life. This is in no small part due to the Scandinavian rule of "public right of access," which gives anyone the right under certain defined circumstances to be temporarily on someone else's land or water area. This applies, for example, to those picking berries or collecting mushrooms (the most common use of public right of access). The rule ensures that the reindeer may move freely across land that is not fenced, and restrictions dictate which land may be fenced. The public-right-of-access rule stipulates that those who move about in nature must not disturb other people or animals, especially reindeer. Public right of access allows camping and mountain biking, but expressly prohibits snowmobiles or any other motorized vehicles. Modern life and tourism appear to have come to Scandinavia and Lapland in a manner that seems idyllic when compared to many other once-pristine parts of the world.[19]

But Lapps still tell a favorite story about the old ways, of a man who has grown too old to follow the reindeer. Of his three sons, the first has joined the army and become an officer, while the second has won a university scholarship. The time has come for the third to choose what he would do.

"Father," he says, "I have decided to become a reindeer herder like you and your father before you."

"At last," says the old man softly. "Now I have a son I can be proud of."[20]

## BOVINE SENSITIVITIES IN TRADITIONAL CULTURES

Cattle are not dull, torpid beasts, as many believe. The effect of training can be striking in cattle, so much so that in the 1800s men wrote of "educating" certain cattle. The Hottentots, a people now found chiefly in southwest Africa and related to the Bushmen, were particularly skilled in training their oxen (castrated, large male cattle); they could manage the animals with great facility and adroitness, making them walk, trot or gallop at their will. According to Robert Hartley, writing in 1842, the historian Youatt wrote in his *Breeds of Cattle* that with the Hottentots "the triumph of the ox is complete. His intelligence seems to exceed anything that we have seen of the horse, and he is but little inferior to the dog."

Youatt describes how a special kind of oxen, the *backelies*, tend to sheep at the command of their masters, keeping the sheep within proper limits while guarding them against any strangers, animal or human. "Even the enemies of the nation these *backelies* are taught to combat," he wrote. "Every army of Hottentots is furnished with a proper herd of these creatures, which are let loose against the enemy. Being thus sent forward, they overturn all before them; they strike down with their horns, and trample with their feet, every one who attempts to oppose them, and thus often procure their masters an easy victory before they have begun to strike a blow." The *backely* was well rewarded; he lived in the same cottage with his master.

When a *backely* died, a village council of old men chose a new one to succeed him. The animal was then "joined with one of the veterans of his own kind, from whom he learns his art, becomes social and diligent, and is taken for life into human friendship and protection."[21]

The desire to form intimate relationships with animals is perhaps instinctive; in the world of the Hottentot and other pre-industrial cultures, survival may have depended upon it. Investigators tell us that today, people who keep pets live longer than those who do not.

India is the setting of another of Youatt's bovine stories, this one concerning the attachment of animals to their keepers. Two men were driving a string of water buffalo loaded with grain and merchandise between two Indian cities when a tiger seized one of them. A nearby herdsman who was tending a herd of grazing buffalo saw what happened, and he ran to the man's assistance. He cut the tiger severely with his sword, and the animal dropped the first man and seized the herdsman. His buffaloes then attacked the tiger, forcing it to release their master and then tossing the beast about until they killed it, but too late, for although the first man recovered, the herdsman died.[22]

Youatt's stories illustrate intelligence and a degree of social affection that should secure for the bovine species far better treatment than they generally receive today.

SETTLED PASTORALISTS:
THE TODA TRIBESMEN OF THE NILGIRI HILLS

From the muggy plains of south central India, the steep jungle slopes of the Nilgiri Hills rise to a plateau that lies an average of six thousand feet above the plains. For hundreds of years, four interrelated and interdependent groups of people—the Todas, Kotas, Badagas and

Kurumba—lived in an isolated five-hundred-square-mile area. The first western visitor was a Portuguese priest in 1602. For almost two hundred fifty years afterward, the peaceful life of the Nilgiri peoples remained unchanged. British engineers built roads into the hills in the early 1800s, an event that shattered the strong interdependence of the groups.

The Badagas, who were the farmers of the plateau, accepted change and merged with the culture of southern India. The Kotas, artists and musicians, had more difficulty adapting. The Kurumbas, woodsmen and sorcerers, remained in their jungle home and kept their old ways. And for many years, so too did the Todas, the dairymen of the hills.

Dr. David Mandelbaum of the University of California at Berkeley visited the peoples of the Nilgiri Hills in 1937 and again in 1968. He gave an account of his visits in "Nilgiri Peoples of India: An End to Old Ties," one chapter in the 1968 National Geographic publication *Vanishing Peoples of the Earth*. The material presented here is largely drawn from his account.

The four Nilgiri groups lived on an area of land about thirty-five miles long and fifteen miles wide. Each group had its own language, traditions and customs, and each played an important role in the life of the others. The Kurumbas brought honey and wood from the jungles and performed feats of sorcery. The Badagas cultivated grain and beans for the others. The Kotas made tools for all and music at religious occasions, festivities and ceremonies. And the pastoral Todas supplied ghee, or clarified butter to the other tribes.

In an intricate network of exchange, every family had close links with a family in each of the other three groups. An example: a Badaga's father-in-law had just died, and the cremation had to be performed quickly. Kota music was needed for the funeral ceremony. The Badaga went to his corresponding Kota family's village and found his Kota busy with a council session. But the Kota quickly gathered up musicians and left for the funeral. Reciprocation would come at harvest time, when the Kota would receive a share of the Badaga's crop.

By the 1960s, the Badagas had increased their numbers to about eighty-five thousand, and had spread far beyond the plateau. They no longer identified with the tribal society. The Kurumbas remained withdrawn in their jungles. The Kotas and the Todas were concentrated in the areas around the towns and villages of the plateau and maintained many of their traditional ways.

In 1820, the first Englishman to write about the Todas described the typical herdsman as "fair and handsome, with a fine expressive countenance, and intelligent eye, and an aquiline nose; his appearance is manly, being tall, strong-built, and well set up; his limbs muscular and finely proportioned." Other Europeans also wrote about the striking appearance of the Todas.

In the 1960s, the Todas still kept three thousand water buffalo, their lives and religion still centered on their animals. The animals and their milk were sacred to the Todas; temples served as dairies and priests as dairymen. Traditionally, the buffalo provided the people with their entire livelihood, and was the foundation of their tribal society. The Todas consumed great quantities of ghee, curds and a type of buttermilk. Their ghee was so essential for the other three groups of Nilgiri peoples that it was the Todas' chief article of exchange.

Todas do not eat buffalo meat; the animals provide only milk. Members of the tribe believe that everything sacred has to do with the buffalo and that everything connected with the care of the animal is sacred. Herds thought to have descended from a particular sacred bloodline may only be tended by priests. When a Toda takes his turn to serve as a priest, he leads an ascetic life to maintain a ritual purity, keeping apart from others and living alone in a temple-dairy.

The temples where butter was churned and made into ghee were off limits to all but the Todas; visitors were denied entry, even holy men of other cultures. The only time outsiders could see the inside of the temple was when the roof was rethatched.

The dairies had two simple rooms. The priest-dairyman lived in one, and in the other he used the clan's sacred lamp, churns and utensils to make clarified butter. Each temple belonged to one of the sixteen Toda clans, but all of the tribesmen came together to celebrate rethatching, the ceremonial renewal of a temple. Temple walls were often decorated with images of the sun, the moon and a four-horned buffalo.

The Todas retained many of their traditional ways when Mandelbaum last visited in 1968. "So long as the Toda herds remain intact as the basis of the people's livelihood and the center of their fond devotion," he wrote, "Toda culture probably will remain intact and retain its vitality."[23]

But the herds did not remain intact. At a workshop called "Toda Tribes, Pastoralism and Conservation of Toda Buffaloes" at Sandynalla, Nilgiris in October of 2001, discussion centered on the status of the Toda buffalo breed, problems faced by the Toda tribes and suggestions for interventions. About one thousand Toda families were reported to be living in about sixty small settlements called mandu, each consisting of a clan of several brothers' families. Each mandu owned from five to fifty buffalo, with a total buffalo population of some eighteen hundred. Rituals involving the buffalo still played a key role in the lives of the Toda, but the buffalo population was shrinking, primarily because government programs had converted over eighty percent of traditionally available pasture lands to croplands.[24]

Pastoral peoples in India have organized in an attempt to stop the erosion and dissipation of their traditional cultures. Because they do not own the land on which their animals traditionally have grazed, pastoralists are dependent on communal and state-owned grazing land. Official neglect has deprived them of their traditional and customary rights to these areas. Because their grazing lands are everywhere in decline, their populations are also declining throughout India.

In March of 2002, India's League for Pastoral Peoples recommended and demanded a number of governmental reforms that would benefit pastoralists, including land use policies to enlarge and protect grazing areas and ensure adequate space.[25] Securing these changes may prove difficult in a time when the bottom line of corporate culture usually overrides considerations of traditional culture.

## DR. WESTON PRICE AND NATURAL DIETARY LAWS

Of all the studies on human nutrition and the effect of foods on human health, that left to us by Weston Price is the most complete and most helpful. Price gave us overwhelming evidence of natural laws concerning dietary needs, laws that operate in human beings everywhere to regulate immunity, reproduction and virtually every other aspect of health. Any reasonable consideration of the role of milk in traditional cultures must incorporate an understanding of Price's work, which provides a foundation for the entire science of nutrition.

This is a strong statement, but not one that I make lightly. Having studied and applied Dr. Price's work for over thirty years, I have found the principles he taught have never failed me or my patients. The fundamental soundness and completeness of his research becomes more and more evident over time, and increasing understanding of his papers and his classic book *Nutrition and Physical Degeneration*, first published in 1939, make ever more apparent the inherent accuracy of his observations and the truth of his conclusions.

In my previous book, *Traditional Foods Are Your Best Medicine*, published in 1987, I explained Price's work in considerable depth. Many other authors now refer to Price and his work, and two non-profit organizations are dedicated to disseminating his findings—the Price-Pottenger Nutrition Foundation in San Diego, California and the Weston A. Price Foundation in Washington, DC. More and more health care professionals and laymen have adopted a nutritional approach that reflects the natural laws Price discovered at work in indigenous cultures throughout the world.

And yet, there is still widespread misunderstanding about what Weston Price learned in his studies of native peoples and how this knowledge applies to us today. The subject of this book is milk, and I do not wish to go too far afield, but a brief review of Price's life and some of his more important conclusions will serve us well in our efforts to understand the role of milk in traditional cultures and in our diets today.

PRICE'S STUDIES OF TRADITIONAL SOCIETIES

Weston Price was born in Ontario in 1870 and raised on a farm. He received a degree in dentistry in 1893 and moved to the United States, where he began his practice. A brilliant scholar and researcher, he also wrote textbooks that became standards in dentistry, as well as scores of articles for publication in professional medical, dental, public health and nutrition journals. For many years, his book *Nutrition and Physical*

*Degeneration* was required reading for anthropology students at Harvard University. The book records his studies of non-industrialized, so-called primitive peoples during the 1930s and 1940s.

Early in his professional career, Price noticed that the children of his patients had problems the parents had not experienced. Not only did these children suffer from more tooth decay than their parents did, they also had teeth that did not fit properly into the dental arch and were, as a result, crowded and crooked. Price referred to these conditions as "dental deformities," and he suspected that changes in nutrition were responsible.

He noticed that the condition of the teeth generally reflected the overall level of health. Considering possible reasons, a revolutionary idea occurred to him: perhaps some deficiency in modern diets caused the problems. Anthropologists had long observed and written about the excellent teeth found in primitive cultures. While others in dentistry looked for causative factors in dental decay, such as bacteria and "soft foods," Price decided to search among primitive people for a nutritional factor that protected them.

His search led him to discover fourteen primitive groups virtually free of tooth decay and dental deformities. He also noted the overall condition of excellent health in these groups. For example, in Alaska, he interviewed Dr. Romig who reported that in thirty-five years of observation, he had never seen a single case of cancer among the natives subsisting on their traditional foods. When natives eating the white man's foods developed tuberculosis, he eventually took to sending them back to their native villages and native foods; they then usually recovered.

Only in cultures that had no access to the white man's foods were the people immune to dental and degenerative disease. Biochemical analyses of their foods showed the diets to be rich in nutrients poorly supplied in modern diets.[26]

The most critical of these nutrients were found in the organ meats and fats of animals—vitamin A, vitamin D and a third fat-soluble nutrient called Activator X, now considered to be vitamin $K_2$, the animal form of vitamin K.[27] How ironic that the foods most vilified by modern medicine, conventional nutritionists and the processed food establishments and their media allies are precisely those that Dr. Price discovered we need the most.

Price described cultures where people following traditional ways and diets lived near kinsmen who had begun to eat the foods of modern civilization—sugar, white flour, canned foods, canned condensed milk and vegetable oils. His time in history was unique for several reasons. The cultures he observed were still truly indigenous, with groups of people living entirely on the local foods. Photographic emulsion was commonly available for the first time, so he could easily record his observations, and world travel too was readily available for the first time for anyone able to afford it. This combination of the old and the new enabled Price to see and record a uniquely enlightening picture of a world that was rapidly vanishing.[28]

His travels took him to the far corners of the earth. He and his wife visited and studied Swiss villagers in high Alpine valleys; Gaelic fisherfolk on islands of the Outer Hebrides; Eskimos in Alaska; Native Americans in the far northern, western and central parts of Canada, and in the western United States and Florida; Melanesians and Polynesians in the southern Pacific; Africans in eastern and central Africa; Aborigines in Australia; Malay tribes on islands north of Australia; Maori groups in New Zealand; and descendants of ancient civilizations in Peru. Whenever possible, he also studied the skeletal remains of ancient people.

He kept meticulous records and photographic accounts of all he saw. His work shows that virtually everyone in traditional cultures had all thirty-two teeth, perfectly fitting into the dental arch and perfectly formed, as long as the people had no access to the white man's foods. Eating refined foods invariably caused dental decay and systemic diseases, and then, in the next generation, crooked and crowded teeth.

In studying the diets of the native people, Price collected over ten thousand samples of native foods and sent them back to America for analysis in his laboratories. He found that traditional diets contained at least four times the minerals and water-soluble vitamins, and ten times the fat soluble vitamins (found uniquely in animal fats) compared to the American diet of his day.

Price was one of the pioneers in developing assays for vitamins A and D. He wrote a textbook on dentistry for the Navy that was carried on every United States naval vessel for many years. His studies on problems associated with root canals, first published in the 1920s, were rediscovered seventy years later and became the basis for the recent book *Root Canal Cover-Up*, which details problems often associated with root canals. His articles appeared in dental journals throughout the twenties and thirties. His observations were not limited to health and diet, for he sought to understand the nature and character of the thousands of people he studied. He came to know many well, and his insights reveal the strength of character of many individuals, a trait he found typical in native cultures. We'll see this in his observations of the Swiss people discussed shortly. First, let's examine the fundamental nutritional principles Price discovered.

## NATURAL LAWS AT WORK IN NATIVE NUTRITION

Native people throughout the world followed dietary regimes that were largely dictated by availability and custom, by what they described as the wisdom of their ancestors. One of the many fascinating discoveries Price recorded was the answer he received whenever he asked native people why they ate the foods they did. The inevitable reply: "So we can make perfect babies."

What were the foods that were considered most important for women and men who wished to conceive a child, for pregnant and nursing women to nourish the child, and for growing children to achieve their optimal physical potential? Price studied this question in great depth. His answer, based on his careful observations, was that foods from one or more of six different groups were absolutely essential:

1. Seafood: fish, shellfish, fish organs, fish liver oils and fish eggs.
2. Organ meats from wild animals or grass-fed domestic animals.
3. Insects.
4. Fats of certain birds and monogastric (one-stomach) animals such as sea mammals, Guinea pigs, bears and pigs.
5. Egg yolks from pastured chicken and other birds.
6. Whole milk, cheese and butter from grass-fed animals.

The foods in the last group were eaten raw and unprocessed, as were a portion of the foods in the other five groups.

These are the foods that native people everywhere said were most important for their strength and health, and for making perfect babies. Seafood and dairy foods were often fermented so that they provided high levels of enzymes. And raw or cooked, all these foods are rich in the fat-soluble vitamins A, D, and $K_2$, in important fatty acids, minerals and a host of other nutrients essential to reproduction and good health.

Price's discoveries cause confusion in many people. For decades food processors, nutritionists, doctors and the media have told us that animal fats and high-cholesterol foods like liver are bad for us. This "medical-industrial complex" has blamed animal fats for the problems caused by sugar, vegetable oils and other processed foods. Let's set aside the propaganda and take a fresh look at the issue.

The health effects of any food that comes from an animal, including the fats, depend on the health of the animal. The animal's feeding and environment completely determine the quality of the food it provides. Healthy animals have always provided humans with healthy food, and they still do. The healthier the animals, the healthier the food they provide us.

Cattle, goats and sheep are ruminants, designed by nature to eat grass. Meat, raw milk, raw cheese and raw butter from healthy, grass-fed, chemical-free animals are wonderful and healthy foods. So are eggs and the fat of chickens and other fowl raised outdoors on insects and pasture. Fish is too, although care should be taken to secure wild (not farm-raised) fish from relatively unpolluted waters. The fatty parts of all these foods carry essential nutrients!

These foods, together with fresh organic plant foods (vegetables, fruit, tubers and nuts), constitute our primitive, ancestral diet. In the last few thousand years, some traditional agricultural cultures have succeeded in maintaining optimal health while incorporating limited quantities of carefully prepared legumes and whole grain foods into the more ancient ancestral diet.

The truth is that animal fats are not the cause of our modern problems. Refined foods are. We actually suffer from a lack of the nutrients that our ancestors obtained in great quantities from the fats of healthy animals.

Several other important principles emerged from the work of Price and other nutritional pioneers who succeeded him. Native diets consisted entirely of whole, unrefined foods. All cultures consumed some of their animal foods raw and all cultures fermented many of their foods. Milk products, if available, were consumed raw or carefully prepared in ways that preserved the enzyme content.

In cultures where grains were available, only whole, unrefined grains were prepared, and bread was made from freshly ground flour. Grains and legumes were also usually carefully fermented, a process that gets rid of the many antinutrient components in these foods. Finally, most cultures made use of the bones, usually by making broth, to obtain calcium and other minerals.

With this understanding, let's continue the story of milk by examining a culture that Price studied where the people thrived on a diet that included substantial amounts of raw dairy foods—the Swiss of the Loetschental Valley.

## SWISS DAIRY FARMERS OF THE LOETSCHENTAL VALLEY

The Loetschental Valley lies nearly one mile above sea level in an isolated part of the Swiss Alps. When Dr. Price and his wife first visited the valley in 1931, it had been the home of some two thousand people for more than a dozen centuries. The people lived in a series of small villages along a river that wound its way through the valley floor. The completion of an eleven-mile tunnel shortly before Price's visit had made the valley easily accessible for the first time in history. The people lived as their forefathers had lived. Wooden buildings, some centuries old, dotted the landscape, with mottoes expressive of spiritual values artistically carved in the timbers. Snow-capped mountains nearly enclosed the valley, making it relatively easy to defend. Though attackers had made many attempts to subjugate these valley dwellers in earlier centuries, the people had never been conquered. They had no physicians, dentists, policemen or jails. Sheep provided wool for homespun clothes, and the valley produced nearly everything needed for food.

The land, much of it on steep hillsides rising from the river, produced the winter's hay for the cattle and rye for the people. Most households kept goats and cows; the animals grazed in summer on slopes fed by glacial waters. Cheese and butter were made from fresh summer milk for use all year, and garden greens were grown in summer. Sourdough whole-rye bread, made in large, stone, community baking ovens, was a staple all year, as was milk and cheese. Most families ate meat once a week, usually on Sunday, when an animal was slaughtered. Bones, organs and scraps were used in soups during the week.

Price examined the teeth of all the children in the valley between the ages of seven and sixteen. Those still eating the primitive diet were nearly free of cavities—on the average, one tooth showing evidence of decay was found for every three children examined. All of the children had naturally straight teeth—there were no dental deformities.[29,30]

Many of the young adults Price examined had experienced a period of tooth decay that suddenly ceased. Of these, all had left the valley prior to this period and had spent a year or two in a more modernized part of Europe. Most never had a decayed tooth before or since their return to their village. In fact, the teeth of many of those who had returned to the valley showed evidence of remineralization.

At this time in Switzerland, tuberculosis took more lives than any other disease. Yet Swiss government officials reported that a recent inspection of the valley had revealed not one single case of TB. Astonishingly, Price's thorough study of local death certificates demonstrated clearly that no deaths had occurred from tuberculosis during the recorded history of the valley. This is evidence of profound natural forces at work and speaks volumes about the power of ancestral diets to prevent chronic disease.

Upon returning to America, Price had samples of the Loetschental Valley dairy products sent to him twice a month throughout the year. A pioneer in developing methods for measuring fat-soluble vitamins in foods, Price had written extensively on the subject and was a recognized authority.

His analysis found the samples to be far higher in minerals and vitamins, particularly the fat-soluble vitamins A, D and Activator X, than samples of commercial dairy products from the rest of Europe and North America.

The Swiss people Price studied recognized the crucial importance of their foods for health. The clergymen told of how they thanked God for the life-giving qualities of each year's first butter and cheese, which were made in June when the cows ate fresh spring grass near the snow line. During a church ceremony, they lighted a wick in a bowl of the first butter made after the cows reached spring pasturage. Price's analysis showed that butter made at that time of year was highest of all in the fat-soluble vitamins.

This spring butter had a special place in the culture and was considered a sacred food. It was rich in the same fat-soluble nutrients found in foods held sacred by other traditional agricultural and hunter-gatherer cultures, foods like fish eggs, organ meats and cod's liver.

In a real and down-to-earth way, spiritual values dominated the people's lives. Part of the national holiday celebration each August was a song expressing the feeling of "one for all and all for one." Price wrote: "One wonders if there is not something in the life-giving vitamins and minerals of the food that builds not only great physical structures within which their souls reside, but builds minds and hearts capable of a higher type of manhood in which the material values of life are made secondary to individual character."[31] He found evidence of this innate spirituality throughout the nonindustrialized world.

The excellent health of the inhabitants of the Loetschental Valley contrasted starkly with the health of those living in the lower valleys and plains country in Switzerland—modernized areas where rampant dental decay, misshapen dental arches with crowding of the teeth, and a high incidence of tuberculosis and other chronic health problems were the norm. The people of the valley were clearly protected by their foods, most importantly their raw milk, rich butter and cheese, which supplied the bulk of the calories and nutrients. Modern, bastardized versions of these foods do not provide the health-building properties of the dairy foods consumed in the Loetschental Valley. Homogenized, pasteurized milk from confinement animals, and butter, cheeses and yogurts made from such milk, may look the same and carry the same name, but the assumption that they are the same as milk products from the Loetschental Valley constitutes an insidious deception perpetrated on the consumers of industrialized food.

# Part II
# Food, Health and Trust

# 9
# Betrayal

*The health of the people is really the foundation upon which all their happiness and all their powers as a state depend.*
Benjamin Disraeli,
English statesman and social reformer

*After generations of this pasteurized, homogenized, two percent spirituality, the body-politic has lapsed into a deep cattlepsy. And without this direct connection to the Fodder, we've allowed a powerful few to bulldoze Mother Nature and seek immortality in their own creations . . . . And that's why the sacred cow is nowhere to be found, but the bull is everywhere.*
Swami Beyondananda, *Duck Soup for the Soul*

Betrayal is a strong word, a word implying disloyalty, treachery, deliberately misleading behavior. My premise in this chapter and the next is that many of our private and public institutions have betrayed our trust. This betrayal is an important element in the story about how the quality of our milk has declined in the course of the past fifty or sixty years.

At the end of World War II, thousands of small farms throughout the country still sold raw milk directly to consumers and through local distribution channels, a situation that would change drastically under relentless official pressure for compulsory pasteurization. A series of articles in popular magazines in 1944, 1945 and 1946 served to frighten the public into support of these efforts. A side effect of this movement was the demise of America's small farms.

The *Ladies' Home Journal* began the campaign in 1944 with the article "Undulant Fever," claiming—without any accurate documentation—that tens of thousands of people in the U.S. suffered from fever and illness because of exposure to raw milk.[1] The next year, *Coronet* magazine followed up with "Raw Milk Can Kill You," by Robert Harris, MD.[2] Similar articles appearing in the *Progressive*[3] and the *Reader's Digest*[4] the following year repeated these outright lies.

The author of the *Coronet* article represented as fact a town and an epidemic, both of which were complete fabrications: "Crossroads, U.S.A., is in one of those states in the Midwest area called the bread basket and milk bowl of America. . . . What happened to Crossroads might happen to your town—to your city—might happen almost anywhere in America." The author then gives a lurid account of a frightful undulant fever epidemic allegedly caused by raw milk, an epidemic that "spread rapidly. . . it struck one out of every four persons in Crossroads. Despite the efforts of the two doctors and the State health department, one out of every four patients died."

But there was no Crossroads, and no epidemic! Author Harris admitted the fabrication in a subsequent interview with J. Howard Brown of Johns Hopkins University.[5] The outbreak was fictitious and represented no actual occurrence.

Harris' own public statements both before and after the *Coronet* article reveal not only the fallacious nature of the story, but also the fact that he knew such a thing could not possibly happen. In an article he wrote in 1941, Harris stated: "Mortality in acute cases of undulant fever was formerly about two percent, but this has been greatly lowered by modern methods."[6] In a 1946 paper he read before the Maine Veterinary Medical Association in Portland, he stated, "The small proportion of deaths from acute illness, varying from two to three percent, rarely higher, can be made almost, if not quite zero."[7]

Undulant fever is another name for brucellosis, an infectious disease that occurs in cattle and other animals and is transmitted to humans primarily through physical contact; it is an occupational hazard for meatpackers, veterinarians, farmers and livestock producers and handlers. Typically the course of illness begins with an acute stage followed by relapses of fever, weakness, aches and pains. In years past, people who drank raw milk occasionally contracted the disease, which was probably transmitted when the organisms causing the disease were shed by grossly infected animals into the milk. A few cases in recent years have been attributed to raw milk cheeses.[8]

Official statistics from the U.S. Public Health Service, which compiles such information on a nationwide basis, show the possible extent of any undulant fever problems associated with raw milk in the years prior to the Harris article. In the years from 1923 through 1944, records for the entire United States show thirty-two outbreaks of undulant fever attributed to milk, with two hundred fifty-six cases and a total of three deaths.[9,10] Clearly, Harris's synthetic epidemic had no basis in reality. The claim that "what happened to Crossroads might happen to your town—to your city—might happen almost anywhere in America" was not only completely false but indeed malicious.

In the ensuing years, these claims and many others like them appeared in subsequent magazine and newspaper articles read by tens of millions of people. Writing in the *Rural New Yorker* in 1947, Jean Bullitt Darlington made a particularly fine effort to set the record straight with a three-part series "Why Milk Pasteurization?" Her articles, "Sowing the Seeds of Fear," "Plowing Under the Truth" and "The Harvest is a Barren One," provided an elegant presentation of the issues. Many of her points are as valid today as they were then.

"Contrary to current popular belief," Darlington began, "pasteurization of milk is not a step forward in nutrition and health. It is a step backward. Certain important nutritional elements such as vitamins, enzymes and minerals are lost. Low standards of milk production are encouraged; incentive for high-grade milk production is discouraged;

competition in distribution is narrowed; monopoly control of producers is made possible; and the dietary value of milk is lowered, while the cost to the consumer is increased.

"These are not statements based on hearsay or guesswork, but upon more than ten years of patient inquiry and diligent study of the evidence, including unbiased scientific research, for the purpose of determining the importance of milk, in relation both to health and economics.

"That pasteurization of milk is not in the public interest can hardly be denied after a study of the subject. Nevertheless, the propagandists would have us believe that disease from unpasteurized milk is so widespread and inevitable that pasteurization should be compulsory. The fallacy of this contention can best be demonstrated by assaying the facts upon which it has been based."

In the first article, Darlington exposes the lies and distortions in the magazine articles referred to above. Her second paper is primarily concerned with the numerous animal and human studies that have demonstrated the superior nutritional value of raw milk compared to pasteurized, and the third presents further arguments in the case against compulsory pasteurization. Much of the evidence Darlington compiled will be examined in Chapter 15 when we compare the safety of raw versus pasteurized milk.

AN INSIDER'S VIEW

Alton Eliason, who began working for Knudsen's, a New Jersey dairy, in 1934, witnessed the betrayal of raw milk from the inside. Knudsen's had no Holsteins in their herd, just Jerseys and Guernseys; consequently their milk contained more cream than that of competitors. Eliason writes: "I will describe the sales method utilized by Knudsen's that boosted their sales and allowed them to add six trucks to their fleet in one year. Virtually all milk was delivered directly to homes during the early morning hours in those days and left on the back porch or sometimes left in an insulated box on the porch to keep it cold until retrieved by the customer. Remember, this occurred in the days before refrigeration. The milk cases were heavily iced to keep the milk cold during warm weather. The few stores having ice boxes or the new refrigerated units usually carried just a few quarts of milk and small bottles of cream for local residents. It was our sales practice to arrange our route so as to follow our competitor and leave a quart sample of our milk next to his. On returning later in the morning we would introduce ourselves and ask the lady of the house whether she had received our sample and would she bring out her regular supplier's bottle so we could demonstrate the greater cream content of our product .... With Knudsen's greater creamline, it was seldom we left without a new customer.

"It was at this time that I witnessed the first step toward the eventual demise of milk as we had known it. While pasteurized milk was rapidly replacing raw, there were still a considerable number of people demanding raw milk. It was the practice in those days for the more affluent to own or rent cottages at the shore for the summer in Connecticut. With the children home from school and mother not needing to get up early to get the children off, many took this opportunity to sleep late into the day. Few women worked outside the home in those days. This created a problem for the dairies, what with the milk standing out in the hot summer sun. While the raw milk rarely went sour, the heat did cause the cream to rise thickly to the top of the bottle and some assumed the milk was sour and called to complain. While turning the bottle upside down a few times would solve the problem, it was usually thought better to replace the bottle rather than risk losing a customer.

"One summer morning, my boss, Chris, asked me to accompany him on such a journey to keep him company. On the trip he remarked that we weren't going to be doing this much longer. I asked him what he meant. He responded, 'We're going to get raw milk outlawed.'

"'How are you going to do that?' I asked.

"'Oh we've got some doctors that are going to testify that raw milk causes diseases,' he responded.

"'But that isn't true,' I pointed out.

"'We don't give a damn whether it's true or not, just so long as we can get these lazy women off our neck,' he said. . .

"In the late 1930s, the corporate powers began the most vicious, unjust wave of adverse publicity ever seen in the health field. They stooped to the lowest denominators to not only prevent the sale of raw milk in public places, but even to stop its sale from the farm. In this effort they hired writers to make the very thought of drinking raw milk seem a lapse in one's mentality. Most doctors have been so brainwashed and indoctrinated with medical school texts that, to this day, if a patient admits that he drinks raw milk, his doctor will insist on knowing where he purchases it. The physician can then report it to the health department. He will often, without further investigation, determine milk as the cause of whatever condition the patient is complaining. Preposterous? No, this scenario was actually experienced by a friend of mine who suffered the same reaction from several doctors she visited. Some even told her not to come back if she continued to drink raw milk. Of course, her affliction had no bearing on her milk drinking."[11]

The smear tactics described above are vivid examples of the role the media and health professionals have played in the banning of raw milk in most places and the almost universal acceptance of compulsory pasteurization. When media portray fiction as fact, and the medical profession accepts that fiction uncritically, the betrayal of public trust is obvious; the more typical slanted stories belie a more subtle betrayal fed by advertising money and the policies of government agencies, professional medical organizations and corporate giants in the food, drug and medical industries. These policies often directly conflict with the best interests of the average citizen. We'll now examine a number ways these groups influence official policy.

ACADEMIC NUTRITIONISTS AND GOVERNMENT POLICY

Many people think of a nutritionist as the person at the health food store who gives advice about vitamins, herbs and other food supplements. This person may have a certificate from a correspondence course, or perhaps a degree in nutrition from an accredited institution. The quality of the advice depends on the individual, and it may be outstanding. But usually it is geared to selling products; most health food stores make the bulk of their profits at the vitamin counter. Legally these advisors may not treat medical problems, but often they act as proxy physicians, a fact usually ignored by authorities. The only influence these individuals have on officialdom is a negative one—the FDA would like to ban retail sales of most supplements and put these people out of business.

On the other hand, academics with advanced degrees in nutrition and dietetics are among the key players influencing the creation of government nutrition policy. The academic nutritionist lives in a world of classrooms, corporations, publishers and government agencies. Academic nutritionists have university degrees, and they have a great deal to do with creating and shaping official government nutrition policies. These policies are reflected in a diverse group of publications, including the Federal Register notices, Congressional hearing reports, Acts of Congress, General Accounting Office reports, agency advisory notices to industry and government agency Internet postings. The media issue reports on these published policies, while the food industry uses them for its own ends, primarily to sell products. Because academic nutritionists play a central role in creating these policies, it is interesting and relevant to consider how they may be influenced in their opinions and pronouncements.

The norm among academic nutritionists is to give speeches at meetings overtly sponsored by food companies or organized by professional societies that receive funding from such companies, and to accept travel funds and honoraria to appear at such meetings. They read journals subsidized by food companies—the *Journal of the American Society of Clinical Nutrition*, for example, receives funding from General Foods, Best Foods and Quaker Oats, among others—speak on panels together with food company representatives, receive grants from food companies and consult for food companies. Does this mean the professors toe the company line? While a tenured full professorship at a major university makes it considerably easier for an academic nutritionist to question the industry agenda, particularly if the individual does not need laboratory facilities or research funding, such individuals rarely speak out, if only to avoid ostracism by faculty members who do rely on industry grants. Yet most nutritionists "are outraged by suggestions that food industry sponsorship of research or programs might influence what they do or say."[12]

NUTRITION ARTICLES IN PROFESSIONAL JOURNALS

Food companies openly enlist academic nutrition experts as their allies. Author Marion Nestle gives an interesting account of these tactics in her book *Food Politics*, describing how the food industry hires "leading experts" as consultants or advisors, and provides grant money for research or projects. She quotes from *The Regulation Game: Strategic use of the Administrative Process*, as follows: "This activity requires a modicum of finesse; it must not be too blatant, for the experts themselves must not recognize that they have lost their objectivity and freedom of action. At a minimum, a program of this kind reduces the threat that the leading experts will be available to testify or write against the interests of the regulated firms."[13]

Most nutrition professionals depend, to varying degrees, on the support food companies give in the form of funds for university nutrition departments and research, professional societies and journals, and meetings and conferences.

This funding is well documented. The Center for Science in the Public Interest (CSPI) maintains a web site that provides the names and university affiliations of hundreds of academics who receive funding from food companies, along with the details of the funding. During the 1970s, CSPI published a survey detailing numerous food company payments to faculty members at university agriculture and nutrition departments for research, grants, consulting, articles, representation at congressional hearings and membership on advisory boards. Advisory board membership is a particularly convenient method for gaining influence; the professional may accept funds merely for having his or her name on a list and taking an occasional phone call from the company.[14]

Corporate money helps pay for the cost of publishing the *Journal of Nutrition Education*, the *Journal of Nutrition* and the *American Journal of Clinical Nutrition*. Sponsors include Slim-Fast Foods, the Sugar Association, Gerber, Nestlé/Carnation, Proctor & Gamble and Coca-Cola. It is difficult to imagine why a company like Coca-Cola would give money to a nutrition journal for any reason other than influencing the journal's content and policies. All of these companies make products that many experts consider clearly detrimental to health, with nutritional "attributes" that even mainstream nutritionists consider debatable and controversial.[15]

A brief foray through the pages of the *New England Journal of Medicine* or the *Journal of the American Medical Association*, both of which publish selected articles on nutrition research, demonstrates why these two prestigious publications are dependent on drug companies for their very existence. Drug company ads fill more pages than the articles in these journals; these ads provide each journal with some twenty million dollars per year.[16] Independent scientists and researchers with papers documenting the benefits of, for example, raw foods in the treatment or prevention of chronic diseases, might find publication in these journals difficult to come by.

Journals aren't the only places where drug companies can buy influence; physicians who accept gifts and travel funds to attend company conferences are more likely than other physicians to prescribe the company's drugs.[17]

The findings of much nutrition research are also suspect because the research is often sponsored by industry grants, much of it undisclosed. In fact, the problem extends beyond nutrition research: a 1996 survey found that nearly thirty percent of university faculty members accepted industry funding.[18] Another survey looked at eight hundred papers in medicine and molecular biology and found that over one-third of the primary authors stood to benefit financially from the research discussed in their papers—some held patents, others served as consultants to the companies involved, and many had financial interests in the companies.[19] The research may not always be biased, and the researchers themselves invariably defend their integrity by rejecting the charge that industry support might bias their work.[20] But the nature of the evidence brings to mind an old story about Henry David Thoreau. During the mid 1800s, milk distributors in Boston were notorious for heavily diluting their milk with water from the Cochituate River, but there was no proof. Thoreau commented, "Some circumstantial evidence is very strong, as when you find a trout in the milk."[21]

## THE FOOD INDUSTRY AND ADVERTISING

The food industry brings more pressure to bear in Washington, where it devotes tremendous resources to lobbying Congress and federal agencies. Food industry operatives form partnerships and alliances with professional nutrition organizations, fund research on food and nutrition, publicize the results of selected research studies favorable to the industry, and sponsor professional journals and conferences. These efforts aim to make influential groups of federal officials, researchers, doctors, nurses, schoolteachers and the media aware of the benefits the industry claims for its products.[22]

The industry is not lacking cash—food companies take in over one trillion dollars in sales each year, about thirteen percent of the U.S. gross national product. They employ seventeen percent of the labor force. Alcoholic beverage companies account for ten percent of these industry revenues, and the rest is split about evenly between food service and retail food companies.

The growth of the food industry was coincident with a gradual but wholesale change in the typical American diet, from one based on locally grown whole foods to one based on processed foods that may come from anywhere. As the industry grew, farming as a lifestyle declined; forty percent of Americans lived on farms in 1900, compared to less than two percent today. Just since 1960, the number of farms has shrunk from over three million to less than two million.

Fifty years ago, hundreds of thousands of farmers raised small flocks of chickens. Today, a few corporations produce nearly all our chicken through a system known as vertical integration: a single corporation owns all stages of production and marketing.[23] Factory farming is the norm. Most people today don't realize that chicken used to taste very different.

Advertising budgets of the largest food companies are mind-boggling. Pepsico, for example, spends over one billion dollars a year promoting foods filled with refined or artificial sweeteners and hydrogenated vegetable oils. Cigarette companies spend hundreds of millions promoting the products of their food divisions, a large portion of which is aimed at children. The industry's response to stiff competition and lower rates of growth (now only about one or two percent per year) is more advertising and more lobbying.[24]

About twenty percent of the retail price of foods goes to the producers. That is the "farm value" of the food. The rest goes to middlemen—distributors, advertisers, packagers and anyone else involved in processing the raw commodity and getting it to the consumer. The cost of the corn in corn flakes is less than ten percent of the retail price. In contrast, eggs, beef and chicken have farm values fifty to sixty percent of retail cost. The biggest profits are in the most highly processed, "value added" foods, and that's why the companies focus their development and marketing efforts on these products.[25] Consider the many food products produced and marketed by Phillip Morris. Consider the other business Phillip Morris is in. Consider the "health claims" made for many of these products, health claims supported by agencies headed by officials appointed by our elected representatives. Consider where those representatives get their campaign funds. Is there something wrong with this picture?

America has an overabundance of food, and one result of the overabundance is that many foods are cheap. We pay less than ten percent of our income directly for food. But we pay in another way; a key reason for low prices is government subsidies for food production. Price supports for milk and sugar are visible. Less obvious support has helped food companies expand while driving millions of small farmers off the land. These methods, all supported by taxpayer money, include market and production quotas, deficiency payments, restrictions on imports, favorable tax rates, water rights, land management, low-cost land leases, marketing and promotion programs for major food commodities and huge federal subsidies for large agricultural corporations. Every company involved in food, from McDonald's to ConAgra, has benefited from these programs, and collectively the food companies spend billions to keep the government providing favorable treatment.[26]

Favorable treatment and advertising mean more sales, and advertising has one fundamental message: eat more. In the year 2000, food and food service companies spent thirty-three billion dollars to advertise and promote their products. One-third of that money goes to direct media advertising, the rest to discount incentives. Most advertising efforts promote the most highly processed foods.[27]

Since 1990, food companies have introduced over one hundred thousand new packaged foods and beverages, over one-fourth of which are "nutritionally enhanced" functional foods that can be marketed as higher in calcium, fiber or vitamins, and low in salt, cholesterol, sugar or fat. Advertising comprises just part of the campaign to market these goods. The companies also use unrelenting pressure to influence health organizations, nutrition professionals and government officials to act in ways that will enhance—or at the least, not harm—the companies' sales efforts. Federal dietary guidelines are a critical component of this strategy, which aims to influence the people who set policy. The methods often involve the transfer of large sums of money in ways that are only marginally legal.[28]

The bottom line is that politics—not good science—govern nearly all government dietary advice and public health policy. Food and drug companies work hard for, and generally achieve, a favorable regulatory environment for their products. Who should decide which foods are healthy and then use taxpayer dollars to promote them? Who should decide whether the public will be warned about the dangers of sugar, additives, vegetable oils or—raw milk? These questions raise issues fundamental to American democracy.[29]

Congress created the United States Department of Agriculture in 1862 to fulfill two functions. Ensuring an adequate food supply was one. The other was to educate people about subjects related to agriculture, which the Department has interpreted as a mandate for issuing dietary advice. Eventually Congress instructed the USDA and the Department of Health and Human Services to issue "Dietary Guidelines for Americans." The first Guidelines came out in 1980. The 2000 Guidelines advise us to "Choose fat-free or low-fat dairy products" as a way to reduce saturated fat intake. Why would the dairy industry favor such advice? Because the dairy industry makes far more profit putting butterfat into ice cream than leaving it in the milk.

Since the early 1900s, dairy lobbyists have influenced many nutritionists to promote dairy products. Many scientists today believe that dairy products accomplish no public health goals. Others believe dairy foods may do more harm than good. Still others see milk as a highly protective food, a view that held sway in the early part of the twentieth century when many people, particularly children, were obviously malnourished. A USDA generic marketing campaign funds the promotional activities of the National Fluid Milk Processor Promotion Board—including the Council's one-hundred-thirty-million dollar "milk mustache" celebrity promotion—and the education and research activities of the National Dairy Council.[30]

Despite widespread controversy about the role of conventionally produced milk and other dairy products in health and disease, the government-backed advertising beat goes on. Alternatives like full-fat grass-fed raw milk never receive consideration, except as a "danger" to the public, which must be "protected."

## THE REVOLVING DOOR

Any legal attempt to influence government policy or action may be considered lobbying. Lobbyists—paid advocates for private interests—naturally promote their client companies' interests, not your interest or mine. According to some commentators, lobbyists even constitute their own branch of government. Lobbyist activities include the provision of "expertise" about proposed policies or laws; legislators claim that these services provide valuable insight and bristle at suggestions that such activities should be curtailed. Through meetings and social events, lobbyists often develop personal relationships with legislators and their staff members. Lobbyists do much more to win friends and influence the right people; they may stage media events and public demonstrations, harass critics, encourage lawsuits and arrange campaign contributions.[31]

Lobbying is big business. According to the Center for Responsive Politics, the number of registered lobbyists reached twenty thousand in 1999, an increase of five thousand since just 1997. These lobbyists spend about one and one-half billion dollars a year on behalf of their clients.[32]

Many lobbyists are former government officials and vice versa—a phenomenon known as the "revolving door." How extensive is this practice? Forty percent of the congressional representatives defeated in the

1992 election became lobbyists, as did substantial numbers of their committee staff directors. A 1998 survey found that about one out of every eight former senators and representatives who left office during the past twenty-five years was listed as a lobbyist. What kind of money is involved? Former Senator Bob Dole belonged to a firm that earned nineteen million dollars in lobbying fees in 1997.[33]

About five hundred agency heads and staff members at the USDA are political appointees. This makes for many revolving-door job switches between the department and food industry lobbyists. In 1971, for example, Earl Butz, the director of Ralston Purina, became Secretary of Agriculture. Departing Secretary Clifford Hardin then became the new director of Ralston Purina. Watchdog organizations have documented hundreds of similar moves over the years, in both upper and lower echelons, raising many questions about government decisions favorable to industry over consumers. This trend continues to the present. In 2001, a lobbyist for the National Cattlemen's Beef Association became chief-of-staff to the new Secretary of Agriculture. The former secretary went to work for a law firm that lobbies for agriculture companies.

The Food and Drug Administration (FDA) also experiences frequent revolving-door job exchanges, and one series in particular directly bears on the agency's ultimate approval of genetically engineered growth hormone in dairy cows. After serving as counsel to the FDA, attorney Michael Taylor went to a law firm that represented Monsanto, the huge agricultural and biotechnology company. He returned to the FDA as Deputy Commissioner for Policy in 1991 to become part of the team that approved the use of Monsanto's bovine growth hormone and issued the agency's very favorable policy on food biotechnology. Questions about his role in these policy decisions led to conflict-of-interest charges and an investigation by the federal General Accounting Office, which eventually cleared him of all charges.[34] Taylor rejoined Monsanto in 1998 as Vice President for Public Policy, where he remained until 1999. Monsanto continues to promote its genetically engineered products relentlessly and aggressively.

## PAC FUNDS AND DAIRY PRICE SUPPORTS

Lobbyists spend lots of money, some of which must be reported and some not. Unreported or "soft" money is often spent on federal officials in the social arena—parties, receptions and so forth. Political Action Committees (PACs) are the vehicles food companies use to disburse most of the "hard" (reportable) money they give to members of Congress. About twice as much agribusiness PAC money goes to Republicans as to Democrats, and the money goes preferentially to members of the Senate and House Agriculture Committees; funds go where they seem likely to have the most influence. Almost all the money from agricultural PACs goes to incumbents, most of it to those with voting records that favor the PAC's sponsor. "In the 1980s, researchers demonstrated that members of the House of Representatives who received PAC funds from dairy industry groups were almost twice as likely to vote for dairy price supports as those who did not. Legislators who favored price supports received 2.5 times more PAC funds than those in opposition, and the more money the members received from dairy PACs, the more likely they were to back price-support legislation."[35]

The Secretary of Agriculture issues milk marketing orders specifying minimum prices and conditions under which milk can be bought and sold within a specified area. In effect, these orders set the price dairy farmers receive from wholesalers (usually cooperatives) for their milk; until recently, the surplus has been so large that prices rarely rise above the minimum set by the orders. Farmers can get an extra ten cents or so per hundredweight if their milk has a somatic cell count under a specified number (three hundred fifty thousand per milliliter in Connecticut). Prices have ranged from around nine dollars to nearly twenty dollars per hundredweight during the last few years; as of late 2002, the price was about twelve dollars, just about a dollar a gallon and only slightly more than farmers received before World War II. (By mid 2008, conventional dairy farmers were receiving about nineteen dollars per hundredweight of milk, as part of a trend towards higher food prices everywhere; their fuel and feed costs had also risen substantially.)

For many years the federal government has also enacted laws that pay dairy farmers subsidies—dairy price supports—if the price they receive for their milk falls below specified levels. The government made up the difference between the price paid the farmer and the price triggering the subsidy. Congress has phased out these subsidies in recent years, though the farmers are lobbying hard for their reinstatement. The marketing orders remain, setting minimum prices. The end of subsidies has meant that more and more dairy farmers are going out of business.

Some people argue that the law of supply and demand dictates that some dairy farmers stop producing. But the matter is much more complex than that, and there are better solutions. For over fifty years, the federal government has done everything in its power to encourage the production of large quantities of cheap milk and cheap food in general—at the expense of quality and at the price of driving millions of small, quality-conscious farmers off the land. If the trend continues, only the biggest agribusiness dairy farms will survive, and quality will continue to suffer. America will still be able to buy two-dollars-a-gallon, two-percent pasteurized homogenized milk. "You might as well be drinking water with chalk in it," says Dan Logue, my neighbor dairy farmer. Like most dairy families, Dan and his family have drunk their own milk raw for fifty-one years.

Quality market milk means raw milk from individual farms, carefully produced with the approval and cooperation of the government— milk that can be advertised and sold as a superior product for a good price, one that educated consumers are more than willing to pay.

CHECK-OFFS FOR THE DAIRY INDUSTRY

Congress has passed various laws requiring producers of certain commodities, including milk and other dairy products, to deduct a fee— a "check-off"—from sales in order to support generic, industry-wide advertising and promotion. The check-off fund for the dairy industry is the largest of any industry—larger, for example, than those for the grain industry, the pork industry and the electric and gas industry. In 1994, dairy check-offs totaled two hundred twenty-eight million dollars. Over one hundred million dollars yearly supports the milk mustache campaign. Some of the money pays for industry-friendly milk research. Although federal law prohibits use of these funds for lobbying, a portion ultimately benefits members of Congress in gray areas not legally defined as lobbying. Smaller producers, legally forced to contribute, have argued that the programs are of no help to them and merely favor industry giants. Their case was presented to the U.S. Supreme Court in 2000 and rejected.

The following example illustrates how USDA policies continue to favor large corporations: in the late 1990s, pork producers obtained the right to hold a referendum on their check-off program (a forty-five-cent mandatory fee on every one hundred dollars of pork sales). In 2000, the smaller producers, who are opponents of the fees, won the vote to discontinue the fees. Factory farms are the giants of the hog industry. The National Pork Producers Council, which represents giant factory hog farms, challenged the vote on vague technical grounds. In 2001, President Bush's new Secretary of Agriculture overturned the referendum, claiming it was "procedurally flawed."[36]

## INFANT FORMULA, BREAST-FEEDING
## AND THE NESTLÉ CORPORATION

For many years, Nestlé has aggressively promoted infant formula worldwide as a substitute for breast-feeding. Company advertisements often subtly imply the superiority of formula to breast milk: "Breast-feed your baby, but when your baby needs a supplement, use our brand of powdered milk." Earlier, less subtle ads—like "Lactogen is the very best milk for your baby"—led to international boycotts of Nestlé products.

To defuse the critics, including international church organizations, the company first accused them of being communists. This drew laughter at a 1977 congressional hearing chaired by Senator Ted Kennedy. While continuing to deny all charges, Nestlé's representative requested that Kennedy ask the World Health Organization and UNICEF (United Nations Children's Fund) to provide the company with guidelines. Kennedy did so, and chosen members of the two organizations drafted the International Code of Marketing of Breast-Milk Substitutes. Nestlé concurrently worked behind the scenes to convince delegate members that any restrictions placed on Nestlé's marketing practices would not be in the best interests of the members' countries. The guidelines, suggesting restrictions on Nestlé's advertising, were nevertheless passed in 1981, with the one dissenting vote coming from the United States. The official U.S. rationale was that the provisions of the Code might violate the Constitution, an excuse often trotted out over the years by various administrations to support egregious actions having no apparent motive other than the appeasement of corporate greed.

As expected, American formula companies lobbied heavily against the Code, and government officials predictably expressed concerns that the Code would set a precedent for regulating drug industry advertising worldwide. The vote told formula companies that the U.S. government would ignore future violations and reassured drug company management that their campaign contributions were well spent.

Nestlé announced that it would follow the Code while embarking on a new series of public relations and advertising campaigns designed to rebuild the company's public image. The international boycott of Nestlé products ended in 1984. The company had replaced advertising as its main marketing tool with a new strategy: free formula placed in maternity facilities. This led to a reinstatement of the boycott in 1988. The U.S. finally signed the Code in 1994. Various publications throughout the 1990s continued to document the fact that Nestlé and other formula companies were repeatedly violating the Code. Corporate strategies had evolved; the companies were now also targeting pregnant women in developing countries throughout the world, while continuing to widely distribute free samples and literature to health care workers, hospitals and mothers. The boycott continued into 2002.

Nestlé and other formula makers have seized advantage of the announcement that AIDS can be transmitted by breast-feeding. Some scientists estimate that nearly half the pregnant women in some African countries carry the AIDS virus and claim they may transmit it to their children through breast milk. Over a decade ago, Nestlé began citing AIDS in their promotional literature as a reason to use formula, ignoring studies showing that bottle-fed children in third-world countries were six times more likely to die from diarrheal diseases.[37]

The reasonable solution is to encourage the production of raw milk from healthy, pasture-fed animals and make it available to the mothers and their infants. Certain whole foods, such as coconut oil and cod liver oil, can be added to make the fatty acid and nutrient profile of cow's milk more like human milk. Mothers can then choose to feed raw milk—the traditional food of many African peoples—to their at-risk infants. So-called lactose intolerance in black people occurs very infrequently when they consume milk that is raw, particularly milk from grass-fed animals. The milk could also be soured, following the culinary tradition of African cattle-herding cultures, a process that breaks down lactose. Mothers who choose to breast-feed would use the milk themselves, enhancing their own health and ensuring the highest quality in their own milk. For more on raw milk for children, see Chapter 16.

## BREAKING OPPONENTS AND BREAKING THE LAW

Besides legal—and sometimes illegal—lobbying, large corporations have two other major weapons they use against the public—lawsuits and price fixing. A lawsuit brought by a giant corporation against a private citizen is an intimidating proposition, one that creates tremendous financial and personal cost. This is a legal way companies silence critics, often with great media fanfare. Instances of price-fixing rarely come to public attention and they often occur in the shadowy world outside the law.

Between 1991 and 1997, thirteen states passed "veggie-libel" laws—laws prohibiting private citizens from giving out negative information about a food unless the charge is backed by certain standards defined by the laws. A South Dakota law, for example, makes it illegal to say that generally accepted agricultural practices might make foods unsafe—whatever those practices might involve. Texas passed the "False Disparagement of Perishable Food Products Law of 1995," prohibiting the dissemination of information indicating a food is unsafe unless backed by "reasonable and reliable scientific inquiry and facts." This ultimately leaves it to a court to decide what is scientific, what is reasonable, and what is fact—and what you or I may say publicly about a food product.

Most of these laws place the burden of proof on the people making the alleged disparaging statements, the reverse of the norm in the American justice system. Thus, the law requires the individuals charged to prove the truth of their statements, rather than requiring the companies bringing the charges to prove the statements are false. Such laws might well have prevented the 1906 publication of *The Jungle*, Upton Sinclair's story about horrific conditions in the meat industry. Even when companies lose their suit, the mere threat of a court action and the associated costs may silence critics. In 1997, cattle ranchers brought a ten-million-dollar class action suit against Oprah Winfrey after her nationally televised comment about hamburgers. She stated that she would no longer eat hamburgers because of the perceived threat of mad cow disease. Ms. Winfrey defeated the suit in court, but her legal fees are thought to have been about one million dollars, quite enough to give the average columnist, talk radio host, independent researcher or writer second thoughts about attacking the food industry.[38]

## GOING AGAINST CORPORATE INTERESTS

In 1998, the *Cincinnati Enquirer* published a detailed account of its investigation into the dealings of Cincinnati-based Chiquita Banana in Latin America, an account that alleged illegal activity.[39] The reporters who wrote the piece admitted to using Chiquita's voice-mail recordings as one of their sources. Chiquita accused the reporters of obtaining the recordings illegally and threatened a large lawsuit, without addressing the allegations made in the article. The *Enquirer* fired the reporters, published an apology and paid a ten million dollar settlement fee. One of the reporters was then sued for defamation. As part of a plea bargain, the reporter then turned over the name of the person who gave him the voice mail recordings. It was then revealed that the judge who assigned himself to the defamation case against the reporter had received campaign contributions from Chiquita executives. Truth indeed is stranger than fiction.

Such corporate behavior teaches us that the press is free only in theory, not in fact. One might ask how "free" any mainstream newspaper or magazine is to publish a story favorable to raw milk, for example. Chiquita Banana is big; the dairy industry is bigger.

PRICE FIXING

Have you ever noticed similarities in the prices of competing brands of the same product? Whether the product is canned peaches or margarine, cereals or soft drinks, two percent milk or processed cheese, one company's price is usually very close to that of every other. We assume that competition in the free market keeps prices reasonable. But occasionally companies are caught price fixing—conspiring to maintain artificially high prices.

For example, government policies have made the infant formula business immensely profitable. Federal subsidies keep cost of the main ingredients, milk and soy protein isolate, artifically low. Furthermore, government purchases for food assistance programs for low-income women and their children account for nearly half of the formula market. Relaxed regulatory control during the 1980s allowed the formula companies to charge government agencies retail prices for food assistance programs. When these agencies demanded competitive bidding, the companies resisted intensely, lobbying both legislators and physicians. Their incredulous argument: competitive bidding would prevent doctors from prescribing certain brands and thus put children's health at risk. The situation prompted seventeen states to investigate the industry's pricing methods. Lawsuits against Abbott Laboratories, one of the largest makers of infant formulas, were eventually settled for over thirty million dollars, a trivial amount compared to Abbott's profits.

A price-fixing conviction has also pestered Archer Daniels Midland (ADM), one of the largest food companies in the world and the largest processor and distributor of soybeans and soybean products. Chairman Dwayne Andreas was well known for plying politicians of both parties with huge contributions. The government learned in 1992 of an ADM conspiracy with competitors in Japan to raise the price of lysine, a one-billion-dollar-per-year animal feed component. A videotape of a meeting between an ADM official and his Japanese competitor corroborated the charges. Said the official: "We have a saying at this company—our competitors are our friends and our customers are our enemies." A federal jury convicted the company in 1998; Andreas resigned as chairman, and three executives went to prison.[40,41]

These two cases represent just the tip of the iceberg; by the year 2000, over thirty federal grand juries were investigating charges of price fixing in the food industry. The Abbott and ADM cases serve to highlight the lengths to which companies will go to enhance the bottom line. If corporations will go to the extreme of overtly breaking the law, what other kinds of surreptitious tactics might they use to enhance sales? Specifically, of the vast amount of university and other research that corporations sponsor—research that almost inevitably enhances their bottom line by making their products look good or competitive products look bad—can any of it be accepted at face value?

POURING RIGHTS:
HOW MUCH FOR AN EXCLUSIVE ON YOUR CHILD?

"Pouring rights" is a term that refers to payments from soft drink companies to school districts for the right to sell the company's products in all of the district's schools, with no competitors allowed.[42] By the year 2000, over two hundred school districts in the U.S. were participants in such agreements.[43] These agreements—shocking when considered coldly—are a product of deliberate industry policy.

Soft drink manufacturers admit that they target children in their advertising campaigns. "All foods can be part of healthy diets," they say, taking a cue from the government's food pyramid. The fact that children have become increasingly obese does not deter the marketing of soft drinks and other junk foods directly to the younger age group. Kids have money; children four to twelve years old spent an estimated twenty-seven billion dollars on their own in 1999, most of it on soft drinks, candy, ice cream and fast food. Huge advertising campaigns aimed at children are both a cause and a result of this spending.[44] The approach taken by soft drink manufacturers has been especially comprehensive.

Pouring rights contracts are merely the latest success story in Coke and Pepsi's search for more profits. The contracts mean big payoffs for the schools, which are increasingly strapped for money. The result is that kids have access to sodas all day long, and soft drinks have largely replaced milk in the diets of American children. A twelve-ounce can of soda contains about one-and-one-half ounces of sugar and fifty milligrams of caffeine. The recent trend is to twenty-ounce bottles with screw caps, perfect for all-day sipping and a ticket to soft bones and rotten teeth. The yearly average consumption of soft drinks in 1997 was forty-one gallons per person, up from twenty-two in 1970—and a great deal of it is consumed by children in schools.[45] During the same years, milk consumption declined from thirty-one gallons per person to twenty-four.

## BEHIND THE BETRAYAL

Commodity subsidies, generic advertising campaigns, price fixing, uncontrolled lobbying and pouring rights contracts represent a massive betrayal of trust. That children should not have access to sodas in school is a simple matter of common sense. Something is seriously wrong with a culture that is unable to prevent corporations from gaining so much power.

Soft drinks in schools is just one example of public, democratic decision-making processes supplanted by private, corporate fiat. It is highly unlikely that the parents in any school district would vote "yes" to sodas in schools, yet they are powerless to stop the companies from coming in. The environmental and sustainable agriculture movements face the same problem of entrenched corporate power blocking attempts to create a cleaner, safer environment and viable alternatives to industrialized agriculture.

Consider a final example, that of genetically engineered foods. The corporations involved have limited the public debate to whether or not these products should be labeled as genetically engineered. But the real issue is who will decide how genetically engineered foods should be used, if at all, and this issue is not even on the table. Government and the courts have allowed the corporations to make this fundamental decision about the most potentially dangerous technology since the splitting of the atom. It is a decision that puts corporate private property rights over individual or communal property, over human and environmental rights.

Dave Henson of the Program on Corporations, Law and Democracy has written elegantly on this subject. Corporate lawyers have gained power for corporations with legal arguments that are "based on the fiction that a corporation is a legal 'person' in terms of constitutional protections. They use the interstate commerce clause of the U.S. Constitution to claim that states, counties and cities have no authority to restrict interstate and transnational commerce. They assert for the corporation the property rights, due process and equal protection guarantees enumerated in the Constitution for real, human persons.

"They have used Fourth Amendment constitutional protections (intended to safeguard natural persons against unreasonable search and seizure by the state) to limit environmental, health and safety inspectors from investigating conditions in industrial farms and factories.

"They have claimed, and legally achieved, First Amendment free speech protection as a way to overturn public initiatives and legislation aimed at limiting billboards, banning advertising in schools and controlling the information agenda on our public airwaves. They have won major U.S. Supreme Court rulings equating financial contributions to political campaigns and political ads with political free speech, disabling 'we the people' from keeping corporate money out of our elections.

"Corporations also receive extensive limited liability, making it nearly impossible to imprison individual corporate managers, board members or shareholders for far worse crimes than those that often result in incarceration of real human persons. If a real person steals a motorcycle for his third felony ('third strike'), California mandates a sentence of 25 years to life in prison. But if, for example, the UNOCAL Corporation, based in California, is convicted for the 15th time for breaking the law (as it has been), it suffers a very small fine and goes on with business as usual.

"It is very important to remember that nearly all of the rights of natural persons, which corporations now enjoy, were handed to them by courts, not legislatures. Most of these rights were neither granted in the U.S. Constitution nor ever voted on by the people.[46]

"A corporation has concern for only growth and profit. That is what it is set up to do. When 'we the people' sit down to discuss how we can develop a sustainable agriculture that strengthens local, diverse culture and restores, not degrades, our Mother Earth, the corporations should be out of the room. It was not so long ago, in nearly every state in the

Union, that corporations were all given limited charters of incorporation (as opposed to today's general charters that grant corporations perpetual life). Typically, a manufacturing charter would be limited to 40 years, a mining charter to 50 years, and other corporate charters to 30 years. After that, the corporation was dissolved, or the corporate officers could apply for a new charter but would then receive public scrutiny of their past actions. The question would be: 'Have they served the interests of the people of our state?' If not, why would we give them a new charter to continue to harm the land or the people?

"A typical early attitude toward charter incorporation was stated in 1834 by the Pennsylvania legislature: 'A corporation in law is just what the incorporating act makes it. It is the creature of the law and may be molded to any shape or for any purpose that the Legislature may deem most conducive for the general good.'

"[Today] the largest of the multinational corporations have gross net incomes greater than many nation states and are at such an inhuman scale that 'enlightened' managers can rarely temper the giant organization's insatiable urge toward growth and short-term economic returns. Trying to change the hearts of CEOs very rarely works. Courts often rule that 'shareholder rights' to maximum profits limit management's prerogative to do the 'right thing,' like stopping the factory farm from polluting the river, or pulling the business out of Burma, or building a child-care center for employees.

"With regard to food and agriculture, the multinational corporations' strategy has been to establish the unchallengeable right to their control over the food system. They have done this through monopolization by strategic underpricing of smaller-scale competition and by developing a revolving door of corruption between corporate management and the very government agencies charged with enforcing regulations."[47]

In Chapter 19, we'll look at strategies for dismantling the mechanisms of corporate rule. For now, we turn to a blatant example of betrayal: the creation of the myth that cholesterol and animal fats cause heart disease.

# 10
# Cholesterol, Animal Fats and Heart Disease: A Modern Myth?

*The purpose of myth is to provide a logical model capable of overcoming a contradiction (an impossible achievement if, as it happens, the contradiction is real).*

Claude Lévi-Strauss

Misconceptions about cholesterol and heart disease prevent many people from fully appreciating the value of raw milk and other vital foods. Many of you believe that cholesterol in foods can cause heart disease and wonder how unprocessed milk, butter and cream can be good for us since they are rich in animal fats and cholesterol. My answer is simple: "Because animal fats and cholesterol are good for you." This is a difficult statement to make because so many of the health professionals and institutions we trust preach otherwise.

It is a surprising fact that the results of the major trials most often cited as evidence for the lipid hypothesis—the idea that cholesterol and animal fats cause heart disease—do not actually prove the theory. On the contrary, these studies contain serious flaws. Trial directors often manipulate statistics, sometimes in subtle ways but at other times in rather obvious ways, to give the appearance of success when results are at best equivocal. Conclusions about the trials often contain claims of success not actually supported by the data. Researchers then cite the summaries of unsupportive trials as evidence for further claims.[1]

The betrayal of trust described in the previous chapter pales in comparison to the campaign to persuade the public that cholesterol and animal fats cause heart disease. The ascendancy of the diet-heart idea has spurred the growth of the processed food industry and the concurrent demise of raw milk. An understanding of the cholesterol controversy will help us appreciate the value of vital foods and the reasons they have been lost.

The lipid hypothesis or diet-heart idea is a powerful and carefully cultivated myth that has played a major role in forcing thirty million farm families off the land since the end of World War II. I hope that having read this chapter, you'll never again hesitate to eat good food, rich in cholesterol and saturated fat.

A MODERN MYTH

The word myth has two meanings. The myths of ancient cultures are traditional narratives involving supernatural or imaginary persons, which embody deeply held ideas about natural or social phenomena. These are the myths that Carl Jung, the great Swiss psychiatrist and scholar, described so eloquently, springing like dreams from the depths of the collective unconscious. Jung, the founder of psychotherapy, called his work "the healing of souls." Myths, said Jung, provided a window to the soul, a means of understanding humanity's most basic truths.

Myth can also mean a widely held false notion. Thus the word myth can refer to something that is profoundly true—or patently false. The cholesterol theory of heart disease belongs to the latter category; it is a popular delusion that has engendered profound cultural changes in western society—from the way we eat and the way we farm to the way we think about our bodies and of nature herself.

We've explored many qualities of milk and other vital foods from domestic animals that live humane, natural and healthy lives. But those qualities are impossible for us to fully appreciate until we clarify issues concerning cholesterol and heart disease. The political and economic trends explained in the last chapter have fostered widespread acceptance of the diet-heart theory, the creature of persistent and unrelenting indoctrination against traditional foods.

The subject of nutrition and human diets—which should reveal its secrets through carefully executed scientific studies—has become highly politicized. The constant denigration of beef, animal fats, eggs, and locally produced dairy foods like raw milk, cream, cheese and butter—all of which were once the products of small farms—has no basis in good science but powerful support from monopolistic grain cartels, food processors, vegetable oil producers and pasteurized dairy manufacturers. Health professionals generally ignore the growing body of evidence indicting the ingredients of processed foods—liquid and hydrogenated vegetable oils, refined sweeteners, refined flour, processed milk products, preservatives and artificial flavorings—which are the largest contributors to modern disease, especially heart disease.

## CHOLESTEROL AND SATURATED FAT: FRIEND OR FOE?

Although the U.S. government's National Cholesterol Education Program portrays cholesterol and saturated fat as villains, these substances are essential components of human biochemistry. In animals and humans, the cell membrane is the living boundary of the cell, the gate that lets the substances of life in and waste products out. Saturated fat and cholesterol are the major constituents of this membrane—without saturated fat and cholesterol, the cell cannot work properly. Saturated fat provides "stiffness" or integrity to the cell wall and cholesterol makes it waterproof. Thus cholesterol provides one of the main engines for life—a different chemistry on the inside and the outside of the cell.

The greatest concentration of cholesterol is found in the brain and nervous system, where electrical impulses course along the cholesterol-rich membranes of the nerve cells. Cholesterol also provides the basic material for the creation of sex hormones and the adrenal hormones, which we use for everything from blood sugar regulation to dealing with stress. As for saturated fats, good science has discovered that they play many important roles—they enhance the immune system, protect us against pathogens, provide energy to the heart and are vital to the function of the kidneys, the liver, the brain and the lungs.[2]

Given the ubiquitous nature of cholesterol, is it not strange that so many of us have come to fear it? True, cholesterol can accumulate in undesirable places, for example in damaged areas of arteries where, along with other substances, it becomes a component of the plaques or atheromas associated with heart disease. Investigators have interpreted the presence of cholesterol in plaque as an indication that dietary cholesterol, found only in animal foods, is the cause of heart disease. But cholesterol is the body's repair substance. Without cholesterol in the bloodstream, tears and irritations in the arteries would soon lead to aneurisms and ruptures. (One of the main constituents of plaque is calcium, but no one is blaming calcium for heart disease.)

In recent years the political and medical establishments have presented the lipid hypothesis as proven fact, an impregnable structure built of the following tenets:

1. Cholesterol and animal fats in foods raise blood cholesterol, and high blood cholesterol causes cholesterol to build up in the arteries causing heart disease.
2. The higher the cholesterol levels in the blood, the faster heart disease occurs.
3. Lowering cholesterol helps prevent heart attacks and extend life.
4. Animal studies prove that cholesterol causes heart disease.
5. The anti-cholesterol campaign is based on good science and has the support of nearly all researchers.

We'll now examine some of the history and research behind these claims.

## FRAMINGHAM AND ANCEL KEYS

Rising numbers of deaths from coronary heart disease occurred during the years following World War II, and a logical strategy for combatting the problem emerged. First, epidemiological studies would identify the risk factors associated with the disease, and then clinical trials would measure the effects of intervention.

The initial government-sponsored epidemiological investigation began in 1948. Researchers recruited two-thirds of the adult population of Framingham, Massachusetts as their living laboratory in order to pinpoint risk factors—observable characteristics or behaviors that demonstrated statistical correlations with heart disease.

It was in the Framingham study that high blood cholesterol first emerged as a risk factor for heart attack. Researchers divided the participants into three groups with relatively low, medium and high levels of blood cholesterol. Individuals in the latter group had slightly more heart attack deaths than those in the other two groups, thus indicating that high levels of cholesterol in the blood was indeed a risk factor, a predictor for coronary heart disease (CHD).[3]

But a risk factor is not necessarily a cause, even though a risk factor may change in parallel with the disease. For example, in the years following World War II, telephone usage increased dramatically in many of the population groups that experienced an increased incidence of heart disease. Telephone usage is a risk factor for heart disease, but obviously not a cause. But if the risk factor is the cause, it must move in parallel direction with the incidence of the disease, without exception.[4] Thus, if butter or animal fat consumption declines while heart disease increases (which is what happened in the U.S.), then scientists must rule out butter or animal fats as a cause.

Although the Framingham study merely indicated that high cholesterol is a risk factor for heart disease (albeit a very weak one), it led to the belief that consumption of cholesterol and saturated fats is a cause of heart disease. Since all animal foods contain cholesterol and saturated fat, avoidance of these foods became the cornerstone of the National Cholesterol Education Program. The diet-heart idea thus allowed food companies to promote vegetable oils as healthy alternatives to traditional fats and a high-carbohydrate diet as a healthy alternative to a diet based on meat.

It was the work of Ancel Keys, the founding father of the lipid hypothesis, that allowed diet-heart proponents to make the leap from the

Framingham study to the dietary guidelines of the National Cholesterol Education Program. As director of the Laboratory of Physiological Hygiene at the University of Minnesota, Keys published a series of articles linking heart disease with animal fat consumption, beginning in 1953. He constructed graphs showing linear relationships between the percentage of calories from fat and the incidence of heart attacks in several countries. In his Six Countries Study, for example, he was able to show an almost perfect relationship between fat consumption and deaths from heart attack in Japan, Italy, England and Wales, Australia, Canada and the U.S.[5] Keys's tidy graphs were enormously influential. But Keys was able to show a perfect relationship only because he selected carefully, choosing the handful of countries that fit his hypothesis and ignoring many others that did not.[6,7]

Although the Framingham study has often been cited in support of lowfat, mostly plant-based diets, the researchers actually found no relationship between the foods eaten and cholesterol levels in the blood. "These findings suggest a cautionary note with respect to the hypotheses relating diet to serum cholesterol levels," they wrote in their summary. "There is a considerable range of serum cholesterol levels within the Framingham Study Group. Something explains this inter-individual variation, but it is not the diet." This statement appears in an unpublished manuscript written by Drs. William Kannel and Tavia Gordon, authors of the official published report.[8]

Actually, Keys himself once stated that there was ". . . no connection whatsoever between cholesterol in food and cholesterol in the blood. None. And we've known that all along."[9] He placed the blame for heart disease on saturated fats alone. But the Framingham investigators found no correlation of blood cholesterol levels with saturated fat either. In a statement published in 1992, Dr. William Castelli, then director of the Framingham project, made the following startling admission: "In Framingham, Mass., the more saturated fat one ate, the more cholesterol one ate, the more calories one ate, the lower the person's serum cholesterol . . . we found that the people who ate the most cholesterol, ate the most saturated fat, ate the most calories, weighed the least and were the most physically active."[10] Most doctors today tell their patients that it is important to exercise. . . but they never mention the fact that eating saturated fats will make it easier to do so.

Today, most researchers admit that dietary cholesterol has only a slight influence on cholesterol levels in the blood—despite broad public acceptance of the dictum that we should restrict intake of cholesterol—because the body's cholesterol level is regulated in the liver according to individual needs. The more cholesterol we eat, the less the liver makes, and vice-versa. Even an extreme diet generally lowers cholesterol by no more than about ten percent in the short run.[11]

I've observed that extended periods of protein deficiency in people who follow vegetarian or near vegetarian diets can lower cholesterol perhaps a bit more, even down to levels around 150 mg/dl for some people. This may be due to the lack of protein, needed for the production of cholesterol. (These patients are then distressed to learn that low cholesterol levels are a strong risk factor for cancer.)

OTHER STUDIES

More contradictory evidence emerged in the 1976 Tecumseh Study.[12] Experienced dieticians questioned over two thousand people in the small Michigan town of Tecumseh and subsequently analyzed the responses. The participants were then divided into three groups according to their blood cholesterol levels. The results: food intake had no relationship with serum cholesterol. The low-cholesterol group ate just as much saturated fat as did the high cholesterol group. No association between diet and cholesterol levels was found in children either, in two studies conducted in 1978, one at the Mayo Clinic in Minnesota[13] and the other in New Orleans.[14]

Two interesting studies involved bank tellers, trained to keep meticulous records. Ninety-nine men weighed all of their food for a week, recording the results. No connection between the food they ate and their blood cholesterol levels appeared. Later in the year, seventy-six of them agreed to do it again, and still no connection emerged. Researchers then selected the tellers whose records were most meticulous—but failed once again to find a connection between what they ate and the levels of cholesterol in their blood.[15]

During the late 1970s and early 1980s, scientists at the National Heart, Lung and Blood Institute tested the idea that restriction of foods high in animal fat and cholesterol will significantly lower blood cholesterol. Researchers screened three hundred sixty thousand men for participation in the massive Multiple Risk Factor Intervention Trial (MRFIT, or "Mister Fit") and chose twelve thousand considered especially prone to heart attack.

The treatment group made drastic dietary changes in hopes of avoiding heart attack and premature death. They cut their intake of saturated fats by one quarter and of cholesterol by half, and they increased their intake of polyunsaturated vegetable oils by one third. Over the course of four years, their cholesterol levels went down by an average two percent, an amount that was statistically insignificant.[16] Moreover, while those who had reduced their cholesterol experienced a slight reduction in deaths from heart disease, they had greatly increased deaths from other causes—cancer, stroke, accidents and suicides. Mr. Fit became Mr. Frustrated.

This trial had unlimited funding and personnel—including dieticians, behavior modification specialists and psychologists—and the results should have put an end to the idea that the boring and unappetizing diet they embraced so enthusiastically could lower cholesterol levels. Instead, the cholesterol proponents promoted their agenda with increasing vigor.

Proof that high levels of cholesterol in the blood lead to formation of plaques in the arteries has also eluded investigators. In 1936, a research team at New York University studied individuals who had died violent deaths. They found absolutely no correlation between the amount of cholesterol in the blood and the amount of blockage in the arteries. Those with low levels of cholesterol had just as much atherosclerosis as those with high cholesterol levels, and many individuals with high cholesterol readings had little or no blockage.[17] The 1968 International Atherosclerosis Project, in which over twenty-two thousand corpses in fourteen nations were examined for plaques in the arteries, showed the same degree of atheroma in all parts of the world—in populations that consumed large amounts of fatty animal products and those that were largely vegetarian, and in populations that suffered from a great deal of heart disease and in populations that had very little or none at all.[18]

When scientists propose a theory, they must also accept the burden of proving that theory. Even one bit of contradictory evidence requires a reformulation of the theory—or its abandonment. But mountains of contradictory evidence have not led to the abandonment of the cholesterol myth, just more obfuscation and shriller voices.

## DIETARY TRENDS

Dr. Paul Dudley White, a Harvard graduate and a brilliant cardiologist, served as physician to President Eisenhower and wrote a textbook, *Heart Disease*, published in 1943. Thirty-five years later, when I was a medical student myself, I discovered these words in White's text:

"When I graduated from medical school in 1911, I had never heard of coronary thrombosis [heart attack]."[19] A surprising statement, I thought, coming from a famous cardiologist. I soon discovered the reason for it: the first article about coronary thrombosis appeared in the *Journal of the American Medical Association* in 1912. Heart attacks were rare in those days, despite the fact that many people lived to advanced ages. When White introduced the electrocardiograph to his colleagues at Harvard, they advised him to focus on a more profitable specialty as heart disease was so rare. The machine recorded unusual patterns in the rhythm of the heart and evidence of possible blocked arteries: the challenge was to find enough patients to make a living with the new invention.

When White began his career, over half of all Americans lived on small farms with their dairy cows, fowl, pigs and beef cattle. Both country people and city folk typically feasted on fatty meats, raw whole milk, eggs and plenty of butter. They cooked in bacon fat and lard, and used lard in pie crusts and pastries. Over eighty percent of the fats in the American diet were animal fats.[20] By 1970, that percentage had fallen to about sixty percent, while cholesterol consumption had not changed. But by that time heart disease caused nearly half of all deaths in America—an increase of about one thousand percent between 1930 and 1970.[21] In other words, while consumption of animal fats declined, the incidence of heart disease increased—these facts alone are sufficient to disprove the theory that animal fats and cholesterol cause heart disease!

During the same years, consumption of refined vegetable oils increased four hundred percent while the use of sugar and processed foods skyrocketed. Many studies have linked these foods to heart disease and cancer, but you never hear about them on television or read about them in the women's magazines.[22]

Comparison of dietary patterns and rates of heart disease in other countries reveals similar inconsistencies. In England, consumption of animal fat remained stable while the number of heart attacks increased one thousand percent between 1930 and 1970.[23] In Yugoslavia, four times as many people died of heart disease in 1965 as in 1955, while saturated fat consumption fell twenty-five percent. During the same period, processed foods had become much more widely available.[24] In Switzerland, heart attacks have declined in the years since World War II, while the consumption of animal fat has increased about twenty percent.[25]

Further evidence that something other than animal fat causes heart disease comes from studies of two tribes in Kenya, the Maasai and the Samburu, discussed in Chapter 8. These tribesmen are shepherds, and their diets consist almost entirely of raw milk, blood and meat. Adult men typically consume almost one gallon of rich milk per day, providing at least one-half pound of butterfat—that's two sticks of butter daily! Heart disease is nonexistent among those on traditional diets and their cholesterol levels are about half the value of those of most Americans.[26] If a diet rich in animal fat and cholesterol is the most important factor in causing heart disease, these people would die of heart attacks at least as often as Americans do.

One popular misconception centers on the notion that the so-called Mediterranean diet is low in animal fat. First promoted by Dr. Keys—who seems never to have heard of salami—this theory has inspired a number of books and articles claiming that the traditional diets of Italy, Greece, Spain, Portugal and France are rich in vegetables, fruit, bread, pasta and olive oil, and contain some cheese and wine but little other animal food and saturated fat.

Anyone who has traveled to the Mediterranean region soon discovers that the inhabitants enjoy eggs, meat, fish, sausage, butter, cream, full-fat cheese, rich patés and lard on a daily basis. In fact, consumption statistics for these countries show that from about 1960 to 1990, saturated fat *increased* an average of about forty-five percent—increased prosperity likely meant more money for the purchase of animal products by more of the population, more money to enjoy the good life. Meanwhile deaths from coronary heart disease *decreased* over the same period by an average of about twenty percent.[27]

Proponents of the lipid hypothesis have singled out eggs as a particularly dangerous component of the diet because egg yolk is richer in cholesterol than any other food. Fear of cholesterol has reached the point that university researchers who want to give healthy study participants two eggs a day must often first consult the university's ethics committee. While this may raise a smile, I do understand it, for my new patients often find it absolutely astounding and all but accuse me of attempted homicide when I suggest that they can eat all the eggs they wish with impunity.

Now that the public is widely fearful of eggs, it should be easy to produce evidence that egg consumption is dangerous. Does research show that individuals who have heart disease have eaten more cholesterol from eggs and other cholesterol-rich foods than individuals with no symptoms of the disease? Not at all! Ten major studies comparing the consumption of cholesterol by heart disease patients and healthy people found no statistically significant differences. The actual figures for the ten studies showed that the heart disease groups had eaten about two percent less cholesterol: the mean cholesterol consumption in the heart disease groups was 506 milligrams per day, and in the control groups it was 518 milligrams per day.[28]

Heart disease is more common in rich countries than in poor ones, and in richer countries people consume more animal food. But within the richer countries, poor people die much more frequently of heart attacks, despite eating far fewer foods rich in cholesterol and animal fats. People in prosperous countries also eat more sugar and refined foods, smoke more, perform less manual labor, eat the products of industrial agriculture and are exposed to more environmental pollution—all factors that could account for the greater incidence of heart disease in rich countries compared to poor ones.[29,30]

Many research trials about heart disease followed in the footsteps of the Framingham study, studies involving hundreds of thousands of people. During the 1950s and early 1960s, most of the trials looked at dietary patterns. The evidence for the lipid hypothesis in those trials was not good. In fact, over thirty published studies involving over one hundred fifty thousand people have failed to show any difference in animal fat consumption between those who develop heart disease and those who do not.[31]

Intervention trials, in which tens of thousands of people were put on cholesterol-lowering diets, have with one exception failed to reduce the number of heart attacks. The one exception was the Oslo trial, published in 1981. Both the researchers and the media drew optimistic conclusions based on these fragile findings, findings that have never been confirmed in other trials.

This lack of evidence is in obvious conflict with popular conceptions and the position of government, medical and pharmaceutical industry spokesmen, but has been well documented by a vocal minority of qualified researchers and authors.[32,33] Uffe Ravnskov, MD, PhD, a Swedish researcher who has extensively studied the literature on the diet-heart idea, lists almost three dozen brave scientists who have published studies describing flaws in the modern cholesterol myth.

Ravnskov points out that in many studies researchers have manipulated statistics in ways that magnify trivial differences to make them appear significant, using a concept called "relative risk."[34] For example, if one person out of a thousand in a group with low cholesterol dies of a heart attack compared to two people in a group with high cholesterol, the difference is only one-tenth of one percent but the "relative risk" of having high cholesterol is said to be one hundred percent, because two is one hundred percent greater than one. These exaggerated figures are then cited in the article summaries—often the only part physicians take time to read.

Despite the lack of evidence and obvious manipulation of trial results, the National Heart, Lung, and Blood Institute insists that "Diet is the cornerstone of treatment of high-risk cholesterol levels," and urges Americans to drastically reduce their consumption of cholesterol and animal fats.[35]

## CHOLESTEROL LOWERING—NOT SUCH A GOOD IDEA

What about the idea that whatever the diet, high cholesterol levels in the blood cause heart attacks, and lowering cholesterol levels can reduce the incidence of coronary heart disease? This is the basic argument used to justify millions of prescriptions for cholesterol-lowering drugs, and for current recommendations that millions more people should be so treated, including children as young as eight years old.[36] It seems reasonable to expect good evidence for this argument.

Earlier, we discussed how high blood cholesterol first emerged as a risk factor for heart disease in the Framingham study. Because individuals with higher levels of cholesterol suffered slightly more heart attacks, researchers concluded that high cholesterol was a risk factor, a predictor for heart disease. But many trials found only a weak association of high cholesterol with heart disease. As with the diet studies, researchers manipulated statistics in ways that magnified trivial differences, and made exaggerated claims in the summaries of the articles to justify unwarranted conclusions unsupported by the actual research.[37]

Many articles promoting cholesterol-lowering measures make reference to the summary of one particular major article about the Framingham study, published in 1987 in the *Journal of the American Medical Association (JAMA)*.[38] But the actual text of the article reveals that nearly half of those who had heart attacks during the Framingham study were in the group that had low cholesterol. Comparing all of the groups, women with low cholesterol died as often as women with high cholesterol. Furthermore, men between the ages of forty-eight and fifty-seven with cholesterol levels between one hundred eighty-three and two hundred twenty-two died more often than those with levels between two hundred twenty-two and two hundred sixty-one. The authors also noted that individuals whose cholesterol had decreased without treatment over the thirty years of the study had a greater risk of dying than individuals whose cholesterol had increased. The crucial statement, "For each

1 mg/dl drop of cholesterol there was an 11 percent increase in coronary and total mortality," was buried in the body of the paper and did not appear in the summary.

In 1990, the following statement appeared in the journal *Circulation*, published by the American Heart Association and the National Heart, Lung and Blood Institute: "The results of the Framingham study indicate that a 1% reduction of cholesterol corresponds to a 2% reduction in CHD risk."[39] Compare this with the quote above from the *JAMA* report that very few have read. No wonder so many physicians are convinced that cholesterol causes heart disease, in spite of the lack of evidence.

The Framingham authors themselves used similar tactics in 1987 to present revised, politically correct conclusions. The following statement appeared in a report concerning thirty years of follow-up, published in the *American Journal of Cardiology*: "The most important overall finding is the emergence of the total cholesterol concentration as a risk factor for CHD in the elderly." The authors made no mention of several studies showing that high cholesterol levels in the elderly are unrelated to heart disease and may even be protective.[40]

Numerous other studies have confirmed the lack of correlation that emerged in the later years of the Framingham project. For example, a study in Sydney, Australia found that cholesterol levels had no predictive value in Australian men over the age of seventy-four.[41] A study at the Albert Einstein College of Medicine in New York produced similar findings. Yet the authors of the latter study concluded, "The findings of this study suggest that an unfavorable lipoprotein profile increases the risk for cardiovascular morbidity and mortality."[42] As indicated earlier, the summaries of articles often contain conclusions having no apparent logical connection with data presented in the body of the paper.

Similar findings on the elderly came to light in work done at Yale University, where researchers studied almost one thousand elderly men and women over a four-year period: twice as many of the participants with low cholesterol had heart attacks as those with the highest cholesterol levels.[43]

These results have led Dr. Ravnskov and other researchers to conclude that high cholesterol may actually be protective.[44] Although such thinking may well seem heretical, it is quite logical; the human body naturally seeks to heal itself, and increased cholesterol may be a normal protective mechanism when the body is under various types of stress. Consider, for example, the results of a French study reported in *The Lancet* in 1989. Women with low cholesterol had a death rate more than five times higher than that of women with very high cholesterol. In fact, the researchers noted that old women with very high cholesterol live the longest.[45] At a 1992 National Heart, Lung and Blood Institute conference on cholesterol in women, participants looked at every study published about the risk of having high or low cholesterol. They concluded that mortality was higher for women with low cholesterol than for women with high cholesterol.[46]

As for men, many studies have similarly failed to show relationships between high cholesterol and heart disease. A research team published their findings in the *Canadian Journal of Cardiology* in 1990 after following over five thousand healthy middle-aged Canadian men for twelve years. Their conclusion: high cholesterol had no relationship with increased risk for coronary heart disease for the period of the study.[47]

Proponents of the lipid hypothesis state that high cholesterol levels are particularly dangerous for individuals who have already had a heart attack, but many studies contradict that notion. A team at the University Hospital of Toronto followed one hundred twenty men for ten years after their heart attacks and found no difference in the incidence of a second attack in those with high cholesterol compared to those with low. Many other published articles confirm these findings.[48]

Such articles have had no apparent impact on the American cholesterol juggernaut. In 1989 the National Research Council published *Diet and Health*, the largest official review on heart disease. The review concluded that there was "a strong, continuous and positive relationship between total cholesterol levels and the prevalence and incidence of, as well as mortality from, atherosclerotic CHD."[49]

These tactics explain how supporters of the lipid hypothesis have convinced people to lower their cholesterol as much as possible. I run a chemistry screen panel on most of my new patients, and most of them express initial pleasure if their cholesterol level is below the new standard of 200 mg/dl. I then must explain that these results are not necessarily positive. Official American medicine appears to practice truth by decree. The practicing physician who does not recommend cholesterol-lowering drugs for, let us say, his elderly female patient who tests a bit above the official norm of 200 mg/dl, is guilty of failing to follow standard-of-care guidelines. He may be subject to disciplinary action from a medical review board and even the loss of his license, or perhaps a civil suit from a zealous family and their lawyers should his patient have a heart attack.

HDL AND LDL

Coincident with the belief that high blood cholesterol causes heart disease is the concept of good and bad cholesterol, HDL and LDL (high density lipoprotein and low density lipoprotein). Lipoproteins are particles composed of fats (lipids) and proteins that carry cholesterol through the bloodstream. HDL is thought to carry cholesterol from the tissues to the liver, where it is used for a variety of purposes or is excreted in the bile. LDL carries cholesterol from the liver, where most of the body's cholesterol is manufactured, to the peripheral tissues.

Because a few studies have indicated that relatively higher levels of LDL are associated with greater risk of having a heart attack, LDL has been dubbed "bad" cholesterol and HDL "good." A low HDL/LDL ratio was thus established as a risk factor for coronary heart disease.

But as we've seen, a risk factor is not necessarily a cause. Many factors that change levels of HDL and LDL, including weight loss, blood pressure, smoking and exercise, appear to also affect heart disease risk. Many studies have attempted to establish prognostic value for levels of HDL and LDL, but with no success. In one of the largest, British scientists looked at seven thousand men for over four years and also reviewed six other large trials before concluding that HDL and LDL levels were not major risk factors, much less causative factors, for coronary heart disease.[50,51]

Yet the U.S. government's *Diet and Health* publication referred to above is unequivocal in its insistence that LDL should be lowered: "LDL has the strongest and most consistent relationship to individual and population risk of CHD, and LDL-cholesterol is centrally and causally important in the pathogenetic chain leading to CHD."[52] One would expect some very good evidence to back up such a strong comment. The authors cite four publications. Dr. Ravnskov analyzed these four and all of the studies to which the four refer, and found that evidence for increased LDL-cholesterol as a risk factor or causative factor for coronary heart disease does not appear in any of them. Ravnskov points out numerous obvious errors and shows how the conclusions of various studies are often at odds with data presented in the papers themselves. Proponents of the lipid hypothesis cite the conclusions of one flawed study after another to support their pronouncements, studies in which statistically insignificant data are repeatedly cited as significant. In short, no evidence indicates that increased LDL-cholesterol causes heart disease or is even a legitimate risk factor—no more a risk factor than high total cholesterol.

HOW TO GIVE A MONKEY A HEART ATTACK

Proponents of the lipid hypothesis often cite animal studies as proof that cholesterol causes heart disease. Thousands of scientists have carried out cholesterol experimentation on laboratory animals. But no other mammal utilizes cholesterol in quite the same way humans do. Vegetarian animals do not normally eat foods containing cholesterol, and when they are force-fed cholesterol-rich foods, the level of cholesterol in their blood skyrockets. Changes may be induced in the arteries of some animals, rhesus monkeys for example, that vaguely resemble atherosclerosis in humans. Eminent scientists have criticized the notion that this observation can be used as proof that animal fats and cholesterol cause heart disease in humans as naïve and ill-founded.[53]

Rabbits are the animals most commonly used in cholesterol experiments. When forced to eat cholesterol-rich food, this vegetarian animal's blood cholesterol rises to levels ten to twenty times higher than the highest ever seen in humans. Cholesterol is deposited in the arteries, among other places, but the deposits do not resemble the lesions of human atherosclerosis. Yet rabbit studies are frequently cited as proof that elevated serum cholesterol in humans causes heart disease.

During the 1960s, scientists used wild rhesus monkeys captured from the jungle in feeding experiments designed to induce what the researchers called atherosclerosis. They fed huge amounts of cholesterol-rich foods to twenty-seven animals who were kept in small individual cages, reinforced with solid metal sheets, in a Chicago basement laboratory. The unhappy monkeys ate little or went on long hunger strikes and threw their food around their cages.

Blood samples were taken from the groin arteries only with great difficulty, for the monkeys resisted violently—screaming, urinating and defecating. After four years of this treatment, one of the monkeys died of a heart attack, an animal reported to be especially hyperactive and extremely nervous. The researchers then published an article, "Fatal Myocardial Infarction in a Monkey Fed Fat and Cholesterol," in the *Archives of Pathology*.[54] The scientists and many others who have cited this study in later papers considered diet and high serum cholesterol levels, and nothing else, to be the factors that led to the monkey's death.

Other scientists with a more integrated view of health and disease, and a more complete understanding of the literature on animal studies, believe otherwise. In a thorough review based on a comprehensive study of the experiments involving cholesterol in animals, William Stehbens, MD, a professor in the Department of Pathology at the Wellington School of Medicine in New Zealand, wrote the following: "Any pathologist of independent mind and free from preconceived ideas would conclude that human atherosclerosis and the lesions induced [in animals] by the dietary overload of cholesterol and fats are not one and the same disease."[55]

## THE PHARMACEUTICAL TRIALS

We've looked at a number of aspects of the Framingham study, but perhaps most important is the light it sheds on today's bottom-line belief that lowering your cholesterol will extend your life. This is the belief that has millions of Americans taking cholesterol-lowering drugs and millions more thinking about it.

The four most important risk factors that emerged from the Framingham study, in order of importance, were age, sex, high blood pressure and elevated cholesterol. Recall that the relationship for cholesterol was quite weak. Among the women in the study under the age of fifty-five, it was not a risk factor at all. For both men and women, the association weakened greatly with advancing age. The majority of heart disease deaths occurred among those with average cholesterol levels and there was no relationship between life expectancy and cholesterol levels for men or women after age forty-eight. The only notable cholesterol link involved the small minority of young and middle-aged men with levels of cholesterol of 280 mg/dl or higher; these men had heart disease at a rate about three times higher than men of the same age with average cholesterol levels.

Other epidemiological studies confirmed the finding that elevated cholesterol was a risk factor, but a weak one. This finding was clear by the early 1960s, but the question of whether or not lowering cholesterol would prevent or alleviate heart disease remained unanswered.[56]

The first great trial to address this question was the Coronary Drug Project, which included over eight thousand men who had suffered at least one heart attack. Sponsored by the National Heart, Lung and Blood Institute, the trial began in 1967 and tested several drugs, including clofibrate, one of the early cholesterol-lowering drugs. Treatment with the drug succeeded in lowering cholesterol levels, but after seven years just as many deaths occurred in those treated with clofibrate as in the control group. Many people in the treatment group suffered from severe side effects.

Follow-up studies years later revealed that the number of heart attack deaths in the group that had received the drug during the seven-year trial was greater than in the control group. Similar findings emerged in the follow-up studies of other large trials with clofibrate—findings that are not mentioned in the many subsequent articles that refer to the original papers.[57]

Another major trial was conducted by the Upjohn Company, this one on their new cholesterol-lowering drug, Colestipol.[58] Doctors in hospitals selected over two thousand patients with high cholesterol and then allowed Upjohn scientists to select which patients would receive the drug and which the placebo—in defiance of proper trial protocol, which calls for random selection. They achieved apparently remarkable results, results never achieved before or after in such trials; the number of heart attacks for men in the treatment group was half the number of those in the control group. However, subsequent analysis of laboratory test records, conducted by independent scientists, showed that the Upjohn scientists had selected a larger number of individuals with familial hypercholesterolemia, an inborn error of cholesterol metabolism, for the control group.[59] These people are much more prone to heart attacks than others, and many die young. By placing larger numbers of these people in the untreated control group, the Upjohn scientists manipulated the protocols so that the treatment group would fare well in comparison. Thus, they managed to achieve the results they wanted in the trial. Scientists can be very clever, as we have seen in the preceding chapter.

A similar trial to test the cholesterol-lowering agent clofibrate was conducted under the sponsorship of the World Health Organization in the 1970s. This trial involved some thirty thousand healthy, middle-aged European men. Researchers selected ten thousand with the highest cholesterol levels, treating half with clofibrate and half with a placebo. Over the course of five years, an equal number in both groups died of heart attacks. But the total number of deaths from all causes was one hundred twenty-eight in the clofibrate group, and only eighty-seven in the placebo group. Five years after the trial, the number of heart attack deaths was also larger in the treatment group.

But clofibrate became a top-selling drug for years, and it is still recommended in many countries. The reason? In the initial five-year trial, one hundred seventy-four of the people taking a placebo were reported to have suffered from a non-fatal heart attack, compared with one hundred thirty-one of those treated with clofibrate.[60] Articles about the trial emphasized this fact, as did promotional literature for clofibrate. But the interpretation of what constitutes a non-fatal heart attack is somewhat subjective; even experienced physicians sometimes diagnose gastrointestinal symptoms or hiatus hernia as a mild heart attack. Given the bias we have seen in many of the studies discussed, it seems quite possible that investigators exaggerated the number of non-fatal heart attacks in the placebo group.

Consistently poor results with cholesterol-lowering drugs did not prevent the National Heart, Lung and Blood Institute from embarking on another massive trial with a new drug in the late 1970s, the Lipid Research Clinics Coronary Primary Prevention Trial (LRC trial). This time cholesterol levels were measured in nearly one half million middle-aged men, and the highest eight-tenths of one percent—about four thousand individuals—became participants in the actual trial. The drug tested was cholestyramine, which half of the men received; the other half took a placebo.

Blood cholesterol in the treatment group went down by over eight percent. Deaths from heart attacks occurred in 1.7 percent of this group, compared to 2.3 percent in the control group. Nonfatal heart attacks numbered ten percent, compared to just over eleven percent in the control group. These results were so close that they could have resulted by chance; they had no statistical significance. The trial was a flop.

But in the summary of the paper, the researchers used the concept of relative risk to make these trivial differences seem important. They compared the absolute number of incidents in the treatment group with the absolute number of incidents in the control group while ignoring the total number of men involved. Fatal heart attacks were said to have been lowered by thirty percent, and nonfatal heart attacks by nineteen percent.[61] Furthermore, there were eleven deaths from other causes in the treatment group, compared with only four in the untreated group, but the researchers failed to mention this fact in the summary. If they had used the relative risk measurement for the side effects, they would have reported a one hundred seventy-five percent increase in deaths from other causes in the group receiving the drug.[62]

If the results of the trial were not due to chance, and if the millions of men in the United States with blood cholesterol as high as those in the trial received the same treatment, perhaps two hundred fewer heart attack fatalities would occur in the country each year. Yet in a 1990 letter that appeared in the *Atlantic Monthly*, Daniel Steinberg, chairman of the conference that initiated the National Cholesterol Education Campaign, cited the LRC trial and claimed that one hundred thousand lives could be saved each year according to "a large number of studies" with statistical significance.[63] In direct contradiction, a few months earlier, the physician who had served as director of the LRC trial stated in a medical journal that the trial had not reduced the number of heart disease deaths, and that "further gains in life expectancy are unlikely."[64]

The side effects experienced in the LRC trial are another story. Normally, the untreated control group receives a placebo that has no side effects. Symptoms unrelated to treatment are then assumed to occur in both the treatment and the control groups with equal frequency. The true percentage of side effects can then be calculated by subtracting the percentage of side effects in the control group from that in the treatment group.

But in the LRC trial the percentage of extremely unpleasant side effects experienced by both groups was alarmingly high. Over two-thirds of the men taking the drug had nausea, vomiting, bloating, abdominal pain and heartburn, and nearly half had constipation or diarrhea. Nearly half of those in the control group experienced similar symptoms, indicating that the placebo contained some sort of active compound (the researchers did not reveal what the placebo was).[65] It is hard to believe that the use of an active placebo was inadvertent and not deliberate.

However, the treatment subjects did suffer more symptoms than the controls, and a greater number were admitted to hospitals for treatment of nervous system disorders. This finding is consistent with other studies in which treatment with cholesterol-lowering drugs resulted in a markedly higher incidence of suicide, depression and violent death. Although it is clear that cholesterol reduction adversely affects the central nervous system, this possibility received no mention in the LRC trial report.

The side effects of cholestyramine (the drug used in the LRC trial) are rarely mentioned. In his letter to the *Atlantic Monthly*, Steinberg wrote, "The drugs in current use for lowering cholesterol levels have remarkably few side effects and, to my knowledge, no fatal side effects."

The relative risk statistical manipulations that researchers used in the LRC trial led to new levels of aggressiveness in the treatment of "high cholesterol." Recall that only men with the upper 0.8 percent of cholesterol values were treated in the trial. Less than one percent of all people have familial hypercholesterolemia, the inborn error of cholesterol metabolism, but a substantial majority of the men treated in the LRC trial had this problem. A treatment that had proved to be of marginal use for these men even with statistical manipulation would now be extended to the general population.

The elderly would be treated, even though there was no evidence that treatment was of any use for them. Women would be treated, even though the LRC trial had not studied women, and all previous studies had indicated that high cholesterol is not a risk factor in women. Men with cholesterol only slightly above normal (by then defined as 200 mg/dl) would now be treated. All of these groups were targeted for treatment in the LRC trial report. Children, bypassed at the time, would be included later.[66]

STATINS EVERYONE? THE CANCER RISK

One of my patients said to me recently, "Well, they used to have some problems with the cholesterol-lowering drugs, but the problems have been solved. The new drugs don't have side effects and they work much better."

New drugs that inhibit the body's production of cholesterol and a number of other important substances were introduced in the late 1980s and have become the drugs of choice for cholesterol-lowering today. Known as the statins, they include Zocor®, Pravachol®, Lipitor®, Lescol® and Mevacor.® These are the new wonder drugs, supposedly free of serious side effects and marvelously effective, lowering cholesterol by as much as forty percent or more. Several large clinical trials have shown small but statistically significant reductions in the number of heart attack deaths and the number of nonfatal heart attacks. Overall mortality has been reduced as well with the drugs, because fewer people in the treatment groups died from stroke.

But ironically, the reports of the trials provide strong evidence that cholesterol levels do not matter and that the statins achieve their results through mechanisms other than lowering cholesterol. Here is the evidence:

* The drugs were as effective for the elderly as they were for younger individuals, and as effective for women as for men; almost all earlier studies have shown that high cholesterol is not a risk factor for women and the elderly.

* Statin treatment reduced the number of strokes; all studies have shown that high cholesterol is a negligible risk factor for stroke.

* Patients who had suffered a previous heart attack gained some protection; previous studies have shown that high cholesterol is at most a weak risk factor for these individuals.

* People with either high or low cholesterol gained some protection taking the statins, indicating that it was not the lowering of cholesterol that afforded protection.

* Finally, it did not matter whether the cholesterol level was lowered a lot or a little; the risk of heart attack was lowered to the same degree in either case.[67]

The likely explanation for the effectiveness of the statins lies in the fact that they inhibit the production of cholesterol by inhibiting the body's production of mevalonate. This substance is the precursor not only of cholesterol but also of a number of other important molecules, including those that regulate the activity of the smooth muscle cells lining the arteries, the platelets that control blood clotting, and substances that slightly reduce the inflammation involved in atherosclerosis. Several researchers have demonstrated that it is these and other statin effects that are responsible for their modest clinical success—and not their characteristic of lowering cholesterol.[68]

Whatever the science, the statins are popular, and more people than ever are now taking drugs to lower cholesterol. But the scientific literature exaggerates the benefits of the statins using the same statistical methods described above.

Keep in mind also that large and expensive trials for these drugs are paid for and conducted by the drug companies. Company money pays for the scores of meetings, conferences and workshops that accompany the trials, and company money pays the professionals to attend and speak at the meetings and do the field work for the trials.[69]

Tens of millions of healthy middle-aged and younger people are now targets for treatment with statins without being told that these drugs may cause cancer. In 1996, an article titled "Carcinogenicity of lipid lowering drugs" appeared in the *Journal of the American Medical Association*. A careful review showed that all of the statins caused cancer growth in rodents, and that the blood levels of the drug associated with cancer in rodents were close to those of patients treated with statins. Because the period between exposure to a carcinogen and the diagnosis of cancer is often ten or twenty years, the authors recommended that the drugs be used only for patients at very high risk for heart disease. They further cautioned individuals with a life expectancy of greater than ten to twenty years to avoid the drugs.[70]

This advice, of course, directly conflicts with advertising promotions now targeting healthy middle-aged and younger people with levels of cholesterol in the 200 mg/dl range.

The effect these medications may have on people over the next twenty years is a great unknown, but the early indications are not good. In one large clinical trial, twelve women in the treatment group got breast cancer during the trial, compared with only one in the control group. "These findings could be an anomaly," the authors of the study wrote.[71] But the difference was highly statistically significant. The package inserts for the statins detail various other side effects—liver problems, muscle wasting, neuropathy, all of which can make life miserable—but make no mention of cancer.

The published results of the first and the largest statin trial to date are even more disconcerting. Preliminary findings in the EXCEL trial, the Expanded Clinical Evaluation of Lovastatin, came out in 1991 after the first year of the trial. In fine print the authors revealed that there had been thirty-two deaths from all causes in the treatment group of six thousand six hundred individuals compared with only three in the placebo group of one thousand six hundred fifty individuals, or two-and-one-half times more deaths in the treatment group, a figure that would be highly significant if it extended throughout the trial.

But in over twenty reports about the trial published since then, none have mentioned the final outcome of the trial, and no further data about the increased mortality seen in the first year in the treatment group have been forthcoming.[72]

## FAILED LEADERSHIP

The cholesterol hypothesis has had an enormous influence on the fate of millions of America's dairy farmers over the last fifty or sixty years. Most Americans no longer understand or want whole raw milk, butter and cheese, all rich in cholesterol, fat and crucial fat-soluble vitamins so lacking in most American diets. This unfortunate dietary change is due in large part to government policies promulgating the diet-heart idea while encouraging the production and marketing of large qualities of cheap, second-rate, reduced-fat milk and impeding the production and marketing of high-quality raw milk. If government policy toward small dairy farmers since around the end of World War II can be characterized as "Let them eat cake," then the demonization of cholesterol and animal fats is the icing on the cake. We turn now to the story of the farms and the farmers.

# Part III
# Milk Today

# 11
# Industrial Agriculture and Dairy Farming in the 21st Century

*Since I started farming, ten million farmers have been removed from the land due to low farm prices. The experts call this technology. I call it planned destruction of rural America by the international conglomerates sanctioned by our government. Our future food supply is in dire jeopardy.*

*Family farming is an endangered profession.*
Anonomous Wisconsin dairy farmers to
University of Wisconsin-Madison researchers, 1999

Modern processed milk comes in the variety of pasteurized homogenized forms available at retail stores everywhere. The way milk is produced, distributed and sold has undergone vast changes during the last one hundred years. Those changes have had profound effects on the lives of millions of farmers, and on the health of nearly everyone, because milk is such a widely used food.

In this chapter, we'll look at the structural changes that have taken place in the dairy industry and the ways that milk production has changed. We'll examine the trend toward confinement dairies in agriculture today and how this affects animal health and the quality of milk; we'll learn how modern milk is produced and how the remaining dairy farmers feel about the milk business. In so doing, we'll see why government policies, regulations, laws and controls on milk sales and pricing have reduced the number of dairy farms in America from almost four million in 1950 to just over one hundred thousand in the year 2000. Over three-and-a-half million farm families left the land during those years.

When I was a child in the early 1950s, the thirty-mile trip to New York City from the small town where my family lived took a little over one hour. The interstate wasn't finished yet, and the rural roads we took went through country dotted with farms. We always played "the animal game." You got points for spotting animals—one point for a dog, cat, bird, or other single common animal, two points for a more exotic species (pig, goat, skunk, rabbit, deer), and three points for a herd of cows. As we drove, everybody watched, and whoever made the sighting first cried out "Dog!" or "Two deer!" or best of all "Herd of cows!" and got the points. The action was fast and furious, and the scores ran into the hundreds.

And the cows were everywhere. Sometimes you couldn't tell where one herd ended and another began. Three points or six? Big argument.

We all know that things have changed since then, but I don't think most of us realize how much. Traveling from place to place on the interstate highways has a way of removing you from the land. You still see barns off in the distance, but herds of cows? Occasionally. But for the most part, dairy cows have disappeared from the landscape. In fact, except for the family pet, and "Wild Kingdom" knockoffs, animals have disappeared from our lives.

How much have things changed? In 1950, almost four million of America's five million farms had milk cows, cows that spent most of the year out at pasture. By 2000, the total number of farms had shrunk to less than two million, and only a small fraction had milk cows.[1] Most of those cows spend most of their time in confinement facilities.

The politics, economics and legal niceties of how government policies have forced millions of farm families off the land and into cities is a subject that requires a book of its own. Here we look at what has happened to the cows and the milk, how some of the farmers feel about dairy farming today, and how modern milk is produced and sold.

CHANGES IN THE DAIRY INDUSTRY

The phrase "Get big or get out" describes the policies and attitudes of the United States Department of Agriculture (USDA) and other federal, state and local government agencies that deal with farmers. Since the end of World War II, the academic agricultural establishment has also preached this policy as an article of faith to farmers in general and dairy farmers in particular. Agricultural colleges have not only favored, but actively promoted an increasing use of pesticides, herbicides and chemical fertilizers, along with the use of large equipment, with large loans to pay for it. Farmers repeatedly hear the claim that high production of milk is required for economic survival. Quality has taken a back seat and so has the health of the cows, which are treated not as sacred beasts but as units of production.

Dairy farmers are paid for the amount of milk they produce. As long as the milk meets certain bacteria count and butterfat standards, they have no incentive to concern themselves with quality. The milk is pooled with that of thousands of other producers. Most farmers cannot market their milk freely and must sell to consortiums under government-regulated fixed contracts. Milk prices fluctuate but in general are so low that most farmers have no choice but to keep their costs as low as possible—difficult to do when bills for feed and veterinary care are high. These economics have meant shrinking numbers of dairy farms; between 1990 to 2000, the number fell from almost two hundred thousand to half that amount. In 2002, sixteen dairy farms went out of business every day.[2]

Meanwhile, the average number of cows per operation has increased from six in 1950 to fifty-two in 1990 to eighty-eight in 2000.[3] Some confinement dairies today have thousands of cows. "Get big or get out." Milk production per cow has also increased. In 1950, the average dairy cow produced a little less than two gallons of milk per day. In 2000, she produced an average of over six gallons per day,[4] thanks to generations of selective breeding and "feeding for maximum production"—pushing the cow with a diet high in grains and additives like bovine growth hormone, which force her to make more milk. The average lifespan for a modern confinement dairy cow is forty-two months, compared to twelve to fifteen years for a cow on pasture.

Technological innovations are one major force driving these changes; new machinery and equipment have replaced manual labor and made for greater "efficiency" in all aspects of milk production, from feeding to milking to "waste handling." Among other problems, what once was fertile manure scattered over pasture has become a waste disposal nightmare.

The other major force behind all these changes is concentration itself, as a widespread shift has occurred from pasture-based milk production to large confinement feeding systems. The startling fact is that in the year 2000, over fifty percent of all milk production in the United States came from operations that house over five hundred cows, and that percentage is growing every year.[5] Before looking at the confinement operations that house most of those cattle, we'll look at the most advanced examples of America's industrial animal agriculture—the facilities that produce nearly one hundred percent of the country's eggs, chicken and pork.

## CONCENTRATED ANIMAL FEEDING OPERATIONS (CAFOs) FOR CHICKENS AND PIGS

René Descartes (1596-1650), often called the father of modern philosophy, claimed that animals were simply machines, incapable of thought or feeling. "To visit a modern CAFO," Michael Pollan recently wrote in the *New York Times Magazine*, "is to enter a world that, for all its technological sophistication, is still designed according to Cartesian principles: animals are machines incapable of feeling pain. Since no thinking person can possibly believe this any more, industrial animal agriculture depends on a suspension of belief on the part of the people who operate it and a willingness to avert your eyes on the part of everyone else.

"From everything I've read, egg and hog operations are the worst.

Beef cattle in America at least still live outdoors, albeit standing ankle deep in their own waste eating a diet that makes them sick. And broiler chickens, although they do get their beaks snipped off with a hot knife to keep them from cannibalizing one another under the stress of their confinement, at least don't spend their eight-week lives in cages too small to ever stretch a wing. That fate is reserved for the American laying hen, who passes her brief span piled together with a half-dozen other hens in a wire cage whose floor a single page of this magazine could carpet. Every natural instinct of this animal is thwarted, leading to a range of behavioral 'vices' that can include cannibalizing her cagemates and rubbing her body against the wire mesh until it is featherless and bleeding. Pain? Suffering? Madness? The operative suspension of belief depends on more neutral descriptors, like 'vice' and 'stress.' Whatever you want to call what's going on in those cages, the 10 percent or so of hens that can't bear it and simply die is built into the cost of production. And when the output of the others begins to ebb, the hens will be 'force-molted'—starved of food and water and light for several days in order to stimulate a final bout of egg laying before their life's work is done."[6]

Pollan's description of hog confinement is equally gut wrenching. "Half the dogs in America will receive Christmas presents this year, yet few of us pause to consider the miserable life of the pig—an animal easily as intelligent as a dog—that becomes the Christmas ham. We tolerate this disconnect because the life of the pig has moved out of view.

"Piglets in confinement operations are weaned from their mothers 10 days after birth (compared with 13 weeks in nature) because they gain weight faster on their hormone- and antibiotic-fortified feed. This premature weaning leaves the pigs with a lifelong craving to suck and chew, a desire they gratify in confinement by biting the tail of the animal in front of them. A normal pig would fight off his molester, but a demoralized pig has stopped caring. 'Learned helplessness' is the psychological term, and it's not uncommon in confinement operations, where tens of thousands of hogs spend their entire lives ignorant of sunshine or earth or straw, crowded together beneath a metal roof upon metal slats suspended over a manure pit.

"So it's not surprising that an animal as sensitive and intelligent as a pig would get depressed, and a depressed pig will allow his tail to be chewed on to the point of infection. Sick pigs, being underperforming 'production units,' are clubbed to death on the spot. The USDA's recommended solution to the problem is called 'tail docking.' Using a pair of pliers (and no anesthetic), most but not all of the tail is snipped off. Why the little stump? Because the whole point of the exercise is not to remove the object of tail-biting so much as to render it more sensitive. Now, a bite on the tail is so painful that even the most demoralized pig will mount a struggle to avoid it."

Pollan took much of this description from the recent book *Dominion*, by Matthew Scully. A Christian conservative, Scully calls CAFOs "our own worst nightmare," names the root cause as "unfettered capitalism," and describes "the cultural contradictions of capitalism"—the tendency of the need for profits to take precedence over moral considerations. The factory farm results from the absence of moral or regulatory restraint. "Here in these places," Mr. Pollan wrote, "life itself is redefined—as protein production—and with it suffering. That venerable word becomes 'stress,' an economic problem in search of a cost-effective solution, like tail-docking or beak-clipping or, in the industry's latest plan, by simply engineering the 'stress gene' out of pigs and chickens. 'Our own worst nightmare' such a place may well be; it is also real life for the billions of animals unlucky enough to have been born beneath these grim steel roofs, into the brief, pitiless life of a 'production unit' in the days before the suffering gene was found."[7]

## CAFOs FOR DAIRY COWS

Confinement facilities for dairy cows are less overtly cruel; cows produce more milk when their suffering is minimized. The caption under a photograph of an "environmentally controlled dairy barn" in the textbook *Dairy Cattle Science* by Dr. M. E. Ensminger reads "a completely enclosed building with air circulation and with temperature, humidity and light control. Environmentally controlled dairy barns are on the increase because they lend themselves to automation and make for the ultimate in animal comfort, health and efficiency of feed utilization."[8]

On the next page we learn that the ultimate in animal comfort often consists of standard stanchion stalls that measure four feet by five feet four inches for a medium sized cow—a large cow is allotted four feet six inches by six feet. (A stanchion is a pair of upright metal bars that run up each side of the animal's head in the neck area to keep the cow in place.) "Less space than is indicated may jeopardize the health and well-being of the animals," the text continues, "whereas more space may make the buildings and equipment more expensive than necessary. The stall barn consists of one or two rows of cows that are usually confined to stanchions. For the most part, concrete floors are used."[9]

Other confinement barns use either tie stalls or "comfort" stalls; the dimensions of both are three to six inches larger than the dimensions of stanchion stalls. In *Dairy Cattle Science*, Ensminger describes these stalls in a starkly realistic way:

"In tie stalls, each cow is individually tied with a strap or chain. This offers cows considerably more freedom than stanchion stalls, but requires more labor. Comfort stalls are a special type of tie stall, designed to give cows more freedom than is afforded by ordinary tie stalls. Each cow is secured with a strap or chain fastened to a curb at the front. Horizontal bars at the front force the cow to stand near the rear of the platform. Stalls are separated by fences made of pipe."[10] Some confinement facilities use free stall systems, where the animals may move about somewhat within the facility and choose from available stalls.

Conveniently, the ultimate in animal comfort also results in efficiency. "Dairy producers automate to lessen labor and cut costs," Dr. Ensminger writes. "Modern dairy equipment has eliminated the pitchfork, bucket and basket. Such chores as feeding, watering, bedding, barn cleaning and milking have been mechanized. Dairy producers are using more self-unloading trucks and trailers, self-feeders, feed bunk augers and belts, laborsaving grain and forage processing equipment. . . automatic waterers and manure disposal units. Automation of the dairy farm will increase."[11] The result of this efficiency and automation is the tasteless two-dollars-per-gallon milk you can buy at any corner store or supermarket.

Let us now consider the consequences of this "efficient" confinement system. Ensminger himself begins his chapter "Dairy Cattle Health, Disease Prevention, and Parasite Control" as follows:

"Without doubt, one of the most serious menaces threatening the dairy industry is animal ill health, of which the largest loss is a result of the diseases that are due to a common factor transmitted from animal to animal. Today, with modern, rapid transportation facilities and the dense dairy population centers, the opportunities for animals to become infected are greatly increased compared with a generation ago." He then admits that "ten percent of all calves are afflicted by calf scours [infectious diarrhea] and 18 percent of all dairy calves so afflicted die. Nearly 40 percent of all dairy cows have some form of mastitis, according to the National Mastitis Council."[12]

This is a shocking admission; some forty percent of our milk comes from cows with infections of the mammary gland. And mastitis is only one of many diseases with which confinement cows are routinely afflicted. The one that contributes most heavily to their suffering is lameness caused by laminitis, a painful condition of the foot that may occur in any hoofed animal. The laminae are soft plates of bone in the lower leg that attach to bones in the foot and bear much of the animal's weight. In laminitis, the laminae become inflamed and swell. The two primary causes of laminitis are excessive grain feeding and concrete floors—the two defining characteristics of the confinement system. The following excerpt is from *Keeping Livestock Healthy, a Veterinary Guide*:

"Almost invariably it is the result of high grain feeding. . . . Because their feet hurt, cattle with laminitis don't gain weight or produce milk as they should. . . . Alleviation of the problem, once it occurs, is difficult. Frequent trimming of the feet to be sure they bear weight evenly is about the best that can be done. Prevention through dietary management is the most important thing."[13] This was written in 1978, before the days of widespread confinement facilities. Back then, dairy farmers knew better than to keep dairy cattle continuously on concrete floors.

More recent publications are emphatic about the role of confinement facilities in causing what now is a major problem in the dairy industry. Veterinarians Jose Santos and Michael Overton are with the Veterinary Medicine Teaching and Research Center at the University of

California at Davis. Their article "Diet, Feeding Practices and Housing Can Reduce Lameness in Dairy Cattle" appeared in the March 2001 *Progressive Dairyman and Hay Grower*.

"Lameness is a major cause of premature culling [removing diseased animals for slaughter] and milk loss in dairy herds," the researchers write. "Several reports have shown that lameness is among the three major reasons for culling of lactating dairy cattle in the USA. Annual incidence of lameness in dairy herds has been reported to range from 15 to over 50 percent." The authors cite laminitis as the most common cause of lameness in dairy herds.

According to Santos and Overton, an over-acid condition of the rumen—the first stomach of a ruminant, in which food is partially digested by bacteria—is a major triggering factor with "a dramatic impact on the incidence of lameness, particularly laminitis. Acidosis is most prevalent following engorgement of large amounts of starch and other rapidly fermented carbohydrates such as pectins and sugars." These are precisely the nutrients found in the high-concentrate, grain-rich diets confinement cows receive to maximize "efficiency" and milk production. With such diets, abnormal concentrations of glucose occur in the rumen. "In the presence of glucose, opportunistic microbes such as Coliforms [bacteria normally found only in the intestines] may thrive." This results in the release of toxins that impair the blood supply to the hooves and promote the development of laminitis.

The authors then describe housing and management factors that influence the incidence of lameness. "The most significant contributing factor is the time spent by cows on concrete," the authors write. Chronic impact on the hard surface bruises the hoof and foot, "leading to an altered foot angle. A vicious cycle often develops that greatly affects the normal weight-bearing ability of the claws. Prolonged overloading leads to inflammation of the laminae. Concussion, trauma and excessive standing increase tissue damage. In addition to the severe pain that may be present throughout the process, the damage may result in sole ulcers of varying depths that are most commonly located in the sole nearest the bulb.

"Hooves of dairy cattle housed on new concrete wore 35 percent faster than those on dirt. Prolonged standing on concrete may compromise the perfusion of blood through the claw and exacerbate any preexisting foot problem. This increased standing has been associated with an increase in sole ulcers and other foot problems. Excessive walking on concrete creates concussion damage and leads to sluggish blood flow and edema." The authors cite a host of other research articles to document their points.

"Any discussion about decreasing the incidence and severity of lameness in dairy cattle should focus on minimizing time spent standing or walking on concrete. . . . Normally, cattle spend about 50 percent or more of their time lying. Of these 12 to 14 hours of desired lying time per day, approximately 30 percent consists of sleep. Confinement on concrete can promote longer standing times if facilities are improperly designed and animals improperly managed."

Overcrowding creates other problems. "An integral part of maximizing cow comfort and minimizing standing time is allowing for normal cow behavior and social interactions. In pasture-based systems, there are usually fewer social encounters and agonistic interactions, and more space to spread out and lie down." Cattle in free stall confinement operations are described as becoming "restless and more likely to engage in dominance aggressive behavior. Increased irritability and agonistic behavior may be seen in total confinement dairies, due to design problems such as dead-end alleys and inadequate water access. Intimidation and fear may cause low ranking animals to spend more time standing without moving or resting, leading to greater pressure within the hoof and greater risk of laminitis."

Other influences on standing time described in the article include management of how the cows are fed, milked, examined and tested. In every case, greater efficiency and milk production seem to lead to more standing or walking on concrete and increased incidence of laminitis. Santos and Overton's conclusion is a quiet but strong plea for consideration of the animals' welfare:

"With current feeding practices to support ever-rising milk production, it is critical to optimize environmental conditions that will maximize lying time and minimize standing time. The incidence and severity of laminitis and other forms of lameness will be reduced only when cows and their environments are managed appropriately."[14] Ironically, this poignant plea comes from men within the academic community, which generally serves the industry.

Other veterinarians have written about the incidence of disease in confinement dairies. Pamela L. Ruegg of the Department of Dairy Science at the University of Wisconsin at Madison is described on the University's web site as a "milk quality specialist." She has written extensively about dairy cattle health, and in her article "Disease Causation and Prevention," she distinguishes between the clinical and subclinical phases of diseases such as laminitis and mastitis:

"The primary disease problem on many farms is 'subclinical disease,' defined as abnormalities of function that are detectable only by diagnostic or laboratory test. The beginning of an epidemic of subclinical disease is not usually clearly defined. The subclinical phases can persist for long periods of time and reduce milk production efficiency. In most instances, there are far more subclinically infected animals and the greatest economic impact is the invisible loss of productivity during the subclinical period."[15]

The writer's obvious concern is economic; subclinical disease means lower milk production. Subclinical disease can be detected in a number of ways, including an elevated somatic cell count (SCC), which is commonly used as a measure of milk quality. Somatic cells are cells from the cow's body present at low levels in normal milk. Some are epithelial cells, which are normally shed from secretory tissue of the udder during milking, while the majority are white blood cells that serve as a defense mechanism to fight infection and assist in repairing damaged tissue. Mastitis (inflammation of the mammary gland) always causes a high SCC count, and a high SCC count is usually associated with mastitis.

Most markets today pay a premium for low-SCC milk, because mastitis and a high SCC count cause undesirable changes in milk composition, including increased whey proteins and decreased casein proteins, resulting in considerably lower cheese yields. Shelf life is reduced and adverse milk flavors result; white blood cells form pus, and though they are killed by pasteurization and then partially removed from the milk in the clarification process, it is logical to assume that they can taint the milk.

SCC levels are monitored to assure compliance with state and federal quality standards, and what those standards reveal is the abysmal quality of most milk produced today. "The SCC level in milk quality regulations must be less than 750,000 per ml to comply with the State and Federal Pasteurized Milk Ordinance (PMO). A violation of the PMO makes the milk non-marketable," according to an article by a veterinarian and an agricultural engineer at the Cooperative Extension Institute of Agriculture and Natural Resources at the University of Nebraska.[16] But in the same article, the authors state:

"The normal SCC in milk is generally below 200,000 per ml, but may be below 100,000 in first lactation animals or in well-managed herds. An SCC above 250,000-300,000 is considered abnormal and nearly always is an indication of bacterial infection causing inflammation of the udder." Ms. Ruegg agrees, stating that counts over two hundred thousand are indicative of mastitis.[17] Another expert, a professor of dairy science at Virginia State University, writes, "Data from the National Mastitis Council show that 6% of the quarters [quadrants of the udder] in a herd could be expected to be infected in a herd with a bulk tank SCC of 200,000. At 500,000 SCC, 16% of the quarters may be infected. Good udder health is essential for quality milk production. The results of many studies suggest that cows with SCC of less than 200,000 are not likely to be infected with major mastitis pathogens, but cows with SCC above 300,000 are probably infected."[18] Remember that federal regulations allow up to seven hundred fifty thousand!

Another dairy expert describes the commonly employed solution: "Intra-mammary infusion of antibiotic into every quarter of every cow following the last milking of lactation, commonly referred to as dry cow therapy, is a proven method of mastitis control."[19] This practice kills off beneficial bacteria in the cows' intestinal tracts and allows pathogens to proliferate, a side effect considered unimportant because the milk will be pasteurized.

The State and Federal Pasteurized Milk Ordinance thus allows the entire milk supply of the United States to come from grossly diseased animals—even according to present-day standards, which have changed dramatically from those of fifty years ago. The fact that standards of what constitutes healthy cows and high-quality milk have changed is indicated by this quote from the *Market Milk Industry*, published in 1950 by a veterinarian and a dairy scientist, both of whom were leaders in their fields:

"Cherrington, Hansen, and Halverson, after analyzing 758 counts, conclude 'that milk from normal udders usually contains less than 50,000 cells per ml, whereas milk from infected udders almost invariably contains more than 100,000 per ml.'"[20]

In Ms. Ruegg's paper, the "Suggested Yearly Goal" for clinical cases of mastitis is twenty-four or fewer cases per year per one hundred cows, with slightly lower percentages for other diseases. Obviously, the industry accepts a substantial amount of disease in confinement cows as part and parcel of the operation; the goal of treatment and controls is not to alleviate suffering but to limit the adverse economic impact of lowered milk production.

Ruegg makes an interesting point: "It is extremely important that a system of unique individual cow identification exists. Without this prerequisite, it is impossible for a health management program to succeed."

The kind of animal care that would ensure milk of high quality is most readily given on a small or moderately sized farm, but is possible on any farm that is pasture-based as long as the first consideration is the quality rather than the quantity of the milk. When the farmer can market directly to consumers or to stores, as licensed raw milk dairy farmers currently do in California, Connecticut, Maine, Washington, South Carolina and Pennsylvania, quality commands a hefty premium over commercial milk and becomes not only an ideal but also a highly profitable practice.

Santos and Overton argue that appropriate management of confinement facilities can result in comfortable, reasonably healthy animals and better quality milk. This becomes obvious in visiting different facilities. Some are clean and obviously run with consideration for the welfare and comfort of the cows, despite the relentless pressure to produce high volumes in order to survive. Too many, however, practice the poor management practices that result in diseased animals and inferior milk.

Ensminger's claim that environmentally controlled dairy barns "make for the ultimate in animal comfort and health" is clearly a pipedream, specious and self-serving. At best, such facilities may minimize animal discomfort, prevent overt disease in most animals, and allow for the production of milk that contains lower numbers of pathogenic bacteria and somatic cells compared to milk from more poorly managed operations. Under no circumstances, however, can a confinement facility produce milk that compares in quality to milk from pasture-fed animals. And in most confinement facilities, unhealthy cows that are often overtly sick produce inferior milk that is "safe" only because it is pasteurized.

Dr. Ensminger's picture appears on title page of his textbook, and three paragraphs describe his achievements and accolades. For example, he is President of Agriservices Foundation, "a nonprofit foundation serving world agriculture." He serves as a Collaborator, U.S. Department of Agriculture, and served as Consultant, General Electric Company, Nucleonics Department (Atomic Energy Commission). He is "the author of 21 widely used books that are translated into several languages and used throughout the world," and received an award "which is recognized as the highest honor that can be bestowed on anyone in the livestock industry."[21]

Modern industrial society and its child, industrial agriculture, generously reward those who support them.

NUTRIENTS IN MODERN MILK

Cows are not the only casualty of the modern confinement system. Increased production has resulted in lower levels of nutrients in the milk. According to an article appearing in the *Journal of Dairy Research*, "the more milk a cow produces, the more dilute the vitamin content of her milk. The goal of the commercial dairy industry is to coax the maximum amount of milk out of each cow through a high-tech combination of selective breeding, confinement housing, synthetic hormones and a highenergy grain diet. It has succeeded admirably. Today's super-cows produce as much as 17,000 pounds of milk per cycle—20 times more than a cow needs to sustain a healthy calf. Unfortunately for consumers, the cow transfers a fixed amount of vitamins to her milk, and the greater her milk volume, the more dilute the vitamin content of the milk, especially vitamins E and beta-carotene. . . It follows that continuing breeding and management systems that focus solely on increasing milk and milk fat yield will result in a steady dilution in the milk fat of these vitamins and antioxidants. . . Dairy cows raised on pasture and free of hormone implants produce less milk than commercial cows, but the milk is therefore richer in vitamin content."[22]

Unfortunately, the modern milk production system does not reward farmers for producing high-quality milk from low-production cows that feed on grass. The industry does, however, recognize that the low-nutrient content of modern milk poses problems. Just as swill dairy milk producers added chalk to the thin milk produced by their sickly cows, the modern industry has proposed another technological solution: fortification. Several companies are developing "functional milk," fortified with calcium and synthetic vitamins, a solution unlikely to benefit consumers as added nutrients, especially synthetic versions, are poorly absorbed and may often have toxic effects. Functional milk will also be fortified with iron, a nutrient not normally present in large amounts in milk and milk products. Iron fortification of cereals, juice and other processed foods is suspected of causing "iron overload," a risk factor for heart disease.[23]

## DAIRY FARMERS TALK ABOUT DAIRY FARMING TODAY

In the winter and spring of 1997, researchers for the Program on Agricultural Technology Studies (PATS) at the College of Agricultural and Life Sciences at the University of Wisconsin, Madison conducted a written survey of Wisconsin dairy farmers. Almost two thousand responded to the survey, and over five hundred included written comments that ranged from one or two sentences to ten page letters detailing their situations and concerns. The PATS staff "could not help but note the expressions of concern and exasperation" and in 1999 published many of the farmers' comments in a report entitled, "In Their Own Words:

Wisconsin Dairy Farmers Talk about Dairying in the 1990s." The information and quotations that follow are taken from that report.

In 1999, there were roughly twenty-three thousand dairy farms in Wisconsin. The average farm had sixty-six milk cows, and about eighty-seven percent of the farms milked fewer than one hundred cows. This situation provides a sharp contrast with states where dairy production is more highly industrialized, like California, Washington, Idaho, New Mexico and Florida. In 1999, the average Wisconsin dairy farmer was forty-seven years old, and eight percent were over sixty-five. Almost half the farms had at least one person working off-farm to enable the farm family to acquire health insurance and additional income.

The farmers responding to the survey represented a broad spectrum of approaches to dairying. About twelve percent reported the use of recombinant growth hormone to boost milk production. At the other end of the spectrum, a growing group of about fifteen percent reported using management-intensive rotational grazing—a grass-based rather than grain-based approach—for several months of the year.

Many of the farmers expressed grave concerns about the future of farming. Here are some of the comments on that subject:

"Family farming is an endangered profession."

"I sure hope somebody does something before it's too late for everybody."

"If farm prices don't improve soon, there will be very few left by the year 2000."

"Where will the people get their food if farmers don't keep on trying to stay afloat?"

The farmers consistently identified low milk prices and rising farm expenses as their most significant problems. The milk marketing system was widely criticized, as respondents emphasized the fact that farmers as a whole had lost their voice in pricing and marketing their products.

"There is not a problem in rural America today that cannot be solved by a fair price."

"We don't want a handout, but we thought supply and demand determined the price. That's a lie! The price is totally controlled."

"It seems like everyone has figured out how to get more money out of us, but we have to take what they want to give us for what we have to sell."

"People are going to have to pay more for quality food."

"The corporate buyers control the price and make the money. Them that got the gold make the rules."

"Kraft and the other big players continue to reap huge profits, while we work extraordinary hours, with great financial investment and yet barely have enough money to survive. If Kraft wasn't allowed to monopolize (control our prices) we would have a better chance. They will do anything to keep raw milk prices as low as possible."

"Farmers are a minority at the mercy of the government, politicians, conglomerates and our own co-ops. Co-ops are more worried about themselves."

"Family farmers should work together for better markets. Unless farm organizations learn to work together for the good of their members there is going to be no future for full-time farmers. The middle man is making all the money."

"It is very painful to travel down any nearby county road and count the farms that are no longer in business. There are more barns sitting idle than in use."

Comments about the quality of life on Wisconsin farms were double-edged, expressing great satisfaction with farming as a way of life and great frustration that it had become so difficult to make a decent living by farming.

"As a way of life, farming is the best and allows even the children to feel a part of the operation."

"I am a small dairy farmer, buying the farm from my Dad. I just want a decent living and a happy family life. No big records and a little time to spend with my family."

"We love what we do for a living—we only wish that we could make a living on it. I find it very disheartening to struggle to make ends meet. Farming is not farming anymore, it is all survival. I think it is terrible to enjoy farming and have to work off the farm to provide a way to feed and clothe my family."

"In my many years of dairy farming I have seen my farm life go from very good to very poor. Now it's all work and no play or pay."

"We all say children on the farm learn to share work and play and get to be around their parents and love it, but farming is not fun like it was years ago."

"I don't think my son should farm. It is simply too much hard work, too many days a week, too many hours a day."

Many farmers questioned the idea that bigger is necessarily better. A few of their comments:

"Large farms use more chemicals and produce milk unfit for consumption. They have extremely high cell counts and mastitis trouble. With too many hired men, no one cares what goes in the tank. Small farms know each cow and each teat that has problems. We are able to keep our milk fit for consumption."

"Everyone would be better off if they'd just find a way to keep small 50-cow herds. With smaller farms there is much less smell. The larger the farms become the less voice farmers will have because of fewer numbers."

"Small family farms can still be very profitable if managed right. I know it works. With the big farms they don't know one cow from the other. I have had very bad dealings with big dairy farms. The farms stink (very bad odor). It's giving farmers a bad name."

"Rotational grazing is the answer for many. It is healthier for the cows. Small farms can stay competitive by using organic farming methods. We were disappointed to find that there were no questions on the survey about the importance of herd health."

"Why make it so hard for the small farmer to make a go of it? It started out as family farms, why can't it be kept that way? Not everyone wants to go big and have all modern equipment."

Comments from the Wisconsin dairy farmers about university- and government-funded agricultural programs generally expressed the feeling that too few public resources were devoted to improving the profitability of small and moderately sized farms.

"There is very little information or new ideas that are useful for smaller farmers. We have been fed a lot of bad information by university and agricultural leaders on how big and getting bigger is the only way. More work should be done on how to stay small and still be profitable."

"We plan to do just the opposite of what the experts say. We downsized and are going organic and quitting using all chemicals."

"We would like to see the university teach more about marketing than production."

"I feel that the government's goal or need to have cheap food for people is one of the biggest things hurting dairy farmers today. We are just a bunch of peons with the government's cheap food policy. The government wants the small farmer eliminated. I guess they will be happy to know that their plan is working very well. Why is the government subsidizing the land for grain farmers, but not dairy farmers?"

"We need a long range plan for agriculture regarding land use, and encouraging small farms and therefore rural communities. The legislature must enact laws which will encourage these goals."

"Since I started farming, ten million farmers have been removed from the land due to low farm prices. The experts call this technology. I call it planned destruction of rural America by the international conglomerates sanctioned by our government. Our future food supply is in dire jeopardy."

"This is a free country and let's keep it free—get the government out of farming. All it does is protect the big farmer and destroy the small. There are too many ridiculous rules and regulations governing dairy farm operations."[24]

The industrialization of agriculture has not been a kind process for millions of American dairy farmers over the past century. The same forces that largely destroyed local production of high-quality milk, cream, butter and cheese in America are now operating in a similar manner in the remaining indigenous cultures throughout the world.

Wendell Berry summarizes the problem succinctly in his book *The Unsettling of America*: "Our government has shown considerable enthusiasm for 'leveling the playing field' in the interest of international corporations. Its enthusiasm for leveling the playing field in the interest of local economies and local ecosystems remains to be demonstrated."[25]

INDUSTRY CLOUT

Political influence is an important weapon in the dairy industry arsenal. Part of this influence is obtained through direct lobbying—dairy industry contributions for 2002 alone totaled almost three million dollars, which are small potatoes for an industry that takes in fifty billion dollars per year.[26]

More subtle influence comes through the "educational" efforts of the National Dairy Council. Dairy industry representation on USDA's dietary guidelines committee resulted in a three-servings-of-dairy-foods-per-day recommendation in the latest USDA dietary guidelines, a fifty percent increase over earlier recommendations for two cups per day.[27] Concurrently, the industry launched a "3-A-Day" advertising campaign aimed at persuading consumers to consume more processed cheese, reduced-fat milk and reduced-fat yogurt.

In September, 2008, the National Dairy Council announced an arrangement with the National Football League to promote increased consumption of lowfat and fat-free dairy. The National Dairy Council will spend one hundred million dollars over five years to support the initiative and an additional one hundred fifty million "on other efforts aimed at improving child health and wellness."[28]

The power of this industry was demonstrated in a recent example involving Martha Stewart. In January, 2008, Martha Stewart aired a segment about raw milk at Smith Family Farm in Maine. The milk industry then conducted "outreach" with Stewart, to "educate" her on the dangers of raw milk consumption. According to a news release by the Midwest Dairy Association, "We discussed our concerns with Stewart's producers at length, and were provided assurances that she will not talk about raw milk throughout her partnership with MilkPEP [Milk Processors Education Program] and additionally, that she will consider changing her overall position and commentary on raw milk in the future."[29]

THE BIG FOUR

Consumers see many brands of milk on supermarket shelves, but behind these brand names, four multinational companies control over seventy percent of fluid milk sales in the U.S.—Land O'Lakes, Foremost Farms, Dairy Farmers of America and Dean Foods. These giants have grown through debt-fueled acquisitions and mergers and by keeping payments to dairy farmers as low as possible. Salaries of corporate officers in these companies typically range in the high six figures, with CEOs garnering one million dollars or more per year. Needless to say, these premium paychecks reward executives for maximizing profits for the corporation, not for ensuring high nutrient values in the nation's dairy products.

Land O'Lakes began as a Minnesota dairy farmers' cooperative in 1921 and soon became the leading supplier of butter to U.S. consumers. In 1987, the company merged with Cenex, another dairy co-op. In addition to butter and milk, the company sells margarine, cheese, ice cream, yogurt, soy oil, wheat flour, animal feed products and "ethanol co-products," the residue from ethanol production. (This residue, which is loaded with chemicals, is then fed to confinement dairy cows—shades of the nineteenth century swill dairies!)

In 2001, Land O'Lakes spent three hundred fifty million dollars to acquire Purina Mills pet and livestock feeds, a move that increased its debt load, reported at eighty-eight million dollars in January of 2003.[30] In October, 2002, Moody's Investor Services downgraded the co-op's debt to "junk" status.[31]

Foremost Farms is a Midwestern dairy cooperative involving over four thousand dairy farmers. It markets five billion pounds of milk per year under various retail brands, including Golden Guernsey Dairy and Morning Glory Dairy. Subsidiary products include flavored milk drinks, pharmaceutical-grade lactose and mozzarella cheese. The company is shifting its operations to the West while closing plants in Wisconsin and

Iowa, accelerating the replacement of independent farmers in the Midwest with large confinement dairies in California.[32]

Dairy Farmers of America is the world's largest dairy cooperative with more than twenty-four thousand members in forty-eight states. The co-op produces nearly thirty percent of the U.S. milk supply. Along with fresh milk and "shelf-stable" (ultrapasteurized) fluid milk, the giant co-op also produces cheese, butter, coffee creamer, condensed milk, dehydrated dairy products, infant formula, nonfat dry milk powder, whey products and Starbucks' Frappuccino coffee drink. The company has grown by "inviting" smaller dairy co-ops to merge with it, and by participating in joint ventures with other dairy corporations, such as Dean Foods. Recently, the co-op joined with two other producers, Glanbia and Select Milk Producers, to build a one-hundred-seventy-million-dollar cheese and whey products facility in the Southwest.[33]

The largest U.S. dairy company is Dallas-based Dean Foods, created in 2001 when industry leader Suiza Foods (also based in Dallas) acquired what was then the number-two fluid milk producer, Dean Foods. The company controls many familiar labels including Adohr Farms, Alta Dena, Borden, Meadow Gold, Nature's Pride, Shenandoah's Pride and Sealtest, and produces the usual line of processed products like coffee creamers, whipped toppings, dips and dressings. Dean Foods owns Horizon Organic Milk and the soymilk maker White Wave. Although the company has two and one-half *billion* dollars of debt, and an uninspired BB+ credit rating, it donated one million dollars to the Dallas Center for the Performing Arts Foundation in July of 2003. In that same year, while more than one hundred dairy farmers throughout America went out of business every week, Gregg L. Engles, the forty-five-year-old CEO of Dean Foods, made three million two hundred thousand dollars.[34]

# 12
# Modern Milk:
# Disasters, Mishaps
# and Disturbing Reports

*Over 16,000 culture-confirmed cases of infections due to* Salmonella typhimurium *were traced to two brands of pasteurized 2% milk produced by a single dairy plant. The number of persons who were actually
affected was estimated to be somewhere between 150,000 and 200,000
. . . eighteen deaths occurred.*
>> *Journal of the American Medical Association,*
>> December 11, 1987

    The overriding reason government officials give for the myriad of
regulations concerning the production and sale of milk, milk products
and meat is public safety. Raw milk is deemed to be so dangerous that
in over twenty states, you may not even purchase it from a farmer, much
less find it in a store. In previous chapters, we've examined the reality behind official campaigns to paint all raw milk as dangerous. In this
chapter, we examine incidents in which millions of people consumed
dangerously contaminated pasteurized milk. Hundreds of thousands
became seriously ill as a direct result, and many died. We then turn our
attention to a number of medical journal reports showing that drinking

modern, commercially produced milk leads to a wide variety of health problems.

## MICHIGAN, 1973: PBB CONTAMINATES THE MILK OF MILLIONS

The story of how Michigan's nine million residents were poisoned with polybromylated biphenyl (PBB), a toxic fire retardant chemical, cuts to the heart of two questions related to milk. First, can we trust the safety of the conventional milk supply? And second, can we trust the pronouncements of government officials about what is safe and what is not, what is good food and what is not?

In 1973, thousands of pounds of PBB were accidentally mixed into livestock feed that was then distributed throughout Michigan. Michigan farmers bought the feed and fed it to their animals, mostly dairy cows. Many cows died within a few months, and many others became obviously but unexplainably ill. Bureaucratic ineptness and corporate malfeasance prevented detection of the mix-up for nearly a year. During that time, milk from Michigan's cows, much of it containing high levels of PBB, remained available for retail sale. Thousands of sick animals culled from poisoned herds were sold for meat. By the time the cause of the problem was discovered, everyone in Michigan and millions of other visitors and consumers of Michigan products in other states had consumed poison. Many became ill.

The discovery of the cause of the problem did not end Michigan's troubles. Six years later, Edwin Chen, staff writer for the *Detroit News*, and author of *PBB: An American Tragedy*, described the incident as "a shameful example of how the government not only failed to protect and help the people but, instead, inflicted further suffering. Even after the astonishing blunder became public, government, university and corporation officials steadfastly downplayed the significance of the accident. They consistently misread and ignored information that came pouring forth in the aftermath of the mix-up. These officials even ridiculed the farmers, accusing them of poor animal husbandry when their prize-winning registered herds sickened and died and, later, accusing them of being hypochondriacs and malingerers when they complained about their own ill health.

"Instead of acting decisively to contain the contamination, the state pursued an undeviating course of suppression, obfuscation and outright deception in order to delay the emergence of the true proportions of the calamity, as each nightmarish prediction by the 'alarmists' became reality and as PBB spread throughout Michigan and beyond. Such stonewalling efforts prolonged, by years, human exposure to the chemical .... Michigan became a vast test tube of nine million human beings."[1]

Dairy farmer Rick Halbert was the first to endure the developing disaster. When milk production started dropping off in September of 1973, Halbert was concerned. The cows didn't seem to be eating. They weren't even chewing their cuds, meaning their digestive systems weren't functioning. Then he noticed that many animals had tears running down their cheeks. During the next few months, Halbert and his vet determined that a mix-up at a processing plant had contaminated the feed with PBB. Many of his animals were dying.

No one at the Michigan State Agriculture Department, the Farm Bureau or Michigan State University would accept his evidence. Veterinarians from all three places told Halbert that tests showed no problems with the feed. In one of Halbert's experiments at home, mice placed on the feed died. Halbert learned that when the Farm Bureau repeated this experiment, the mice there died also. When Halbert told the Bureau's veterinarian about this, his comment was, "This is cattle feed, not mouse food." Meanwhile Halbert's animals continued to die, and his wife and children had become ill. His vet performed autopsies on the dead animals, and all had enlarged livers and inflamed kidneys.[2]

The Agriculture Department and the Farm Bureau continued to deny any problem. At Halbert's request, the U.S. Food and Drug Administration (FDA) conducted a health survey of farm families. Although their investigators found widespread and serious problems, the FDA did not disclose their findings, and publicly stated that they had found no problems of statistical significance.

Two years later, independent physicians and scientists would discover that about one-third of the people they examined showed symptoms of PBB toxicity. By then it was painfully obvious to everyone involved that dairy cows and other animals throughout the state had eaten

contaminated feed, and that tens of thousands of livestock were affected.

Early on, Halbert had hired independent laboratories to look for
the problem ingredient in the feed. About a year after the problem began, some of these scientists found that the feed contained high concentrations of PBB. Halbert then told the state and the Farm Bureau what
his laboratory investigators had discovered. No longer able to deny the
problem, both the state and the company shifted to a strategy of minimi-
zation. The state announced that if contaminated animals tested above a
threshold for PBB, the state would pay for killing them and burial. However, the farmer was still responsible for trying to collect damages from
the Michigan Chemical Corporation and the Farm Bureau—no easy task
with thousands of farmers involved. Many farmers meanwhile had sick
and dying animals with PBB below the threshold level; they could not
even get a free burial site for their animals, much less reimbursement.
State Department of Agriculture officials fought to keep the threshold
level high and thus minimize the economic impact of the entire incident.

The result was chaos. If the state tested a herd and found PBB levels to exceed the threshold, they quarantined the herd; the milk could
not be sold, and the animals could not be sold for meat. Knowing this,
many farmers did not test for PBB levels; they simply shipped their sick-
est animals to market as meat and kept milking the rest. Others who had
animals with levels above the threshold sent their animals to designated
state killing and burial sites. And hundreds of other farmers who tested
their animals found levels of PBB below the threshold for quarantine.
Most of these animals continued to provide milk and meat, although a
few farmers shot their sick animals and buried them on their own land,
rather than sell them into the market.

Regulations involving milk production and PBB were even more
diabolical. The Department of Agriculture took the position that even if
a biopsy of the cow's fat showed PBB in excess of the government standard, she could still be milked. The only test that mattered was the level
of PBB found in the bulk milk tank for all the cows from the herd. If that
level exceeded the state's standard, the farmer could remove enough

animals with particularly high levels to get the bulk milk back below the standard.

PBB contamination thus continued to spread for years after the problem came to light, primarily because the Michigan State Department of Agriculture first procrastinated and ignored signs of the problem and then tried to protect the agriculture industry by refusing to acknowledge that PBB was a serious threat to public health. Throughout the incident, the Department withheld crucial information from both farmers and the public. Prompt identification of the problem and removal of the animals from the milk and meat markets, with fair compensation for the victimized farmers, would have eliminated most of the contamination that occurred.[3]

The extent of the state's duplicity emerged in the sequence of events that unfolded after May of 1974, when the Department of Agriculture learned from farmer Halbert that PBB was in the feed. By then the Department knew that nearly all of the state's eight thousand dairy farms and tens of thousands of farm animals had been contaminated, and that people had been consuming the milk and meat for at least a year. Yet on May 13, after learning of the contamination, the Department issued a press release saying that "only a very few" of the state's dairy farms were involved, and "thus there is little need for concern about the public milk supplies." On the same day, the agriculture director wrote a letter to the governor, claiming, "We can safely say that the public milk supply is cleaner, safer and more wholesome than at any time in history." Within weeks, the Department's own investigators discovered PBB in every part of Michigan, and within two years, over five hundred dairy herds would be quarantined. PBB concentrations in milk tested ranged from two to almost one hundred thirty-four parts per million. Samples of dairy feed showed up to seven thousand seven hundred parts per million.[4]

Independent scientists have been unequivocal about the toxicity of PBBs. Daniel Nebert, MD, is the editor of *Interface: Genes and the Environment*, published by the Center for Environmental Genetics at the University of Cincinnati. In the Spring, 1998 issue, Dr. Nebert and a co-author wrote: "PBBs. . . have been implicated and extensively studied with regard to their role in overt environmental toxicity (e.g. immunosuppression) and cancer. It has not been appreciated, however, that exposure may lead to subtle neurological and central nervous system toxicity and alterations in behavior, including changes in IQ. . .

"The earliest clinical signs that a disaster had occurred [in Michigan] included amnesia, confusion and somnolence (farmers forgot the location of their tractors, were unable to find their way home at the end of the day, and fell asleep in the fields) and lowered white blood cell count, i.e., evidence of immunosuppression. Decreased birth weights, increased respiratory illnesses, and lower IQ values among children born to Michigan mothers exposed in 1973-74 have been reported, and the mental development of these children continues to be followed into adulthood."[5]

After the 1973 incident became known, dairy plants in Michigan refused to buy milk from the contaminated farms. Instead, farmers sold a great deal of milk to manufacturers of processed dairy foods. Some lots of cheese, evaporated milk and butter were found to contain upwards of one thousand parts per billion of PBB. How much of these foods were shipped all over the country, both before and after the accident was discovered, is impossible to estimate. Even in 1978, five years later, a farm in Michigan was found to be shipping highly contaminated products to an Indiana food processor.

Contaminated meat was also shipped far and wide. As late as 1978, feeds in Minnesota, Illinois and Indiana still contained up to two hundred forty parts per billion PBB, and farmers there suffered from symptoms of PBB poisoning. Apparently the feeds reached these other states through feed brokers. And evidence indicates that over fifty million doses of Parke-Davis flu vaccine produced between 1974 and 1976 were contaminated by tens of millions of PBB-containing eggs used in the production of the vaccine.[6]

Perhaps most frightening is the fact that the Michigan story could so easily be repeated—anywhere and with any number of toxic substances. If you buy cartons of commercially produced milk, as most Americans do—or any processed food, for that matter—can you be confident that they aren't contaminated? Can you trust the public health authorities to do their jobs? And, most important, can you trust them to give honest, unbiased and responsible information about the kind of milk you should or shouldn't drink?

ILLINOIS, 1985: PASTEURIZED MILK DISASTER

"Massive Outbreak of Antimicrobial-Resistant Salmonellosis Traced to Pasteurized Milk" was the title of an article that appeared in the *Journal of the American Medical Association* on December 11, 1987. Over 16,000 culture-confirmed cases of infection due to *Salmonella typhimurium* were traced to two brands of pasteurized 2% milk produced by a single dairy plant. The number of persons who were actually affected was estimated as close to two hundred thousand. This was the largest outbreak of salmonellosis ever identified in the United States.[7]

Buried deep in the body of the paper is the statement that nearly three thousand people were hospitalized. "Eighteen deaths occurred," the authors stated.[8]

State and federal health agencies had begun an investigation in March, 1985, when large numbers of people began appearing at emergency rooms complaining of nausea, abdominal pain and diarrhea. The implicated dairy plant was one of the largest in the Midwest, processing about one and one-half million pounds of milk daily from cooperatives in southern Wisconsin and northern Illinois and delivering most of it to one large retail chain. Products from the same plant may have also caused an August, 1984 outbreak of about two hundred cases of salmonellosis, but the results of that investigation were not conclusive.

The strain of salmonella causing the infections was highly resistant to antibiotics, leading investigators to conclude, "The original source of this multiple-resistant strain may well have been dairy cattle; use of antimicrobials on dairy farms can lead to emergence of resistant strains. The precise method by which the milk was repeatedly contaminated could not be proved." Investigators proposed the theory that small amounts of highly contaminated raw milk somehow moved into cross-connections between raw and pasteurized milk during processing.[9] Individuals who had used antibiotics in the month prior to drinking the contaminated milk were much more susceptible to infection and illness.

The concluding paragraph of this article raises some important issues: "The trend toward food production by a relatively small number of large companies rather than by many small businesses achieves economies of scale, permits maximum use of modern technology and may ultimately decrease the amount of food-borne disease that occurs. However, large producers must be especially careful to prevent contamination of their products because the consequences of such contamination can be truly catastrophic."

The Illinois salmonella incident may appear to be a strong argument for pasteurization, and indeed such shabbily produced milk could not be safely distributed without being pasteurized. But pasteurization is obviously no guarantee of safety, and even less so of quality and healthfulness. How much more sense it makes to have numerous local small dairies producing milk for local markets, with raw milk available for those who desire it. Milk of superior quality would command a premium in the marketplace. Any problems that might occur would be small and easily traced to their source.

AFLATOXINS IN MILK :
A POTENTIAL DISASTER IN THE MAKING

*Applied Dairy Microbiology* is the most comprehensive reference and text in its field, providing "a thoroughly updated and expanded treatment of dairy microbiology." The editors have advanced degrees in bacteriology, food science and microbiology, and the contributing authors to the book's fourteen chapters are leading experts in various aspects of dairy science. One chapter, "Public Health Concerns," is written by Elliot T. Ryser, PhD, of Michigan State University. Dr. Ryser's primary interest, according to the university's web page, is the "microbiological safety and quality of fermented and non-fermented dairy products."

Ryser has a great deal to say about the dangers of raw milk, and we will be examining his concerns in Chapter 15. In this chapter, we will focus on what he has to say about aflatoxins—a "major public health concern based on the potential impact of chronic exposure."[10]

Aflatoxins are toxic substances produced by certain molds from the genus *Aspergillus*. "First identified in England in 1960 during an outbreak that involved the death of more than 100,000 turkeys from liver disease, the aflatoxins have become recognized as extremely potent liver carcinogens for both animals and humans," Ryser writes. The most potent aflatoxins are produced when animal feeds containing corn or other grains become moldy, and when cows ingest contaminated feed, aflatoxins are excreted in the milk. "As of 1987," Ryser continues, "at least 34 countries had active or proposed legislation regarding aflatoxin limits in animal feed, with the United States and many European countries also having legislated maximum acceptable levels in fluid milk and dairy products. . . . Present evidence indicates that levels in milk and dairy products are relatively unaffected by pasteurization, sterilization, fermentation, cold storage, freezing, concentrating or drying[11]. . .

"Concern regarding human exposure to aflatoxin is based on results from animal feeding trials. Acute toxicity of aflatoxin is well documented in laboratory animals. Gross liver failure is the normal cause of death in animal studies. Long-term exposure in feed (1 ppm) usually leads to terminal liver cancer with mutagenic and teratogenic effects also widely recognized. Milk from cows that received aflatoxin-contaminated feed produced liver lesions and kidney damage in day-old ducklings. In early feeding studies using rainbow trout, 60 percent of fish on a continuous diet of 20 micrograms (millionths of a gram) per kilogram of body weight developed liver carcinomas within 12 months[12]. . .

"Milk surveillance programs have been conducted in the United States and elsewhere. During the fall of 1977, 43% to 80% of milk samples collected in Alabama, Georgia, North Carolina and South Carolina contained a trace to greater than 0.7 micrograms, with a heavily contaminated corn crop being largely responsible. A similar peak was again observed in late 1988 and early 1989, with a midsummer drought blamed for high levels in midwestern feed corn. More recently, high levels of aflatoxin also forced a Georgia dairy to recall more than 24,000 gallons of pasteurized dairy products during January of 1991. . .

"In European surveys conducted during the late 1960s and 1970s, 11% to 82% of the milk samples examined contained levels of 0.2 to 6.5 micrograms per kilogram, with fewer positive milk samples recorded during the summer grazing period."[13]

This brings up a very important point: aflatoxin contamination of milk is strictly the result of feeding grains to cows, and these grains are often moldy. As discussed in the previous chapter, over half the dairy cows in the United States are now kept in confinement facilities and fed high-grain diets designed to maximize milk production. The amount of aflatoxins in the milk depends on the extent to which stored feeds become moldy and the amount of grain fed. How are we to prevent aflatoxins in milk from causing an epidemic of cancer and other diseases? "Minimizing the presence in milk and dairy products is entirely dependent on careful control and monitoring of mold growth and levels in animal feed," Ryser tells us; federal requirements about the allowable amount of aflatoxin per gram of animal feed will "if observed, consistently yield acceptable milk."

Ryser has nothing else to say about reducing or eliminating the dangers of aflatoxins. There is not a word about the desirability of grass feeding or the possibility of utilizing pasture-based systems, or even the importance of using less grain in feeding. His chapter meanwhile contains numerous passages—mostly misleading and often inaccurate—describing the alleged dangers of raw milk and championing the need for compulsory pasteurization. As mentioned above, pasteurization does not change the toxicity and carcinogenicity of aflatoxins. Since Ryser's primary interest is said to be the "safety and quality of fermented and non-fermented dairy products," one must wonder why Ryser focuses so little attention on aflatoxins and puts so much emphasis on the alleged dangers of raw milk.

In Chapter 18, we will address the issue of milk quality as we examine the work of a number of scientists who have studied soil and animal health from an integrated and holistic perspective. Their work forms the foundation for the movement called sustainable agriculture. The so-called experts today—the Rysers in academia and government who have supported the rise of industrial agricultural "efficiency"—appear to have no true interest in either the health of the animals or the safety and quality of their milk. Aflatoxins are a particularly potent example of all that is wrong with modern milk. The "scientists" who brush off the problems of aflatoxins and other poisons—while denigrating and outlawing the viable alternative of raw milk from healthy animals—belong to the circle of corporate "experts" who hew to the party line and serve those in positions of great economic power.

ANTIBIOTICS IN MILK

The high incidence of mastitis, laminitis and other diseases in cows kept in confinement facilities leads to widespread use of antibiotics. Again, quoting Dr. Ryser: "As of May 1992, at least 60 different animal drugs were approved for use. However, at the same time, 52 non-FDA approved, residue-producing drugs were also suspected of being used illegally. . . . Because milk from various farms is typically commingled, unsafe or illegal animal drug residues can contaminate large volumes of milk, with the FDA estimating that milk from a single sulfamethazine-treated cow can contaminate the milk from 70,000 cows when pooled. Two widely publicized 1989 surveys published in *The Wall Street Journal* highlighted the scope of this problem with 20% and 38% of the retail milk samples tested containing animal drug residues and other nonapproved drugs."[14]

Penicillin G is one of the most popular drugs used on dairy farms; no prescription is required, and it is commonly infused directly into the inflamed mammary glands of mastitic cows. This practice "leads to almost total excretion in the milk," Ryser writes. "Most reports suggest that penicillin G and its derivatives are relatively resistant to heat . . . . Penicillin also has the distinction of being the most allergenic drug known, with approximately 10% of the human population reportedly being sensitive. Because several early reports traced allergic dermatitis to tainted milk, a maximum legal limit of 0.01 ppm has been established for penicillin in fluid milk[15] . . .

"The sulfonamides, another important group of antimicrobials, have been used to treat systemic and cutaneous infections in farm animals for more than 50 years. . . . Like the penicillins, the sulfonamides are also resistant to most food processing conditions, with activity being retained during prolonged heating. . . . One particular sulfonamide banned for use in lactating dairy cattle, namely sulfamethazine, is a suspected human carcinogen based on animal studies. Considerable public concern was raised in 1988 when trace levels of sulfamethazine were detected in the United States milk supply. . . . Other commonly used drugs, including chloramphenicol and ivermectin (an anti-worming agent), have been associated with aplastic anemia (an irreversible and potentially fatal bone marrow disease) and various neurological disorders.[16]

"In 1988, 71% of retail and tanker truck milk samples tested in the northeast United States were contaminated with sulfonamides at levels of at least 5 ppb. Half of the positive samples contained greater than 25 ppb sulfonamide, with one sample having 15,000 to 20,000 ppb. Sulfamethazine was the dominant sulfonamide detected and was sometimes present at levels as high as 40 ppb, eight times higher than the maximum allowable level. In another survey involving retail milk from 10 major United States cities, sulfonamides were detected in 36 of 49 samples . . . . However, in Prince Edward Island, Canada, where sulfonamides are not sold over the counter, 1000 tanker truck samples tested negative for these drugs."[17]

Other authors have cited poor dairy herd management, inadequate record keeping on mastitic cows and inappropriate use of the drugs in question as the prime reasons for the high incidence of antibiotic residues in milk.[18,19] The use of recombinant bovine growth hormone in the United States (Canada has banned the drug), discussed in the next section, has resulted in a higher incidence of disease in dairy cows and even more widespread use of antibiotics.

The development of new antibiotic-resistant bacterial pathogens as a result of long-term exposure to antibiotics in milk is another problem. The milk that caused the salmonellosis outbreak involving nearly two hundred thousand people contained a rare strain of salmonella that was resistant to fourteen different antibiotics, including eight that are commonly found as drug residues in milk.[20] This development highlights the inherent dangers of the confinement dairy system—the animals are often so sick that only the overuse of antibiotics allows milk production to continue in otherwise intolerable conditions.

RECOMBINANT BOVINE GROWTH HORMONE

The FDA in 1985 approved commercial sales of unlabeled milk and meat from cows treated in large-scale trials with synthetic recombinant

Contented cows graze on green pastures in this 1909 Carnation Milk ad. Consumers recognized the fact that healthy milk came from healthy cows, but may not have understood how the heat-intensive production of condensed milk compromised nutrients.

Mr. W. A Batman delivers raw milk in 1944, produced on his 40-acre farm. Note the inscription "TB and Bang [brucellosis] Tested." Even in 1944, farmers knew how to guarantee safe, raw milk.
Courtesy Country Magazine.

"Milk! Real milk from a cow!"

One of several National Dairy Products Corporation ads appearing in the National Geographic 1944-45. The text reads: "This GI's appetite for milk has been officially encouraged from the start of training for the sake of good nutrition. Service menus provide generous portions of all dairy products—and help make service men huskier and healthier than ever before in history." The ad also praises ice cream, butter and cheese as products that can be shipped to troops in combat areas.

A modern dairy herd is kept indoors on cement floors and fed dry feed while green grass, nature's perfect food for cows, grows outdoors.
Photo by Marcus Halevi

Holstein cows crowded into "comfort stalls" approximately five feet by six feet where they spend their entire lives. Lameness is common and the average life-span is 42 months, compared to 12-15 years for a cow on pasture.
Photo by Marcus Halevi.

Replacing downer cows is one of the major costs in the modern dairy industry. Much fast-food hamburger meat comes from cows that become lame in confinement operations.
Photo by Marcus Halevi.

A tanker truck delivers milk to the processing plant.
Photo by Marcus Halevi.

A modern milk factory, designed and operated by chemical engineers.
Photo by Marcus Halevi.

Inside the milk factory, miles of pipes carry milk in various stages of processing. All these pipes must be cleaned and residues invariably end up in the milk.
Photo by Sally Fallon Morell.

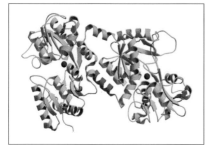

Elegant complexity is revealed in this diagram of lactoferrin, an enzyme in raw milk that protects against pathogens and ensures complete assimilation of iron in the milk. The rapid heating of pasteurization warps and distorts this fragile, three-dimensional structure, rendering it ineffective and possibly toxic. .

A Jersey cow grazes contentedly on green grass. The milk of a Jersey cow has a much higher butterfat content than that of modern Holstein cows. Photo by Marcus Halevi.

Bunching and munching, cows demonstrate the herd tendency as they move across fresh pasture. Photo by Sally Fallon Morell.

Pale butter made from cream of confinement cows compared to rich yellow butter from cream of cows on pasture. The natural yellow color indicates higher levels of fat-soluble nutrients. Commercial butter appears yellow because coloring is added. Photo by Linda Joyce Forristal

Modern raw milk delivery truck in Italy. A vending machine dispenses raw milk from the side of the truck. Similar vending machines are installed in schools and office buildings throughout continental Europe.

bovine growth hormone (rBGH) manufactured by Monsanto, American Cyanamid, Dow Chemical, Upjohn and Eli Lilly. By 1990, evidence from published and unpublished industry sources had raised questions about the safety of rBGH milk. Increased incidence of mastitis in rBGH cows led to higher levels of white blood cells (pus) in their milk, and contamination with antibiotics used in treatment. The structure of rBGH differs significantly from the natural growth hormone, and milk from rBGH cows contains excessive levels of insulin-like growth factor (IGF-1), which is associated with cancer.[21]

In spite of these unresolved concerns, the FDA approved large-scale commercial use and sale of rBGH milk in 1993. Subsequent regulatory guidelines effectively banned the labeling of such milk. In Canada, meanwhile, a massive grassroots mobilization opposed Monsanto's push for approval by the Health Protection Branch of Health Canada and helped gain a one-year moratorium on approval in 1994. When that moratorium ended, over three hundred organizations officially called for an extension to the ban. More than one hundred thousand individual Canadians sent post cards and letters to the federal health minister, and a health food magazine collected five hundred thousand names on a petition opposing the use of rBGH.[22]

The moratorium did end in July, 1995, but Health Canada asked the manufacturers for more research on animal safety before making a decision. Over three years of controversy and turmoil within Health Canada followed, but on January 14, 1999, the agency announced that it would not approve rBGH for sale in Canada. Agency officials noted that the decision was based on more than nine years' review of studies on rBGH and animal and human safety. Veterinary experts cited a twenty-five percent increased risk of mastitis and a fifty percent increased risk of laminitis and associated lameness associated with use of rBGH. These and other health problems led to a twenty to twenty-five percent increased risk of culling from the herd. "The findings of the animal safety committee, when combined with our own assessment," a key official at Health Canada declared, "made it quite clear that Health Canada had to reject the request for approval to use rBGH in Canada. It presents a sufficient and unacceptable threat to the safety of dairy cows."[23]

Samuel Epstein, MD, Professor of Environmental Medicine at the University of Illinois School of Public Health and Chairman of the Cancer Prevention Coalition, has detailed the human risks of rBGH. Epstein cites industry studies showing "that rBGH milk may contain more than a 10-fold increase in IGF-1 concentrations."[24] He is particularly concerned with increased risks of gastrointestinal and breast cancers from exposure to IGF-1. After detailing the physiological mechanisms involved, Epstein quotes from an article in *Cancer Research*, ". . . the possibility exists that increased levels of circulating IGF-1 may contribute to breast tumor growth."[25] His conclusion emphasizes the fact that we simply do not know what the long-term effects of rBGH may be:

"In short, with the active complicity of the FDA, the entire nation is currently being subjected to an experiment involving large-scale adulteration of an age-old dietary staple by a poorly characterized and unlabeled biotechnology product. Disturbingly, this experiment benefits only a very small segment of the agri-chemical industry while providing no matching benefits to consumers. Even more disturbingly, it poses major potential public health risks for the entire U.S. population."[26]

JOHNE'S DISEASE

Johne's (pronounced yo-neez) disease or paratuberculosis is a common ailment of cattle, resulting in chronic or intermittent diarrhea, emaciation and death. Identified over a century ago, the disease causes losses estimated to exceed one and one-half billion dollars per year. The infectious organism, *Mycobacterium avium paratuberculosis* (Map) resides in the intestines of dairy cattle, disseminates to the udder and is excreted directly into the milk of infected cows. Surveys indicate that forty percent of dairy herds in the U.S. are infected and the rate is increasing. According to a website sponsored by several U.S. government agencies, "Every time animals are moved, new herds become infected, and if nothing changes with regard to a Map control program in the U.S., the dairy herd infection rate may reach 100%."[27]

Although few members of the public have heard of Johne's disease, it is the subject of intense scientific debate within the world of milk production. This debate centers not on its presence in dairy herds—a problem now widely acknowledged among scientists and about which farmers are becoming more aware—but on the effect the Johne's bacterium has on human beings. According to Kurt Gutknecht, writing for the *Wisconsin Agriculturist*, the dairy industry has been slow to admit the possible relationship between Johne's disease in cattle and Crohn's disease in humans. "The public health issue has been on the periphery of the dairy industry's agenda for years, a nagging concern that's never made it to the front burner. Most medical researchers studying Crohn's disease think it's an autoimmune disease. Nevertheless, a core of researchers continue to provide troubling evidence of links between Johne's and Crohn's disease. And many of those afflicted by Crohn's disease are starting to pay attention—and some are embittered by the dairy industry's perceived reluctance to tackle the issue openly."[28]

The Map bacterium is difficult to detect and culture, and only a small percentage of infected animals with no microscopically visible organisms will react positively to an immunological test. Similarly in humans, the microbe often goes undetected because it is difficult to identify using standard laboratory procedures. Nevertheless, according to Dr. John Hermon-Taylor, chairman of the department of surgery, St. George's Hospital Medical School, London, England, and an internationally known expert on Crohn's disease, "When the evidence is considered, it's difficult to argue the case that the organism is not involved. It is certain that *M. paratuberculosis* can be pathogenic in humans and that it's very likely that it causes a significant proportion—even a substantial proportion—of Crohn's disease in humans."[29]

The FDA and the dairy industry argue that pasteurization is the only way to completely rid milk of pathogenic organisms; but the Johne's bacterium survives pasteurization! "The ability of infected animals, even those not showing any symptoms of infection, to shed the organism and its detection in 7% of the pasteurized milk tested in England between 1990 and 1995 shows that humans are exposed to intact *M. paratuberculosis*, and that the possibility that some of these *M. paratuberculosis* are still viable is very high," says Dr. Hermon-Taylor.[30]

In response, the industry is moving slowly towards mandatory testing and disclosure (Wisconsin passed such legislation in the early

1990s), research into pharmaceuticals to combat the disease. . . .and ultrapasteurization involving higher temperatures to kill the organism. Whether the organism will become resistant to the higher temperatures remains to be seen, but meanwhile the obvious answer to the problem is to return our dairy animals to pasture (confinement dairies are made-to-order for spreading diseases like Johne's) and to consume our milk raw. Beneficial bacteria in raw milk can take care of pathogens, and because raw milk is so easy to digest and provides such superior nourishment, it does not create the conditions allowing Map to take hold in the gut.

INSIDE THE MILK PLANT

The modern confinement dairy system sends its milk to modern processing plants. A rare glimpse into today's milk factory is provided by Emily Green, writing for the *Los Angeles Times*: "Visitors are not allowed in modern milk processing plants, where hygiene is of utmost importance. . . . Inside the plant, all you can see is stainless steel. Inside that machinery, milk shipped from the farm is remade. First it is separated in centrifuges into fat, protein and various other solids and liquids. Once segregated, these are reconstituted to set levels for whole, lowfat and nonfat milks. What is left over will go to butter, cream, cheese, dried milk and a host of other milk products. Of the reconstituted milks, whole milk will most closely approximate original cow's milk. When fat is removed, it is replaced with protein- and vitamin-rich skimmed milk powder or concentrate. Standardization ensures that milk is consistent, that one glass of any given type tastes exactly like the next.

"The milk is then sent by tanker trucks to bottling plants. At the plants 6400-gallon tankers disgorge milk into silos. Before entering the bottling area, workers must dip the soles of their shoes in antiseptic baths. Staff members wear smocks, hairnets, jackets for the cold and ear plugs against the roar of machinery. Conveyor belts foam with anti-bacterial lubricant. Banks of computers chart the milk flow so raw milk cannot contaminate cooked. The milk is pasteurized at 161 degrees for 15 seconds by rushing the milk past a superheated stainless steel plate. If the temperature is 230, it is called ultrapasteurized. This will have a distinct cooked milk taste but it is sterile and can be sold on grocery shelves. It does not even require refrigeration. As it is cooked, the milk is homogenized by a pressure treatment that breaks down the fat globules so the milk won't separate. Once processed, the milk will last for weeks, not days."[31]

And because it will last for weeks, modern milk is shipped all over the country. Texas, which used to have a thriving sector of small dairy farms, now gets its milk from Wisconsin. Restaurants in the rich farm country of Pennsylvania get their butterpats from Illinois. And shoppers in supermarkets all over the country may get milk that is several weeks old and comes from thousands of miles away.

PROTEIN ENRICHED

While Green describes the nonfat dried milk added to lowfat milks as "protein- and vitamin-rich," this additive actually compromises the nutritional quality of commercial milk in many ways. Production of nonfat dried milk involves forcing skim milk out a tiny hole at high temperatures and pressures, a process that not only destroys nutrients but also causes the production of nitrates—which are potent carcinogens. Furthermore, the process causes oxidation of the cholesterol in milk. As I have discussed, cholesterol in food does not present any adverse effects; in fact, cholesterol is an important nutrient, especially for the growing child. However, oxidized cholesterol has been shown to initiate the process of injury and pathological plaque build-up in the arteries; in animal experiments in which large amounts of cholesterol induce atherosclerotic lesions, researchers use oxidized cholesterol, not the undamaged cholesterol that occurs normally in food.[32] Thus the obedient consumer who drinks reduced-fat milk in order to avoid heart disease and cancer actually increases his intake of substances that cause heart disease and cancer.

It is true that the nonfat dried milk added to reduced-fat milks is "protein-rich," but therein lies another danger of commercial milk. The body needs vitamin A to assimilate protein. When we consume foods rich in protein without the supporting fats—as in reduced fat milks to which nonfat, high-protein dried milk is added—the body draws on the vitamin A stored in the liver. Eventually these stores become depleted, ushering in a host of diseases—from autoimmune disease to cancer. In growing children, diets rich in protein but low in fat result in rapid spindly growth, poor posture, lack of muscle tone and poor eyesight[33]—a kind of Ichabod Crane syndrome. This is exactly what we are seeing in America today as government and industry have joined to promote consumption of "protein-rich" lowfat milks to growing children.

Nonfat dried milk does not appear on the label of commercial reduced-fat milk because this practice spans the entire industry. The FDA considers the addition of nonfat dried milk an "industry standard" and does not require labeling.

In September of 2008, an outbreak of kidney failure in Chinese babies made the world aware of another problem with dried milk—the presence of the additive melamine. Over six thousand babies were afflicted and several died.[34]

Melamine is an industrial compound used as a pesticide and fire retardant. Its addition to milk can make milk appear to contain more protein than it actually contains, to help pass quality testing. In China, the compound was added by local dealers to whom farmers sold the milk. Melamine ingestion causes not only kidney stones, but may lead to reproductive damage. It is a common additive to fish and livestock feed, especially in China, so it can end up in milk even if not purposely added. Spray drying concentrates the melamine in the milk—and babies getting milk-based formula as their only food would be most at risk—but melamine can show up in fluid milk and other milk products as well.

The incidents and reports described above make it clear that commercially produced milk often contains a wide variety of undesirable substances, many the result of accidental contamination but others deliberately added. We'll discuss other disturbing incidents involving pasteurized milk when we compare the safety of raw versus pasteurized milk in Chapter 15.

# 13
# Lactose Intolerance and Modern Milk

Lactose, or milk sugar, is the carbohydrate in milk. Some people lack the ability to make adequate amounts of lactase, the enzyme that digests lactose by splitting it into the simple sugars galactose and glucose, and they may experience a variety of symptoms when consuming milk products. When undigested lactose reaches the large intestine, it is fermented by microflora in the colon. The result may be intestinal cramps, flatulence and diarrhea.

Virtually all infants produce adequate lactase to digest mother's milk in the small intestine. But in many people, lactase production declines at age three or four. The greatest decline takes place in individuals from cultures that have not kept dairy animals nor used milk beyond weaning, such as Australian Aborigines and the indigenous peoples of North America. Other cultures, including many Asian cultures and most native Africans, have kept some dairy animals but used milk in insignificant amounts in the adult diet; these peoples exhibit a marked decline in the ability to digest lactose as adults.

Those least likely to develop lactose intolerance are the descendants of European, Middle Eastern, East African and Asian pastoral cultures. The explanation for this tolerance to lactose is that over the centuries, the genes for lactose tolerance increased in populations in which adults consumed non-fermented milk. Intermarriage between these cultures also has increased lactose tolerance in cultures originally lactose intolerant, because the gene conferring tolerance is dominant.[1]

Fermented milk products such as cheese, buttermilk, clabbered milk, kefir and yogurt are products in which a portion of the lactose is transformed into lactic acid. Traditional dairy cultures everywhere, particularly in more southern regions, have always made most of their milk into these fermented products.

The enzyme lactase is not produced in adults of any animal species except humans, who are thus uniquely adapted to digest lactose as adults. Human milk is richer in lactose than cow's milk, with seven and one-half grams per one hundred grams, compared to four and one-half grams in cow's milk.

Raw milk contains lactase, but the enzyme is destroyed by pasteurization. Pasteurization also destroys beneficial bacteria, which are the source of lactase in raw milk and which can produce lactase in the digestive tract.[2] This is one reason why raw milk is much easier to digest than pasteurized; in fact, most children and adults unable to digest pasteurized milk and diagnosed as lactose intolerant digest raw milk beautifully. This has been the case for hundreds of individuals I have worked with professionally, an observation recently validated by a survey conducted in the state of Michigan. Over eighty percent of respondents diagnosed by their doctors as lactose intolerant indicated that they could drink raw milk without problem.[3]

On the other hand, one must keep in mind that intolerance in infants may be related to various disorders, including cystic fibrosis, celiac disease and toxicity caused by drugs or immunizations.

TESTING FOR LACTOSE INTOLERANCE

Lactose intolerance tests administered to Afro-American and Caucasian Americans in 1965 found that only about ten percent of whites showed symptoms of intolerance, compared to about seventy percent of blacks. Tests in Africa showed twenty percent of pastoral, cattle-herding tribes to be intolerant, compared to eighty percent of non-pastoral tribes. By 1970, numerous papers reported general intolerance to lactose among various ethnic groups, including Eskimos, Israeli Jews, Japanese and other Asians, and native South Americans. According to these tests, real adult lactose tolerance was found only in northern Europeans and their descendants (including most white Americans), as well as descendants of African pastoral tribes.

In considering the meaning of such tests, however, it is important to keep in mind that since raw milk contains lactase, many individuals who tolerate neither a dose of lactose in a test, nor a glass of pasteurized milk, digest raw milk without any problem, especially if raw milk is introduced slowly.

In cultures where milk was important, traditional peoples typically consumed milk not only raw, but also fermented. Fermentation breaks down at least half the lactose, while leaving intact the lactase and beneficial bacteria that aid in digesting the lactose that remains. The diagnosis of "lactose intolerance" in individuals who consume these foods as part of a healthy traditional diet but who fail to digest a test dose of lactose has no practical significance. Unfortunately, such academic studies are typical because of a refusal on the part of the research community, dominated as it is by food-industry funds, to even consider the advantages and health benefits of raw milk and its fermented products.

## LACTOSE INTOLERANCE IN AFRICAN TRIBES

Differences in the ability of various population groups to digest lactose are reflected in the ways they utilize traditional raw milk and its products. The Fulani people of Nigeria, who may have originally come from Asia, have followed a pastoral way of life for thousands of years. During the last three hundred years, some moved into villages and towns and intermarried with a group that did not keep cattle, the Hausa. Two groups of Fulani people with distinctive lifestyles resulted, the pastoral Fulani, who continued to live with their cattle in the countryside, and the Hausa-Fulani of the towns. In 1972, a *Scientific American* report by Norman Kretchmer described the differences in lactose ingestion between the two still interdependent groups.[4]

The pastoral Fulani milk their cows in the early morning and drink some milk fresh. Much of the remaining milk is cultured and sent to the Hausa-Fulani in the towns and villages for use, often later the same day. This fermented milk is a kind of yogurt called *nono*, allowed to culture in the morning sun until it becomes completely fermented and watery; fermented grain such as millet is added as a thickener. Virtually no lactose remains in the nutritious final product.

Most of the Hausa and Hausa-Fulani townspeople were found to be intolerant of lactose test doses, while most of the pastoral Fulani were tolerant. But people from both of the groups who tested intolerant of pure lactose were able to eat *nono* without trouble.

Kretchmer found that areas of Africa where dairying took place coincided with areas of general lactose tolerance. The blacks brought to America were mostly from areas of West Africa where there was no dairying, and they were originally intolerant to lactose. This intolerance declined over the years through the intermingling with northern European genes.[5]

A WIDESPREAD MISCONCEPTION

Why did some groups of humans develop greater tolerance to lactose? The development of dairying itself may be the simple explanation. At least ten thousand years ago, small groups of humans began to milk cattle, sheep, goats and reindeer. Chance genetic mutations may have given some people high enough lactase activity to digest more nonfermented milk as adults, and this may have provided selective survival advantages. People with the mutation could utilize their animals' milk as food, and then sell it in fermented form to others who were less lactose tolerant.[6] Studies indicate that lactose tolerance is transmitted genetically and is a dominant trait, that is, genes for tolerance from one of the parents are sufficient to make the child tolerant to lactose.

An interesting paper most relevant to the issue of lactose intolerance appeared in a 1984 article published in the *American Journal of Clinical Nutrition*. The authors wrote: "The use of fermented dairy foods is most common in areas of the world where lactase deficiency is prevalent. Recently, we have shown that the digestion of lactose in yogurt is enhanced as compared to that from [pasteurized] milk. This enhanced digestion is apparently due to inherent B-galactosidase in yogurt, which is active in the gastrointestinal tract after the consumption of the yogurt. Furthermore, yogurt is well tolerated by lactase-deficient subjects resulting in little or no gastrointestinal distress. . . . Furthermore, pasteurization of the yogurt eliminated the enhanced digestion of lactose and reduced the inherent lactase activity of the yogurt by 10-fold."[7]

This research shows that yogurt and fermented milk products are easily digested, not only because much of the lactose has been broken down during the fermentation process, but also because the enzyme B-galactosidase in these products enhances the digestion of the remaining lactose. Enzymes are, of course, lost when the yogurt is pasteurized. The team did not work with raw milk but their research strongly implies that enzymes in raw milk are helpful in its digestion, and helps show why raw milk is so often well tolerated by individuals who get sick when they drink pasteurized milk. A survey commissioned by the Weston A. Price Foundation indicates that about twenty-nine million Americans are lactose intolerant, about twenty-four million of whom could drink milk without problem were raw milk widely available.[8]

The belief in widespread lactose intolerance is a misconception; most people are simply intolerant to the pasteurized homogenized milk products commercially available. People who test positive for lactose intolerance and have problems with commercial milk often digest raw milk with no problems at all, especially raw milk from animals fed mostly grass. Raw fermented products such as yogurt, kefir, and cheeses properly made from such milk are wonderful foods that are easily digested by almost everyone.

The incidents and reports discussed above reinforce and confirm my professional experience—pasteurized dairy products are neither desirable nor healthy, and at times are unsafe. Even small amounts cause aggravation in individuals with medical problems. Avoidance is the best course, with a focus on securing a source of high-quality raw milk.

# 14

# Milk Homogenization and Heart Disease

*Milk has been changed over the years by processing into an unrecognizable physicochemical emulsion which bears very little resemblance to the original, natural, and nutritional milk.*

> Kurt Oster, MD, Chief of Cardiology
> and Chairman of the Department of Medicine,
> Park City Hospital, Bridgeport, Connecticut

*Pasteurized homogenized milk? Might as well drink water with chalk in it.*

> Dan Logue, Dairy Farmer, Woodbury, Connecticut

*Things are never what they seem,*
*Skim milk masquerades as cream.*
> William S. Gilbert

Although almost all commercially available milk today is sold in either plastic bottles or plastic-lined cardboard containers, for many years milk came in glass bottles. And before the commercial introduction of the glass milk container in 1878, distributors sold milk received from outlying farmers or city dairies in ten-gallon bulk cans. The dairyman himself was often the milkman, bringing his product into nearby towns.

In the early days of milk delivery, customers met the milkman with their own containers, to be filled with fresh milk.

Later, larger containers equipped with stirrers and faucets replaced the ten-gallon can. The stirrers were needed to mix the milk and keep the cream from rising to the top, avoiding the problem of one customer receiving mostly cream while others received mostly skim milk.[1] Milk is a natural emulsion; when shaken, the fat globules disperse throughout the rest of the fluid. When allowed to stand, the cream in unhomogenized milk comes to the top because it is lighter than the rest of the fluid. Homogenization fixes the emulsion: no more cream at the top.

The process of homogenization was first invented to emulsify margarine. Then in 1899, milk homogenization began; a process that forced milk through hair-like tubules was patented as a way to fix the fat in milk into an emulsified state. Pasteurization made it possible to transport milk for long distances, and that made homogenization desirable for the industry because homogenization solved the cream separation problem that occurred during transport. Homogenization crushes milk by forcing it under high pressure and temperature through holes in a die. The fat particles that result are much smaller than fat globules that occur in natural milk. The combination of pasteurization and homogenization meant that milk could be transported over long distances and stored for a long time.

CONSUMER RESISTANCE

For many years, the public refused to cooperate and purchased little homogenized milk. Skeptical consumers were disturbed both by the change in flavor and the absence of the cream line at the top of the bottle; the amount of cream and its color had always provided a way for consumers to judge the quality of the milk. Public acceptance of homogenization proved evasive for over thirty years. Finally, in 1932, in the midst of the Great Depression, the McDonald Dairy in Flint, Michigan began a new campaign to sell the public on an old product.

Quite a campaign it was. The dairy hired men to do tests in milk-company laboratories; some drank pasteurized but unhomogenized milk, while others drank pasteurized homogenized milk. After controlled periods of time, they regurgitated the milks, which were examined for curd formation. Milk company spokesmen claimed that the curd in the group drinking homogenized milk was much better digested. The curd from both groups was preserved in formaldehyde, and milk salesmen then carried the specimens around as proof of homogenization's advantages. This and other techniques helped homogenized milk gain market share; by 1940, one-third of the states recognized homogenized milk in their regulations and about one-third of the milk sold in America was homogenized. By the late fifties nearly all milk was homogenized.[2]

The tenacity of the milk industry in pushing homogenization is instructive. Despite massive public resistance for several decades, milk companies eventually succeeded in convincing Americans to accept a product designed solely for the profit and convenience of manufacturers and distributors. The mantra "Progress is our most important product," advertising slogan of the General Electric company and the *zeitgeist* of the post-war era, hastened the demise of traditional foodways, of which milk with the cream on top was one. Ronald Reagan, a former B-movie leading man, destined to become Governor of California and later President of the United States, was the chief salesman for Progress; Reagan hosted the immensely popular TV show "The General Electric Theatre" throughout the 1950s. Homogenized milk was progress. Today most Americans have never known anything else.

The promotion of homogenization received not a little help from the media, always friendly toward an industry that provided millions yearly in advertising revenues. Scientists hired by the dairy companies and their allies pitched in, and industry press releases and publications trumpeted the party line. Referring to a collaborative 1938 study at Children's Hospital of Philadelphia, dairy-industry spokesman Ralph Selitzer concluded: "The results established the digestibility of homogenized milk. This fact, coupled with the consumers' preference for the creamy texture and better taste of homogenized milk, increased the product's popularity."[3]

Nevertheless, resistance to homogenization continued among a small number of health-conscious consumers, bolstered by the writings of a doctor and scientist named Kurt Oster.

TWO HEART ATTACKS
AND ONE REBEL CHIEF OF CARDIOLOGY

Kurt Oster fled Nazi Germany to America in the late 1930s. He was a graduate of two of Europe's most distinguished universities, with a medical degree from the University of Cologne and a graduate degree in chemistry from the University of Berlin. Before coming to the United States, he had served as chief resident in pediatrics in a large hospital in Berlin. He began his research work in this country in New York City, first at Mount Sinai Hospital and then at the College of Physicians and Surgeons at Columbia University. He collaborated with internationally renowned scientists, including Charles Lieb, a co-discoverer of prostaglandin precursors. During this phase of his career, he and his colleagues published a number of important medical and biochemical papers.[4]

During World War II, Oster went to work for a large pharmaceutical company in Fairfield, Connecticut. He was involved with the production of penicillin, the first antibiotic, for the armed forces and rose to become medical director of the company. At the same time, he also began to work at nearby Park City Hospital in Bridgeport, where he would become Chief of Cardiology and Chairman of the Department of Medicine.

Over the next twenty years, he enjoyed success at many levels. But this eminent cardiologist suffered two heart attacks. He had followed the medical establishment's low-fat and low-cholesterol edicts before the first heart attack, and even more carefully during his recovery. But after the second attack, he decided that he and other heart specialists did not understand the causes of heart and circulatory diseases. With the ancient admonition, "Physician, heal thyself!" as his credo, he decided to concentrate his research on atherosclerosis, the disease of the arteries that leads to many health problems, including heart attacks.[5]

In his thorough search of the medical literature he did not find a single study validating the notion that dietary cholesterol and saturated fats played a major role in causing heart and circulatory disease. He concluded that special interest groups, by exploiting the unproven hypothesis, made a mockery of the scientific method.

## XANTHINE OXIDASE

Oster began studying and comparing the structure and biochemistry of healthy and diseased arterial tissue. He decided to investigate plasmalogen, an essential fatty component of many cell membranes in widely scattered tissues throughout the human body. Plasmalogen makes up a substantial part of the membranes surrounding heart muscle cells and the cells that make up the walls of arteries. It is also present in the myelin sheath surrounding nerve fibers and in a few other tissues. But it is not found in other parts of the human anatomy.

Plasmalogen had been discovered by the German biochemist Robert Feulgen, known as the father of plasmalogen research, and it had been studied much more extensively in Germany than anywhere else. In 1968, Oster visited the most prominent researcher at the University of Cologne. Oster's fluency in German and his personal contacts afforded him considerable insight into plasmalogen's possible role in heart and circulatory disease. His trained mind sensed a relationship between plasmalogen and atherosclerosis.[6]

Oster and his research team at Park City Hospital analyzed surgical specimens and autopsy tissue. They discovered that heart and artery tissue that should contain plasmalogen often contained none. It is well known that atherosclerosis begins with a small wound or lesion in the wall of the artery. Oster reasoned that the initial lesion was caused by the loss of plasmalogen from the cells lining the artery. Fatty streaks, gelatinous lumps and small blood clots come next, followed by the plaque of advanced atherosclerosis, deposits composed of cholesterol, fibrin and calcium. The plaques grow, leading to hemorrhages and blood clots.

The big question was what caused the lack of plasmalogen in the heart muscle and the tissue lining the arteries. From his research at Columbia some twenty-six years earlier, Oster knew that the enzyme xanthine oxidase (XO) has the capacity to oxidize or change plasmalogen into a different substance, making it appear that the plasmalogen had disappeared. The body makes XO, but XO and plasmalogen are not normally found in the same tissue; the heart, therefore, normally contains plasmologen but not XO. Oster's own research, published in 1944, had shown that the presence of XO in the liver and in the mucous membrane of the small intestine was directly responsible for the natural absence of plasmalogen from the cell membranes at these sites. If XO somehow made its way to the heart and its arteries, that might explain the absence of plasmalogen in the surgical specimens and autopsy tissues from pathological hearts. But Oster could see no reason why the body's own XO would travel to the heart and cause damage. Because many foods contain XO, he began to consider a dietary explanation. Meanwhile, he spent weeks in the laboratory studying the effects of XO on living tissue. He confirmed the reaction he had noted between XO and plasmalogen years before at Columbia. His next challenge was to identify XO when it was present in living tissue, and to establish XO's presence in the heart and artery tissue where plasmalogen disappeared.

But this was not an area where Oster had technical expertise. By chance, however, he met Dr. Donald Ross of Fairfield University in November of 1969. Ross's doctoral dissertation had been on xanthine oxidase in Japanese beetles. The men teamed up and worked together for over twenty years.

Years of laboratory research followed their initial meeting. The team confirmed the presence of biologically active XO in tissue samples from diseased areas of arteries and in heart muscle tissue. No one had ever searched for XO in plasmalogen-rich artery tissue before because XO and plasmalogen were known to be incompatible. Oster and Ross reported their surprising results in the *Proceedings of the Society for Experimental Biology and Medicine* in 1973. The title: "The Presence of Ectopic [out of place] Xanthine Oxidase in Atherosclerotic Plaques and Myocardial Tissues."

What was the source of the XO found in the autopsy tissues? Normal human serum (the fluid part of the blood) does not contain XO. Oster and Ross considered two possible sources. One was liver cells; patients with acute liver disease showed increased serum levels of xanthine oxidase, and those with chronic liver disease occasionally showed moderate elevations. Another potential source was cow's milk, ". . . presently under investigation in this laboratory since it has been shown that milk antibodies are significantly elevated in the blood of male patients with heart disease."[7]

It seemed unlikely that XO would travel from one part of the body to another, from the liver to the heart, to the arteries in particular, especially in people with no history of liver disease. The presence of milk antibodies in the blood of heart disease patients signaled that foreign proteins in milk (XO, like all enzymes, is a protein) had entered the system and triggered an immune response. Oster asked himself, "Which widely consumed food contains large amounts of XO?"

Cow's milk is the most widely consumed food containing high levels of XO. Thorough cooking destroys XO, but pasteurization destroys only about half of the XO in milk. Knowing this, Oster now looked for a link between XO in milk and the loss of plasmalogen in arteries and heart muscle tissue.

He knew that people have drunk milk for upwards of ten thousand years, and that milk and milk products were central in the diets of many cultures. But the epidemic of atherosclerosis was recent. These facts argued against traditional milk and milk products as the culprit. But the homogenization of milk became widespread in America during the 1930s and nearly universal in the 1940s—the same decades during which the incidence of atherosclerotic heart disease began to climb. Oster theorized that the homogenization of milk somehow increased the biological availability of XO.

Oster found support for his theories in the science of epidemiology—the study of the incidence and distribution of diseases, and of their control and prevention. Using 1970 data from a variety of sources, he gathered and compared information about death rates from atherosclerotic and degenerative heart disease with the consumption of milk, butter and cheese in thirteen countries. Homogenized milk consumption correlated with death rates from atherosclerosis; butter and cheese consumption did not. Finland and the United States had the largest consumption of homogenized milk; the death rates in these two countries were over two hundred per hundred thousand people. The French drank about the same amount of milk per capita, but almost none was homogenized. The death rate for the French was less than one-fifth that of the Finns and the Americans, about forty-two per hundred thousand. The French also ate three times more cheese and five times more butter than the Americans—one must wonder how the cholesterol-saturated fat hypothesis ever gained any credence at all! The Swiss drank about the same amount of milk per capita as Americans, but only a fraction of it was homogenized; the death rate for the Swiss was about seventy-six per hundred thousand.[8]

According to Oster, the XO that remains in pasteurized, unhomogenized milk is found on the exterior of the milk fat globule membrane, where it is broken down during digestion. XO in raw milk is similarly digested. Homogenization, however, reduces the fat globules to a fraction of their original size, and according to Oster, the XO is encapsulated by the new outer membrane of the smaller fat globules which form during the homogenization process. Oster claimed that this new fat globule protects the XO from digestive enzymes, allowing some XO to pass intact within the fat globules from the gut into the circulatory system when homogenized milk is consumed.[9]

Oster referred to the smaller fat globules produced during the homogenization process as liposomes and claimed that they were small enough to enter the bloodstream intact, carrying their cargo of XO with them. After entering the circulation, they travel to the capillaries, he said, where the lipoprotein membranes appear to be digested by the enzyme lipoprotein lipase. This frees the XO for absorption into the body, including the heart and artery tissues, where it would interact with and destroy plasmalogen.

In 1974, Oster and Ross published a double-blind study in *American Laboratory* entitled "Immune Response to Bovine Xanthine Oxidase in Atherosclerotic Patients."[10] According to Oster, the antibodies found in the blood of milk drinkers indicated that XO from cow's milk may be absorbed and may enter the circulation; the data indicated that individuals with signs of atherosclerosis have greater amounts of milk protein antibodies than those with no signs of atherosclerosis and that levels of these antibodies are proportional to the volume of homogenized milk consumed. A research team at the University of Delaware later confirmed this observation and concluded that small quantities of cow's milk XO absorbed over a lifetime "may be biologically very important."[11]

The medical community had known since 1953 that American youths were prone to atherosclerosis. In that year, an article entitled "Coronary Disease Among United States Soldiers Killed in Action in Korea" was published in the *Journal of the American Medical Association*. Researchers performed autopsies on the bodies of three hundred American soldiers with an average age of twenty-two who had died in combat. The young men showed "gross evidence of coronary atherosclerosis." In fourteen of them, two or more of the main branches of the coronary arteries were ninety percent or more blocked.[12] Oster and Ross's work seemed to provide an explanation about what appears to be a major cause for the prevalence of atherosclerosis in Americans of all ages. But the same study also showed that Koreans had lots of atherosclerosis—and they drank no milk. This indicates that other factors besides the homogenization of milk may be involved in the etiology of atherosclerosis.

## FLAWS IN OSTER'S THEORY

Oster had many critics who disputed parts of his theory. He defended himself with vigor, pointing out that many studies contradicting his theories were funded, at least in part, by the dairy industry. Nevertheless, the arguments of his opponents point to some serious inconsistencies in Oster's work and conclusions.[13]

In essence, Oster's theory replaces cholesterol as the cause of heart disease with another mechanism, summarized as follows:

1. Homogenization causes xanthine oxidase, a supposedly noxious enzyme, to be encapsulated in a liposome, which can be absorbed intact.
2. XO is released by enzymatic action and ends up in heart and arterial tissue where it causes the destruction of a specialized protective membrane lipid called plasmalogen, leading to lesions in the arteries and the development of plaque.

A fundamental flaw in Oster's theory involves the difference between a fat globule and a liposome. Fat globules basically contain triglycerides and cholesterol encapsulated in a lipid bilayer membrane composed of proteins, cholesterol, phospholipids and fatty acids. They occur naturally in milk in a wide range of sizes. The fat globules in un-homogenized bovine milk are both very small and very large, ranging in size from one thousand nanometers to ten thousand nanometers. After homogenization, the average globule size is about five hundred nanometers with a range from two hundred nanometers to two thousand nanometers.

Oster considered homogenization of cow's milk to be a "procedure which foists unnaturally small particles on our digestive tracts."[4] Yet sheep's milk fat globules are reported to be "very small. . . [and consequently]. . . easier to digest," and in fact globules from this milk are described as "naturally homogenized." The milk fat globule membrane from sheep's milk does not separate and butter cannot be made from such milk even though there is twice as much fat in sheep's milk as in cow's milk. The fat globules from goat's milk are similarly small. Once again, goat's milk is considered easier to digest than cow's milk for this reason. So there is nothing unnatural about small milk fat globules.

Fat globules of all sizes are broken down during digestion, releasing the hundreds of thousands of triglycerides as well as any enzymes they contain. (Milk fat globules actually contain more than seven enzymes, of which XO is one. The other major ones are $NADH_2$, iodonitrotetrazolium, 5-nucleotidase, alkaline phosphatase, phosphodiesterase and gamma-glutamyltranspeptidase.) The triglycerides are broken down into individual fatty acids and monoglycerides while the proteins and enzymes are usually broken down into individual amino acids (enzymes are specialized proteins).

Although Oster described these small milk fat globules in homogenized milk as liposomes, several researchers have pointed out that liposomes are very different in basic composition. Liposomes are typically two hundred nanometers or less in size and do not contain complex protein components.

Liposomes do not occur in nature but were developed by scientists as a way of delivering components such as drugs to the cells in the body. They are composed of a phospholipid layer in which the phosphorus part is on the outside and the lipid part is on the inside. The layer encapsulates a watery liquid, not fatty acids.

It is true that liposomes are not broken down during digestion. For this reason, scientists have looked at liposomes as a way of delivering oral medications to the cells. In fact, a 1980 study led by Ross reported that liposome-entrapped insulin affected blood sugar-lowering in diabetic rats.[14] Ross claimed that this proved that large molecules could be absorbed.

A team led by A. J. Clifford looked carefully at Oster's theories. In a study published in 1983,[15] they noted that "neither liposome formation during homogenization of milk nor absorption of intact liposomes from the gastrointestinal tract has been demonstrated." In reviewing the major published findings, Clifford reported that "absorption of dietary xanthine oxidase has not been demonstrated." Clifford's team cited studies showing lack of activity of serum xanthine oxidase from pigs and humans fed diets that did and did not include milk.[16,17] Further, Clifford's team noted that "a relationship between intake of homogenized 'dairy foods' and levels of xanthine oxidase activity in the blood has not been established."

One study even showed an increase in serum xanthine oxidase when corn oil was fed, whereas milk and cream showed no such increase.[18] Oster had argued that homogenization came into widespread use during the 1930s and 1940s, the same years during which heart disease incidence went up dramatically. But these were the same years in which vegetable oils came into widespread use. (And if Oster's theories are correct, then only those who drink modern milk would get heart disease, a conclusion that is obviously untenable.)

As for Ross's study on insulin, Clifford argued that recent evaluations by others showed the insulin phenomenon to be an artifact of the methods used and not due to the delivery of insulin to the cells. Thus, one of Oster's published proofs turned out to be erroneous. (In fact, scientists have subsequently tried to use liposomes in humans as a way of delivering insulin taken orally to the cells but without success. However, liposomes have been used successfully to deliver an enzyme needed for the treatment of Gaucher disease.) When the Clifford team examined the electron micrograph presented in Ross's 1980 paper, they reported that it did not match the typical liposome stucture as described by a noted authority on liposomes.[19]

This does not mean that XO in milk is not absorbed—intact proteins do pass through the gut when poor nutrition or candida overgrowth damages the intestinal wall. But these same conditions could also contribute directly to heart disease for a variety of reasons. The presence of high levels of serum XO in patients with heart disease does not necessarily mean that XO directly causes heart disease. Like cholesterol, XO may simply be a marker for other conditions.

In the second part of his theory, Oster maintained that XO causes the destruction of plasmalogen. However, Clifford's team reported that "a direct role for xanthine oxidase in plasmalogen depletion under physiological conditions has not been established." They cited animal studies where bovine xanthine oxidase was given intravenously in large doses.[20] This treatment failed to deplete plasmalogen in the arteries or in the coronary tissue, nor did it introduce the formation of plaque.

IS PASTEURIZATION THE CULPRIT?

Oster cites a number of epidemiological studies in support of his theory, but the changes that ushered in homogenization accompanied many other changes in the western diet—increased amounts of sugar, white flour, additives, processed vegetable oils (shown to increase xanthine oxidase). . . and pasteurization. In fact, the publicity that has bolstered Oster's theories—even up to the present—has overshadowed the work of British scientist J. C. Annand, who argued forcefully that it is the heating of milk protein that renders it atherogenic.[21] Noting, as did Oster, that many heart disease patients have increased levels of milk antibodies compared to controls, he looked at the effects of pasteurization on bovine immunoglobulin, a protein in milk. Laboratory examination of milk pasteurized by an earlier technique that heated it to 145 degrees Fahrenheit for thirty minutes (called the Holder method), showed marked denaturation; there was less denaturation of bovine immunoglobulin in milk processed by the more modern flash pasteurization method, in which milk is heated for about seventeen seconds at

160 degrees Fahrenheit. Annand did not foresee the advent of ultra-high temperature (UHT) pasteurization; almost certainly this method, which heats milk to 230 degrees Fahrenheit (above the boiling point!) for one or two seconds, causes much more denaturing than regular flash pasteurization. But if the dairy industry has carried out any research on the effects of these high temperatures on the proteins and vitamins in milk, they are keeping it a secret. Annand also noted that antibodies to a variety of heated milk proteins, not just bovine immunoglobulin, have been detected in humans and that pasteurization can increase allergenicity of these proteins one hundred-fold.[22]

MODERN HOMOGENIZATION

The fact that Oster's theory has been disproven does not mean that homogenization is benign. The University of Guelph Department of Dairy Science and Technology, Ontario, Canada, provides the following description of the process.

"Auguste Gaulin's patent in 1899 consisted of a three-piston pump in which product was forced through one or more hair-like tubules under pressure. The size of fat globules produced was 500 to 600 times smaller than the tubules. There have been over 100 patents since, all designed to produce smaller average particle size.

"Consider a conventional homogenizing valve. As milk enters the valve, its velocity is increased to 120 meters per second. The homogenization phenomenon is completed before the fluid leaves the area between the valve and the seat. The whole process occurs between two pieces of steel in a steel valve assembly.

"Energy, dissipating in the liquid going through the homogenizer valve, generates intense turbulent eddies. Globules are thus torn apart by these eddy currents. The product then passes through a second stage valve similar to the first stage. While most of the fat globule reduction takes place in the first stage, there is a tendency for clumping or clustering of the reduced fat globules. The second stage valve permits the separation of those clusters into individual fat globules. In addition, heat pasteurization breaks down the cryo-globulin complex, which tends to cluster fat globules that would otherwise cause them to rise.

"The milk fat globule has a native membrane, picked up at the time of secretion in the cow. During homogenization, there is a tremendous increase in surface area and the native milk fat globule membrane is lost."[23]

The new membrane that is formed incorporates a much greater portion of casein and whey proteins than the original fat globule. These proteins, as well as the fats, have undergone treatment in "intense turbulent eddys" concurrent with the high temperature of pasteurization. What effects these processes may have on the structure and integrity of these molecules is anybody's guess. The incorporation of proteins into the fat globule membrane alone may account for the increased allergenicity of modern processed milk.

Scientists have recently discovered a number of highly beneficial components in the milk fat globule membrane (MFGM), components that help suppress pathogenic organisms and protect against multiple sclerosis, Alzheimer's disease, depression and stress.[24] These components are disturbed even when cream is churned into butter, so they would obviously be eliminated (or even rendered toxic) during the process of homogenization. The benefits of the MFGM are only available when we consume cream or unhomogenized milk.

One fact is beyond dispute: homogenization prevents the consumer from realizing just how little fat is contained in modern processed milk, even "full fat" milk. Before homogenization, milk purchasers looked for milk that had lots of cream—a sign that the milk came from healthy cows, cows on pasture. Old-fashioned milk contained from four to eight percent butterfat, which translated into lots of cream on the top. Modern milk is standardized at three and one-half percent, no more. Intensive advertising campaigns have convinced most consumers to purchase reduced-fat milk; intensive lobbying in the name of heart disease and obesity prevention has led to the elimination of full-fat milk for growing children in school lunch programs.

Butterfat brings bigger profits to the dairy industry as an ingredient in ice cream than as a component of liquid milk. The consumer has been cheated, but with homogenization, he can't tell.

# 15
# The Safety of
# Raw versus Pasteurized Milk

*It is very difficult to get a man to understand something when his salary depends on not understanding it.*

Upton Sinclair

*Drinking raw milk is like playing Russian roulette with your health.*

John F. Sheehan, Director
U.S. Food and Drug Administration
Division of Dairy and Egg Safety

Several issues are central to the raw milk controversy in America today. Some are scientific and some essentially legal. Even the scientific issues are shrouded in legalities and politics, but we'll approach them in a straightforward and practical manner. One issue is the question of safety: How safe is raw milk? We'll answer that question by considering the historical records of both raw and pasteurized milk as agents associated with disease, and by looking at scientific evidence delineating the numerous components in raw milk that kill pathogens and strengthen the immune system.

Another scientific issue involves the health benefits of raw milk compared to pasteurized—a subject that has been explored in many of the preceding pages. We'll look at this issue again in Chapters 16-18 as we explore why and how green pastures and contented cows produce nature's most nearly perfect food for children and adults.

Legal issues surrounding the raw milk controversy are complex and many of their ramifications are beyond the scope of this book. But we'll consider a number of practical questions. Is the alleged evidence about the dangers of raw milk so strong that the government should prohibit its being sold or even given away, as indeed has occurred in some states and countries? Even more fundamental, does our constitutional government have the right to make laws outlawing a food that has sustained much of humanity throughout recorded history? In the face of restrictive and unfair laws, what legal structures exist that may allow dairy farmers to legally make raw milk products available to consumers for reasonable compensation? How are producers and consumers of raw milk working together to change existing laws that prevent farmers from selling raw milk and its products on the open market?

The answers to these questions are shaping the way a determined minority of Americans has built a grassroots movement to make a ready supply of raw milk and raw milk products available for themselves, their families and anyone else who desires it. These committed individuals— farmers, consumers, activists, alternative medical practitioners and their patients, journalists, local, state and federal government representatives and others in public life—and the legal issues they are confronting are the subject of Chapter 19. For now, we consider a more straightforward matter: the safety of raw versus pasteurized milk.

The position of the public health and conventional medical communities on raw milk is unequivocal: they are dead-set against it. In 1986, an FDA ruling banned the interstate shipment of raw milk, butter and cream across state lines. For many years, officials in every state have pushed for laws banning all sales of raw milk, with strong support from the Centers for Disease Control (CDC) and the FDA. Within the last thirty years, legislation has banned retail sales of raw milk in most states and restricted sales to the farm where the milk is produced in many others. But no state has passed legislation against the purchase, possession or consumption of raw milk. This fact alone argues that the incentive to ban raw milk sales is based on economic rather than public health concerns. FDA assertions that raw milk is "inherently dangerous and should not be consumed"[1] serve as a smoke screen for legislation that helps centralize the dairy industry and eliminate competition from small independent farmers.

Health officials frequently draw attention to studies claiming that raw milk has caused illness—most often issuing press releases against raw milk during outbreaks caused by other foods. However as we shall see, most of these published reports exhibit extreme bias on the part of investigators and contain numerous flaws. In fact, many studies claiming this "inherently dangerous" food as a cause of disease actually exonerate raw milk as a culprit.

RAW MILK IS INHERENTLY SAFE

While government officials have painted raw milk as a dangerous soup of pathogenic bacteria, a great deal of obscure, peer reviewed research has revealed a very different picture. After all, raw milk is the first food of every mammal on the planet. The calf that is born in the muck and manure immediately gets up and begins to suck on its mother's unsanitary teat; likewise, the puppy crawls across filthy bedding to find its mother's unwashed nipple. If raw milk is an inherently dangerous food, how is it that the family of mammals has survived?

Mammals including humans have survived because raw milk contains multiple, redundant systems of bioactive components that can reduce or eliminate populations of pathogenic bacteria while also strengthening the immune system of the suckling infant.

Early researchers recognized factors responsible for the germicidal property of raw milk, as described in the 1935 textbook *Fundamentals of Dairy Science*.[2] In 1938, researchers found that raw milk would not support the growth of a wide range of pathogens, noting that heated milk supports the growth of harmful bacteria by inactivating "inhibins."[3]

Today we have detailed knowledge about these "inhibins." The two major components, which form the backbone of this amazing system, are the enzymes lactoperoxidase and lactoferrin. The lactoperoxidase enzyme uses small amounts of free radicals to seek out and destroy bad bacteria.[4] It is found in all mammalian secretions including tears and saliva.[5] Levels tend to be higher in animal milk—goat milk contains ten times more lactoperoxidase than human milk.[6] So effective is lactoperoxidase at killing pathogens that officials in other countries are exploring the possibilities of using lactoperoxidase for ensuring the safety of other foods, and even as an alternative to pasteurization.[7]

Peroxidase enzymes such as lactoperoxidase are common in the living tissues of plants and animals and play an important role in innate immunity to infection. They are harmless to animal and plant tissue but strongly inhibit the bacterial membrane enzymes that are critical to bacterial survival. These enzymes initiate the production of powerful oxidizing agents (peroxides), which are based on sulphur groups.

Lactoperoxidase was discovered in milk one hundred years ago when cheesemakers observed that at certain times of the year starter bacteria added to milk would not work. This took place during the blooming of certain grasses high in sulphur compounds, which are readily oxidized to thiocyanates by lactoperoxidase. The thiocyanates formed are so strongly antimicrobial, they inhibit not only the pathogenic and spoilage bacteria but also the lactic acid bacteria used by the cheesemakers.[8]

The second major antimicrobial enzyme in milk is lactoferrin, which works by stealing iron away from pathogens and carrying it through the gut wall into the blood stream. Thus, this enzyme does a double duty, killing off a wide range iron-loving pathogens while helping the infant to absorb all the iron contained in the milk. In addition, lactoferrin stimulates the immune system.[9]

According to a recent review in the *Journal of Experimental Therapeutics and Oncology*, lactoferrin exhibits fungistatic, bacteriostatic, bactericidal and antiviral properties and inhibits the growth of parasites. It is effective against *E. coli*, *S. typhimurium*, *Bacillus subtilis*, *Pseudomonas aeruginosa*, *Vibrio cholerae*, *Haemophilus influenzae*, *S. aureus*, *Klebsiella pneumoniae*, *Candida albicans*, *Candida crusei*, *Tinea pedis*, *Toxoplasma gondii*, *Plasmodium falciparum*, *Herpes simplex*, hepatitis C virus, human papillomavirus and various other pathogens.

It is not effective against beneficial bacteria such as bifidobacteria and lactobacillus species.[10]

One of the main iron-loving pathogens is the tuberculosis bacillus. In a study involving mice bred to be susceptible to tuberculosis, treatment with lactoferrin significantly reduced the burden of TB organisms.[11] Another iron-loving microorganism is *Candida albicans*, a yeast ubiquitously present in the digestive tract, which can cause serious health problems when conditions favor its overgrowth. Mice injected with *Candida albicans* had increased survival time when treated with lactoferrin.[11] Other research indicates that lactoferrin can be used to cut visceral fat levels by as much as forty percent, and that the compound has many other health benefits.[12] You can even purchase lactoferrin as a supplement—or benefit from its actions simply by drinking raw milk.

In 2004, the FDA approved lactoferrin for use as an anti-microbial spray to combat virulent *E. coli O157:H7* contamination in the meat industry! The FDA press release praised the product as an innovative way to protect the nation from food-borne illness. "Innovative technology is a critical building block in preserving the strong foundation of the U.S. food supply," said Dr. Lester Crawford, Deputy Commissioner of the Food and Drug Administration. "We must continue to encourage scientific research and new technology to maintain this nation's safe food supply."[13]

Since the dawn of mammalian history, nature has provided this "innovative technology" to nursing infants to protect their vulnerable and sensitive digestive systems from the insults of invading pathogens. Perhaps this is one reason why responsibly handled raw milk rarely leads to genuine cases of food-borne illness.

Physicians from earlier times often referred to milk as white blood, a designation that modern science proves to be correct. A key player in raw milk's anti-microbial and immune support system is white blood cells, or leukocytes, exactly the same as those found in blood. Leukocytes form the basis of milk's safety net, consuming foreign bacteria, yeasts and molds. They also produce hydrogen peroxide to activate the lactoperoxidase system and anaerobic carbon dioxide, which blocks aerobic microorganisms.[14] Raw milk contains B-lymphocytes, a type of white blood cell that aids the immune system by producing specific antibodies; macrophages, which engulf foreign proteins and bacteria; neutrophils, which kill infected cells and stimulate the immune system; T-lymphocytes, which multiply when bad bacteria are present and produce immune-strengthening compounds; and immunoglobulins (IgM, IgA, IgG$_1$ and IgG$_2$), or antibodies, which transfer immunity from the animal producing the milk to the animal or person consuming the milk, especially in colostrum.[15]

Many other components in raw milk play the dual roles of fighting pathogens and supporting the immune system. These include polysaccharides, which encourage the growth of good bacteria in the gut and protect the gut wall; oligosaccharides, which protect other components in raw milk from destruction by enzymes and stomach acids while preventing bacteria from attaching to the gut lining; medium-chain fatty acids, which disrupt the cell walls of pathogens while strengthening the immune system; lysozymes and other enzymes that disrupt bacterial cell walls; hormones and growth factors, which stimulate maturation of gut cells and prevent "leaky gut;" fibronectin, which increases the antimicrobial activity of macrophages and helps repair damaged tissues; B$_{12}$-binding protein, which inhibits bacterial growth in the colon by reducing levels of vitamin B$_{12}$, while also helping the infant absorb all the B$_{12}$ in the milk; glucomacropeptide, which inhibits bacterial and viral adhesion, suppresses gastric secretion and promotes the growth of beneficial bacteria; bifidus factor, which promotes the growth of *Lactobacillus bifidus*, one of the helpful bacteria families that crowd out dangerous microorganisms; and the lactobacilli themselves, which proliferate in raw milk over time and crowd out bad bacteria.[16]

All these factors work together to inactivate pathogens "individually, additively and synergistically," as one researcher put it.[17] These protective factors "can target multiple early steps in pathogen replication and target each step with more than one antimicrobial compound." At the same time, these compounds work to strengthen the immune system and the gut wall.

Of course, this marvelous synergistic system can be overwhelmed if milk is produced in filthy conditions, but when the cows are healthy and the production methods clean, they ensure a product that is inherently safe.

Pasteurization largely wipes out these numerous protective factors, inactivating the various leukocytes, antibodies, enzymes and binding proteins, while reducing the activity of medium-chain fatty acids, lysozymes, oligosaccharides, hormones and growth factors, and beneficial bacteria. Ultrapasteurization—most milk is ultrapasteurized these days—inactivates lysozyme, and all but the medium chain fatty acids are inactivated in infant formula.[18]

Lactoperoxidase loses biological activity at 178 degrees Fahrenheit. It therefore survives pasteurization (about 160 degrees Fahrenheit) but not the ultra-high heat treatment (UHT) of 230 degrees Fahrenheit used in the production of today's long-life milks. However, even at regular pasteurization temperatures, lactoperoxidase will be greatly reduced in potency because pasteurization partially destroys the hydrogen peroxide present in the milk and also destroys the two systems that generate hydrogen peroxide, namely leukocytes and lactic acid bacteria.[19]

In a publication denouncing the consumption of raw milk, the FDA cites one study claiming that pasteurization does not inactivate lactoferrin.[20] But the authors of this study used not milk but purified lactoferrin, with its iron component removed. Although lactoferrin is more heat-stable when the iron is removed, accomplishing this removal of iron requires incubating purified lactoferrin with citric acid at 41 degrees Fahrenheit for twenty-four hours and running it through a gel filtration system. Such a "lactoferrin product" bears very little resemblance to the lactoferrin in raw milk.

In 1977, researchers showed that the original lower-temperature, longer-time pasteurization of human milk at 145 degrees Fahrenheit for thirty minutes destroys sixty-five percent of the lactoferrin.[21] They did not evaluate the antibacterial efficacy of the remaining thirty-five percent, which may have been damaged or completely destroyed. Heating human milk to 185 degrees Fahrenheit for fifteen minutes caused ninety-six percent destruction of its lactoferrin. Again, we do not know whether the remaining four percent retained its antibacterial potency. (Remember, ultrapasteurization takes milk to even higher temperatures.)

Thus, pasteurization largely inactivates raw milk's built-in safety system. Proof of raw milk's anti-microbial properties comes from what are known as "challenge tests," where pathogens are added to raw milk and then monitored over time. For example, when the pathogen campylobacter is added to raw milk, the levels decrease—in chilled milk from thirteen thousand per milliliter to less than ten per milliliter in nine days. At room temperature, the decline is even more rapid.[22] In one study, researchers credited the action of lactoperoxidase in killing added fungal and bacterial agents, but decline in pathogen numbers is most likely due to the whole complex of antimicrobial factors.[23] Recently in California, Organic Pastures Dairy Company subjected their raw milk and colostrum to challenge tests monitored by an independent laboratory. Pathogen counts declined over time and in some cases were undetectable within a week. The laboratory concluded, "Raw colostrum and raw milk do not appear to support the growth of salmonella, *E. coli O157:H7* or *Listeria monocytogenes.*"[24]

Milk's anti-microbial properties can be very frustrating to researchers. In 1985, a team of scientists tried to blame raw milk for an outbreak of *Campylobacter jejuni* in a village where virtually everyone drank raw milk from a single farm. They found the organism in rubbish heaps and watering holes, but not in the milk or milk filters. Frustrated with this result, they cultured samples right on the farm instead of carrying them in sterile containers to a sterile working space in the laboratory as is usually done, and the milk and milk filters proved contaminated. They claimed the reason they had to culture the milk on the farm was because the *C. jejuni* was unable to tolerate the "natural antibacterial effect of fresh milk" for the several hours it took to transport the milk to the lab, but they offered no explanation of how the milk could have made anyone sick if all the *C. jejuni* within it died within hours of milking. When they tried quantifying two of the positive samples after some unspecified time, the milk turned up negative. When they tried subtyping two other samples soon after collection, they failed because the bacteria could not survive long enough for them to finish the procedure.[25]

Pasteurized milk will not pass these challenge tests. Should pathogens contaminate pasteurized milk, very little of the protective system remains to keep them in check. And since pasteurized milk comes from large factories with wide distribution networks, contaminated pasteurized milk often results in hundreds if not thousands of illnesses and even a few deaths, as we shall see.

## RAW VERSUS PASTEURIZED BREAST MILK

Much of the research that has revealed the amazing anti-microbial and immune supportive properties of raw milk has been carried out on human milk. However, these discoveries apply to the milk of all mammals; in fact, as we have seen, protective components such as lactoperoxidase are often higher in the milk of animals.

Human milk requires the same antimicrobial system as animal milk because human milk is not pathogen-free. The notion that human infants suckled a sterile product, as scientists for many years believed, has given way to the realization that human milk contains many pathogens. For example, scientists in Finland detected several strains of *Staphylococcus aureus*, "known as a causative agent of maternal breast infections and neonatal infections" in human breast milk samples.[26] Scientists in Canada report that breast milk "is a body fluid capable of transmitting blood-borne pathogens when ingested."[27]

In fact, in a screening program for expressed breast milk in China, testing revealed "the alarming fact that our study group had the highest rate of contamination ever reported."[28] Pathogenic bacteria in the milk included enterococci and *Staphylococcus aureus*. The research team speculated that the high rate of contamination "could be due to the Chinese tradition of avoiding bathing for one month after childbirth." Apparently, mother's milk picks up numerous pathogens from the skin; and one theory holds that immune signals for pathogens are also transferred to breast milk via ducts that connect with the digestive tract.[29]

The protective factors in milk inhibit not only existing pathogens but also "anticipate new mutations and new pathogens . . ."[30] The immunological factor IgA, for example "appears to reflect long-term maternal immunologic memory."[31] This explains the Chinese wisdom—shocking to investigators—of not bathing for a month after giving birth. When the infant suckles milk containing pathogens, the immunological factors in that same milk can program the infant for protection against a myriad of pathogens, and can protect him for life! These studies can only inspire awe and wonder at the exquisite processes that support biological life.

Other studies on human milk show that heating reduces the ability of milk to protect against infections. In 1984, researchers in India carried out a randomized controlled trial involving two hundred twenty-six high-risk newborns, given combinations of formula and raw and pasteurized human milk. The highest rate of infection occurred in the group given pasteurized human milk plus formula (thirty-three percent). Those given raw human milk plus formula had a sixteen percent rate of infection and those given pasteurized human milk alone had just over a fourteen percent rate of infection. The lowest rate of infection was about ten percent in the group given raw human milk only.[32]

Scientists in Africa looked at ways of storing human milk. No growth of pathogens was observed in raw human milk stored four hours at high temperature (eighty-six to one hundred degrees Fahrenheit), eight hours at room temperature (fifty nine to eighty-one degrees Fahrenheit) and twenty-four hours at refrigerator temperature (thirty-nine to fifty degrees Fahrenheit).[33] They concluded that "although freezing temperature (thirty-two to thirty-nine degrees Fahrenheit) seemed safest for breast milk storage, short-term storage in a freezer was not recommended due to the likely hazards of the thawing process." Another study found that raw human milk was safe for human consumption for up to seventy-two hours refrigerated.[34] Longer-term storage by freezing did not cause safety problems.

Unfortunately, human milk donated to breast milk banks is routinely pasteurized before freezing, thereby destroying the many protective mechanisms that human milk can confer on premature babies. And accidents do happen. A recent outbreak of *Pseudomonas aeruginosa* in a neonatal intensive care unit caused by a contaminated milk bank pasteurizer resulted in thirty-one cases of infection and four deaths.[35]

Pasteurization not only compromises the safety of breast milk, it also compromises its nutritional value. For example, researchers in 1986 published a randomized controlled study to assess the effect of pasteurization of breast milk on the growth of very-low-birth-weight infants.

Infants bottle fed untreated milk from their own mothers grew more rapidly than those fed pasteurized pooled preterm milk.[36] Another study carried out in the same year also found reasons for concern about the effect of heat sterilizing breast milk. Researchers compared the results of feeding pooled pasteurized breast milk with their own untreated mother's milk to very-low-birth-weight babies. Those receiving unpasteurized human milk had significantly more rapid weight gain. Researchers attributed the lower weight gain in babies fed pasteurized human milk to the destruction of lipase, an enzyme needed to utilize milk fat.[37]

From a study published in 1977 we learn: "Human milk was subjected to heat treatments of graded severity and examined for its content of immunoglobulins, lactoferrin, lysozyme, vitamin $B_{12}$- and folate-binder proteins, and lactoperoxidase. Holder pasteurization [146 degrees F for 30 minutes] reduced the IgA titer by 20 percent, and destroyed the small content of IgM and most of the lactoferrin. Lysozyme was stable to this treatment, but with an increase in temperature there was progressive destruction, to near 100 percent at 212 degrees F. The same was broadly true of the capacity of milk to bind folic acid and protect it against bacterial uptake; with vitamin $B_{12}$ the binder was more labile at 167 degrees F than at 212 degrees F. The [heat-treated] milk contained no detectable lactoperoxidase."[38]

Government officials widely support giving raw milk to infants—as long as that raw milk is human breast milk. According to a document posted at the Centers for Disease Contol website, "Mother's milk is the safest food for young infants. Breastfeeding prevents salmonellosis and many other health problems." Yet the same website contains the following warning against salmonella: "Cook poultry, ground beef, and eggs thoroughly before eating. Do not eat or drink foods containing raw eggs, or raw unpasteurized milk."[39] For mothers who are unable to breastfeed for whatever reason, or who simply choose not to do so, the logical alternative is homemade formula based on raw milk from another mammal, but official government policy adamantly opposes giving raw milk from animals to infants, recommending manufactured formula instead, a product that is highly synthetic and which has its own safety issues. Between 1982 and 1994 alone, there were twenty-two significant recalls of infant formula in the United States due to health and safety problems.[40] (For more on infant formula based on raw milk, see Chapter 16.)

Thus, while research on human milk has revealed numerous protective components in raw milk, the bureaucrats in our government agencies are mired in forty-year-old science. Next time one of these unenlightened souls tells you that the milk you give your children has to be pasteurized for their protection, ask them whether the pathogen-loaded breast milk mothers give their infants needs to be pasteurized as well.

THE DANGERS OF PASTEURIZED MILK

Public health officials claim that pasteurization is "the only way to ensure that milk is safe to drink." Indeed, milk in general—both pasteurized and raw—is a particularly safe food. For example, in 1997, milk and milk products accounted for only two-tenths of one percent of all reported cases of food-borne illness.[41] Barring post-pasteurization contamination, residual amounts of protective factors that remain after pasteurization are probably adequate to combat most heat-resistant pathogens found in commercial milk.

Nevertheless, pasteurized milk sometimes causes illness, and when it does, the outbreak usually involves many individuals. A 1976 outbreak of *Yersina enterocolitica* from pasteurized chocolate milk sickened thirty-six children, sixteen of whom required appendectomies.[42] In 1982, the same organism sickened seventeen thousand pasteurized milk consumers in several states. The tainted milk was traced to a pasteurizing plant in Memphis, Tennessee.[43] A 1983 outbreak of *Listeria monocytogenes* sickened forty-nine people in Massachusetts and caused fourteen deaths.[44] Almost two hundred thousand individuals may have been sickened from the outbreak of *Salmonella typhimurium* that took place in the Midwest in 1984-85,[45] discussed in Chapter 12.

During the 1990s, the most serious incidents included an outbreak causing over two thousand *Salmonella enteritidis* illnesses from pasteurized ice cream in Minnesota, South Dakota and Wisconsin[46] and an outbreak of *Yersina enterocolitica* in pasteurized milk that sickened ten children, three of whom were hospitalized.[47]

And there have been recent outbreaks as well. In 2000, *Salmonella typhimurim* from pasteurized milk sickened almost one hundred individuals in Pennsylvania and New Jersey.[48] *Campylobacter jejuni* from pasteurized milk sickened two hundred inmates in a Colorado prison in 2005[49] and almost sixteen hundred inmates in a California prison in 2006.[50] In 2007, three people in Massachusetts died from *Listeria monocytogenes* in pasteurized milk.[51] Yet no one from the FDA or other government agencies describes pasteurized milk as "inherently dangerous" or calls for its removal from the marketplace.

THE DANGERS OF OTHER FOODS

According to a Center for Science in the Public Interest (CSPI) report, between 1990 and 2004 the following outbreaks occurred:

31,496 illnesses, 639 outbreaks from produce
16,280 illnesses, 541 outbreaks from poultry
13,220 illnesses, 467 outbreaks from beef
11,027 illnesses, 341 outbreaks from eggs
9,969 illnesses, 984 outbreaks from seafood

The largest percentage of outbreaks came from seafood (thirty-three percent of the total) while the largest percentage of illnesses came from produce (thirty-eight percent of the total). While dairy foods (both pasteurized and raw) contribute to less than one percent of all reported food-borne illnesses, the risk from other foods is large.[52]

According to Robert Tauxe, CDC Chief of the Food-borne and Diarrheal Diseases Branch, food-borne pathogens such as campylobacter, *E. coli O157:H7, Yersina enterocolitica*, cryptosporidium and listeria, have emerged only within the past twenty-five years. In contrast, the five pathogens that plagued the early decades of the 1900s, when pasteurization was implemented, those causing brucellosis, botulism, typhoid fever, trichinosis and cholera, combined account for only one one-hundredth percent of food-borne illnesses today. Most of those are associated with foreign travel.[53]

Tauxe reports that thirteen recently emerged pathogens are responsible for a majority of the seventy-six million cases of food-borne illness, three hundred thousand hospitalizations, and five thousand deaths annually, and he estimates that one in four Americans experiences a food-borne illness every year. The following are some major pathogens and their reported cases per annum:

| | |
|---|---|
| Campylobacter | 1,963,000 |
| Salmonella | 1,342,000 |
| E. Coli O157:H7 | 92,000 |
| Yersina enterocolitica | 87,000 |
| Listeria | 2,000 |

The majority of food-borne illness is caused by Norwalk-like viruses (noroviruses), which account for over nine million cases per year. These viruses are resistant to both freezing and high temperatures. CDC currently does not conduct active surveillance to monitor outbreaks of gastroenteritis caused by noroviruses.

Many factors common to modern life explain the emergence of these new pathogens—overuse and misuse of antibiotics, crowded feedlots, low-quality and low-cost animal feed, globalization of the food supply, and reduced human immunity due to poor nutrition.

The CSPI statistics may be an underestimation. Eggs contaminated with salmonella—we looked at how nearly all eggs are produced in Chapter 11—are said by some authorities to sicken three hundred thousand and kill hundreds of Americans each year.[54] A nationwide study published by the USDA in 1996 found that over seven percent of ground beef samples taken at processing plants were contaminated with salmonella and almost twelve percent were contaminated with listeria.[55] In contrast with the situation in this country, Sweden began a program over forty years ago to eliminate salmonella from its livestock, and only about one-tenth of one percent of Swedish cattle harbor salmonella today. Salmonella has also been almost completely eliminated from Swedish eggs.[56]

It's not just salmonella and listeria that taint American meat and processed foods. Thirty percent of ground beef samples taken at processing plants were contaminated with the pathogen Staphylococcus *aureus* and over half with *Clostridium perfringens*. "All of these pathogens can make people sick," wrote Eric Schlosser in *Fast Food Nation*. "Food poisoning caused by Listeria generally requires hospitalization and proves fatal in about one out of every five cases. In the USDA study, 78.6 percent of the ground beef contained microbes that are spread primarily by fecal material. The medical literature on the causes of food poisoning is full of euphemisms and dry scientific terms: coliform levels, aerobic plate counts, sorbitol, MacConkey agar and so on. Behind them lies a simple explanation for why eating a hamburger can now make you seriously ill: There is shit in the meat."[57]

And it's also in white meat. Over seventy percent of chicken samples tested in Washington, DC grocery stores in 1999-2000 came back positive for campylobacter; almost fifteen percent of turkey samples contained the pathogen. By contrast, the same survey found that less than two percent of pork samples tested positive for the organism and only one-half percent of beef samples.[58]

Organisms that cause illness are ubiquitous—and tenacious. *E. coli* and *Salmonella enteritidis* can survive on coins for a week or more, and *Salmonella enteritidis* can survive on glass or Teflon for up to seventeen days.[59]

Milk substitutes also harbor pathogens. A 1998 survey found five types of microorganisms in four brands of stored soy milk samples. During storage at forty-one degrees Fahrenheit, microbial counts increased sharply after two to three weeks.[60] Dry, powdered foods are not safe either. A 1978 survey found salmonella in many "health food" products including soy flour, soy protein powder and soy milk powder.[61]

The same thing that contaminates our meat and eggs—manure from confinement animal operations—is also a major source of contamination in fruits and vegetables. Documented outbreaks of human infections associated with consumption of raw fruits, vegetables and unpasteurized fruit juices have increased dramatically in recent years. According to the Centers for Disease Control and Prevention, in the U.S. the number of reported produce-related outbreaks per year doubled between the period 1973-1987 and 1988-1992. These include salmonellosis linked to tomatoes, seed sprouts, cantaloupe, apple juice, and orange juice; *Escherichia coli O157:H7* infection associated with lettuce, sprouts and apple juice; enterotoxigenic *E. coli* linked to carrots; shigellosis linked to lettuce, scallions and parsley; cholera linked to strawberries; parasitic diseases linked to raspberries, basil and apple cider; hepatitis A virus linked to lettuce, raspberries and frozen strawberries; and Norwalk or Norwalk-like virus linked to melon, salad and celery.[62] In 1997, fruits, vegetables and salad contributed to thirty-six outbreaks compared to only nine for chicken, three for eggs and two for milk.[63]

In the fall of 2006, a particularly virulent outbreak of *E. coli O157: H7* traced to spinach grown in California's Salinas Valley sickened over two hundred individuals and caused three deaths.[61] This was followed by a lettuce outbreak that made seventy-one people ill.[65] In both outbreaks, many people ended up in the hospital, most with bloody diarrhea, but in a few cases, the bacteria released toxins into the bloodstream that caused the kidneys and other organs to shut down.

Investigators noted that potential environmental risk factors for *E. coli* contamination at or near the fields included the presence of wild pigs, the proximity of irrigation wells used to grow produce for ready-to-eat packaging and surface waterways exposed to feces from cattle and wildlife.[66] In other words, infected manure from animals and wildlife was the likely cause of the outbreak. And the most likely source of infected manure—which is used as fertilizer and also ends up in well water and irrigation water—is confinement animal operations, including confinement dairy operations.

The Centers for Disease Control cites increased consumption of fruits and vegetables, which Americans are urged to eat as "part of a healthy diet," as a factor in the huge increase in food-borne illness from plant foods. There are no requirements for pasteurizing these foods we're supposed to eat more of; in fact, consumers are encouraged to eat them raw. FDA advises consumers that all produce should be thoroughly washed before it is eaten, but in the latest outbreaks, washing the produce would not have prevented illness. That's because these bacteria can grow inside the leaves of lettuce, spinach and other vegetables and fruit, where surface treatments cannot reach. In addition, microbes can organize themselves into tightly knit communities called biofilms, which coat fruits and vegetables and protect the bacteria from water and anti-microbial solutions.[67]

The raw milk movement provides a real solution to the problem of food-borne illness—because raw milk consumers make sure their milk comes from small, pasture-based farms and healthy animals unlikely to harbor pathogens and unlikely to contribute to water polution; and because raw milk builds immunity to disease-causing organisms that are simply a natural part of the world in which we live.

REPORTS OF ILLNESS FROM RAW MILK: A HISTORY OF BIAS

So if raw milk is inherently safe, why do we so often hear that raw milk causes illness? What about all the reports in the scientific literature linking outbreaks of disease to raw milk? The answer lies in the attitude of bias against raw milk held by most scientists and government officials. So ingrained is this prejudice that researchers may not even be aware of their lack of impartiality. Yet a careful reading of the published literature reveals a long history of unfounded assumptions, inappropriate sampling techniques and tortured conclusions used to build a case against raw milk. Often a single biased report that finds an association of raw milk with illness—and an association is not the same as a proven cause—serves as justification for shutting down a raw milk dairy or passing more restrictive laws. In fact, the pattern of raw milk "incident" leading to restriction of access to raw milk happens so frequently that some raw milk activists have raised the spectre of deliberate sabotage.

For many years, the state of Georgia was a raw milk state, due in large part to the persistence of Mathis Dairy in Dekalb, one of the last certified raw milk dairies in the country. Numerous attempts to pass legislation against raw milk in the state had failed, thanks to the popularity of the dairy and its iconic mascot, Rosebud the cow. But a 1983 outbreak of campylobacter in Atlanta gave authorities the ammunition they needed. Raw milk was banned in Georgia as a result of the incident. The report on the outbreak, published in the *American Journal of Epidemiology*, noted that "extensive testing failed to find campylobacter or any other pathogens in any milk products from the dairy. All safety measures had been followed faithfully." Yet the authors concluded, "The only means available to ensure the public's health would be proper pasteurization before consumption."[68] Ironically, this study was published shortly before the massive 1984-85 outbreak traced to a pasteurizing plant in Melrose Park, Illinois, in which almost two hundred thousand midwesterners were sickened by salmonella from *pasteurized* milk.

Raw milk sales are not allowed in the state of Wisconsin. But in June of 2000, the owners of Clearview Acres in Sawyer County started a cow share program to meet the burgeoning demand for raw milk. The program had approval from the Wisconsin Department of Agriculture, Trade and Consumer Protection (DATCP), which suggested a format used by another state-authorized cow-share program in Wisconsin. However, Clearview owners were not satisfied with the two-page contract that DATCP suggested, finding that it did not contain enough provision for testing and safety. The revised contract allowed for greater safety protocols, and the program was soon supplying milk to three hundred individuals.

During a twelve-week period beginning November 10, 2001, an outbreak of *Campylobacter jejuni* caused diarrhea, abdominal cramps and fever in hundreds of people in northwestern Wisconsin. Officials blamed the outbreak on the consumption of raw milk from Clearview Acres, an accusation formalized in a DATCP report issued June 28, 2002 and posted on the CDC website.[69] According to a report, seventy out of seventy-five persons confirmed with the illness drank unpasteurized milk from the dairy.

The owners of the dairy did their own research by contacting emergency rooms in the area. According to their estimates, the campylobacter infection afflicted as many as eight hundred individuals—most of whom did not drink raw milk—throughout northwest Wisconsin. Reports of illness continued for eight weeks after provision of raw milk to cow-share holders had ceased.

Only twenty-four of three hundred eighty-five cow-share owners became ill—eight confirmed cases and sixteen probable family members of the eight confirmed. Most of these had consumed hamburger at a local restaurant. No illness occurred in the remaining three hundred sixty-one individuals consuming raw milk from Clearview Acres dairy.[70]

The discrepancy in government figures and those of Clearview Acres was due to interview tactics by local officials. Afflicted individuals who showed up at the nearest local hospital were questioned as to whether or not they drank raw milk. Medical personnel tested only those who answered yes. All others were given an antibiotic and sent home without further investigation—and thus not included in the official count of those who got sick. Reports of illness in other hospitals were ignored.

Clearview Acres was a Grade A dairy with an excellent history of cleanliness. In fact, in October 2001, Clearview Acres received the second highest rating of all farms receiving federal inspection. The rating was ninety-nine out of a possible one hundred. The dairy regularly tested its milk for the presence of pathogens. All tests, including those for campylobacter, had been negative. During the outbreak, DATCP tested Clearview Acres milk for campylobacter in state laboratories and claimed the results were positive. Clearview Acres' own tests were negative.

Documents released in the court case involving Clearview Acres indicate that the state instituted an undercover operation shortly after the cow-share program began, with the express purpose of shutting down the operation. When state tests of Clearview Acres milk consistently came up negative, the state attempted to take away the farm's Grade A permit, but was stymied for lack of jurisdiction. Finally, DATCP blamed Clearview Acres milk on the local campylobacter outbreak and issued a cease-and-desist order.

The bias in sampling techniques, underreporting of widespread illness, suspicious results of the state's campylobacter test and the documented clear intent on the part of officials to shut down the cow-share operation would prevent any honest investigator from concluding that the raw milk from Clearview Acres had caused the outbreak. Yet this report still remains on the CDC website, and officials often cite the Wisconsin outbreak as an argument against the consumption of raw milk.

Ohio has prohibited the sale of raw milk since 1997 with a grandfather clause allowing any farmer licensed to sell raw milk before 1965 to continue. The last farm to hold a raw milk permit, Young's Dairy in Yellow Springs, voluntarily gave it up in January of 2003 after an outbreak of salmonella that sickened forty-seven people, sixteen of whom worked on the farm. The strain originated elsewhere in the state and officials could not positively attribute the problem to Young's.[71] Nevertheless, the state put considerable pressure on the dairy—threatening to take away their Grade A license and close down the pasteurized portion of their business—which then closed down the raw milk portion of their operation.

The outbreak and subsequent decision by the dairy came just one week after the Ohio Farm Bureau Federation voted to support an effort aimed at permitting more people to sell raw milk. The majority of the more than four hundred delegates to the group's annual meetings, all active or retired farmers from across the state, stated that farmers who wanted to sell raw milk should be able to obtain a license to do so. Then came the incident at Young's Dairy. Coincidence? We think not.

LISTERIA AND RAW MILK: BUILDING A CASE IN PENNSYLVANIA

*Listeria monocytogenes* is a dangerous pathogen that can cause fever, muscle aches and gastrointestinal symptoms such as nausea and diarrhea. But although raw milk has been blamed for many types of illness, it has not historically been associated with *Listeria monocytogenes* (*L. mono.*). In response to a freedom of information request by the Weston A. Price Foundation, submitted in early 2007, the Centers for Disease Control provided data on raw milk outbreaks for the period 1973-2005. The report listed no cases of food-borne illness from fluid raw milk caused by listeria during the thirteen-year period.[72] (There were a number of cases that linked Mexican-style raw milk cheese with listeria—more on this later.)

Suddenly, however, raw milk and listeria were in the news. On April 7, 2007, the Pennsylvania Department of Agriculture (PDA) issued a press release stating that raw milk from the farm of Clark and Elaine Duncan had tested posivive for *L. mono.* The milk inspector had taken the sample on March 31 and obtained the results on April 4. Up to that point, PDA policy allowed raw milk sales to continue unless a second milk sample also came back positive, but the new head of dairy safety, Bill Chirdon, immediately suspended milk sales after the single negative test. The Duncans sent a sample to a private lab the week following their suspension and that came back positive as well. However, there were no reported illnesses from the dairy's customers.

On April 4, the same day the Duncans' test results came back positive, PDA told Arnold and Esther Diller of Piney Ridge Farm in northwestern Pennsylvania that they were suspending their raw milk sales because their milk had tested positive for listeria. Arnold Diller subsequently sent a sample to an independent lab, which came back negative. As a condition for resuming sales on their farm, their inspector gave them a list of tasks to accomplish for reinspection. After repeatedly failing to clean a piece of milking equipment to the satisfaction of the inspector, the Dillers turned in their license to PDA.

The Dillers had obtained their permit not long before, in 2006, in response to increasing consumer demand, and thus became one of the few permitted raw milk dairies in western Pennsylvania—most Pennsylvania dairies holding permits are in the eastern part of the state. Some of the Dillers' customers picked up the milk at a local health food store. Shortly before the state's positive listeria tests, a Pennsylvania food and safety inspector witnessed the raw milk in a walk-in cooler and voiced disapproval, even though no law prohibits the practice. One of their customers was a state representative who had earlier told PDA officials how happy he was to be able to get raw milk from the Dillers. In what seemed like an attempt to discourage the lawmaker from remaining a customer, the night before PDA issued the press release about the positive test results, the agency faxed a copy of it to the representative.

Not long after their sales were suspended, the Dillers were told by a state employee from Harrisburg that if they voluntarily gave up their raw milk license, their problems with the state would clear up. Instead, the Dillers re-applied, and in response to considerable pressure from the local chapter leader of the Weston A. Price Foundation, who insisted on a meeting with Bill Chirdon, their permit was reinstated—after considerable foot dragging—in August of 2008.

The most suspicious example of biased PDA policy involved the Beulah Land Jersey Farm, owned by Dennis and Joanne Wenger. The Wengers sold milk for pasteurization to Dairylea and also had a raw milk permit. On April 8, both U.S. Dairy (a state-approved independent lab) and the PDA took samples from the bulk tank. The next day, the milk hauler for Dairylea picked up milk. On April 11, PDA informed the Wengers that their test was "presumptive positive" for listeria and requested they discontinue selling raw milk. Additionally, the PDA test results showed a somatic cell count (SCC) of over one million. On April 14, the PDA called to say that the test had confirmed "positive" for listeria and that they would have to discontinue raw milk sales. By this time the Wengers had received the results from both U.S. Dairy and Dairylea showing SCC under two hundred thousand. The Wengers faxed copies of these test results to PDA.

On April 15, 16 and 17, MicroBac (another state-approved independent lab) came to the farm to take samples from the bulk tank for listeria testing. On April 16, Dennis Wenger called two state senators to inform them about the large discrepancy in somatic cell counts between PDA's test results and those of U.S. Dairy and Dairylea. Later that day, Mr. Wenger received a call from Bill Chirdon, who insisted that the PDA laboratories "never made a mistake."

After some discussion, Chirdon offered to retest the Beulah Land Jersey Farm milk. The next day, on April 17, the state came to take samples. The SCC test results for this sample were considerably lower than the first PDA test but still much higher than those obtained by the other two labs.

On Saturday, April 19, the Wengers received the test results from the first sample taken by MicroBac—negative for listeria. On the following Monday, the state lab made a highly unusual call to MicroBac to find out the results of the Wengers' samples. MicroBac refused to release the information without the Wengers' consent. The state then called the Wengers to inform them that their sample was negative. This was followed by a call from MicroBac saying that the second and third samples had also tested negative. PDA reinstated the Wengers' raw milk permit on April 22.

It is important to stress the fact that not one of these dairies' customers got sick from listeria, in spite of the PDA's positive test results. Yet press releases linking raw milk with listeria remain on government websites and now abound on the internet. The sudden advent of findings raises the strong suspicion that the PDA wanted to build a case linking raw milk with *L. mono.* where none existed before. As a result of these incidents, many farmers have turned in their permits or have not renewed them, and are claiming their constitutional right to sell milk directly to consumers without a license. As Dennis Wenger stated, "I never questioned the state inspection system before, but now I don't trust them at all."

Health officials have withheld another important fact: microbiologists currently believe that only a few of the hundreds of types of *L. mono.* are actually pathogenic.[73] Thus, when initial tests for *L. mono.* come back positive, those charged with testing protocols for raw milk should stipulate further tests to determine the specific strain. Unfortunately, such testing is expensive and never definitive. Read on.

THE SOFT SCIENCE OF MICROBIOLOGICAL TESTING

Most people have a high regard for science, and they assume that the results of laboratory tests are precise—that they are the Truth with a capital T. However, in reality, microbiological testing is more art than science, and fraught with pitfalls. Every step of testing procedures provides the possibility for error: samples can be contaminated, mishandled or even mislabeled and analytical results can be misleading and misinterpreted. Most important, testing requires personal skill and judgment that can significantly impact the ultimate results.

Microbiological testing must accomplish three things: determine whether a bacterium is present; then determine the specific type of bacterium from thousands of others with similar characteristics; and if present determine how many there are. In other words, find, distinguish and count.[74]

The typical laboratory technique for finding bacteria begins with sample collection—which must be performed carefully to avoid contamination and prevent the numerous ways in which the sample's content may be changed. The sample is then inoculated into an enrichment liquid to encourage growth of certain bacteria and suppress others. To isolate individual bacteria colonies, the enrichment liquid is streaked across a petri dish containing nutrients solidified in agar. Standardized careful streaking—usually done by hand—helps create individual bacteria colonies containing thousands of bacteria and make them visible. This traditional means of "isolation" is based on the idea that if spread thin enough, each separate colony will grow from a single bacterium. If there were different types of bacteria in the sample, so the thinking goes, each would separate out and develop into individual colonies that could be further tested for identification.

Counting often involves making careful serial dilutions so that one tube contains low enough numbers to make counting possible, and then performing several tests on each. One traditional counting technique relies on tables to determine the "most probable number." For example, if the table gives a count of ninety-three colony-forming units per milliliter, the statistical analysis acknowledges that the actual number in this example could be as low as eighteen or as high as four hundred twenty.

Variability in results is constantly present. For example, samples taken from the same bulk tank will vary according to how the sample was collected, whether the milk was thoroughly stirred, whether the samples were kept in the inspector's pocket, how long before the sample was tested and whether they were tested in the same or different laboratories. When counting is performed using highly advanced automated machines, additional errors can be committed by the lab technician, or result from machine dysfunction or incorrect calibration of the equipment.

To determine the type of bacteria present once they have isolated a colony, technicians use various tests to detect the production of a metabolite, gas or enzyme, a change in pH or hemolysis (the breaking open of red blood cells). For example, coliform colonies produce gas and turn blue when a special compound is added to a manufacturer's specially formulated petri dish.

There are literally hundreds of test kits available to determine the kind of microorganism present, all intensely marketed by the manufacturers. If funding or patience is limited, wrong kit choices on the first few attempts may result in a failure to identify the specific type of bacteria. And as every step of the testing procedure must be defined and followed exactly, and requires the personal skill, judgment and honesty of the technician, opportunities for error are numerous. Simple clerical error in recording test results is one of the most common sources of incorrect results.

And then there is the problem of deliberate bias. As explained by Dr. Ted Beals, a pathologist with many years of laboratory experience, when investigators have preconceived ideas about what they are looking for, they have ways of finding it. They can

* Stop pursuing a question as soon as they get the answer they want;
* Keep trying until they get the answer they want;
* Fail to admit to possible misinterpretation if they get the answer they want;
* Say nothing if they don't get the answer they want.

During the period of alleged *L. mono.* contamination described earlier, officials from the Pennsylvania Department of Agriculture spoke with pride about their newly equipped state laboratory, which uses a rapid testing system, the VIDAS 30, developed by the food industry, to get quick preliminary results. But even this system requires overnight incubation of samples and specialized growth conditions, and often further "gold standard" testing fails to confirm the results obtained by the rapid testing system. In addition, the equipment was developed by the industry to err on the side of false positives. This is appropriate for internal quality testing by the food company. For industry, some false positive results for pathogens are acceptable using the rapid testing system. The food company can then play it safe by withholding food from distribution until further confirmation, or nonconfirmation, is obtained. However, false positive preliminary results used by regulators, to force the shut down of a dairy operation before confirmation, is scientifically inappropriate and can be devastating to small family dairies.

There is also the question of whether such rapid testing techniques are even appropriate for use on a living food like raw milk, which naturally contains bacteria that can confuse a machine programmed to detect a short list of characteristics that might be present in organisms that do not cause disease. And standard operating procedures are extremely specific for each test, each sample type and each type of equipment. Rapid testing equipment was not developed for fresh raw milk intended for direct consumption. It has been standardized for raw milk intended for pasteurization or pasteurized milk, so it is neither fair policy nor good science to use the same testing protocol for the two products.

If preliminary test results are positive, such as for listeria, the laboratory then uses a culturing technique intended to suppress the growth of anything in the culture other than bacteria like listeria. This is a fair test if the milk is pasteurized, because pasteurized milk is a dead food with no good bacteria to out-compete pathogens. Australian microbiologist Ron Hull, PhD, has carried out tests showing that in raw milk, the threat of listeria goes away with time because good bacteria gradually increase and eventually render listeria harmless.[75]

Furthermore, only a few strains of *Listeria monocytogenes* are associated with disease outbreaks.[76] Once *L. mono.* has been detected, additional (and often expensive) tests are needed to determine whether the bacteria are of the virulent type that causes illness in humans. And even if a laboratory finds a small number of pathogenic organisms—some new techniques are so sensitive they can find a single bacterium in very large samples—this does not mean that the consumption of a glass of raw milk testing positive will necessarily cause disease. With most organisms, it takes thousands or even millions of virulent organisms to make someone sick.

Comparing raw milk to pasteurized milk is like comparing a fresh product with a cooked product. For this reason, a zero tolerance approach is appropriate for pasteurized milk but not for raw milk, because raw milk contains good bacteria present to overwhelm any pathogens present. What's needed are studies to quantify how high the infectious dose in raw milk would have to be before it could cause illness in humans consuming the product.

USDA publishes an infectious dose for most food-borne pathogens even though they acknowledge that it is unlikely to be the same in all foods or in different people.[77] But the agency has never conducted studies to determine what the infectious dose for pathogens would be in fresh raw milk intended for human consumption.

The current zero tolerance standard for listeria in raw milk is not appropriate because, as the experience in Pennsylvania has shown, large numbers of people consuming raw milk reported as testing positive for listeria are not getting sick. The policy causes economic hardship for raw milk producers and supply interruptions for consumers. The fact that the Pennsylvania Department of Agriculture did not until recently suspend a raw milk permit when the first test was positive shows a fundamental acceptance of this concept—that the tolerance levels for listeria and other pathogens in raw milk is not zero.

According to Dr. Beals, microbiological testing should be used on the farm, where a farmer can use routine periodic testing to monitor the health of his herd, the handling of milk and the cleanliness of the containers and equipment. The appropriate use of laboratory testing for pathogens occurs *after* an illness is reported. Then testing samples from the sick person can be used to track the specific virulent bacteria to determine whether food was the source of the infection. Sophisticated fingerprint characteristics can be essential to pinpoint the exact source and allow for corrective actions to minimize risk to other people without unnecessarily harming the precarious cash flow of small farmers.

SURVEY TECHNIQUES: MORE BIAS

When investigators put together a report on an outbreak of foodborne illness intended for publication in a scientific journal, they depend not only on laboratory test results, but also on data about the individuals who got sick. And this data can be chosen and manipulated in such a way as to give the conclusion the investigators are seeking. Dr. Beal's postulates listed above apply equally well to sampling methods as they do to testing protocols—ask questions that elicit the answer you want, stop asking questions when you get the answer you want, deny any possibility of misinterpretation when you get the answer you want, and say nothing about data that conflict with the answer you want. . . then proclaim the answer you wanted to the public via scientific articles and alarmist press releases.

If health officials can possibly link an incidence of disease with raw milk, they will. The outbreak in northern Wisconsin, described earlier, provides a typical example. Hospital personnel were able to create a statistical association between illness and raw milk by excluding those who were sick but did not drink raw milk. Food questionnaires used to determine the source of illness always contain a question about raw milk consumption. Often it is the first question.

At a Pennsylvania Senate hearing on raw milk held in September, 2007, one attendee related the following story. After consuming underdone chicken in a local restaurant, her daughter became violently ill and was taken to the hospital. The diagnosis was listeriosis. Several weeks later she received a call from the health department. Their first question: "Did your daughter drink raw milk?" The woman assured the health department that her daughter did not drink raw milk and told them she suspected the underdone chicken her daughter had eaten. But the questioner was distinctly uninterested in the chicken. After repeating the question several more times, "Are you sure your daughter did not consume raw milk?" the official terminated the conversation. This occurred during the period, described earlier, when the Pennsylvania Department of Agriculture (PDA) was claiming that milk from several raw milk dairies was contaminated with *Listeria monocytogenes.*

Here's another disturbing report from a Pennsylvania activist, which occurred during the same period: "Recently I had occasion to speak with a dairy farmer who had been in the news and was the subject of harassment by the Pennsylvania Department of Agriculture. I learned that a family member had been harassed by telephone when her baby came down with salmonella poisoning. The rest of the family had eaten chicken from a fast food restaurant and drank raw milk from this particular farm, yet only the baby became ill. The baby had not consumed either food but was on formula—not breast milk, not raw cow's milk, not store-bought cow's milk. Yet the daily harassment by phone from the Pennsylvania health department had brought the mother to near collapse as she tried to care for her several healthy young children and the ill baby. The health department tried to trick, cajole and bully her into saying that the baby could have or might have had some raw milk from this farm. Upon a call from the farmer asking them to contact the farm's lawyer instead of harassing the family, PDA harassment subsided. However, other farm clients were also harassed. One patient said he had not been to get milk because of an illness so he had not even had any raw milk in the house when he became ill with salmonella."[78]

In the Ohio incident that led to the closing of Young's Dairy, the infection was known to have begun elsewhere in the state; and the dairy was also a petting zoo. Visitors to farms and petting zoos, especially children, often get sick if they do not have any natural immunity to a farm environment. If they happen to drink raw milk at the same time, the milk is blamed, not the farm.

A major source of food-borne illness is runoff water from confinement farms. Yet investigators rarely test the water when searching for a culprit. In fact, in most cases of food-borne illness where raw milk is a suspect, investigators rarely have a sample of raw milk to test. The wheels of bureaucracy move slowly and by the time an investigation has begun, the necessary sample has been consumed or poured down the drain.

Then there is the problem of selective reporting. Cases of food-borne illness that occur within a reasonable time after the consumption of raw milk are likely to be reported at a much higher rate than other cases of food-borne illness because of the aggressive campaign that the FDA, CDC, and various state agencies have waged to monitor raw milk closely and "educate" the public about its dangers. This alone could cause a statistical association to appear, one that proves nothing except the existence of reporting bias.

A document published by the Weston A. Price Foundation provides the following hypothetical scenario. "A large outbreak of salmonella affects ten thousand people. Most of them have minor symptoms ranging from queasiness to diarrhea. Ten of them call their doctors and ask whether they should worry about it. The doctors ask them if they have recently drunk raw milk, eaten raw meat or poultry, visited a petting zoo or played with a turtle—the usual suspects. Most of them have not, so the doctor says not to worry about it and to call back in a week if it persists or in a few days if it gets worse. But when one patient responds that he has drunk raw milk, the doctor is alarmed. She takes a stool sample and alerts the health authorities so they can monitor the populace for an outbreak. The authorities run a news campaign suggesting a possible association between salmonella and raw milk from a local farm, and reiterate the warning that 'drinking raw milk is playing Russian roulette with your health' and that salmonella infections can produce permanent disabilities such as 'reactive arthritis' if they go untreated. Out of the ten thousand people suffering from queasiness or transient diarrhea, about one hundred have drunk raw milk; thirty of them panic and call their physician or the health authorities. The nine thousand nine hundred who did not drink raw milk take comfort in the fact that they only eat safe foods such as cooked chicken and rinsed spinach and therefore only report their illness at the usual rate of one-tenth of one percent. Presto: a statistical association is born."[79]

And, as any statistician can tell you, correlation does not prove causation. According to author Gary Taubes, "What we derive from epidemiologic studies are associations and hypotheses. . . You cannot prove any hypothesis true. All you can do is refute the hypotheses and see which ones you have left."[80]

Or, as the saying goes, "Epidemiology is like a bikini. What is revealed is interesting. What is concealed is crucial."

MEXICAN-STYLE RAW MILK CHEESE: AN EASY TARGET

Several serious outbreaks of disease have involved Mexican-style raw milk cheese—so-called "suitcase cheese" or *queso fresco*—which is a particularly easy target for investigative bias. Consider an epidemic of listeriosis in Los Angeles County, which involved one hundred forty-two reported cases between January 1 through August 15, 1985. Ninety-three cases occurred in pregnant women or their offspring. There were forty-eight deaths: twenty fetuses, ten neonates and eighteen nonpregnant adults. Most of the victims were Hispanic.

In a 1988 report on the epidemic, entitled "Epidemic listeriosis associated with Mexican-style cheese," lead author M. J. Linnan and his team wrote, "An investigation of the cheese plant suggested that the cheese was commonly contaminated with unpasteurized milk."[81] But there was never any evidence that the contamination of this cheese—which was sold as a pasteurized product—was related to contaminated raw milk![82]

The initial investigation found that, compared to uninfected controls, infected patients were over five times more likely to have eaten Mexican-style cheese, over four times more likely to have engaged in sexual intercourse in the preceding month (remember, many of those who became sick were pregnant, therefore were likely to be married or have partners), and just over four times as likely to have consumed a root vegetable called jicama (remember, most of the victims were Hispanic).

A secondary investigation found that the association with cheese was due specifically to the use of a cheese produced by Jalisco Mexican Products. The investigators did not pursue the associations with sexual intercourse or jicama any further.

Investigators found the matching strain of listeria in multiple unopened packages of the cheese on June 12, 1985 and initiated a recall of the product the following day. Despite the recall, the outbreak continued producing new cases at full force through the end of July.

The team then tested the cheese for alkaline phosphatase (ALP) activity. Complete destruction of the enzyme ALP is considered the standard test for successful pasteurization. They found excessive ALP activity in nine out of eighty samples of cheese. But investigation of the factory showed that the pasteurizer was working properly.

The authors provided no data showing a relationship between ALP levels and contamination with live listeria, and of twenty-seven dairy farms that supplied raw milk to the cheese plant, they found no cases of listeriosis in any of the herds. Furthermore, all raw milk samples tested negative for the organism. Yet the researchers concluded that the outbreak was caused by cheese "commonly contaminated with unpasteurized milk."

The presence of ALP in some of the cheese samples allowed the authors of the Linnan report to blame raw milk for the outbreak. But three years later, researchers showed that Mexican-style soft cheeses contain both heat-stable and heat-labile forms of microbial ALP.[83] Moreover, some cheese bacteria produce ALP that cannot be differentiated from ALP indigenous to milk. In 2007, the industry introduced a new detection method to correct this problem.[84] Thus, this test when performed in 1985 was not a valid means for demonstrating inadequate pasteurization in this type of cheese. The milk or cheese was clearly contaminated at the cheese manufacturing plant, either before pasteurization, after pasteurization, or both.

Jalisco sued Alta Dena Dairy, one of its suppliers, for a portion of the estimated one hundred million dollars in damage claims filed by victims of the listeriosis epidemic. In 1989, however, a jury absolved Alta Dena of all responsibility for the epidemic, citing complete lack of evidence that its raw milk was contaminated.

According to the Linnan report, this outbreak of listeria was the third one traced to a specific food product. The first occurred in 1981 and was traced to coleslaw. The second, in which forty-nine patients became ill and fourteen died—occurred in 1983 and was traced to pasteurized milk. Health officials often warn pregnant women not to consume raw milk or Mexican-style cheese—but never about the dangers of consuming coleslaw and pasteurized milk.

Mexican-style cheese was the whipping boy for a large outbreak of listeriosis that occurred in North Carolina between October, 2000 and January, 2001. Several years later, in 2005, a team led by P. D. MacDonald published a report on the epidemic.[85] The results of their case-control study may have been biased from the beginning as "During the study, rumors spread that the suspected vehicle of infection was homemade Mexican-style cheese." The patients were questioned several months after the event, and "rumors" may have helped them selectively remember consuming *queso fresco*.

Nevertheless, investigators found that case patients were almost five times as likely as controls to have eaten hot dogs. According to a 2003 risk assessment jointly published by the FDA, USDA and CDC, non-reheated hot dogs are over three hundred eighty times as likely as fresh, soft cheese to cause listeriosis.[86] No hot dogs were tested for the presence of listeria, even though during the period of the outbreak, a massive recall of listeria-infected hotdogs—nine hundred thousand pounds of them—took place in ten southeastern states.[87] Barbequed chicken was also recalled at the time—but the company producing the product refused to comply with the recall.[88]

Instead, the MacDonald team pointed the finger at the raw milk used to produce soft cheese. The title of their report: "Outbreak of listeriosis among Mexican immigrants as a result of consumption of illicitly produced Mexican-style cheese."

In the body of the report, we read, "For Hispanic women, we recommend targeted education and dietary counseling about the hazards of eating fresh cheese, undercooked hot dogs, deli meats and other ready-to-eat meat products implicated as vehicles for listeriosis during pregnancy." But only "illicitly produced Mexican-style cheese" got star billing in the title.

Of the several sources of raw milk used for the cheese, listeria was present in the bulk tank raw milk of one manufacturing-grade dairy, and it matched isolates recovered from ten female case patients, from cheese bought from a door-to-door vendor and from unlabeled cheese from two Hispanic markets. MacDonald and his team fail to mention whether they obtained matching isolates from the listeriosis-infected hotdogs.

Unlike the Jalisco case in California, where listeria was found in unopened packages of factory-made cheese, some of the samples tested in North Carolina were already opened and came from the refrigerators of individuals who had become ill. The finding of listeria in the cheese does not, therefore, mean that the cheese caused an illness. It is equally likely that the sick person contaminated the cheese. And because the *queso fresco* in this case was an artisan product, likely vectors of disease include cutting boards, kitchen counters and food preparation utensils in small kitchens where the standards of sanitation may not be ideal. But since the outbreak occurred in a Hispanic community where everyone consumed Hispanic food, including Mexican-style raw cheese, it was easy for the researchers to create a statistical association of raw milk cheese with the outbreak.

THE PUBLISHED LITERATURE ON RAW MILK OUTBREAKS:
BUILDING THE CASE AGAINST RAW MILK

The National Conference on Interstate Milk Shipments is a non-profit organization that represents the interests of the dairy industry. The group meets every other year to discuss topics of concern to conventional milk processors. At the group's May, 2005 meeting, Cindy Leonard, MS, of the FDA's Division of Dairy and Egg Safety presented a PowerPoint presentation prepared by John F. Sheehan, head of the division.The presentation aimed at defusing the arguments of raw milk proponents, namely that raw milk is inherently safe and more nutritious than pasteurized milk. Mr. Sheehan's take-home message: raw milk provides no nutritional advantage over pasteurized, and the only way to make raw milk safe is to pasteurize it.[89]

Sheehan refers to fifteen studies linking illness with raw milk or Mexican-style raw cheese. Of the fifteen papers referenced, eighty percent linked raw milk to illness without a positive milk sample, and two-thirds found no valid statistical association with raw milk. The FDA presentation misrepresented the findings of almost half the reports. In a third, the authors discovered alternative likely sources of infection but did not pursue them and in thirteen percent of the studies, investigators found no evidence that anyone had even consumed a raw milk product. In one study, the outbreak did not even exist![90]

More to the point, not one of the fifteen studies demonstrated that pasteurization would have prevented the outbreak. (We'll examine the claim that raw milk has no health benefits in Chapter 16.)

Another review of cases alledging illness caused by unpasteurized milk and cheese comes from the Centers for Disease Control.[91] For the period 1998 to 2005, the agency lists thirty-nine outbreaks associated with raw dairy products resulting in eight hundred thirty-one illnesses, sixty-six hospitalizations and one death. Of these, more than half are newspaper reports and health department press releases, not articles published in the scientific literature. In eighty-two percent of cases, there was no valid milk sample and in seventy-eight percent, officials could not provide a valid statistical association with raw milk. In ninety-seven percent of the cases, no evidence is provided to indicate that pasteurization would have prevented the outbreak. Two of the incidents were traced to pasteurized milk and one to pasteurization failure. Three of the reports cited were either unpublished or not verifiable. Most importantly, the death reported in the summary appears nowhere in the table.[92] More sloppy government work accepted as gospel in the court of public opinion.

Bill Marler is a high-profile attorney who specializes in food-borne illness litigation. His law firm won the highly publicized Jack-in-the-Box and Odwalla juice cases, in which dozens of people in Washington State became ill and several died from *E. Coli O157:H7*. In 2008, Marler focused his attention on raw milk, posting a blog[93] and publishing two position papers full of FDA-inspired language against raw milk and raw milk products.[94]

Interestingly, up to that point, Marler had lost the one raw milk case he had taken, which involved a 2001 outbreak of *E. coli O157: H7* that sickened at least two hundred people at Prospect Elementary School in rural Robeson County, North Carolina. An epidemiological report blamed the outbreak on homemade butter made from raw cream served to students as a classroom demonstration. The judge ruled that the school had governmental immunity and could not be sued.[95]

One of Marler's position papers contains a list of one hundred two references from scientific journals purporting to implicate raw milk in disease. It is obvious that the list was compiled by an intern or law student who simply did a search for "raw," "milk" and "outbreak" without actually reading the studies. Only seventy-three out of the total report on actual illnesses; eight report on the presence of pathogens in the milk of bulk holding tanks (hence milk destined for pasteurization) and twenty-one are reviews, editorials or letters to the editors of scientific journals. In fact, a number of the citations are reports of outbreaks traced to pasteurized milk, reviews focusing on the dangers of pasteurized milk, or letters to the editor supporting the right of consumers to purchase raw milk.

Of the studies implicating raw milk in food-borne illness, a full ninety-six percent had either no valid positive milk sample or no valid statistical association. Several of the studies served as a platform to hurl insults at raw milk advocates or discuss methods for hurting the commerical interests of farmers. One study author complained that because raw milk advocates "have lost their case in the scientific and medical communities," they have turned to the legal and political arena to take advantage of the "current climate of heightened concern for personal liberties and freedom of choice, and frequent rejection of science."[96]

## SALMONELLA IN RAW MILK AND OTHER FOODS: THE DOUBLE STANDARD

Infection with salmonella species accounts for a substantial portion of food-borne illness in this country, with an estimated million and one half cases and five hundred deaths annually.[97] An infective dose of salmonella requires at least one million organisms. Ground beef is a common and persistent source; USDA regulations allow for up to ten percent of the samples taken at a given plant to contain salmonella, but these limits are often exceeded. High levels of salmonella in ground beef indicate high levels of fecal contamination.

Meanwhile, known sources of salmonella are routinely fed to cattle. Quoting again from *Fast Food Nation* by Eric Schlosser: "A study published a few years ago in *Preventive Medicine* notes that in Arkansas alone, about 3 million pounds of chicken manure were fed to cattle in 1994. According to Dr. Neal D. Barnard, who heads the Physicians Committee for Responsible Medicine, chicken manure may contain dangerous bacteria such as salmonella and campylobacter, parasites such as tapeworms and *Giardia lamblia*, antibiotic residues, arsenic and heavy metals."[98]

An example of the difficulty USDA officials have in enforcing regulations against the meatpacking industry is provided by the 1999 case of a ground beef plant in Dallas, owned by Supreme Beef Processors, which failed a series of USDA tests for salmonella. Up to forty-seven percent of the company's ground beef contained salmonella—nearly five times higher than what USDA regulations allow. Yet the USDA continued to purchase large quantities of meat from Supreme Beef for use in schools. Indeed, Supreme Beef Processors was one of the nation's largest suppliers to the school lunch program, annually providing nearly half of its ground beef to schools. On November 30, 1999, the USDA finally removed inspectors from the company's plant, shutting it down.

The next day, Supreme Beef sued the USDA in federal court, claiming that salmonella was a natural organism, not an adulterant, and contending that the USDA should not have removed inspectors from the plant. Federal Judge A. Joe Fish ordered inspectors back into the plant, pending resolution of the lawsuit. The plant shutdown lasted less than one day. Six months later the judge issued a decision, ruling that the presence of high levels of salmonella in the plant's ground beef was not proof that conditions there were "unsanitary."

"Fish endorsed one of Supreme Beef's central arguments: a ground beef processor should not be held responsible for the bacterial levels of meat that could easily have been tainted with salmonella at a slaughterhouse. The ruling cast doubt on the USDA's ability to withdraw inspectors from a plant [and thus shut the plant down] where tests revealed excessive levels of fecal contamination. Although Supreme Beef portrayed itself as an innocent victim of forces beyond its control, much of the beef used at the plant had come from its own slaughterhouse in Ladonia, Texas. That slaughterhouse had repeatedly failed USDA tests for salmonella."[99]

In contrast, consider the story of raw milk and salmonella in California. The California State Health Department and several county health departments, most notably those of Los Angeles and San Diego counties, conspired for some thirty years to harass Alta Dena Dairy and nearly every other raw milk dairy in the state, and to put them out of business. The Steuve brothers—Ed, Harold and Elmer—founded Alta Dena in Monrovia in 1945 with sixty-one milk cows and two bulls. Dr. Pottenger was a regular customer. In 1950 the family purchased a much larger operation in Chino. The dairy became certified for raw milk production in 1953 and grew rapidly. By the 1980s, the dairy milked over eight thousand cows daily and owned eighteen thousand animals. With eight hundred employees, Alta Dena was the largest producer-distributor in the nation, selling over twenty thousand gallons of certified raw milk daily. Alta Dena products, including raw milk and raw butter, buttermilk, ice cream, kefir and yogurt, were sold in health food stores in every state. For over forty years, Alta Dena proved that safe and healthy raw dairy products could be produced and distributed on a large scale with literally no proven cases of illness caused by their products. This fact did not deter the various county health officials and the California State Health Department from their campaign to destroy Alta Dena. Eventually, the Department's chosen weapon would be salmonella, a weapon they used only after failing with the alleged threat of a number of other diseases to generate fear of raw milk in the public and a costly ongoing legal morass for Alta Dena.

The first assault occurred in 1965, when a San Diego County health officer named Askew summarily issued an order banning all raw milk in the county, claiming to have found *Staphylococcus aureus* in Alta Dena milk. While these bacteria can be involved in everything from skin infections to pneumonia, they are ubiquitous in the environment and are carried by about half of the human population. Many pasteurized dairy products contain low levels of *S. aureus*, with residues of higher levels present before pasteurization.[100] *S. aureus* poisoning is usually traced to processed foods such as ham and cream-filled pastries. Although *S. aureus* can cause mastitis in cows and staphylococcal poisoning has on occasion been attributed to a wide variety of dairy products in the past, the only four major outbreaks reported in the United States since 1970 have involved dairy products, namely processed butter products and pasteurized two percent chocolate milk.[101]

Illness caused by *S. aureus* is brief and intense, with nausea, vomiting, diarrhea and cramps. Acute symptoms last only a few hours, with the patient fully recovered within a day or two.[102] No one had become ill when Alta Dena milk was banned in San Diego County. "The health officer stated publicly that he was going to do away with raw milk in the state of California," writes Dr. William Campbell Douglass in *The Milk Book*, "if it was the last thing he ever did."[103]

According to Douglass, health officer Askew was asked at a hearing of the County Board of Supervisors whether to his knowledge anyone had ever become sick from drinking certified raw milk in San Diego County. He answered, "No, but it could happen." The Board urged him to lift the ban, yet he refused to do so. The country's largest producer-distributor dairy could not sell its raw milk in San Diego County, and the ban remained in effect for three years. Finally, after a three-year battle, the Fourth District Court of Appeals ruled that the health officer had exceeded his authority. Meanwhile, in 1967, the California Medical Society passed a resolution calling for the pasteurization of all milk in California. Three other counties summarily banned raw milk, but vociferous public opposition succeeded in removal of the bans.

It was in January of 1969 that the Los Angeles County Health Department attacked Alta Dena. The *Los Angeles Times* announced, with banner headlines based on information supplied by the Health Department, that Alta Dena raw milk was banned with the presumption of contamination by the organisms that cause Q fever. This obscure viral-like disease is caused by the parasite *Coxiella burnetii*, which is carried in ticks and sometimes in the ruminant animals that ticks infect.

The parasite causes no symptoms in the animals; most cases of Q fever occur in farmers and meat factory employees who work in close contact with animals, and the disease appears to be transmitted by inhalation of the parasite. The symptoms are fever, pain and intense headache, and most patients recover fully with two to four weeks of antibiotic treatment.[104]

*C. burnetii* has been found in milk from cows carrying the parasite, and regular consumers of raw milk sometimes have antibodies to the parasite without showing any evidence of disease. This implies that exposure stimulates the immune system to develop resistance. Two reports in the medical literature have linked raw milk consumption with a few dozen cases of Q fever (one article was published in 1968, a few months before the Los Angeles County leveled charges), but the association remains totally unproven. In fact, Eliott Ryser states that "in one study in which contaminated raw milk was ingested by human volunteers illness did not occur." Other studies showed that the parasite survived the temperatures normally used for pasteurization for most of the twentieth century.[105] On balance, it appears unlikely that Q fever has ever been transmitted by the consumption of raw milk.

No one in Los Angeles County had reported any symptoms of Q fever. Alta Dena defied the LA County Health Board ban, continuing to sell raw milk in the county, and was taken to court. Meanwhile the dairy labeled its raw milk as "pet food, not for human consumption." Harold Steuve, president of the dairy and the mayor of Monrovia at the time, was arrested for contempt of court. Only when Alta Dena's expert witnesses testified that Q fever was caused by inhalation of the parasite and not by consumption of raw milk did prosecutors drop the charges.

A 1966 Los Angeles County Health Department report on Q fever proves the health department's bias. The report describes seven cases, six of which lived "in or around dairies." None of the seven drank raw milk. Contact with animals and subsequent airborne spread, the report admitted, was the vector for infection, but claimed that "the most practical solution now available" was the universal pasteurization of all milk.

The California State Health Department led the next attack, in 1974, with a statewide ban of Alta Dena's raw milk, citing the threat of brucellosis. All Alta Dena cows had of course been vaccinated against the disease and were routinely tested as an extra precaution. The ban forced the dairy to go to court once again and to retest the entire herd. No brucellosis was found, and Alta Dena resumed sales of raw milk. But, once again, the Steuves lost thousands of dollars in legal and testing expenses, and an untold amount of sales due to adverse publicity.

Having failed to show that Alta Dena raw milk had ever caused any of the classic milk-borne illnesses, the state zeroed in on salmonella. In the mid 1970s the state made numerous statements claiming that salmonella-contaminated raw milk was produced by Alta Dena and other California raw milk dairies. In 1978, the Steuve brothers led California raw milk producers in seeking a California state Senate bill requiring the State Health Department to oversee raw dairy foods in a manner similar to that of other food products. On June 4th, a week before the Senate bill was to come up for debate, a state laboratory claimed to have found salmonella in Alta Dena milk. The State Health Department delayed five days before releasing the information, while the public bought and consumed the milk—milk the state would subsequently declare a public health hazard. Then on June 9th, two days before the Senate debate was to begin, the Department notified the press of the alleged contamination, claiming that an epidemic of salmonella poisoning was imminent.

The only epidemic was an outbreak of inflammatory news reports. From San Rafael to Sacramento, from Ventura to Vallejo, raw milk producers stood accused: "Raw Milk Warning," "Some Raw Milk Found to be Contaminated," "Contaminated Raw Milk Ordered Off Shelves." Radio announcements warned the public not to drink raw milk from Alta Dena dairy. No one got sick, but in the hysteria the Senate bill failed.

A few days later, after reviewing relevant documents, the *Los Angeles Herald Examiner* accused California State Health Department officials of falsifying bacterial reports in order to defeat the Senate bill. Two independent laboratories—one that did testing for the Los Angeles County Medical Milk Commission and the other that did considerable testing for the state—returned negative results for salmonella. The Health Department laboratory had either falsified its results, or the testing methods had been so sloppy that the milk samples were contaminated during the testing procedures. The *Herald Examiner* article hinted at a conspiracy to eliminate raw dairy products among members of the State Health Department.

Other State Health Department tactics bolstered the conspiracy charge. In several instances, products for which there was no evidence of contamination at all—falsified, inaccurate, or otherwise—were destroyed. Officials forced a food store manager to pour ninety gallons of certified raw milk down a toilet. Health officers punched holes in Alta Dena raw cheese, and poured Chlorox over it. The Department leaked a "staff report" to *New Age*, a widely read California magazine, which published excerpts in August 1978. "Evidence points to a continuing health hazard to the public consuming Alta Dena's raw certified milk," reported *New Age*, and quoted a medical epidemiologist who claimed that Alta Dena raw milk was killing cancer patients.

The epidemiologist and two of his colleagues, both of whom worked with the California State Health Department, published a report in the *British Medical Journal* stating that twenty-two patients, mostly with leukemias and lymphomas, had died between 1971 and 1975, sometime after "exposure" to Alta Dena raw milk.[106] Publication in a foreign journal made the authors relatively immune to lawsuits. Since then, the article has been widely quoted as scientific fact in American journals.

The governor's office in California received over seventeen thousand letters, telegrams and phone calls in defense of Alta Dena within two months of the *Herald Examiner* report. The furor died down, but the number of letters alone grew to over fifty thousand. The State Health Department was undeterred, repeating unconfirmed allegations of salmonella contamination later in 1978 and again in 1979. Both times, newspapers generated the usual scare headlines: "Poisoned Milk Recalled," "State Issues Warning About Alta Dena Milk," and "Tainted Milk Ordered Off Market Shelves." Again the allegations were false, no one got sick and Alta Dena carried on. But one by one, other raw milk producers in the state went out of business.

In 1983, Nevada state inspectors seized Alta Dena raw milk from a health food store and claimed it contained salmonella. The milk was twenty-one days old, past its expiration date. Four different labs, including the California State Health Department lab and one county lab, subsequently analyzed the milk and found no salmonella. The FDA spent three days investigating the Alta Dena Dairy and found nothing of importance. The California State Health Department nevertheless issued warnings to the people of California not to drink Alta Dena raw milk, or even give it to their pets.

Also in 1983, the report describing five serious salmonella cases at the Veterans Administration Medical Center in San Diego was published.[107] Three of the five patients were regular consumers of Alta Dena raw milk, and one of them, a patient with advanced cancer who had been receiving extensive chemotherapy, died with an acute salmonella infection.

Ignoring all the evidence on the benefits of raw milk and the desire of many people to consume it, the Department used the *possibility* of occasional salmonella contamination as an excuse to wage a vendetta against Alta Dena and California's other raw milk producers.

In 1984, an article in *Vogue* headlined "A Raw Milk Warning: A New and Dangerous Health Fad" featured statistics published in the newsletter of an organization called California Council Against Health Frauds. The report claimed that raw milk drinkers were at increased risk of salmonella infection, "which can result in high fevers and bloody diarrhea." These symptoms are extremely rare for most salmonella infections. People who drink raw milk are one hundred eighteen times more at risk, said the article. This exaggeration was obtained by manipulating figures originally published in 1944.

In 19, Consumers Union of the United States joined with California's conventional dairy producers to file suit against Alta Dena Dairy for advertising, allegedly falsely, that raw milk was healthful and pasteurized was not. The State Health Department concurrently claimed that raw milk products were a public health hazard and prohibited Alta Dena from distributing and selling its raw milk pending settlement of the Consumers Union suit. In 1992, the court ruled that Alta Dena's health claims were illegal and ordered all raw milk sold in California to carry a government warning. The Steuves then sold Alta Dena Dairy, but continued to produce and distribute raw dairy products under the Steuve's Natural label.

In 1997, John Leedom, MD, one of the six members of the Los Angeles County Medical Milk Commission, publicly stated that not only licensed grade A raw milk but also certified raw milk should be banned in Los Angeles County. Alta Dena produced licensed grade A raw milk that was also certified by the Commission; California's other licensed grade A raw milk producers were not certified. Three other commissioners sided with Leedom. According to James Privitera, MD, one of the two commissioners who favored keeping raw milk available, the majority implemented regulations so restrictive and prejudicial that it became impossible for raw milk producers to stay in business. Alta Dena's new owners at that point stopped selling raw milk, and Steuve's Natural raw milk has not been available since May, 1999. We'll pick up the story of what's happened with raw milk in California later in this chapter.

DEATHS ATTRIBUTED TO RAW MILK: MORE BAD SCIENCE
Illness attributed to raw milk tends to be mild and of short duration; occasionally, however, a report links raw milk with death. One of the most widely cited involves the cancer patient at the Veterans Administration, mentioned above, who consumed Alta Dena milk. Her death was attributed to a virulent form of the bacterium, *Salmonella dublin*

(*S. dublin*). As with most infections, people with suppressed immune systems (such as AIDS patients or people taking corticosteroids or chemotherapy) have the greatest risk from organisms like salmonella.

The report, published in the *Western Journal of Medicine* in May, 1983 was entitled "Invasive *Salmonella dublin* Infections Associated with Drinking Raw Milk."[108] The author conducted a year-long study in 1980 and 1981 at the Veterans Administration Medical Center (VAMC) in San Diego. During that year, fourteen cases of salmonella infection had been diagnosed at the hospital; five of them were *S. dublin* infections. The ages of these five individuals ranged from fifty-six to ninety-seven, and all but one had a serious preexisting chronic disease or were taking immunosuppressive corticosteroid or chemotherapy drugs. Three of the five had drunk raw milk from Alta Dena dairy within the previous two weeks.

The eighty-five-year-old woman had chronic leukemia, diagnosed in 1979. To quote from the article, "In September 1981 she was treated for the first time with cyclophosphamide [a highly toxic chemotherapy agent which impairs natural immunity to infection] and prednisone three times a day. A week later diarrhea, fever and chills developed and she had a syncopal episode [temporary loss of consciousness due to a fall in blood pressure]. . . blood, urine, and stool cultures all grew *S. dublin* . . . she died on the 17th hospital day. . . This woman's immune status was compromised by both the leukemia and the therapy. She presented in shock with an overwhelming Salmonella bacteremia [bacteria in the blood]." Three of the other four patients with *S. dublin* infections were sick enough to require antibiotic therapy and admission to the hospital; one was hospitalized for several weeks.

This story presents another example of the gulf between biased science and the facts of the case. The doctors offered no proof that the raw milk the woman drank carried salmonella. And whatever the source of infection, were it not for the immunosuppressive drugs, none of the individuals would have become infected with salmonella. How long had the eighty-five-year-old woman been drinking raw milk with impunity before her first week of chemotherapy, at the end of which she became deathly ill? The article does not address this question. About the many benefits of raw milk, the author says only, "I will not comment on the validity of the nutritional claims that are made for raw milk."

Another case occurred in 1975 and involved an infant who was switched from breast-feeding to raw goat milk at two months. The child began to have loose green stools with some streaking of blood and a purplish discoloration of the gums. After receiving a DPT immunization at five months, the child began to vomit three or four times a day and was admitted to the hospital one week later. On the eleventh day after admission, he received a blood transfusion using blood that had evidence of a *Toxoplasmosis gondii* infection, and this evidence was found in the child a few days later. The infant was severely deficient in folic acid, which is present at only one-fifth the level in goat milk as it is in cow milk or human milk.

The report on his death carried the title, "Toxoplasmosis in an infant fed unpasteurized goat milk."[109] None of the milk samples tested positive for *T. gondii*, but the authors blamed the infant's symptoms on *T. gondii* supposedly acquired from drinking raw milk anyway, and offered no discussion of how his severe folic acid deficiency may have contributed to his symptoms.

Other deaths attributed to raw milk are found in reports on infection allegedly due to Mexican-style raw milk cheese. As discussed earlier in this chapter, raw Mexican-style cheese is an easy target. In the California outbreak, raw milk was exonerated by a jury; in the North Carolina outbreak, investigators ignored other more likely vectors of disease, based their conclusions on tests of opened samples, and engaged in interview techniques designed to achieve the foregone conclusion that raw milk was to blame.

## TYPHOID FEVER, SCARLET FEVER AND DIPHTHERIA: BAD SCIENCE FROM THE PAST

While illness attributed to raw milk in modern times involves acute gastrointestinal episodes that are usually short-lived and do not require medical treatment, fifty or one hundred years ago, raw milk was routinely blamed for a host of diseases often depicted as deadly. These diseases included typhoid fever, scarlet fever, diphtheria, tuberculosis and undulant fever. Although these diseases occur only rarely today—many have not been linked to milk at all since the 1950s—they are often trotted out in official publications, media stories and hearings on legislation affecting the sale of raw milk. Public health officials imply that should raw milk become more widely available, the old diseases would be back with us, threatening many people with disease.

An example is found in Elliot Ryser's chapter "Public Health Concerns" in *Applied Dairy Microbiology*:[110] "Outbreaks of milk-borne illness date from the inception of the dairy industry. Bacterial infections including diphtheria, scarlet fever, tuberculosis and typhoid fever predominated before World War II and were almost invariably linked to consumption of raw milk.. . ." No reference is given for this incorrect information. Nor is there mention of the fact that pasteurized milk caused the worst milk-borne outbreak of typhoid fever ever; in 1927 in Montreal, almost five thousand people were stricken and four hundred fifty-three died during a four-month period in an epidemic that was traced to negligence at a local pasteurizing plant.[111]

Ryser continues: ". . . early surveillance efforts soon led to passage of the first Model Milk Ordinance, which stressed nationwide pasteurization and the eventual reduction in the incidence of milk-borne enteric diseases with no milk-borne cases of diphtheria, scarlet fever, tuberculosis, or typhoid fever reported in more than 40 years. . . . Banning the interstate shipment of all raw milk products, both certified and noncertified, in 1986 helped reduce the number of raw milk-related outbreaks. Sporadic illnesses continue to be reported, however, particularly among farm families who routinely consume milk from their own dairy herds." Again no references are given, this time for the statement about farm families. Taken together, these passages are not only misleading but also very confusing. Let's examine them and see why.

First we have the sentence "Bacterial infections including diphtheria, scarlet fever, tuberculosis and typhoid fever predominated before World War II and were almost invariably linked to consumption of raw milk." Dr. Ryser appears to have told us that raw milk caused most cases of these illnesses. That assertion would be blatantly untrue—but that is not quite what he is telling us. For if we check back to the sentence before ("Outbreaks of milk-borne illness date from the inception of the dairy industry"), we see that he may be referring only to cases of the diseases that were milk-borne.

But as indicated above, Ryser does not reference the "almost invariably" statement. How much milk-borne disease was actually attributed to raw milk in the years leading up to and during World War II? In her series of articles "Why Milk Pasteurization?" published in the *Rural New Yorker*, Jean Bullitt Darlington provided some revealing statistics published by the Ontario Department of Health and the U.S. Public Health Service. For the years 1934 through 1941, the total number of cases of typhoid fever reported for the province of Ontario, from all causes, was just under two thousand, with two hundred forty five deaths. The total number of cases reported as milk-borne was sixteen, with two deaths.[112] The records do not tell us how many of these few cases were associated with raw milk and how many with pasteurized. But it is clear that Ryser's association of typhoid fever with raw milk is highly misleading. In fact, less than one percent of the total cases of typhoid in the eight-year period were reported as milk-borne, and less than one percent of the deaths were from cases that were reported as milk-borne.

Figures for the United States demonstrate that Ryser's contention that milk-borne diseases ". . . were almost invariably linked to consumption of raw milk" not only has no basis in fact, but presents a picture that is the opposite of the facts. The U.S. Public Health Service reported that in twenty-two years, 1922-1944 inclusive, reports linked a total of almost thirty-eight thousand cases of all kinds of diseases to all varieties of milk and milk products, pasteurized and raw, with an average of seventeen hundred twenty-six cases per year. For 1944 in particular, there were one thousand four hundred forty-nine milk-related cases, of which only four hundred thirty were attributed to raw milk. There were twenty deaths—only one of which was attributed to the consumption of raw milk.[113, 114]

As noted above, Ryser reports, ". . . the eventual reduction in the incidence of milk-borne enteric diseases with no milk-borne cases of diphtheria, scarlet fever, tuberculosis, or typhoid fever reported in more than 40 years. . . . Banning the interstate shipment of all raw milk products, both certified and noncertified, in 1986 helped reduce the number of raw milk-related outbreaks." Here it appears that banning raw milk had the effect of reducing the incidence of diphtheria, scarlet fever, tuberculosis and typhoid fever. But since Ryser has just told us that there have been no milk-borne cases during the last forty years, he is actually claiming a reduction in the "number of milk-related outbreaks" of "enteric diseases" (typically mild gastrointestinal illness). His next sentence is, "Sporadic illnesses continue to be reported, however, particularly among farm families who routinely consume milk from their own dairy herds." The implication once again is that these sporadic illnesses include diphtheria, scarlet fever, tuberculosis and typhoid fever when in fact they are "enteric diseases," a few days of diarrhea. Ryser provides no reference to document this assertion. It is impossible to say with certainty whether this writing is deliberately misleading or simply inept.

In this and earlier chapters, we've examined gross exaggerations by public health authorities on the extent of problems caused by raw milk—a constant theme through the medical literature of the past one hundred years. In Chapter 5, I described part of a 1929 address by William Dodge Frost, PhD and Doctor of Public Health, in which he analyzed the question of how many of the cases of typhoid, scarlet fever and diphtheria in the United States in the years 1906 through 1925 could be attributed to the consumption of milk. Here I quote some of the actual figures that formed the basis of Dr. Frost's conclusions:

"The table shows that the proportion of milk-borne typhoid to the total amount of typhoid varies from 0.17 to 0.94 of 1 percent and that the average for the 20-year period is about one-half of 1 percent (0.53 percent).

"In the case of scarlet fever, the yearly percentages range from 0.05 to 0.37 of 1 percent with an average of 0.106 percent.

"The percentages for diphtheria range from 0.0 to 0.18 of 1 percent, with an average of 0.028 percent.

"The milk-borne are 0.221 of 1 percent of the total [for all three diseases] or practically 1 case milk-borne to 450 cases acquired some other way."[115]

This evidence about typhoid fever, scarlet fever and diphtheria should be considered along with that of Mrs. Darlington. Consider too the fact that there have been no milk-borne cases of these diseases reported during the past forty years, despite the continued legal availability of raw milk in some thirty-five states, and the fact that millions of farm families during the last forty years have continued to drink raw milk. Is it not abundantly clear that any allusion to potential problems with these diseases today, as a warning against raw milk becoming more widely available, is a complete and utter smokescreen?

Once again quoting Mrs. Darlington, whose 1947 articles remain as relevant today as ever: "If evidence for the case for [compulsory] pasteurization is so difficult to find that it must needs be distorted and in some cases even invented—which is clear from the most recent publicity on the subject—an honest mind cannot fail to grasp that the case for [compulsory] pasteurization is a very weak case indeed."[116]

## RAW MILK AND *E. COLI O157:H7*

Small social gatherings used to be the source of most cases of food poisoning. Such outbreaks still do occur, but new kinds of outbreaks are more typical now, outbreaks caused by changes in the way food is produced. According to Dr. Robert V. Tauxe, head of the Food-borne and Diarrheal Diseases Branch at the CDC, America's centralized, industrialized system of food processing has created outbreaks that have the potential to sicken millions of people.[117]

Food-borne illness from milk products usually involves gastrointestinal illness precipitated by the bacteria salmonella and campylobacter. Incidents involving these two organisms have accounted for most dairy-related illnesses reported since the early 1980s. Recently, the new virulent form of *E. coli* (*E. coli O157:H7*) has caused dairy-related outbreaks of illness, which have received considerable attention because of the particularly severe or fatal complications sometimes produced by the organisms. (Most forms of *E. coli* do not cause illness, and in fact play a beneficial role in the digestive tract, and even with *E. coli O157: H7*, only a few of its strains are pathogenic.) In *Applied Dairy Microbiology*, Ryser reports, "at least 60 cases of raw milk-associated illness" due to *E. coli O157:H7*. In the same paragraph, he documents more than

500 hamburger-related cases of *E. coli O157:H7* illness that caused the deaths of four children in 1993—the now famous Jack-in-the-Box case that occurred in Washington state. At least fifteen additional outbreaks linked to the consumption of undercooked ground beef occurred in the 1980s. In Canada, sixteen hundred cases were reported in 1992, and fourteen hundred were reported in the United States in 1994.[118]

Ryser also documents a number of *E. coli O157:H7* outbreaks that involved pasteurized milk, citing faulty pasteurization or post-pasteurization contamination. As usual, Ryser cites these outbreaks as additional reason for compulsory pasteurization. Writing of one outbreak involving eighteen severe cases in Montana in 1994, however, he actually provides us with fair warning that one should avoid all pasteurized dairy products (though this was certainly not his intent): "This outbreak does raise serious new public health concerns regarding the possible presence of toxic strains of *E. coli* in factory environments and their entry into finished products as post-processing contaminants."[119] It appears that what's in the milk is the same thing Eric Schlosser told us is in the meat.

One outbreak attributed to raw milk and often cited in the scientific literature took place in 2001 on Vancouver Island in British Columbia. The report, entitled "*Escherichia coli O157* Outbreak Associated with the Ingestion of Unpasteurized Goat's Milk in British Columbia," describes five cases of *E. coli O157:H7*.[120]

The first case occurred in a one-year-old child who had consumed raw goat's milk and also had visited a petting zoo—a common source of illness. The authors did not describe any follow-up of the petting zoo lead. Two children of the same family became ill soon after, but the authors did not report whether they had drunk raw milk. Three months earlier, the family had joined a cooperative that supplied them with the milk, of which eighteen other families were members, none of whom reported illness. Two children of another family who visited the cooperative farm became ill, but the authors did not report whether they had purchased or consumed any raw milk.

Two out of seven bottles of milk purchased by the first family were tested for the organism, one of which was found "presumptively" positive after "enrichment" with a testing substance; the other sample tested negative. The authors did not report whether the infected bottle had already been opened, nor did they report testing any milk obtained from the farm itself. They did not discuss the possibility that the infected persons had contaminated the milk after becoming ill, nor did they report testing any other foods from the family's house or the water on the farm. The investigation provides an excellent example of the methodology described above: look until you find the answer you want; stop looking when you find the answer you want.

While health officials build a case against *E. coli* in raw milk, the fact remains that other foods, such as undercooked meat, are the most likely candidates to cause the type of epidemics that Dr. Tauxe of the CDC is most concerned about—those that sicken millions of people.

The organism was first identified in 1982. This pathogen has become widely dispersed in the food supply with the rise of huge feedlots, slaughterhouses and hamburger grinders. Meat production in America is ever more centralized: most of the beef consumed in the United States is now slaughtered in thirteen large packing houses. Eric Schlosser, author of *Fast Food Nation*, provides the following description: "The meat-packing system that arose to supply the nation's fast food chains—an industry molded to serve their needs, to provide massive amounts of uniform ground beef so that all of McDonald's hamburgers would taste the same—has proved to be an extremely efficient system for spreading disease. The large meatpacking companies have managed to avoid the sort of liability routinely imposed on the manufacturers of most consumer products. Today the government can demand the nationwide recall of defective sneakers, but it cannot order a meatpacking company to remove contaminated, potentially lethal ground beef from fast food kitchens and supermarket shelves."[121]

Another danger from confinement farms is runoff water, which carries *E. coli:O157:H7* onto crops and into households. This is a particularly serious problem in Washington, a state in which a disproportionate number of cases has occurred. Between 1990-1999, twenty-three such outbreaks were reported in Washington state, afflicting at least two hundred eighty-eight individuals, from sources as diverse as fish, lettuce and lasagna, as well as from ground beef.[122] The worst outbreak occurred in October 1996, when seventy individuals became sickened from contaminated apple juice—the famous Odwalla juice case. This highly publicized outbreak led to federal regulations requiring the pasteurization of all fruit juice sold in retail outlets.[123]

In late November of 2005, an outbreak of illness attributed to virulent *E. coli O157:H7* afflicted eight Washington state individuals who had consumed raw milk, sparking a flurry of news reports, vaulting the subject of raw milk into the national media—and also raising the spectre of deliberate sabotage.

The milk came from Dee Creek Farm, a small family farm near the town of Woodland in Cowlitz County, in southwestern Washington State. The owners, Anita and Michael Puckett, operated a cow share program, one of several in the state. State officials knew about the Pucketts' operation—the Pucketts described their operation earlier that year, in July, to Claudia Coles, head of the Department of Agriculture's safety program, at a conference on small farm operations. Coles listened and asked leading questions but did not express disapproval. A later report quoted her as saying, "We can't do anything about it unless there is a health problem."

The Pucketts were new to dairying. They did not have fancy facilities but were careful to follow good sanitary practices as recommended by several other dairymen in the area. The cows grazed on pasture but came into a barn for milking. The Pucketts washed the teats with iodine and milked with a milking machine into a closed stainless steel bucket which they carefully washed before milking. They then transported the buckets into their kitchen where they transferred the milk into gallon-sized glass jars owned by the shareholders. It was the shareholders' duty to provide clean jars, but the Pucketts then washed the jars again in the dishwasher, just to be safe. The filled jars went immediately into the freezer for ninety minutes and then into the refrigerator.

The various shareholder families had organized themselves into groups for milk pick-up. Each day of the week, one family picked up milk at the farm for a dozen or so other shareholders. When the pickup person arrived at the farm, the Pucketts placed the glass jars into a large cooler with blue ice. Each group of families had a pickup location, such as a front porch, where the cooler was left unattended. Families for each group had a window of three to nine p.m. to come by and retrieve their milk from the cooler. The Pucketts had explained the pickup system to agents from the Department of Health and the Department of Agriculture on one of their visits to the farm; the officials offered no feedback, neither positive nor negative.

Michael Puckett often picked up the empty cooler early the following morning, on the way home from his night job. About two weeks before the incident, he was somewhat unnerved by the presence of a car parked across the street of the pickup house. A driver sat behind the steering wheel. Puckett stalled to see how long the car would remain. Twenty minutes passed, at which time a police car arrived and the waiting car moved off.[124]

The first Dee Creek shareholder to become sick was a child from a family that picked up milk on Monday from the milking of November 26 or 27, at the pickup house where Michael had noticed the parked car. Soon other children fell ill and several were hospitalized. Health officials quickly confirmed the culprit as a strain of virulent *E. coli O157:H7*.

The newspapers reported seventeen or eighteen confirmed cases of food-borne illness from virulent *E. coli* in Dee Creek Farm shareholders—the first of many exaggerations to appear in the media. According to the Washington Department of Health, there were only seven; according to a farm spokesperson, there were actually eight confirmed cases, six people (from four families) from the Monday pickup group of thirteen families and two from the Tuesday pickup group of six families. In all, five were hospitalized, from three families, all from the Monday pickup group. One was released after treatment with IV for dehydration, one was released after three days and one after five days, but two of the children, from two different families, remained hospitalized in serious condition for around a month. One member of the Puckett family tested positive but did not get sick, and three other individuals among the shareholder families had symptoms but did not test positive. In fact, of the other eleven "cases," at least eight of them specifically tested negative. One important point: Dee Creek Farm stopped distribution and advised their shareholders to cease consumption of their milk days before the Department of Health even acknowledged that they knew about the issue and contacted the farm.

The Washington State Department of Agriculture (WSDA) visited the farm three times during the week of December 12 to conduct a thorough investigation, taking samples of milk and swabs from all five cows on the farm. At that point, the Pucketts had put away the equipment they used for their share holders and were milking only for their pigs. This they explained to the inspectors, noting how they did things differently when they milked for human consumption. Mrs. Puckett had to remind the inspectors to hose down and sterilize their boots before they entered the milking barn—the farm was very muddy at the time, as were all farms in the region, because of a record-breaking rainy season. WSDA included embarassing photographs of mud-splattered cows and equipment in their report on the investigation.

Predictably, the media coverage of the incident leaned heavily on health department reports, described as "a showcase of sensationalism and unprofessional journalism." However, TV interviews did include many consumers who expressed passionate support of raw milk. In one, a shareholder poured a glass of Dee Creek Farm's milk that she still had in her refrigerator for her family to drink. The newspapers reported that the law offices of William D. Marler had contacted two of the three afflicted families.

On December 21, the Clark County Health Department issued a report stating that the Washington State Department of Agriculture had confirmed *E. coli O157:H7* in Dee Creek Farm milk—Clark County was the scene of an outbreak of *E. coli O157:H7* at a county fair earlier in the year. Claudia Coles left two telephone messages, one to the Pucketts and one to their daughter, apologizing for the Clark County report and stating that at that point, they had found no specific pathogens in the milk.

It was at a press conference on January 16 that Washington State officials announced a positive finding of *E. coli O157:H7* in two samples of milk and five environmental samples from Dee Creek farm, of a strain that matched those cultured from the stool of the sick children. The report stated that "Raw milk bought and distributed from Dee Creek Farm was consumed by all affected people prior to their becoming ill," and that

"Dee Creek Farm illegally sold raw milk." The state report concluded: "The WSDA FSP investigation along with the epidemiological work by the County Health Departments demonstrates that the illegal raw milk provided by Dee Creek Farms was the source of the *E. coli O157:H7* that sickened at least 18 people in Washington and Oregon."[117]

While state officials expressed confidence that the outbreak was caused by raw milk, they ignored many important facts. First, and most important, was the fact that independent labs testing Dee Creek's milk, following the same testing protocol used by the state, found no *E. coli O157:H7*, not even in the same samples the state claimed tested positive.

Another fact: there was at least one concurrent outbreak of infection from *E. coli O157:H7*, affecting several family members, in the area. One boy ended up in the same hospital as the Dee Creek kids, in critical condition, and was still there after a month, possibly with long-term brain, nerve and kidney damage. Several of his family members were also confirmed with *E. coli O157:H7*.

Neither the state nor the media thought it relevant to report these illnesses. We can only guess whether there were other unreported cases of *E. coli O157:H7* at the same time. (All three raw-milk drinking children have since recovered.)

One more fact: just two months before the Dee Creek incident, in September 2005, *E. coli O157:H7* was found in water samples in a north Spokane water district, prompting a health alert.

Then there are the tactics of the Washington State Department of Agriculture—reminiscent of those used against Alta Dena in the 1970s and 1980s. The state kept its final report secret until the day before the introduction of new raw milk legislation banning cow shares and announced "proof positive" at a press conference. Dee Creek Farm and others involved learned of the final report and the press release from the media, not the state.

To make their case for the new legislation, officials claimed that Dee Creek had barred entry to the farm. In fact, the Pucketts had never barred entry to the farm, only requested that inspections take place when they did not have other obligations (such as meeting with their attorney or visiting the doctor), to which officials agreed. (When confronted with these lies, Michael Tokos of WSDA apologized and agreed that the Pucketts did not ever bar entry.) The whole affair smacks of well-planned orchestration, perfectly timed to influence anti-cow-share legislation.

Another particularly virulent outbreak of *E. coli O157:H7* illness, one we discussed earlier, occurred in California during a ten-week period, beginning in August, 2006. Over half the two hundred four victims were hospitalized; thirty-one cases involved a type of kidney failure called hemolytic uremic syndrome (HUS), and there were three deaths. HUS, by the way, usually occurs when the patient afflicted by virulent *E. coli* is given antibiotics, which can lead to a build up of Shiga toxin that can cause kidney failure.[125]

Using PFGE analysis, investigators finally matched the particular strain of *E. coli O157:H7*—out of over thirty-five hundred known unique *E. coli O157:H7* strains—to fresh salad spinach grown in the Salinas valley and also to cattle feces from a cattle ranch uphill of the spinach fields.[126] Several companies voluntarily recalled their spinach as the industry scrambled to find ways to prevent future outbreaks—spinach growers alone suffered two hundred million dollars in lost sales in 2006 and more in earlier outbreaks.

But the problem is complex. If, as most investigators suspect, run-off water from confinement farms is a source of the organism, it will be a continuing source of infection—which apparently cannot be washed off, as *E. coli* can reside within the tissue of the leaves as well as on the surface. Clorox rinses and cold storage have proven equally ineffective in preventing illness.[127]

Virulent *E. coli* almost certainly originates with the confinement of livestock, so it is ironic that a lot of the media attention during the outbreak focused on a raw milk dairy farmer from Fresno who grazes his dairy cows on grass. Mark McAfee, the outspoken president and founder of Organic Pastures Dairy, even developed a mobile milking parlor so his cows could always be on pasture. His raw milk products, including butter, cream, yoghurt, kefir and cheese, sell in health food stores throughout California, where retail sales of raw milk and raw milk products are legal. It was raw milk products from Organic Pastures Dairy that replaced those from Steuve's after California health officials forced the closure of the Steuve brothers' raw milk business.

McAfee instituted a private testing program when he went into business in 1999, frequently subjecting the milk products, the farm environment, the cows and their manure to laboratory analysis. At the time of the outbreak, he had performed over thirteen hundred tests, not once finding a human pathogen.

Then came reports that several children had been hospitalized from *E. coli O157:H7*, all of whom had consumed raw milk. According to the FDA, five were ill and four hospitalized. In reality, only two were hospitalized, both of whom had been given antibiotics in spite of express instructions on their armbands forbidding antibiotics. McAfee visited both children in the hospital. The mother of one child denied the illness had anything to do with raw milk and the other child had consumed spinach two days before the illness.

"Just to be safe," the California Department of Food and Agriculture (CDFA) quarantined all Organic Pastures raw milk products. A state team dressed up in protective gear showed up at the farm and tested and retested the cows, the milk and the manure on the farm. They found pathogens only in two heifers, which were not being milked. McAfee had purchased the heifers from a confinement dairy—he says the pathogen finding taught him a lesson, and he will never bring outside cows into his herd again. In any event, the strain from the heifers did not match the strain that had sickened the children. The state lifted the quarantine two weeks later and eventually paid a partial compensation to Organic Pastures for loss of sales.

But the link between California raw milk and *E. coli O157:H7* died a slow death. An FDA anti-raw milk PowerPoint presentation posted on the Internet several months later contained several slides linking a "California raw milk dairy" to four HUS hospitalizations from *E. coli O157:H7*. The slides were removed after an angry letter from McAfee threatened the agency with a lawsuit.[128] In a June, 2008 court case involving raw milk, attorneys for the Maryland Department of Health and Mental Hygiene cited "children in California drinking raw milk, getting sick from *E. coli* and almost dying," in arguments opposing cow-shares agreements.

And when attorney Bill Marler convinced two of the victims to sue the dairy, more reports about the case appeared in the newspapers. Marler placed an inflammatory video, full of distortions, about the sick children on YouTube.com, but removed it after receiving a letter from McAfee enumerating its errors. Still, all the free publicity at the time of the outbreak led to a twelve percent increase in sales for Organic Pastures.

THE SAFETY OF RAW VERSUS PASTEURIZED MILK

We now come to the sixty-four thousand dollar question. What is the risk of illness on a per-serving basis for raw milk compared to pasteurized milk and also to other foods? The obvious bias in published reports makes this a difficult question to answer, but we can try.

From a joint USDA/FDA/CDC paper on *Listeria monocytogenes*, published in September, 2003, the authors estimated that there are five hundred fifteen times more illnesses from *L. mono.* per year due to deli meats and twenty-nine times more illnesses from *L. mono.* per year due to pasteurized milk compared to raw milk.[129] On a per-serving basis, the authors estimated that deli meats are ten times more likely to cause illness than raw milk—yet we hear no warnings from the FDA that "Deli meats are inherently dangerous and should not be consumed."

The CDC attributes nineteen thousand five hundred thirty-one illnesses to the consumption of pasteurized milk and milk products from 1980-2005, just over ten times the number of illnesses attributed to raw milk during the same period. The CDC estimates that 3.5 percent of American households drink raw milk on a regular basis. Using this estimate, there are over twice as many illnesses attributed to raw milk compared to pasteurized milk on a per-serving basis. Adjusting for bias in the numbers attributed to raw milk, however, pasteurized milk may be over five times more dangerous than raw milk on a per-serving basis.[130] One statistician concluded from the CDC numbers that you'd have to drink over three million glasses of raw milk before you might expect to get an illness of any kind due to the milk.[131]

Here's another way to crunch the numbers. There are about sixty government-reported illnesses from raw milk per year—a number that is probably greatly exaggerated—and about one-half million raw milk drinkers in the U.S.—a number that is conservative. But using these figures, the rate of illness from raw milk can be calculated at about one one-hundredth of one percent per year—the actual percentage is probably much lower. The rate of illness from other foods is about twenty-five percent—seventy-six million cases per year in a population of about three hundred million. Thus even using inflated government statistics on illness from raw milk, you are over twenty-five hundred times more likely to contract illness from other foods than from raw milk.

JUST HOW DANGEROUS ARE PATHOGENS, ANYWAY?

A recurring theme in this book has been the importance of each individual's immunity in resisting the potentially harmful effects of pathogenic bacteria. This topic emerged in a January 5th, 2000 *Los Angeles Times* article titled "The Great Egg Panic: New proposals rekindle the debate over eggs' safety. But some scientists say the fears are overblown."[132]

"New government proposals designed to check salmonella poisoning could force routine pasteurization or irradiation of the American egg supply," the article reads. Officials argue that because three hundred thousand Americans are sickened and hundreds die each year from salmonella in eggs, eggs should be irradiated. "Today's egg, the new wisdom dictates, is too frequently contaminated with a bacterium called *Salmonella enteritidis* to be eaten as eggs always have been: sunny side up, in mayonnaise, cracked raw over hot pasta and grated with Parmesan cheese or simply soft-boiled and spooned worshipfully from a cup." Other officials disagree, including Peter Barton Hutt, former chief counsel for the FDA. He calls the statistical modeling that produces the food poisoning statistics "the closest thing I can think of in this modern age to a Ouija board." Now a lecturer on food safety at Harvard University, Hutt says, "The statistics are all over the place because none of them are any good. They are all wild guesses."[133]

So while it is clear that many commercially produced eggs contain salmonella, it's not at all clear how many, or how many problems this may lead to, or why some people are afflicted while most are not.

According to John R. Roth, a professor of biology at the University of Utah, who has been studying salmonella for forty years, ". . . probably it [salmonella] exists in very many organisms at a low level where it's not a pathogen but living as part of the gut flora." The idea of banishing it, he says, is absurd. "Salmonella is distributed pretty widely, and if you're willing to look closely enough, you'd probably find it almost everywhere. Sometimes it makes a mistake and gets across the gut wall and into an organism. Then it has all these mechanisms for surviving known as virulence."[134]

In the vast majority of cases, that virulence manifests as an irritation in the gut wall where the immune system fights off the bacteria, and symptoms range from loose stools to flu-like illness. In rare cases, the infection reaches the bloodstream, and occasionally these cases may be fatal. Salmonella-induced fatalities almost always involve individuals who are immunosuppressed from previous drug therapy. According to the Centers for Disease Control in Atlanta, between 1985 and 1998 there were seventy-nine verified deaths from this cause, about five per year—one-tenth the number of people killed in the U.S. each year by lightning.[135]

Roth's assertion that salmonella is literally everywhere is important, for it confirms two things. First, there is no point in sanitizing the food supply, because contamination with salmonella and other organisms can just as easily occur after pasteurization, irradiation or whatever other process is used to sanitize. Second, the individuals who become ill as a result of exposure do so because their immune systems are functioning abnormally.

Actually, regular exposure to organisms such as salmonella can build resistance and immunity. In effect, we can make ourselves stronger and healthier by eating raw foods that may contain organisms considered "pathogenic." That is why regular raw milk drinkers are much less likely to become ill during outbreaks of illness attributed to raw milk than first-time raw milk drinkers. According to a 1985 report, "Persons, regardless of age, who are routinely exposed to *Campylobacter jejuni* by vehicles such as raw milk may develop some protective immunity. [This is] supported by several serological studies . . ."[136]

During one campylobacter outbreak ". . . none of the chronic raw milk drinkers became ill after ingesting large amounts of the same milk that caused a high attack rate among those persons who were acutely exposed . . . . Presumably this phenomenon is due to previous exposure to Campylobacter with subsequent development of immunity . . . this investigation confirms the presence of these antibodies [to Campylobacter] in persons chronically exposed to raw milk and for the first time, to our knowledge, shows an association between high antibody levels and immunity to infection under field conditions."[137]

Quite simply, these studies confirm the fact that raw milk drinkers develop powerful immunity and resistance to pathogenic organisms. The same journals that provide this information have continued to demand a complete ban on raw milk, including a ban on farmers giving the product away to neighbors and friends. Yet in this age of widespread threat from virulent microorganisms, raw milk proves to be the one food that can provide immunity to the pathogens in the other foods we consume.

GRASS-FED, FULL-FAT RAW MILK IS SAFEST

Back in 1936, Edwin Jordan, author of *A Textbook of General Bacteriology*, pointed out that "The character of pasture was early observed to affect the kind and abundance of the species [of bacteria] found in milk; the lack of pasture in more recent years has been demonstrated to have a profound effect."[138] Numerous studies have confirmed the fact that current feeding methods utilizing large quantities of grains have had a profound influence on the kind and abundance of bacteria found in milk, much to the detriment of the health of the animals and the quality of the milk.

Of particular relevance is the development of acid-resistant strains of bacteria in modern cattle. According to a 1998 *Science* magazine article, cattle fed mostly grain have a lower (more acidic) intestinal pH and are more likely to harbor pathogenic bacteria than cattle fed mostly grass and hay. The abnormally low pH in which the bacteria develop makes these bacteria acid-resistant. "The ability of bacteria to act as food-borne pathogens depends on their capacity to survive the low pH of the [human] gastric stomach and to colonize the intestinal tract of humans," the authors write. "Cattle that were fed grain had one million-fold more acid-resistant *E. coli* than cattle fed hay."[139]

These acid-resistant pathogenic bacteria from heavily grain-fed, overly acidic cattle have an increased ability to survive the acid environment of the human stomach and subsequently colonize the intestinal tract and cause disease. This is a major reason why raw milk (or meat) from grass-fed cows is so much safer than milk from animals kept largely or entirely in confinement and fed mostly grains.

The butterfat in milk is another factor that protects us from illness. In addition to containing antimicrobial short- and medium-chain fatty acids, butterfat is a carrier for important vitamins that strengthen the immune system. Another substance, called glycosphingolipids, protects against gastrointestinal infections, especially in the very young and the elderly. In a study involving pasteurized milk, children who drank skimmed milk had diarrhea at rates three to five times great than children who drink whole milk.[140]

Milk was designed by nature to be a perfect food—but in order for milk to be a perfect food, and a completely safe food, it should be produced and consumed as nature intended. . . from cows on pasture, with all the butterfat, and unpasteurized. Natural, rich and raw!

# 16
# Raw Milk and Children

*The child on raw milk is very fit. Chilblains are practically elimi-nated. The teeth are less likely to decay. The resistance to tuberculosis and other infections is raised.*

*The Lancet*, May 8, 1937, page 1142

*Raw milk should not be consumed by anyone, at any time, for any reason.*

John F. Sheehan, Director of Dairy Food Safety
Food and Drug Administration, Testimony before the
Maryland House of Delegates, March 15, 2007

Government officials speak with one voice in their warnings against raw milk, especially noting that it should not be given to infants and children; they can be abruptly distainful of reports from parents on how switching to raw milk helped alleviate serious health conditions in their children. These reports are not science, they say, only anecdotes.

Let's begin our discussion of raw milk for children with some rep-resentative anecdotes from the files of the Weston A. Price Foundation.

ANECDOTAL EVIDENCE

A physician who prescribes raw milk to his patients describes a dramatic case involving a nine-month-old boy who had suffered three ear infections in three months. The mother had fed the child a number of formulas based on processed cow's milk and soy protein, and she had even tried pasteurized goat milk. With each formula the child suffered recurrent vomiting, diarrhea, failure to gain weight and thrive, and he had been ill with either viral or bacterial infections almost continuously since early infancy. After the mother switched to a formula based on raw goat milk, however, the diarrhea and vomiting ceased and the child began to gain weight. His growth became normal and at one year he was perfectly healthy.

A Weston A. Price local chapter leader reports on a two-year-old boy with very serious asthma. After the mother put the boy on raw cow's milk, the child went through the entire winter without a visit to the doctor for any reason and no asthma attacks—except for one, a serious attack that occurred after the boy consumed pasteurized milk while on a family trip.

Another report describes an autistic eight-year-old boy who had not spoken a word since the sudden onset of autism at the age of two. After two months on raw cow's milk, all autistic behavior disappeared and the child began to babble as a prelude to speech. The only dietary or treatment change was a switch from pasteurized to raw milk.

Imagine the joy and relief that raw milk has given to these children, and the families of these children—an end to suffering, an end to worry. Family life can be peaceful and happy again, and the child now has the possibility of a normal life. Make no mistake, the official stance is that these children do not have the right to consume raw milk, even that parents who give raw milk to their children are guilty of child abuse because they are exposing them to serious risk.[1]

Written up by a physician and published in a medical journal—something most unlikely to happen in today's anti-raw milk climate—these anecdotes would be called "case histories." But coming from parents, they are simply anecdotes, with the implication that parents lack the judgment to distinguish between good science and the placebo effect. But for parents observing their children, motivated first and foremost by the desire to see their children healthy, these "anecdotes" are pure observational science.

According to John Sheehan of the FDA, "Claims that raw milk has miraculous disease-curing properties are not supported by the scientific literature."[2] Note that Mr. Sheehan does not say that raw milk's miraculous disease-curing properties do not exist, only that they are not described in the scientific literature. And why is there so little in the scientific literature about the health benefits of raw milk? Why have scientists not studied this fascinating subject? The answer should be obvious. No scientist would risk his or her career to focus on such an unprofitable area of research, and no journal would challenge the dictum that raw milk is dangerous. It's almost as though the FDA has promulgated an unwritten commandment: "Thou shalt not study raw milk."

Yet raw milk has been studied and the few published papers present a consistent body of evidence on raw milk's benefits, especially for growth, that is, especially for children. Most of these studies are old studies, carried out before the Second World War—but that does not mean these studies should be discounted. No one would jump off a tall building just because Newton formulated the laws of gravity several hundred years ago. Good science is good science in whatever age we live, and the body's requirements for nutrients are the same now as they were hundreds of years ago.

EARLY HUMAN STUDIES

In 1926, when pasteurized milk and raw certified milk co-existed (and health officials still thought the certification of raw milk was a life-saving service), the *Archives of Pediatrics* published a study of two hundred twenty-four children whose parents obtained milk from the Boston Dispensary. Children received either raw certified milk; Grade A pasteurized milk; Grade A pasteurized milk plus cod liver oil; or raw certified milk plus cod liver oil and orange juice. Compared to those on pasteurized milk, children who received raw certified milk had better weight gain and greater protection against rachitis, a childhood disease, similar to rickets, caused by deficiency of vitamin D and sunlight, and associated with impaired metabolism of calcium and phosphorus. Interestingly, the addition of cod liver oil and orange juice did not improve the results for children on raw milk, but did allow those on pasteurized milk to have better weight gain and more protection against rachitis. According to the authors, "The use of certified milk [raw] without orange juice or cod liver oil gave a considerably greater percentage of weight development than either pasteurized milk alone or pasteurized milk with orange juice and cod liver oil." They concluded that "a larger use of certified milk in infant feeding should be encouraged by the medical profession."[3]

The journal published a similar study three years later. The researchers compared two groups of infants. Group I (one hundred twenty-two babies) received raw milk; group II (one hundred twelve babies) received pasteurized milk. Those receiving raw milk had better weight gain than those on pasteurized milk. Rickets occurred more frequently in the group on pasteurized milk and the cases of rickets that did occur in the raw milk group were milder. There were twenty-four cases and nine deaths from diarrhea in the raw milk group compared to thirty-six cases and fifteen deaths in the pasteurized milk group. Mortality was ten percent in the raw milk group and sixteen percent in the pasteurized milk group.[4]

A 1931 study on the growth of Scottish school children was published in *Nutrition Abstracts and Reviews*.[5] Children drinking raw milk had a significantly greater increase in height and weight compared to those drinking pasteurized milk. ". . . [P]asteurized milk was only 66 percent as effective as the raw milk in the case of boys and 91 percent as effective in the case of girls in inducing increases in weight; and 50 percent as effective in boys and 70 percent as effective in girls in bringing about increases in height."

The authors gave the following explanation for the results, referring to another study that had previously appeared in the *Journal of Biological Chemistry*: "Kramer, Latzke and Shaw obtained less favorable calcium balances in adults with pasteurized milk than with 'fresh milk' and made the further observation that milk from cows kept in the barn for five months gave less favorable calcium balances that did 'fresh milk' (herd milk from a college dairy)."[6]

Also in 1931, health officials in Scotland reported on a project to determine whether milk could improve growth of impoverished children in the Lanarkshire schools. It was a large and ambitious study—following twenty thousand children ages five to twelve. Five thousand received three-fourths pint of raw milk per day; five thousand received three-fourths pint of pasteurized milk per day for four months. The control group of ten thousand children received no milk.

In the final report, published in the journal *Nature*, March 21, 1931, the research team noted better growth in those children receiving milk but stated that "the effects of raw and pasteurized milk on growth in weight and height are, so far as can be judged from this experiment, equal."

However, two scientists, Fisher and Bartlett, looked carefully at the data and followed up with a critical evaluation in the April 18, 1931 issue of *Nature*. They found that the initial evaluation was highly biased and that growth, especially in boys, was better on raw milk than pasteurized—and this on less than one pint of raw milk for only four months!

Further compelling evidence of the superiority of raw milk appeared in *The Lancet* in 1937, in a report on the work of the medical officer to a group of orphanages. The physician gave pasteurized milk for five years to one group of seven hundred fifty boys, while giving raw milk to another group of seven hundred fifty. All other conditions were alike except for this one item. During that period, fourteen cases of tuberculosis occurred in the boys fed pasteurized milk, while only one occurred in those fed raw milk. It was studies like these, plus the observations of physicians in both America and Europe, that led to the following statement in the *The Lancet* the same year: "The child on raw milk is very fit. Chilblains [a serious problem in houses without central heating] are practically eliminated. The teeth are less likely to decay. The resistance to tuberculosis and other infections is raised."[7]

The orphanage study contains an interesting comment on the dental health of the children brought up on raw milk: "Dr. Evelyn Sprawson of the London Hospital has recently stated that in certain institutions children who were brought up on raw milk (as opposed to pasteurized milk) had perfect teeth and no decay. The result is so striking and unusual that it will undoubtedly be made the subject of further inquiry."[8] Instead, the report has been conveniently forgotten; today, official pronouncements recommend fluoride, not raw milk, for protection against tooth decay.

EARLY ANIMAL STUDIES

Early studies on raw versus pasteurized milk in animals confirm the findings of early studies on human beings. In an earlier chapter, we discussed Francis Pottenger's work. His experimental findings from feeding cats various raw and pasteurized milk diets had been noted by a professor at Ohio State University in the early 1940s, who observed the same pathologies Pottenger described in cats fed pasteurized milk. As did Pottenger's, the professor's raw milk cats thrived.[9]

A rigorous controlled experiment in 1941 with calves at the West of Scotland Agricultural College at Auchincruive produced equally dramatic results. "Two groups, each of eight calves, were fed, one group on raw milk, the other on pasteurized milk . . . . The experiment covered a period of 90 days. All the animals in the raw milk group finished the trial without mortality. In the pasteurized milk group, two died before they were 30 days old, and a third died on the 92nd day; that is, two days after the experiment." The remaining calves in the pasteurization group were in ill health at the end of the experiment, while all of the animals in the raw milk group were in excellent health.[10]

The results of other animal experiments performed in England to determine the relative nutritional value of raw and heated milk were reported in 1931 in *The Lancet*: "Our results show definitely that some dietetic factors are destroyed when milk is sterilised, and to a definite but lesser degree when it is pasteurised, and that although fresh milk is capable of supporting sustained growth and reproduction in rats, heated milk is no longer capable of doing so."[11]

Five years later, the same authors reported that rats fed pasteurized milk showed loss of hair while those fed raw milk did not. The type of milk also influenced the comparative reproductive capacity of the rats: "Two females which had received sterilised milk for about eight months showed remarkable improvement after receiving raw milk for about eleven weeks and one gave birth to a litter when mated to a buck from the raw-milk group. Previous to this, 15 matings had been attempted with does and bucks both reared on sterilised milk, and no signs of pregnancy were shown on any one of these occasions."[12]

Those who consume pasteurized and especially ultrapasteurized milk who wish to have children should consider themselves warned.

In 1931 Dr. Ernest Scott and Professor Lowell Erf of Ohio State University compared the effects of raw and pasteurized milk in rats. Those given whole raw milk had good growth, sleek coats, clear eyes and good quality blood; those given whole pasteurized milk had rough coats, slow growth, loss of vitality and weight and anemia.[13] The lack of anemia in the raw mlk-fed rats is significant because, according to a discussion by Scott and Erf, the scientific concensus at the time was that all milk, raw and pasteurized, could cause anemia if it were consumed as the only food. The observed anemia in the pasteurized milk-fed rats is undoubtedly due to the destruction of lactoferrin during pasteurization, as well as the denaturation of vitamin A in the butterfat—vitamin A supports iron assimilation.

Anemia in young children is a serious condition and manifests as follows: "Infants with chronic, severe iron deficiency have been observed to display increased fearfulness, unhappiness, fatigue, low activity, wariness, solemnity, and proximity to the mother during free play, developmental testing and at home. In a recent preventative trial in Chile, ratings after 30-45 minutes of developmental testing showed that, compared with infants who received iron supplementation, a greater percentage of unsupplemented infants never smiled, never interacted socially, and never showed social referencing."[14]

The presence or absence of anemia in the rats may explain the marked differences in observed behavior patterns between the two groups. Those on raw milk had "excellent dispositions" and did not show signs of stress when they were picked up and petted. Those on pasteurized milk were very irritable, often showing a tendency to bite when handled. This finding mirrors frequent reports from parents that their children's behavior improves when they make the switch from pasteurized to raw milk.

Researchers Wulzen and Bahrs reported on their work with rats at Oregon State University during the early 1940s. "In all experiments," they wrote, "the growth of the rats fed raw milk was superior to that of similar experimental groups fed pasteurized milk." Autopsies showed that the raw-milk-fed animals had no abnormalities, while in many cases it was "noted that the nuclei of heart cells from pasteurized-milk-fed animals were shrunken." The authors found various other degenerative changes in the adrenal glands, muscles and livers.[15]

These researchers then performed another series of similar experiments with guinea pigs. They reported that "Animals fed raw whole milk grew excellently and at autopsy showed no abnormality of any kind. Those on the pasteurized milk rations did not grow as well and developed a definite syndrome, the first sign of which was wrist stiffness. On pasteurized skim milk ration the syndrome increased in severity until the animals finally died in periods ranging from a month to a year or more. They showed great emaciation and weakness before death."[16]

Health officials insist that pasteurized milk has the same level of nutrients as raw, and for many of the nutrients this statement is technically correct. Raw and pasteurized milk from the same source contain the same amount of calcium, for example. But the real issue in growing children is how the calcium is used. In a series of experiments carried out at Randleigh Farm, an experimental dairy farm in upstate New York, during the late 1930s, researchers compared rats on raw and pasteurized whole milk. The raw milk-fed rats were larger and more robust, with good, healthy fur; those on pasteurized milk had hairless patches, called acrodynia, due to vitamin $B_6$ deficiency.[17]

The most serious difference showed up on autopsy. Those rats on raw milk had longer bones, and the bones were much denser. Typically the bones of the pasteurized milk-fed rats weighed one hundred forty-six grams while those on raw milk weighed two hundred six grams—they were about thirty percent denser. So while the amount of calcium in the two types of milk was approximately the same, it was utilized more effectively in the raw milk-fed rat. In humans, bone density for life is acquired in childhood and translates into a more robust constitution, greater height and more attractive facial structure.

The researchers at Randleigh Farm also compared the internal organs of the raw and pasteurized milk-fed rats. Their findings were similar to those of Dr. Pottenger. Those on pasteurized milk had poor color and compromised integrity of the intestine, liver and other organs—their insides were mushy.

In 1941, when researchers Wulzen and Bahrs performed autopsies on guinea pigs fed pasteurized whole milk, they found muscles streaked with calcification and calcium deposits under the skin and in the joints, heart and other organs, a pathology that was absent in guinea pigs fed raw milk. This finding gives us a good idea of what happens to the calcium that does not get built into the bones—it ends up in the soft tissues, where it does not belong. The researchers attributed the inappropriate calcium utilization to the destruction of a hormone-like factor in butterfat called the Wulzen factor.

After the Wulzen and Bahrs study, the track goes cold. As laws for mandatory pasteurization were put into place, a chilly wind swept over the universities, and research into this fascinating subject came to a halt.

The one exception is the research on raw versus human milk described in Chapter 15. But in a serious lapse of logic, public health officials assume these studies on raw human milk have little relevance to raw animal milk. In any event, they did no good. Even though the research clearly showed that it was better to give human milk to babies raw, milk banks routinely pasteurize this precious, life-saving food.

## A FAMOUS PEDIATRICIAN
## EXHORTS AMERICANS TO GIVE UP MILK

In 1983, long after health officials had forgotten about certified raw milk, Frank Oski, MD published what became a very influential book entitled *Don't Drink Your Milk*. Oski was Chairman of the Department of Pediatrics at the State University of New York Upstate Medical Center; he subsequently became Director of the Department of Pediatrics at the Johns Hopkins University School of Medicine and Physician-in-Chief at the Johns Hopkins Children's Center. He has been characterized as America's leading pediatrician.

"Milk has been linked to iron-deficiency anemia in infants and children," Oski writes. "It has been named as the cause of cramps and diarrhea in much of the world's population, and the cause of multiple forms of allergy as well; and it may play a central role in the origins of atherosclerosis and heart attacks.

"Among physicians, so much concern has been voiced about the potential hazards of cow milk that the Committee on Nutrition of the prestigious American Academy of Pediatrics, the institutional voice of practicing pediatricians, released a report entitled, 'Should Milk Drinking by Children Be Discouraged?'"[18]

About one-fifth of all infants under two in America suffer from iron-deficiency anemia, about half of which, according to Oski, is due to low-grade intestinal bleeding induced by sensitivity to milk. The amount of blood lost is too small to be detected visually, but is enough to lead to anemia.[19] Oski did not know about the Scott and Erf experiments, which showed that raw milk does not cause anemia.

Oski links a number of other symptoms to milk allergies including persistent or recurrent nasal congestion, asthma or chest infection, skin rashes and otherwise unexplained vomiting or diarrhea. These are all problems that I too have seen in many infants and children who consumed regular store-bought milk and milk-based formulas. Other investigators have linked kidney disease, eczema and rheumatoid arthritis to milk, and this too is consistent with my experience; I've long observed that regular pasteurized milk is one of the worst and most obvious triggers for children with eczema or rheumatoid arthritis.

Other investigators have published studies linking modern milk consumption to multiple sclerosis, amyotrophic lateral sclerosis (Lou Gehrig's disease), antisocial behavior in children and juvenile diabetes.[20,21] Of course, neither Oski nor any of these other investigators appear to have considered the possibilities of raw milk.

ALLERGIES AND ILLNESSES
ASSOCIATED WITH PASTEURIZED MILK

For many individuals allergies are the clearest manifestation of acute illness caused or aggravated by milk and other dairy products. Many articles in medical journals describe allergies to milk in babies and young children. The authors never mention the fact that the allergies are almost always to pasteurized milk; the alternative of raw milk goes unrecognized and unmentioned. In one study, fifty-nine of seven hundred eighty-seven babies studied were found to have the classic allergic symptoms of recurrent nasal congestion and bronchitis, eczema, diarrhea or repeated vomiting in response to pasteurized milk or milk-based formula. In other studies the percentages of babies allergic to milk have been even higher. These children saw their doctors much more frequently and required hospitalization more often than children who were non-allergic. The earlier the babies were exposed to pasteurized milk, the more likely they were to show signs of intolerance.[22]

A more serious complication was described by investigators who worked with ten- to thirteen-year-old children with a kidney disease called nephrosis, which involves the loss of excess amounts of protein from a damaged kidney. Fluid accumulation with swollen hands and feet is commonly the result, and the problem can lead to permanent renal disease and death. When pasteurized milk was removed from the diet, the children showed signs of marked improvement, and when the milk was reintroduced, the problems returned. The researchers concluded that sensitivity to milk and other foods played a prominent role in causing the disease. Unfortunately, in this as in other studies, the investigators made no attempt to give raw milk and note the results.[23]

Other physicians have observed additional relationships between pasteurized milk and allergic disease in children. Eczema, musculoskeletal pain ("growing pains"), rheumatoid arthritis and strep infections are just a few of the problems pediatricians have alleviated by eliminating milk from the diet.[24] In my own experience, there is not a single problem that occurs in infants and young children that cannot be helped by eliminating pasteurized milk and dairy products from the diet. Upper respiratory symptoms, frequent ear infections and asthma are often the most obvious symptoms, but virtually any complaint may be a manifestation of allergy to pasteurized milk, as well as to other processed foods. Of the hundreds of children I've treated, virtually every child whose parents have been willing to eliminate these foods from the child's diet has seen marked improvement in symptoms, often with subsequent progress to vibrant good health.

Physicians have also noted a number of interesting and disturbing relationships between the consumption of pasteurized milk and several serious chronic diseases. Investigators at the Baylor College of Medicine found that the factors that characterized patients with Lou Gehrig's disease included exposure to lead and mercury and high consumption of pasteurized milk.[25] A number of pediatricians have noted milk allergy in juvenile rheumatoid arthritis. In *Don't Drink Your Milk*, Oski quotes pediatrician Dan Baggett:

"I have had several children with signs and symptoms of early rheumatoid arthritis. Without exception, during the past eight years, I have had the good fortune to relieve them and watch their certain return to good health by simply eliminating all traces of milk from their diet."[26] Oski notes that many other pediatricians have had similar experiences. He also comments on the "many subtle and puzzling forms" that milk allergy may take.

Other investigators have found a relationship between heavy milk drinking and antisocial behavior. Young criminals were found to drink almost ten times more milk than those in a control group.[27]

It is against this background of ever increasing problems with pasteurized milk that we turn to a remarkable series of studies carried out in Europe between 2001 and 2007. These studies looked at "farm milk"— that is, raw milk—as one of several factors that might protect children against allergies and asthma. These were the first studies on the effects of raw animal milk to appear in the literature since the 1940s, and they were published in prestigious journals. Significantly, they were carried out in Europe, not the U.S.

In the first, published in *The Lancet*, 2001, which involved twenty-six hundred families, researchers found that "Long-term and early-life exposure to stables and [raw] farm milk induces a strong protective effect against development of asthma, hay fever and atopic sensitization [rashes]."[28] In the second, published in the *Journal for Allergy and Clinical Immunology*, 2006, researchers concluded that children who even infrequently drank raw milk had significantly less current eczema symptoms and a greater reduction in atopy [allergic hypersensitivity]."[29]

The third study, called the PARSAVAL study, looked at almost fifteen thousand children ages five to thirteen. Researchers found that consumption of raw milk was the strongest factor in reducing the risk of asthma and allergy, a stronger factor than living on a farm or having a pet. These findings were published in 2007, in *Clinical and Experimental Allergy*.[30] Health officials can no longer claim that "all the studies on raw milk are old studies."

Asthma is a crippling, even life-threatening condition. Over five thousand people in the U.S. die from asthma per year. According to the CDC, asthma is the second most prevalent chronic condition among children, afflicting at least five million. It results in approximately fourteen million days of missed school each year and carries the specter of toxic inhalers and emergency room visits. The European studies point to a safe and easy solution to the problem of asthma: give children raw milk and give it to them early in life. It is difficult to find words to describe the character of those who proclaim that raw milk provides no benefit to children.

## THE PROTEINS IN MILK

Milk proteins are very fragile, three-dimensional objects with complicated precise folding, and even precise variations in surface electric charge. The rapid heating of pasteurization warps and distorts these proteins so that the body no longer recognizes them; instead it is forced to mount an immune response. Pasteurization affects not only the two main proteins in milk, casein and whey proteins, but also the various enzymes, because enzymes are basically proteins. A growing child, let alone a mature adult, must expend a lot of energy dealing with this assault on the immune system—such an effort explains the irritable behavior of the rats studied by Scott and Erf—and of children on pasteurized milk. Very frequently, parents report an improvement in behavior in children after a switch to raw mik from pasteurized. (By contrast, meat proteins are very tough and bundled into tight coils, and they survive various forms of heat treatment fairly well.[31])

The distortion of milk proteins by pasteurization also provides a partial explanation for the growing list of disorders associated with pasteurized milk—gastrointestinal problems, frequent ear infections, allergies and rashes, early onset diabetes, auto-immune disease, attention deficit disorder and autism. As the destruction of proteins by pasteurization means the destruction of raw milk's whole system of immune support, the child drinking pasteurized milk is subject to a double whammy—a large burden on the immune system coupled with lack of immune system support.

NUTRIENT LOSSES

During the early days of pasteurization, researchers showed that scurvy often resulted when pasteurized milk replaced raw milk in the diet of infants. "Pasteurized milk gradually induces infantile scurvy, unless antiscorbutic diet is given in addition," wrote Alfred Hess in a 1916 issue of the *American Journal of Diseases of Children*. "This disorder quickly yielded to the substitution of raw for pasteurized milk."[32]

The following year, Hess wrote of the situation in Berlin, "A large dairy in that city established a pasteurizing plant in which all milk was raised to a temperature of about 60 degrees C. After an interval of some months, infantile scurvy was reported from various sources throughout the city."[33]

Thus from the earliest days of pasteurization scientists demonstrated that heat treatment had a profound effect on the health-giving properties of milk. A loss of nutrients other than vitamin C was demonstrated in subsequent studies. One article, "The effect of heat on the solubility of the calcium and phosphorus compounds in milk," was published in 1925 in the *Journal of Biological Chemistry*.

The author's conclusion was unequivocal: "There is a loss in the soluble calcium and phosphorus contents of the milk due to heat and the amount of the loss depends upon the temperature to which the milk has been heated."[34] Other studies showed that pasteurization caused the loss of significant percentages of many of the B vitamins and nearly all of the enzymes in milk.[35]

One study, published in the *Journal of Dairy Science* in 1934, documented the loss of thirty-eight percent of the B-complex vitamins.[36(41)] Similar findings were published in a 1979 master's thesis at the University of Georgia—the losses from pasteurization of vitamin $B_6$, thiamin (vitamin B$_1$) and folic acid were determined to be 34.4 percent, 33.8 percent and 24.1 percent, respectively.[37(42)]

High-quality raw milk contains significant amounts of vitamin C, estimated in 1936 to be twenty to twenty-five milligrams per liter.[38(43)] Hess wrote in 1932 that the amount of vitamin C in raw milk was "dependent entirely on the vitamin content of the food or fodder of the animal" and that pasteurization destroyed at least fifty percent of the vitamin C in milk.[39(44)] Researchers in the Department of Chemistry at the University of Wisconsin confirmed these findings several years later: "Commercial raw milks contained an anti-scorbutic potency which was only slightly less than fresh raw milks. Pasteurized milks on the average contained only one-half the latter potency."[40(45)]

Others estimated much higher rates of destruction. In a 1938 report titled "Infantile Scurvy," one expert wrote, "The vitamin is present in varying concentration in cow's milk and, since it is a fragile substance, is largely destroyed by pasteurization."[41(46)] In 1941, the U.S. Government Printing Office published the *Proceedings of the National Nutrition Conference for Defense*. That document stated that " . . . the cows of the country produce as much vitamin C as does the entire citrus crop, but most of it is lost as a result of pasteurization."[42(47)] In an article published in *Pediatrics*, 2001, we read, ". . . without doubt. . . the explosive increase in infantile scurvy during the latter part of the 19th century coincided with the advent of use of heated milks. . ."[43]

Proponents of pasteurization admit the loss of vitamin C but claim that "infants can get it from other sources." But what other sources of vitamin C are there for the infant—sugar-laden orange juice? Raw milk can resolve scurvy without putting other burdens on the growing infant, both the full blown condition and the subclinical variety, with its surreptious damage to the blood vessels and the organs, especially the eyes; pasteurized milk cannot.

Pasteurized milk contains similar levels of minerals as raw milk, but these minerals are not as well absorbed after milk has been heat treated. We saw how pasteurization inhibits proper calicum and iron assimilation—and it is a good working hypothesis that pasteurization inhibits the assimilation of other minerals as well. Pasteurization destroys the beneficial bacteria in raw milk, which enhance mineral absorption.[44] Iodine, critical to thyroid function, is lower in pasteurized milk.[45]

The Randleigh Farm studies demonstrated that animals on pasteurized milk develop vitamin $B_6$ deficiency. This nutrient is absolutely critical to hundreds of biochemical processes, necessary for the production of red blood cells, hydrochloric acid, receptors and feel good chemicals. It supports the heart, liver, brain, kidneys and nervous system and can alleviate symptoms as diverse as epilepsy, skin problems, multiple sclerosis, asthma, tooth decay, celiac disease and proneness to sunburn. Shouldn't all children be given the best possible source of vitamin $B_6$, raw milk?

Pasteurization inactivates the carrier protein for folate[46] and vitamin $B_{12}$.[47] It destroys lipases, enzymes needed for fat utilization.[48] Vitamin D is present in milk in protein-bound form; thus pasteurization is likely to inhibit utilization of the sunshine vitamin.[49] Heat degrades vitamin A and also beta-lactoglobulin,[50] a protein that increases absorption of this nutrient, which is needed for growth, mineral metabolism, hormone protection and protection against infection, among numerous other roles.

RAW MILK AND BONE STRUCTURE

Author Joann Grohman tells the following family story about raw milk and bone structure in *Keeping A Family Cow*:

"I have a large family. Pictures of my descendants are all over the house. These young people, eight children and nine grandchildren, all have something in common besides a mother and a grandmother. They have excellent bone structure.

"I'm a painter and also a farmer. As an artist I'm trained to see bone structure. It's the foundation of beauty. Straight legs, an erect carriage with well-set shoulders, well proportioned facial bones with straight teeth, these are the basics and they can't be picked up at spas or beauty salons. You develop them in childhood.

"As a farmer I know that good bone structure is no accident. The quality of the diet is the main determinant. Ethnic (we farmers call them breed) differences exist, but we (and our animal friends) are born with the birthright of excellent bone structure whether it's a stocky or elongated bone. This is our genetic potential.[47(18)]

"The teeth of children raised on the milk from their family cow are always straight. I'm making this rather sweeping statement because I have never run into any exceptions. I have had letters from my readers also describing the freedom from decay their family enjoys now that they keep a cow."[51(19)]

## RAW MILK FOR AUTISTIC CHILDREN

Autism is a heartbreaking condition in which the child is unable to engage in normal social and emotional reactions with those around him. Once extremely rare, today it afflicts as many as one in one hundred fifty children, causing untold suffering and misery—a kind of living death—for both the victims and their families. Autistic children suffer not only from neurological impairment but also severe digestive disorders. Removal of casein and gluten (in milk and wheat) is the prescribed treatment. One theory holds that opiates in milk induce autistic behavior.

A recent interesting discovery is the fact that autistic children have higher-than-normal levels of blood ammonia and that treatment with lactic-acid bacteria can lower these levels. Ammonia is produced by certain gram-negative bacteria inhabiting the gut; these types of bacteria exist in very high levels in the autistic child. Lactobacilli produce very little ammonia and will displace these pathogenic bacteria in the intestinal tract.

A fascinating paper by Linda Carlton and Mary Brauninger, both parents of autistic children, presents the theory that exposure to heat-killed bacteria can induce an innate immune response resulting in autism. They note that the first known cases of autism were reported during the 1940s, at the time when pasteurization of milk became nearly universal and immunization programs were instituted. Pasteurized milk introduces heat-killed bacteria into the gut, and vaccinations introduce heat-killed bacteria directly into the bloodstream.[52(96)] They suggest a diet containing raw milk, raw fermented milk and other fermented foods for autistic children.

Mrs. Carlton reports: "My colleague. . . and myself have been feeding our children daily raw milk—either the raw cow's milk, or the raw goat's milk. In addition to raw milk, we also have been fermenting the raw milk with kefir grains. The changes in our children are incredible!

"However, we cannot spark any interest among other parents with autistic children, because they are deadly afraid of milk's theorized opioid effect.

"In August 2002, we began to research opioids and their behavioral effects. It is almost a tragedy that this fallacious theory as the explanation for autism's symptoms had to be challenged by two mothers and not some research scientist. . . .

"If you have never tried the real kefir grains, then you are in for a treat. Actually, the first time we tried them, we all experienced an elevated temperature and cleansing, presumably due to real detoxification. In any event, our families have greatly benefited from raw fermented milk products. . .

"The pasteurization of milk has damaged the gift of life and health. Even heating milk above 100 degrees to make [modern] yogurt causes protein cross-linking where amino acids become fused together. Poor lysine really goes through a beating!

"You will never heat milk again after studying heat treatments, nor will you want to consume pasteurized beer, pasteurized soy sauce, pasteurized fruit juices or pasteurized eggs."[53(97)]

PASSIONATE MOMS

Raw milk is a perfect food, and an especially perfect food for growing children. If you have read this far and still think that raw milk is a bad idea, put yourself in the shoes of a mother with small children. Every instinct, every fiber of her being desires good health for her growing child. Yet she is surrounded by forces that work toward the detriment of her children's health—processed and highly sweetened foods that are advertised to children, sold to children, pushed on children. Even if she prepares all the family meals—and many mothers lack the time, energy or skills to do so—she still worries about getting proper nutrition into her youngsters.

And many children are picky eaters—milk is often the one food that picky children will actually consume.

And if she can't or won't breastfeed, or if her infant isn't thriving on breastmilk, what are her choices? Artifical, processed infant formula full of high fructose corn syrup, mono- and di-glycerides, vegetable oils, powdered protein and synthetic vitamins? Or a homemade formula based on raw milk, the closest thing in nature to human milk and the only food designed to kickstart the immature immune system?

Thousands and thousands of mothers have discovered that raw milk is the one food that allows them to give a sigh of relief, a food that helps their children grow normally, puts color in their cheeks, calms their behavior, gives them energy and focus, protects them against infection, cures allergies and asthma, and offers them the promise of a normal life. We call these passionate moms, and passionate moms are the strongest force on earth.

Yes, Mr. Sheehan, raw milk is a miraculous food, and there is a host of passionate moms out there who are determined to get it for their families, whether you like it or not.

# 17
# The Magic of Fermented Milk

*And because of the abundance of the milk they give, he will have curds to eat. All who remain in the land will eat curds and honey.*

Isaiah 7:15, 22

Raw milk has many magical properties and one of those properties is its power to support a diverse range of beneficial microbiological life. Most of these microorganisms feed off the lactose in milk and produce lactic acid as a byproduct. Thus, over time, sweet fresh milk becomes sour.

When raw milk sours at warm temperatures, it first turns into a yogurt-like gel and then separates into semi-solid curds and liquid whey. During the process, lactic acid inhibits putrefying bacteria.

Fermented milk products are esteemed everywhere for their therapeutic qualities. In the East, Persian legend has it that Abraham was shown how to prepare a yogurt-like drink by an angel; the drink was reputedly responsible for his fertility and longevity.[1] Kefir was known in ancient times as the champagne of milk and later the "drink of the Prophet," for legend names Mohammed as the one who introduced this fermented drink to his people.

Many villages of ancient Europe, North Africa and Asia had their own names for yogurt, made from the milk of cows, sheep, water buffalo, goats, mares, lamas, reindeer, yak and other animals. The names often signified health and long life, as *laban* or *leben* in the Middle East, *lab-ben raid* in Egypt, and *lebeny* in Assyria.

The thirteenth century historian Lemgo traveled throughout the Middle East and Asia. He described a special area of the Shah's palace in Persia that was reserved for the preparation of *masslo*, a fermented milk drink similar to *tayer*, a favored food of the Jews. Both these foods reputedly prevented epidemics. *Mosab* was another popular fermented milk product, valued by Persian women for its beneficial effect on the skin.

The near universal use of fermented yogurt-like drinks is shown by their various names in the many countries and regions in which they were popular. A few examples include *skyr* in Iceland and the Arctic, *langemilk* in Sweden, *hangop* in Holland, *hochen milk* in Denmark, *bassmilch* in some Alpine regions, *huslanka* in the Carpathian Mountains, *glumse* in Scandinavia, *taetioc* in Lapland and *mezzoradu* in Switzerland. Many of these drinks date to ancient times, as do other forms of fermented milk products, which include *urgutrik* from Bohemia, *matsoon* from Armenia, *gooddu* from Sardinia, *tarho* from the Balkans, *or-jan* from Greece, *dahi* from India and *skuta* from Chile. The word yogurt itself has many variations including *yoart* in Turkey, *yo-urt* in Slavic countries and *yalacta* in Norway.[2]

Traditional peoples usually kept their fermented milk strains in pure form as they passed the cultures from one generation to the next. Often the products served as medicines; many were secret formulas used by celebrated physicians of antiquity, particularly in the treatment of diseases affecting the gastrointestinal tract and its associated organs. Galen noted special qualities in fermented milk that were not present in fresh milk.[3]

Because Ireland was well suited for livestock, many traditional Irish and Gaelic people practiced semi-nomadic pastoral farming, and used fermented milk products as important foods. Curds called *bonac-labbe* were especially popular. Butter was an essential part of the diet, and in times of plenty was buried in cool, damp bogs for future consumption.[4]

## FERMENTED MILK AND LONGEVITY

Many stories attribute longevity to the consumption of fermented milk, but that of Thomas Parr is perhaps the grandest. "Old Parr" was an English peasant reputed by some accounts to have lived one hundred fifty-two years, though modern researchers argue that one hundred two may be closer to the truth. He died in 1635, having lived a lusty life on a diet of "sub-rancid cheese and milk in every form, coarse and hard bread and small drink, generally sour whey," wrote William Harvey.[5] Harvey, the physician who discovered the circulation of the blood, performed an autopsy on Parr, which was said to have verified his great age. Parr's legend includes stories of extraordinary sexual endowment. At the alleged age of one hundred five, he was ordered to do public penance for indecent sexual overtures to a woman, and seventeen years later, he married for a second time and fathered a child.[6,7]

In his book *The Prolongation of Life*, author Ilya Metchnikoff attributes longevity to yogurt and fermented milk products. Metchnikoff, a 1908 Nobel Prize winner, described the longevity of the people living in Bulgaria and other Balkan countries, attributing it to their regular consumption of fermented dairy foods.

Reports of populations that remain vigorous into extreme old age come from three localities in the world—Vilcabamba in Equador, Hunza in the Himalayas and Caucasian Georgia. In all three, fermented raw milk products formed an important part of the diet.[8] Of particular note is the fact that well into the twentieth century, the animals in these places were pasture-fed year round and in all three, pasture land was fed by the mineral-rich runoff of melting glaciers.

## HEALTH BENEFITS

Considerable modern evidence indicates that yogurt and other fermented foods may have a highly beneficial influence on health and longevity. The U.S. government, however, has long maintained the opposite. The 1965 U.S. Department of Agriculture Yearbook, *Consumers All*, in a section titled "Food Quackery," states unequivocally, "Yogurt has no food or health values other than those present in the kind of milk from which it is made."[9]

But a wealth of scientific evidence demonstrates this statement to be false. Writing in *American Practitioner and Digest of Treatment* in December 1950, Harry Seneca, MD and his co-authors abstracted articles from the *Bulletin of the Society of Pediatrics* and other journals. Seneca noted that the biological value of milk protein increases during the culturing of yogurt. In addition, lactic acid produced by fermentation of lactose acts as a digestive antiseptic and a tonic to the nerves of the intestinal tract.[10] Another article in *Dairy Council Digest* described reports indicating that infants fed kefir, a fermented milk beverage from the Caucasus region, retained more calcium, nitrogen, phosphorus, iron and fat than infants fed regular milk.[11] Yet another article showed why this is true: the fermentation process renders calcium and phosphorus (and perhaps other nutrients) more available for absorption.[12]

The work of Russian researchers on fermented milk products was reported in *Chemical Abstracts* of 1963. Riboflavin increased about seventy percent from winter to summer milk. When the milk was fermented into *chekka* (curd) and *kurut* (salted, dried chekka), the riboflavin content tripled.[13] Spanish investigators reported that yogurt showed an increase in folic acid. Other Russian workers reported that *koumiss*, fermented mare's milk, contained far more vitamin $B_{12}$ than the milk from which it was made. *Koumiss* was reported to be particularly helpful for patients with tuberculosis.[14]

Fermented milk products also have powerful bactericidal properties.[15] *Salmonella typhi* (the agent for typhoid fever) added to yogurt disappeared within thirty to forty-eight hours. Shigella species, agents for dysentery, disappeard within two hours. *Escherichia coli* did not develop; *Salmonella paratyphi* (an agent for recurrent fever and diarrhea) and *Corynebacteriae diphtheria* lost their ability to cause disease, as did *Neisseria meningitides* (an agent for meningitis) and *Vibrio comma* (the agent for cholera).

*Dahi*, the fermented milk product in India, is similar to yogurt. When *E. coli*, streptococcus, and staphylococcus were added to *dahi*, the organisms soon died off.[16]

In general, pathogenic bacteria simply disappear two to four days after they are added to yogurt containing from 1.65 to two per cent lactic acid; lactic acid hinders the growth of or kills most pathogenic organisms, which cannot live and develop in an acid medium.[17]

In 1965, the World Health Organization issued a report on the use of a fermented milk product called *airig* in tuberculosis sanitariums in Mongolia. Patients received one liter of *airig* daily. A special research group from the Mongolian Academy of Sciences found that *airig* had a specific effect against tuberculosis.[18] Several years later, another investigator reported that the *Lactobacillus acidophilus* and other organisms (including species of beneficial yeasts) found in kefir inhibited the growth and multiplication of the organisms that can cause tuberculosis and typhoid.[19]

Fermented milk is an excellent treatment for diarrhea in infants and young children. Its value as a preventive during an *E. coli* epidemic was reported in the *Journal of Dairy Science* in 1972.[20] That same year, a group of physicians from the University of Laval in Quebec reported that fermented milk prevented diarrhea in newborns. They also noted that ear and throat infections and pneumonia occurred far less often in the fermented milk-fed infants, and that the hospital's antibiotic expenses dropped by over seventy-five percent when fermented milk was introduced.[21]

In 1950, American physicians reported that fermented milk was the preferred food for weaning children in the Soviet Union. Soviet pediatricians and nutritionists based their recommendations on extensive research.[22] Prior to this, physicians in Sophia, Bulgaria studied the effects of sour milk on both healthy and sick infants for over twelve years. They reported that sour milk caused the usual bacteria of the stools to gradually change, with great benefit in the prevention and treatment of diarrhea.[23]

*Lactobacillus acidophilus* occurs widely in nature and in the human mouth, vagina and intestinal tract. These bacteria, which transform lactose in milk into lactic acid, inhibit the growth of various pathogenic organisms, including those that cause dysentery. These properties of acidophilus were described in a 1959 article entitled "Nature's Gastrointestinal Antibiotics." The authors wrote, "In the Near East, despite high incidence of Shigella and Salmonella dysentery among visitors in

Lebanon, Syria, Egypt and Turkey, the natives seem to be comparatively free of these diseases. These people consume *leben* daily, a composite of curds cultured with *L. acidophilus.*"[24]

Research articles published in a number of medical journals during the 1930s, including the *Bulletin of the Society of Pediatrics*, reported the usefulness of fermented milk products in the treatment of many gastrointestinal problems associated with belching, abdominal distension and gas. In addition to diarrhea and dysentery, problems successfully treated included ulcers, inflamed gall bladder, colitis, acute inflammation of the lining of the stomach and intestines (often diagnosed as gastroenteritis or irritable bowel syndrome), and poor digestion due to lack of hydrochloric acid and pepsin.[25] In 1957, two British physicians reported in England's preeminent medical journal, *The Lancet*, that "there is considerable evidence that for some complaints (e.g., gastroenteritis, colitis, constipation, biliary disorders, flatulence, migraine, nervous fatigue) cultured milk can be especially valuable."[26] Earlier, the *American Journal of Digestive Diseases* had reported that chronically ill institutionalized patients experienced numerous benefits when fed plain yogurt, including relief from constipation to the point of no longer needing laxatives. These patients also had better skin tone and improvements in skin rashes and diabetic ulcers.[27]

As noted above, *L. acidophilus* occurs naturally in the human intestinal tract. The use of fermented milk products encourages optimal populations of this friendly bacterium. Metchnikoff believed this organism and *L. bulgaricus* were largely responsible for the protective effects yogurt exerted against invading pathogenic bacteria.

Today, instead of fermented milk products, doctors prescribe antibiotics and similar drugs, which destroy normal intestinal flora. A host of side effects has become widespread in the process, often including constipation or diarrhea. Fermented milk products restore normal intestinal flora, a known beneficial effect, while inhibiting the multiplication of pathogens; the antibiotic value of yogurt has been compared to that of penicillin.[28] A 1972 report in the *Journal of the American Medical Association* detailed the therapeutic use of yogurt to mitigate the toxic effects of combined antibiotic therapy,[29] and a 1960 report in *Clinical*

*Medicine* described the effectiveness of *L. acidophilus* in reestablishing normal intestinal flora after antibiotic treatment.[30]

A 1964 article in the *Journal of Oral Therapeutics and Pharmacology* provides further proof of the usefulness of *L. acidophilus*, even in oral capsules. Two capsules four times daily were given to eleven patients with acute infectious inflammation of the gums and mouth. Patients with painful lesions poured the powder from the capsules directly on the lesions before rinsing it down with a few ounces of milk. "Within twelve hours," the authors wrote, "all patients reported relief of pain; in twenty-four hours, eating without difficulty was restored; and, after seventy-two hours, the patients were lesion-free. No side effects and no complications were encountered."[31] One wonders how many dentists today inform their patients of this simple, inexpensive, and highly effective treatment of herpetic gingivostomatitis—the medical name for this problem—rather than prescribing an antibiotic.

WHEY IS THE WAY

Whey is the yellowish liquid that forms when sour or cultured milk separates into "curds and whey." The concentration of curds into hard cheeses results in the release of additional whey, called cheese whey.

Research indicates that fresh whey acts like yogurt and other soured milk products in killing nearly all pathogenic bacteria tested, including a wide variety of Salmonella organisms, *E. coli*, *Brucella abortus* (the agent for undulant fever), *Klebsiella pneumoniae* (an agent for acute bacterial pneumonia) and *Corynebacteriae diphtheria*.[32]

But the dairy industry considers whey, particularly cheese whey, a waste product, one that it has turned into a profit with the manufacture of powdered whey as a dietary supplement. However, of the two major proteins in milk, whey and casein, whey is the more fragile. Its amino acids, enzymes and immune supporting properties are largely denatured by the spray drying process. In addition, most commerical whey is derived from commercial, confinement-dairy milk used in the commercial cheese-making process, and is therefore likely to carry the many adulterants that we have discussed. Also, as we have seen in Chapter 15, no powdered product is sterile; but any beneficial bacteria in fresh whey made from raw milk will be destroyed during high-temperature processing.

However, fresh whey obtained from the culturing and separation of raw milk has an important place in any kitchen, as it can serve as a starter culture for lacto-fermented—traditionally pickled—vegetables (such as sauerkraut), fruits (such as chutneys) and other meat products (such as salami). As with milk, sugars and starches are converted into lactic acid during the fermentation process, preserving the food for long periods.

Good things happen to lacto-fermenting foods besides preservation. Lactobacilli, the organisms that make lactic acid, proliferate and enhance digestibility and increase the amounts of many vitamins. Enzymes multiply as well, along with substances that have antibiotic and anticancer properties. Lactic acid itself not only preserves the food but also promotes the growth of healthy flora in the intestinal tract.

Since the earliest times, many cultures throughout the world have enjoyed lacto-fermented vegetables, fruits and meats. Cabbage, cucumbers, beets, turnips, herbs, grape leaves, green tomatoes, peppers and lettuces all were fermented in Europe and Russia. Asian cuisines featured pickled cabbage, eggplant, cucumber, onion, carrot, squash and turnip. In America, relishes originated as lacto-fermented products. Hard sausage products and preserved fish, such as *gravlax* (lacto-fermented salmon), have an important place in cuisines from around the world.[33]

Furthermore, many cultures produced whey-based beverages such as small beer. These hold great promise as an alternative to modern soft drinks. Healthy, probiotic versions of root beer, ginger ale and cream sodas can be produced using whey as a culturing agent.

People living in traditional cultures throughout the world, without refrigeration or modern sanitation, enjoyed outstanding health and freedom from disease because lacto-fermentation preserved food in a way that was safe and healthful.

## FERMENTED MILK FOR THE LACTOSE INTOLERANT
Some individuals do not digest large quantities of lactose easily.

Even some individuals of northern European descent, who would be expected to be lactose-tolerant, have trouble with milk. Loose stools, congestion and intestinal gas may be typical after consuming a few ounces of fresh milk, even high quality raw milk. These adults produce lactase at only about ten percent of its original level.[34] Clabbered milk, yogurt, kefir, buttermilk, cheeses and other lactic-acid fermented milk products are very low in lactose and easily digested by nearly all of these individuals. These products should be made at home or by small manufacturers using whole raw milk gently heated only to room temperature or slightly above, and without the additives and fillers found in commercial yoghurt products.

CHEESE: THE BASIS OF CULTURE

Cheese is a secondary and long-life product of fermented milk, produced by removing the liquid from milk curds, culturing with specific organisms and often adding salt. There are literally thousands of types of cheese from around the world, ranging from soft cheese that must be eaten within a few weeks of production to hard aged cheeses that can last unrefrigerated for many years.

Whereas traditional fermented milk products nourished the town or village in which they were produced, hardened and aged cheese can be stored, carried and traded. In fact, raw cheese from pastured cows is the perfect storage food, containing calcium, phosphorus and other minerals, fat-soluble vitamins, B vitamins and even vitamin C in easily assimilated form. Cheese can sustain crews on ships, armies on the move and travelers on long journies.

Cheese is also an excellent value-added product, bringing farmers and artisans the highest possible price for their milk. Cheese can bring prosperity to farms, towns and regions. Commerce in cheese contributed to the growth of wealth and flowering of culture in Europe, especially in Germany, Switzerland, Holland, Italy and France.

And because good cheese, the kind for which consumers are willing to pay a lot of money, can only be made by artisans, cheese supports economic independence for the common man and for rural economies. It is not too much of a stretch to claim that cheese production and consumption supports the spirit of independence that led to the American revolution and de-centralized, constitutional government in many parts of the world. As Charles de Gaulle stated in a 1951 address: "How can one be expected to govern a country with two hundred forty-six kinds of cheese?"

Our historical and scientific review of the healthfulness of fermented milk products brings into clear focus the fact that nearly everyone can enjoy remarkable benefits by making raw and fermented milk from healthy, grassfed animals a central part of the diet. The conclusion that such foods are far superior in every way to conventionally produced milk products is inescapable for any serious investigator willing to objectively examine the evidence.

# 18

# Why Whole, Raw,
# Grass-Fed Milk is Best

*And I will send grass in thy fields for thy cattle, that thou mayest eat and be satisfied.*

Deuteronomy 11:15

A 1909 advertisement for Carnation milk shows a small herd of Holsteins grazing on green pastures along a stream, with evergreen trees and a glacial mountain in the background. "Carnation Milk. From contented cows. Green grass the year 'round on the North Pacific Coast," the copy reads. A very straightforward ad.[1] Today most milk promotion avoids reminding us about the living conditions of cows.

Instead, we learn all about milk from famous people. What do these celebrities have in common? Larry King, Martha Stewart, Van Halen, Spike Lee, Ivana Trump, Danny Devito, Jay Leno, Lauren Bacall, Tony Bennett, Vanessa Williams, Joan Rivers, Angela Lansbury, Dennis Rodman, Christie Brinkley, Britney Spears and Pete Sampras? They've all graced billboards in the milk mustache campaign, the Milk Industry Foundation's multi-million dollar attempt to reverse 30 years of declining milk sales. The object: make milk cool. The milk mustache became an icon of the nineties and a part of pop culture.[2] Each celebrity poster carries a different four-line message about an alleged benefit of milk.

Few advertisers today conjure the image of cows at pasture—an image that represents an archetype of good health. Even people who have never seen a live cow sense that contented cows spend their time in the sunshine eating fresh grass—and contented cows are associated with good milk. Purveyors of organic milk, one of the biggest growth industries of the nineties, have often used pictures of cows at pasture on their milk cartons; for this, one consumer group sued an organic dairy company, charging false advertising.[3]

The Horizon Milk Company is a one-hundred-million-dollar plus Colorado corporation that controls some seventy percent of the retail market for organic milk. Comparing the image Horizon presents on its labels with the reality of the lives the Horizon cows lead is instructive. A Horizon milk carton in use in the year 2000 featured a cartoon-like drawing of a cute cow, with the words "A clean living cow. . . makes real good milk" framing the image. "Our milk is produced on certified organic farms where no dangerous pesticides or chemicals are ever used," the copy continued. "We feed our cows 100% organically grown corn, grain, hay and other healthy foods. . . . We allow our cows to make milk the natural way, with access to plenty of fresh air, clean water and exercise. After all, cows are mothers, too. . . "[4] Horizon's "natural way" does not include a word about grass.

At Horizon's factory farms, mostly in California and other western states, thousands of cows spend their days fenced in dry lots where they never see a blade of grass, eating their certified organic grains and some hay.[5] These cows are heavy producers, but because they are not let out to pasture, they are particularly susceptible to mastitis, organically fed or not, a condition that requires antibiotic treatment. Because organic dairy standards stipulate at least a few months of separation between treatment of a cow with antibiotics and her return to an organic herd, cows with clinical mastitis are generally culled from the herd for slaughter.

The Organic Cow of Vermont, based in the Northeast, is another producer of organic milk. Horizon bought out the company in the late 1990s and rewrote the label. The new Organic Cow label still features the company's "Happy Cow" logo, but no longer mentions happy cows and Vermont family farmers. The label instead describes the benefits of ultrapasteurization, which allows the milk to be shipped all over the country with an extended refrigerated shelf-life of fifty days. Most of Horizon Dairy's and Organic Cow's milk and milk products are ultrapasteurized.

As we have discussed, ultrapasteurization is a high-heat process that totally destroys all enzymes and considerably more vitamins and carrier proteins than regular pasteurization. In conventional pasteurization, milk is heated to 145 degrees Fahrenheit for thirty minutes (the Holder method) or about 160 degrees Fahrenheit for fifteen seconds (flash pasteurization). Most pathogens and other microorganisms are killed but some benign varieties that can sour milk remain alive.

Ultrapasteurization, also known as UHT (ultra-high temperature) pasteurization, targets these microorganisms by heating the milk to temperatures of 230 degrees and even as high as 285 degrees Fahrenheit—way above the boiling point! All microorganisms and spores that might spoil the product are destroyed, but so are all the antimicrobial and immune-supporting properties. Ultrapasteurization followed by rapid cooling of the milk is coupled with aseptic packaging to yield boxed milk and other products that can be stored unopened at room temperature for about six months. Nevertheless, the milk is sold from the refrigerator section of the grocery store, just like regular pasteurized milk. American consumers would be unlikely to purchase milk if they knew it required no refrigeration.

Ultrapasteurized organic milk now sells for premium prices in thousands of supermarkets and health food stores throughout the country. This milk is probably less nutritious than regularly pasteurized conventional milk.[6] Yet Horizon assures us on their website that "there is no difference in the nutritive value and the delicious taste" between their conventionally pasteurized and ultrapasteurized milks.[7]

To the credit of Horizon and other organic agribusiness outfits, thousands of acres are farmed without pesticides or herbicides in order to supply the grain for organic milk. However, that same land dedicated to pasture feeding and small scale raw milk production would result in increased soil fertility, reduced erosion and a very different economic model, as we shall see.

THE NEW SWILL DAIRIES

In Chapter 5, we described the infamous "milk problem," the feeding of brewery swill to confinement cattle in urban areas, which led to the death of about half of all inner city infants during the 19th century. The resulting milk was filthy and so thin that unscrupulous purveyors often added chalk to it, to mask its original bluish color. The latest agricultural model takes us right back to the swill dairies, with confinement dairy farms located close to ethanol plants so the byproducts can be fed to the dairy cows. The fermentation process in the modern ethanol plants isn't anything like the fermentation process the moonshiner uses to make whisky, nor even like the fermentation process used in the inner city breweries. Today the process is chemical-driven and done in record time. To purify the ethanol requires a number of chemical processes and the resulting mash (which the industry actually calls "sludge") is a reeking mass of chemical residues, including sulfuric acid.[8]

A recent article in *Stockman Grass Farmer* lists three dangers of byproduct feeding.[9] One is a type of polio that creates brain lesions in the cows due to high sulfur levels in the feed. The disease has symptoms similar to mad cow disease.

Second, the ethanol byproducts are highly susceptible to potentially deadly molds called mycotoxins. "The residual mash produced [from ethanol production] is both hot and wet, which is an ideal environment for mold growth. It is dumped out of the centrifuge onto a concrete floor and a front loader loads it into a dump truck for transport to a dairy or feedlot. The factory floor, the tractor bucket and the interior of the truck are all potential sources of yeast infection, which initates mold formation, and must be constantly kept disinfected to prevent contamination . . . Because this feed is rendered bacterially sterile by the production process, any mold that alights on it can grow extremely rapidly and can reach problematic levels in just a few hours." Aflatoxin can actually survive the ethanol production process, can pass through into cows' milk and is not killed by pasteurization. It is a potent liver poison and major carcinogen.

Third, research at Kansas State has found that cattle eating brewer's grains from beer manufacturing were six times more likely to harbor the virulent form of *E. coli* than cattle fed corn—and cattle fed corn are more likely to harbor the organism than cattle on grass. Adding chalk to the milk is not going to solve this problem.

To facilitate shipping of distillery waste to dairies located in other parts of the country, ethanol manufacturers turn the sludge into dry, extruded pellets. The cows will not eat these pellets unless they are sweetened, so manufacturers spray them with corn syrup, the product of another chemically driven corn processing method.[10]

Unlike the swill dairies of the 1800s, these dairies are out of sight, out of mind—and out of range at which they can be smelled! Located in sparsely populated rural areas, they are too far away from the general public to cause an outcry, much less reveal the connection between what we feed our dairy cows and the declining public health.

ACTIVATOR X

But does it really matter what we feed our cows? Even if we go back to small scale production, can't we just give our cows dry hay and grain?

To answer this question, we must turn again to the work of Weston Price, who discovered that the primary cause of dental decay and other degenerative disease was a lack of certain nutrients not adequately provided in modern diets. He presented evidence in his book, *Nutrition and Physical Degeneration*, showing that healthy primitive peoples, with their striking smiles of straight, white teeth, had very high levels of fat-soluble vitamins from certain animal sources in their diets.

One of these was a previously unrecognized fat-soluble substance, which plays an essential role in optimal mineral assimilation, bone structure, dental health and growth, and he demonstrated its presence in the butterfat of milk, in fish eggs, and in the organs and fats of grazing animals. He measured the amount in dairy products, and found that the substance was present only in butter from cows eating rapidly growing green grass. In his extensive records, he used the term Activator X for this substance.

Price analyzed over twenty thousand samples of dairy products from various districts throughout the United States, northwestern Canada, Australia, Brazil and New Zealand. The greatest influence on the content of nutrients, including Activator X, ". . . was found to be the pasture fodder of the animals. Rapidly growing grass, green or rapidly dried, was most efficient."[11] These periods of high-vitamin content were more directly related to whether or not the grass was growing rather than to the amount of sunshine or the temperature. In temperate climates, these periods occur in the spring and early fall.

Price also studied the mortality data from the various districts, and he carefully constructed graphs plotting the number of deaths versus the amount of vitamin A and Activator X in the dairy products. His conclusion has fascinating implications: "A study of the data of the health departments of all these districts regarding mortality for heart disease and pneumonia disclosed that the curves were always found to be lowest when the vitamin content of the dairy products was highest." In other words, when people were taking in a lot of vitamin A and Activator X, they had much lower levels of heart disease and pneumonia.

Price developed an "X Factor" butter oil by centrifuging butter at room temperature to produce an oil that was much richer in Activator X than whole butter. In his studies on the control of dental caries he found that while the consumption of butter was an aid in mineral metabolism, the high-potency oil yielded much better results. Used in conjunction with high-vitamin cod liver oil, Price was able to reverse tooth decay and cure many diseases.

Rickets, a disease of children characterized by softening of the bones leading to bow-legs, was prevalent in Price's time. Price demonstrated that rickets in rats could be healed by adding butter oil concentrate, in the amount of two percent of the calories in the diet, to an otherwise deficient diet. The quantity of oil used was equivalent to about one-half ounce (one tablespoon) for a child eating two pounds of food a day. Price describes his treatment of a four-year-old boy suffering with a fracture and rampant tooth decay. The boy had also suffered from convulsions for over eight months and had broken his leg in a fall to the floor during a convulsion three months earlier. The fracture had not healed. The minister who brought the boy to Price had been called to the home to baptize the boy for burial because the child was near death.

The boy's diet had consisted primarily of white bread and skimmed milk. Price's only treatment was a change in diet: he prescribed whole raw milk and gruel made from freshly ground whole wheat with a large spoonful of butter-oil concentrate poured over it. "After his first meal," Price wrote, "the boy slept his first night without a convulsion. He was fed five times the next day on the same diet, and had no convulsions. Recovery was very rapid. Without any treatment on his teeth, dental caries were controlled. He grew to be an athletic young man, active in sports, particularly baseball."[12] X-rays taken before and after Dr. Price's dietary treatment demonstrate the healing of the fractured femur.

An experiment with turkeys further demonstrated the importance of Activator X. Supplements of both cod liver oil and butter oil concentrate, rich in Activator X, were given to turkeys eating stock food diets. Turkeys given butter oil and cod liver oil grew more than twice as rapidly as those supplemented with cod liver oil alone. Within just one week there was an obvious difference in condition and appearance, along with marked changes in the calcium and phosphorus content of the blood.

Price also found significant changes in the chemical constituents of the saliva and the growth of *L. acidophilus* in human subjects who added butter rich in Activator X to the diet. "Clinically," he wrote, "the use of butter high in Activator X, in conjunction with a favorable selection of natural foods, as shown through a period of seventeen years, is highly effective in the control of dental caries. Primitive races controlled dental caries with diets high in body-building factors which included Activator X."[13]

Activator X is of course found in whole milk from grass-fed animals—the food Price called "Nature's only complete diet for mammalian infants and by far the most important single item of food for growing human beings in all periods of stress."[14] But the richest source is butter oil concentrate carefully made from such milk. In Chapter 19, we'll meet a dairy farmer who is producing just such a product.

For years the identity of Activator X remained a mystery, but some careful detective work by Chris Masterjohn, a researcher for the Weston A. Price Foundation, has revealed that Activator X is most likely the same substance as the animal form of vitamin K, called vitamin $K_2$.[15]

Dairy cows and other animals produce vitamin $K_2$ out of vitamin $K_1$, the plant form of vitamin K, which is present in green grass. Vitamin $K_2$ occurs in the same foods found to be good sources of Activator X—certain seafoods such as shellfish and fish eggs, and the fats, butterfat and organ meats of grass-fed animals.

Originally scientists considered vitamin $K_2$ important only for blood clotting, but today, after a decade of research, they have uncovered a great many other roles for the substance; and this research dovetails perfectly with Dr. Price's findings. Vitamin $K_2$ activates proteins responsible for the deposition of calcium and phosphorus in the bones and teeth; its presence in the saliva protects against dental caries. And vitamin $K_2$ contributes to infant and childhood growth by preventing the premature calcification of the cartilaginous growth zones of the bones. A specific marker for vitamin $K_2$ deficiency is a small and sunken-in nose, what Dr. Price referred to as the "underdevelopment of the middle third of the face." Just as Weston Price described, vitamin $K_2$ plays a critical role in building attractive, wide faces with teeth that are naturally straight and greatly resistant to tooth decay.

Vitamin $K_2$ has other roles that mirror the properties of Activator X. It is crucial to reproduction, for example. The brain contains one of the highest concentrations of vitamin $K_2$, where it is involved in the synthesis of the myelin sheath and other components needed for a healthy nervous system—witness the child's freedom from seizures after Dr. Price had treated him with the butter oil—and it contributes to learning capacity.

Most startling of all are the findings of Dutch researchers, which show that vitamin $K_2$ protects against the calcification and inflammation of blood vessels and the accumulation of atherosclerotic plaque.[16] The intake of vitamin $K_2$ is inversely associated with heart disease, exactly what Dr. Price discovered.

The past fifty years have witnessed an epidemic of infertility, learning disorders and heart disease, while the narrow face has become so commonplace as to be considered normal—most children today need braces to straighten their teeth. The underlying cause—predicted by Dr. Price and confirmed by modern research on vitamin K—can be attributed to the industrialization of agriculture, which has taken our dairy cows and other domestic animals off grass, and the campaign against butter and other animal fats, ostensibly to prevent heart disease!

MORE BENEFITS FROM GRASS-FED BUTTER

The other two important vitamins Dr. Price found in high amounts in nonindustrialized diets were vitamins A and D. As with Activator X, vitamins A and D will be present in butterfat in appreciable amounts only if the cows are outside on pasture—vitamin D comes from sunlight and vitamin A comes from the conversion of carotenes in green grass. These two nutrients work synergistically with vitamin $K_2$—vitamins A and D tell the cells to make certain proteins and then vitamin K activates these proteins after signaling by vitamins A and D. This finding explains why Dr. Price did not get good results using cod liver oil (a source of vitamins A and D) alone, but achieved many remarkable recoveries with a combination of cod liver oil and high-vitamin butter oil (a source of vitamin $K_2$ as well as vitamins A and D).

Vitamins A and D have a myriad of uses in the body, including mineral metabolism, homone production, protein metabolism and the health of virtually every organ. Both A and D are necessary for calcium metabolism so that the calcium in milk is effectively absorbed and built into the bones and teeth.

Another nutrient found in the fat of grass-fed ruminant animals is conjugated linoleic acid (CLA), which in recent years has been shown to play an important role in disease protection and the maintenance of optimal health. Nonfat dairy products contain no CLA. A recent article in the *Journal of Dairy Science* reported that milk from grassfed cows contains up to five times more CLA than milk from conventionally fed cows. Other workers found that to produce milk with the highest possible CLA content, the cows must be fed no grain at all; feeding fifteen pounds of grains per day lowered the CLA content of the milk to the level found in the milk of confinement cows.[17,18,19] Only whole milk from cows on grass contains significant amounts of CLA.

Studies have shown that CLA has strong anticancer effects. For example, rats fed CLA at one and one-half percent of their total calories showed reduction in tumor size of up to sixty percent.[20] Even relatively small amounts of CLA may have significant effects; one researcher has estimated that eating one serving daily of grassfed meat, one ounce of cheese and one glass of whole milk from a grassfed cow, will significantly lower the risk of cancer.[21] CLA also appears to have fat-burning and muscle-building characteristics—in other words, it helps you lose weight.

GRASS FEEDING AND THE ENVIRONMENT

In August, 2005, a manure lagoon in an upstate New York dairy farm collapsed, depositing three million gallons of liquid manure into the Black River, killing at least one quarter million fish and creating an environmental nightmare. The dairy kept forty-five hundred cows in confinement.[22]

In February, 2001, two young workers passed out from exposure to hydrogen sulfide and ammonia while working on an underground pump; they drowned in liquid manure. The workers were employed by a seventeen hundred-cow dairy in California's Central Valley. The cows produced about two hundred thousand gallons of waste each day, washed from the pens through the underground shaft to be pumped into a holding lagoon.[23]

The dairy could have hired a professional crew for six hundred dollars to clean the pump but elected to use low-cost workers for the job. The first, a welder, descended into the shaft without safety equipment, and the second lost his life trying to save his buddy.

The accumulation of liquid manure on confinement dairy farms poses an obvious threat to the environement—to our rivers and streams and to the air iteslf—and to the safety of farm workers. These dangers do not exist on small dairy farms that practice pasture-feeding.

Recently cows have taken the blame for a host of environmental ills, from erosion and soil depletion to global warming. Certainly a system that depends on monocropping, as does the confinement dairy system, will lead to erosion and pollution with pesticides and herbicides; but managed pasture grazing for beef and dairy cattle helps build soil, minimizes erosion and sequesters carbon.

As explained by Matthew Rales, writing for the Weston A. Price Foundation, "We are told by the global warming gurus that the earth is heating up due to excess carbon dioxide in the atmosphere. Through specific grazing strategies we can sequester this excess carbon and form rich, productive topsoil in the process. We do this not by planting more trees, or even by setting aside more wildlife preserves. We do this with domesticated ruminants—pulsing the landscape with large numbers of animals for short periods of time.

"In nature, bison and wildebeest graze in huge mobs, remaining in one location briefly, and then they move on to fresh ground. They keep bunched together tightly for fear of pack-hunting predators. These ruminants are Nature's soil-building and fertility management mechanism. We also know that the soils under which these animals graze are our largest land-based carbon sinks on earth. All we need to do, then, is to mimic these native grazing patterns with our domestic stock, and we have an easily achieved, rapid solution to the excess carbon in the atmosphere.

"The hoof action, manure, urine and saliva all act as bio-stimulants on the pasture, encouraging the grass plants to thicken, bare spots to fill in, and species diversity and succession to accelerate forward from simplicity to complexity. The productive grasslands of the world and the massive herds of herbivores that grazed them coevolved together. One cannot exist without the other. The grass relies on the ruminant for its full expression just as much as the ruminant relies on grass. Without ruminants to fertilize the soil and break down cellulose in dry climates, prairies quickly become deserts; and with managed grazing of ruminant animals, deserts can be restored to productive land."[24]

GRASS FEEDING, RAW MILK AND RURAL ECONOMIES

At Tennessee Senate hearings held in September, 2005, state senator Frank Niceley argued for liberalization of raw milk laws on economic grounds. "When I grew up, you could drive through the backroads of Tennesses and see dairy farm after dairy farm, all with grazing cows, beautiful barns and well-kept farm houses. Today when you drive across the state you never see a cow. The houses are abandoned and the barns are dilapidated. Much of the pastureland has reverted to scrubby forest." Just after World War II, there were almost ten thousand dairy farms in the state of Tennessee; today there are about five hundred.

Throughout America, and particularly in the South and Midwest, travelers are greeted with the sight of barns falling down and small towns unkempt and largely abandoned. Many factors have contributed to this decline, of which mandatory pasteurization laws coupled with the industrialization of agriculture are certainly among the most important. Laws mandating pasteurization deny rural communities the number one value added agriculture product—raw milk and raw milk products. And the confinement model, in which grains and other high-density feeds are carried to cows in confinement, puts an insurmountable financial burden on the farmer.

Consider a small dairy farmer with thirty cows. In the conventional model, he feeds grains for high production, and each of his cows produces about one hundred ninety hundredweight of milk per year. Because of mandatory pasteurization laws, he is forced to sell to the dairy company that controls the area in which he resides. He will receive anywhere from ten to twenty dollars per hundredweight for his milk. Ten dollars per hundredweight is the price farmers got for their milk at the end of World War II. If he receives the average, fifteen dollars per hundredweight (about one dollar twenty cents per gallon), his gross income is about eighty-five thousand dollars. But his expenses are high—feed costs, veterinary bills, and the cost of replacement cows can easily wipe out his income. Often his wife must work for extra income to obtain health insurance. If the cost of feed rises or the price of milk drops, the farm comes to the end of its precarious existence.

As small dairy farms become an endangered species, the large dairies have filled in the gap. These farms have the same high costs as the small dairy, but there is a difference: they are subsidized. For example, the mega-dairy industry in California has sales of over six billion dollars per year and gets more than one-quarter that amount—one billion six hundred million dollars—back in subsidies.[25]

By contrast, the thirty-cow model works very well economically when the cows are grazed on pasture and the farmer can sell his raw milk and raw milk products directly to the consumer, even though his cows produce only half as much milk. He can sell his fluid milk for between four and thirteen dollars per gallon—the typical price is six dollars per gallon, at least four times more than the conventional model. If he makes yoghurt or cheese, he can make forty to fifty dollars per gallon. A conservative estimate of his gross income for dairy products is one hundred fifty thousand dollars per year. And his costs are much lower—his vet bills are low, he has much lower feed costs and he spends no money on replacement cows—the cows replace themselves, with some leftover, which he can sell. And there's an added bonus. If he makes butter, cream or cheese, he will have whey and skim milk as a by-product, which make an excellent protein source for pasture-fed hogs and poultry. If customers are coming to his farm to purchase raw milk products, they will be delighted to buy pasture-fed eggs, pasture-fed chicken, and bacon, ham and pork chops from pasture-fed hogs as well. And if he wants to sell beef, honey and garden vegetables, he has a ready market for these products also.

This model can bring the farmer a gross income two or three times more than his income in the conventional model, with much lower costs. The multiplier effect for each dollar earned on the farm is five to seven dollars for the local community and the potential for growth in the local service industry is large.

A return to traditional pasture-based dairying and local, direct sales of raw milk presents the potential of vigorous rural revival, of prosperous small farms and thriving local communities. The thriving market towns of Europe were built on just such a model. Consider the town of Parma, with its economy based on locally produced ham and raw Parmesan cheese. The farmers live in large houses called villas, and the opera house in the center of town has a gold-plated dome.

Let's now look as some farmers who are pioneering the pasture-based raw milk dairying movement, who are preparing the way for a revival of rural prosperity and a renaissance of indigenous cultural life.

# 19
# Raw Milk Today:
# Green Pastures, Contented
# Cows and Contentious Issues

*People need this milk. They want it real bad. You should hear the
stories they tell me.*

> Anonymous farmer in a state
> that outlaws all sales of raw milk

*Never doubt that a small group of thoughtful, committed citizens
can change the world; indeed, it's the only thing that ever has.*

> Margaret Mead

## LOCAL FARM, CONNECTICUT

Some of the finest raw milk in Connecticut is produced on Debra
Tyler's Local Farm in West Cornwall. Ms. Tyler tends twelve to fourteen
cows and calves on thirteen fertile acres of pasture. Health food stores
in Connecticut have sold Local Farm milk for many years, but Debra
recently downsized her herd and now sells only on the farm. Hers is
one of about a dozen licensed raw milk dairies among Connecticut's two
hundred dairy farms.

The cows at Local Farm are Jerseys. The most popular dairy cow in

America are Holsteins, which provide more milk, but with less protein, fat and calcium. Jerseys were originally bred by the French to produce milk for cheese making. The fat content of Debra's Jersey milk varies seasonally but averages about 4.8 percent, well above the normal 3.5 percent for whole milk. Debra is a grass farmer; her cows eat mostly grass plus a little hay in the spring, summer and fall, and mostly hay (plus a little grass) in the winter, when each cow consumes one forty-pound bale per day.

Local Farm used to be certified organic. Certification costs several hundred dollars a year in fees and periodically requires several hours of paperwork. Maintaining certification also meant that Debra sometimes had to pay more for certified feed from faraway places than for locally produced feed she knows to be pesticide-free but which is not certified organic. A couple of years ago, she let the organic certification lapse. "People who come here can see what they're getting," she told me.

Bottled in glass and rich in cream, Local Farm raw milk carries the sweet flavor of fresh milk from grass-fed Jerseys. It's the most popular raw milk in Connecticut, and demand at local natural food stores has always exceeded the supply. To Debra's knowledge, no one has ever become ill drinking Local Farm milk. A few years ago, stores recalled about three dozen half-gallon bottles when the state reported campylobacter bacteria in one sample of milk from Debra's tank following the monthly bacteriological testing. Follow-up testing found no traces and no one became ill. The farm's bacteria counts are consistently low.

Debra taught enrichment programs for all children, and special programs for the gifted, in kindergarten through the eighth grade in the public schools for four years before retiring in 1992 to become a dairy farmer. She home schooled her daughter. Recently, Debra founded Motherhouse, a support group for women during pregnancy and motherhood. "Cows are the ultimate nurturers," Debra says. "They teach the essence of mothering and nursing."

Teaching has become more and more a part of her farm work as well. She organizes two or three "family cow" workshops each year, and in the last few years has sold several cows to families that have decided to keep a family cow.

The workshops are well attended, and one June day several years ago, I joined about fifteen other people at Local Farm to take part in the proceedings. By the end of the day each of us, including the eight-year-old daughter of a couple from Massachusetts, took a turn milking three-year-old Daisy Lavender. We drank warm fresh milk, made cottage and farmer's cheese and churned sweet butter. We then shared a lunch of sourdough bread and homemade dairy products.

We started the day by going out into the pasture—mostly lush green clover and Kentucky blue grass—which grows adjacent to the barn and the three-sided, hay-floored shelter that served as our headquarters. Verdant rolling hills stretched out before us to the country road that cuts through the mini-valley below Local Farm.

Fifteen people, eleven cows, and three calves gently intermingled. One of the cows, Rebecca, would present her massive head, horns and all, to one person after another for a scratching. Daisy Lavender was for sale, and she would nose about potential owners, sometimes moving quietly behind one and nuzzling him. Portulaca, dry at the time but due to calve in July, would move steadily towards us when Debra called her name. Along with a number of other people, I got my first up-close lesson about the gentle intelligence and sweet dispositions of well-cared-for cows.

The author of *Breeds of Cattle* tells the following story, one illustrative of maternal affection mixed with a process akin to rational thought. Mooing loudly, a cow runs toward a man walking through a field. Alarmed, the man suspects madness, but as she nears him the cow turns and heads back, still looking back over her shoulder at the man and mooing. He walks on, and she again approaches him, gazing at him, appearing anxious, again mooing. Then she trots away in the same direction as before. Curious, the man follows her, and she leads him to the far end of the field, where her calf lies fallen into a ditch, nearly drowned. He rescues the little animal, and the mother awkwardly but joyfully skips and prances about.[1]

Such is the intelligence, reasoning faculty and affection of the animals Debra Tyler has grown to love. Debra intends to continue to phase down the milking—she hopes another raw milk farmer will come along to satisfy the demand she has helped create throughout the area—and phase up the breeding, raising and placing of family cows.

ORGANIC PASTURES DAIRY, CALIFORNIA

Three thousand miles away at Organic Pastures Dairy, Mark McAfee is phasing up every aspect of America's largest raw milk dairy. From May 1999, when Steuve's Natural stopped producing raw milk for sale to the public, until McAfee began in January 2002, California had only one licensed raw milk producer, Claravale Dairy, a small farm with about thirty-five Jerseys in the San Francisco Bay area town of Watsonville. The California State Health Department's vendetta against Alta Dena, the Steuve brothers and other producers sent a message to other potential producers, and a system of hefty fees imposed on raw milk farmers for the tests the state requires further ensured that no one would enter the arena.

None of that has deterred McAfee. Organic Pastures Dairy is California's first certified organic, fully pasture-grazed raw milk dairy. Founded in 2000 as an extension of an organic farming operation that has been in operation since 1988 as McAfee Farms, the family-owned-and-operated dairy is located near Fresno in the fertile San Joaquin Valley. McAfee is now bottling 10,000 half gallons of raw milk each week and selling them in health food stores all over California along with thousands of pints each of raw cream and colostrum weekly. The dairy's creamery produces more than one thousand pounds of raw butter each week; the skim milk left over is sold to outside organic creameries for pasteurization and yogurt. A recent addition to the product list is a truly raw Cheddar cheese. The dairy does not outsource its dairy products and uses all of its own fluid raw milk in its own products.

McAfee grows organic apples, almonds and alfalfa on one hundred fifty of the farm's six hundred acres; the remainder is divided up into a series of paddocks through which he rotates his Holsteins, Jerseys and Ayrshires—about four hundred cows in all. The animals eat thirty pounds of dry alfalfa hay and eight to ten pounds of grain, mostly rolled corn, each day; the rest of their diet is a mix of fresh-growing green grasses. McAfee is crossing his Holsteins and Jerseys with his Ayrshires.

"The crossbreeds have a better immune system," he told me. "They live longer—over ten years—they're healthier, they pasture well and have no hoof problems."

Mark invented and built the farm's mobile milking parlor, which is pulled by truck to a new location every week. This eliminates the need to hold cows in manure-filled pens prior to milking. Waste lagoons typically used at confinement dairy operations are unnecessary at Organic Pastures. Cows are not forced to spend time on concrete, which eliminates most problems with lameness. The result is healthy animals and low bacteria counts in the milk. The milk goes directly from the cow through a chilling and double filtering process—it's flash chilled to thirty-six degrees Fahrenheit within thirty seconds of leaving the cow, another key to low bacteria counts and Organic Pastures' long shelf life of fourteen days.

As I approached Fresno and Organic Pastures Dairy on a late December day, endless tracts of agricultural land stretched all about me to the horizons, dotted by huge combines that moved slowly across the landscape. The heart of industrial agriculture (if it has one) lies in the San Joaquin Valley. Occasionally I passed conventional dairy farms, with hundreds of cows crowded into huge fenced pens, often knee deep in black muck, without a blade of grass in sight. I wondered how many of these operations were producing organic milk for ultrapasteurization.

Organic Pastures is miles off the main road. I parked in front of the modest building housing the dairy's offices, next to the small bottling facility and creamery. Behind the buildings, cows grazed on green pastures. McAfee's Spanish-style ranch house, with a roof of red clay tiles pitched over white stucco walls, stands two or three hundred yards down a dirt and gravel drive cut through the pastures.

McAfee greeted me. We went inside, sat down and talked animatedly about cows and raw milk. Mark is a zealot—an enthusiastic and extreme partisan—without being a fanatic. McAfee was a paramedic for sixteen years before making a career switch in his late thirties and returning to the family farm. Like a character out of the popular television show ER, he exudes the confidence of a superbly trained professional who knows what he has to do in any situation and is prepared to act.

"My attitude toward the state health board people," he told me, "is to just cooperate fully and give them whatever they ask for, and more. They still test us two to four times a month and the fees are about two thousand dollars a month—that includes inspection of the creamery. But we do our own testing and post the results on the web every day. We hold every tank of milk for eight hours before bottling or making it into cream or butter—time enough for our tests to run. We've never found a pathogen and neither has the state."

McAfee then showed me laboratory reports of the tests he'd recently run. He had introduced pathogens into his milk and they simply did not multiply. In many cases they died off.

Mark spoke of CLA and the health benefits of raw milk. He had a real feel for the value and importance of what he's doing as he described his plans for Organic Pastures.

I asked him whether he felt he'd influenced other California dairy farmers. Was anyone else thinking of applying for a raw milk license? "Not as far as I know," he said. But sooner or later, others will become interested because Mark is getting around sixty-five dollars per hundredweight for his raw milk, about six times more than farmers get for conventional milk.

His influence in many circles is already growing. Media attention has sparked renewed public interest in raw milk and sales of Organic Pastures products are increasing rapidly. McAfee spoke of movie industry sources for financing expansion. He also mentioned a movie script about an organic raw milk dairy overcoming the challenges and political pressures of the conventional dairy industry.

As Organic Pastures has prospered, California officials have kept quiet. . . until the *E. coli* outbreak from raw spinach in September, 2006. We described the quarantine imposed on Organic Pastures in Chapter 15. That was the first of several attempts to shut down McAfee's operation.

In November, 2007, McAfee learned from reading a routine informational email sent from California State Assembly woman Nicole Parra, that the California legislature had quietly passed AB 1735, which mandated a ten-coliform-per-milliliter limit on raw milk at the point of sale. All other states with the coliform limit of ten for retail raw milk test at the bulk tank. Since coliform bacteria rapidly divide and multiply whenever milk is sent through pipes in the bottling process, and also increase in numbers in raw milk on the shelf, McAfee knew that his milk could not consistently pass the standard. Besides, most coliforms are beneficial bacteria, and that is what his customers wanted in their raw milk. Neither Organic Pastures Dairy nor Claravale Dairy, the two licensed raw milk dairies in California, were notified of hearings on the bill, characterized as a "sneak attack" on raw milk. The law was signed by Governor Schwarzenegger on October 8, 2007 and took effect on January 1, 2008.

The passage of AB 1735 galvanized raw milk supporters throughout the country, who wrote letters, made calls and contributed to legal expenses. Represented by the Farm-to-Consumer Legal Defense Fund, Organic Pastures and Claravale Dairy obtained a temporary restraining order against enforcement of the bill in the San Benito County Superior Court. Meanwhile, Senator Dean Florez sponsored SB 201 to replace AB 1735. The legislation mandates a hazard analysis (HAACP) plan for raw milk production and frequent testing for actual pathogens—coliforms are not pathogens and coliform testing does not reveal the presence of pathogens such as campylobacter. The bill passed unanimously out of three committees, the Assembly without one dissenting vote, and the Senate with only four dissenting votes.

Meanwhile, in March, 2008, two of McAfee's employees received surprise visits from federal agents, who attempted to coerce them into testifying against the dairy at a grand jury investigation on Organic Pastures' sale of raw milk as pet food across state lines. Three years earlier, McAfee had responded to an FDA warning letter by sending the agency a copy of the labels he intended to affix to unpasteurized dairy products shipped in interstate commerce. The labels indicated that the products were for "cat or dog food only." The agency answered McAfee's response by referring him to an FDA guidance document on marketing a pet food product. The document stated that "there is no requirement that pet food products have premarket approval by FDA." The agents asked one of the employees to wear a wire; the employee refused.

Mark responded to the investigation by immediately publicizing the news on the Internet and on raw milk-friendly blogs, while his lawyers contacted the U.S. Attorney's office in Fresno, offering to share documents and other exculpatory evidence in an attempt to dissuade them from continuing the grand jury investigation. Apparently in response to the offer, the U.S. Attorney cancelled the grand jury testimony of the two employees and temporarily suspended the proceedings of the grand jury. Meanwhile, McAfee had stopped shipping fluid milk products in interstate commerce but continued to ship his milk-plus-colostrum products, which appeared to be unaffected by the investigation since they are regarded under federal law as dietary supplements, not as dairy products. FDA has since closed this loophole.

In August, 2008, California Governor Arnold Schwargenegger vetoed SB 201, stating the official CDFA position that it would "weaken food safety standards in California." Nevertheless, raw milk remains on the store shelves even though CDFA is strictly enforcing the ten-coliform limit. This causes the two California raw milk dairies, Organic Pastures and Claravale, to be shut down every six to eight weeks for two or three days to allow for retesting to meet the standard. The dairies have learned to live with the shutdowns—Organic Pastures makes cheese with their milk during the shutdowns—and that is why raw milk is still available for retail sale in California.

MOUNTAIN BROOK FARM, CONNECTICUT

Southbury, Connecticut, a pretty little New England town, is a curious mix of farms, modest houses, churches, antique shops, a shopping center, stately country homes, stores and a retirement community. Close by lies Tapester's Mountain Brook Farm, one of Connecticut's two goat farms licensed to sell raw milk. The milk sells in nearby health food stores, and I've recommended it to many people.

In the spring of 2002, I met Liz Tapester in Hartford at the state Environmental Committee's hearing on raw milk. There she spoke with great emotion about the care that went into her production of milk and how her customers depended on her milk. She pleaded with the members of the committee not to allow the state to ban the sale of raw milk.

A few days later the Committee voted to kill the bill. Raw milk and Liz's dairy would survive in Connecticut for at least one more year.

"Mountain laurel, rhododendron, and azalea—you've got to watch out for those three, they're toxic for goats, and your goats may eat them if they get a chance," Liz speaks softly as we walked up the hillside near her house. "These are my boys," she said, gesturing toward the top of the yard near the edge of the woods. Three male Nubian goats stood in an irregularly shaped enclosure with a shed in the center. Beyond the goat pen several acres of wooded hillside angled upward. "My girls all graze up there," Elisabeth said. "Goats are browsers, and they browse everything they can reach, including the bark of the trees. The trees where they've browsed will all die eventually.

"You can pet these guys if you want, but let me warn you, they smell. They urinate all over themselves, and each other. They're pretty gross. I keep these guys for breeding, they take care of my girls." The three black-and-tan males stared at us, two from a few feet away and the third with his face pressed against the wire fence directly in front of us, his beard hanging a full foot below his chin, seeking another rub on the head.

We walked slowly across the yard behind the house toward another enclosure at the opposite side. Twelve or fifteen smaller goats moved toward us, clamoring about as we approached the wire. "These are some of my girls. Some of them are milkers, and others will be soon. Some I'll sell as pets, for fifty or a hundred dollars. Mostly the 4-H-ers buy them, and that's all they can afford. A few will go to other farms for milking and breeding, but there isn't much of that happening. I'm just about the last one in Connecticut selling raw goat's milk. Can you believe it? Are you guys going to buy some of my girls and keep it going?

"There's only one man I'll sell them to for meat. He takes good care of them, loves them right up to the day he slaughters them. I don't trust anyone else to treat them right. I have some I really shouldn't keep, but I'm terrible at business."

We moved toward the barn adjacent to the pen, which held the goats, at the side of the yard and at the same level as the house. A child came out from behind the barn, a lovely black-haired Asian girl who looked to be four or five. She moved among the female goats, touching them, talking to them. She waved to us and called out, "Hi Mommy!"

"That's my daughter," Liz said. "She grew up with the goats, she loves them. We want to adopt more children, but we don't make enough money. A family has to make at least forty thousand dollars to adopt. I think adopting children is the most wonderful thing in the world."

The small barn held another twelve or fifteen goats lying or moving about in the hay-covered open stalls and floors. "We feed them mostly hay," Liz said, "plus they browse the woods. We use another kind of hay for their bedding. Last year we spent about seven thousand dollars for feed hay and seven thousand dollars for bedding, and we took in fourteen thousand in milk sales. We sell some to people who come here to pick it up,and the rest to the stores."

I asked about distributors and customers, trying to make it add up to pay the bills.

"One of the ladies who picks up here owes me hundreds of dollars. She says she doesn't have it, but needs the milk for her kids. I just can't say no to her. I hope she'll pay me, but . . . The distributor owes us too, twelve hundred dollars. Another raw dairy farmer we know said she told him if he didn't pay up, no more milk, and he paid. But I haven't done that. Maybe I will! But I'm really not very good at business."

"This is the milk room," Liz said as we entered the lower barn. "Everything has to be just so, clean and in the right place. I am so meticulous, I'm a fanatic. Of course, you have to take care of everything carefully because you never know when the dairy inspector might show up, he has a way of surprising you. But I go further, I make my milk cans and all my equipment spotless. That's partly how I get my bacteria counts so low."

At the time, the state allowed a standard plate count of ten thousand per milliliter in milk to be sold raw (increased to thirty thousand in 2005). Since obtaining her raw milk license, Liz has had bacteria counts above two hundred fifty only four times, and the highest of those four was three thousand five hundred. Liz has an automatic milking machine and uses it at times, but prefers to milk by hand. "Besides keeping the milk extra clean, by milking by hand I can tell if there's anything at all unusual in my goats. If there's even a little beginning of changes in the teats that might turn into mastitis, I can tell, and take care of that animal. It takes longer to milk by hand, but that's how I like to do it. I spend three hours in the morning and three in the evening."

Liz also works off the farm three days a week for a law office in town. As we walked back up the steps toward the house, Liz's husband Lee arrived home from work, and we all sat at a picnic table between the upper barn and the house.

"I used to attach a little label to each milk bottle that tells about the farm, and the names of the goats," Liz said. "I should start making labels again, but there's never any time."

I asked Liz how much her milk sells for. "Five dollars a half-gallon, and the stores sell it for seven dollars fifty," she replies. "I'm milking seventeen goats now, and get about fourteen gallons a day. But we don't sell it all."

We talk about the state's attempts to ban the sale of raw milk, and a proposed labeling regulation that would require raw milk producers to label each bottle, "WARNING: This raw milk product is unpasteurized and may contain disease-causing bacteria." I pointed out that though such a label might hurt the sales of raw milk, the statement was true.

"It's true of everything!" Lee gently exclaimed.

"You're right," I said. I realized instantly that I'd been wrong in thinking that such a label was not unreasonable. Other food—hamburgers, chicken, commercial dairy products—can contain disease-causing bacteria. These products are not required to carry a label declaring them dangerous. It is ludicrous to require producers of high quality raw milk to label their products in a way that is more likely to put them out of business than to protect anyone.

We also talked about why small farmers need to work together for common goals. Like small farms everywhere, raw milk producers in Connecticut are hanging on by a thread. Most of the legislators on the Environmental Committee grew up on raw milk; that may be the only thing that keeps a bill to ban raw milk from going to the floor of the legislature and passing. Meanwhile, the few raw milk farmers left are struggling, and a number have gone out of business or retired. Liz loves her animals and loves providing healthy milk for people, but six hours a day (just for the milking) three hundred sixty-five days a year for no profit is tough.

As we said goodbye, I remembered what Liz told me about adopting children, that she and Lee can't adopt any more because they don't make enough money. As we headed back down the rocky road, Liz and Lee headed for the barn. It was time to milk the girls.

DAVID WETZEL, NEBRASKA

Until he purchased his farm in late 1999, Dave Wetzel was the vice president of a steel company. Now, he and his wife Barb live over an hour from the nearest town and farm three hundred twenty acres of Nebraska grasslands, milking about seventy-five pasture-fed shorthorn cows seasonally from April to October. Although his entire operation is what Dave calls "beyond organic," he originally sold much of his milk through normal commercial channels.

"Organic is a commercial term but does not describe a sustainable farming practice that takes animal welfare as the optimum concern," Wetzel says. "Organic is used to maximize return because it is commercially recognized. Our focus has never been to optimize return."

Dave feeds no grains; his animals get only grass and hay. His calves are raised suckling milk and move on to alfalfa grazing at about fifteen weeks. The Wetzels chose milking shorthorn and milking Devon cattle as the breeds best suited for their needs. Milking shorthorns, also known as Durhams, were introduced to America in the late 1700s. They're known as dual-purpose cattle, valued by the early settlers for their milk and their meat, as well as their willing power for the wagon and the plow. The females can be counted on for a calf every year. The Wetzels sell thirty or forty calves each year and ten to fifteen cows and bulls.

Wetzel has a mechanical bent and figured out how to centrifuge butter at low temperature to produce the Activator X-rich butter oil concentrate Weston Price describes in his book *Nutrition and Physical Degeneration*. The product had not been available since Price retired; Wetzel brought it back and now markets it in eight- and sixteen-ounce bottles as "X-Factor Oil."

"We irrigate one hundred sixty acres," Dave told me. "With enough moisture, we always have rapidly-growing grass from April through October, a mix of clovers, alfalfa and a number of other species. Rapid growth is the key to the Activator X content, and irrigation is key to constant rapid growth. Rotational grazing then yields a constant supply of X Factor in the milk. It takes eight or nine pounds of skimmed cream, equivalent to five or six pounds of heavy cream, to make eight ounces of X Factor Oil."

A few customers travel to the Wetzels' farm each week to buy raw milk. Nebraska law allows farmers to sell raw milk on the farm, but the state agriculture department forbids advertising or soliciting raw milk sales in any way, even by a phone call. The local agricultural extension agent, however, is one of their customers. Several farmers Wetzel knows are talking to state officials and legislators about changing the law to allow expanded sales of raw milk.

"Many of the agriculture people we know drink raw milk," Barb Wetzel tells me, "but until we started making X-Factor oil, most of this wonderful grass-fed milk we produced was pooled with other commercially produced milk. We're so far from towns that very few people can come out here for our milk, even if they know about it. It's sad." Today the Wetzels recycle the skim milk left after making butter oil by spraying it on their pastures. Rich in calcium and probiotic bacteria, it makes a wonderful fertilizer.

Dave Wetzel doesn't like the laws governing the sale of raw milk and raw milk products. "But the law is the law," he told me, "and it's my duty as a citizen of this state to follow it, like it or not. That's just the way I feel." I ask how he would feel if the authorities pass a law forbidding the farmer from giving his raw milk even to his own family, as they have in Canada. "No comment," Dave replies.

FOXFIRE FARM, CONNECTICUT

The first structure you see after driving up the rocky road to Foxfire Farm is an open-ended aluminum shelter—about one hundred fifty feet long, fifty feet high and fifty feet across—a huge cylinder that had been sliced in half lengthwise and then placed on the ground. Cattle move about under the structure and over the adjacent ground at both ends. Beyond this modern structure is the farmhouse, a traditional two-story dwelling with a massive stone chimney and a broad front porch.

Elisa Santee and her husband Bill Trietch have been farming the one hundred thirty acres at Foxfire in Mansfield Center, Connecticut for ten years. Their card reads "Foxfire Farm & Fence Company: A Certified Organic Farm & Dairy. Cheese, milk, vegetables, plants, breeding stock, fencing."

Elisa was a city girl. "I'm from Stamford," she told us. "I milked my first cow when I was thirty, after we bought the farm." Elisa teaches math at the local community college on Mondays and Wednesdays, and on Fridays she makes raw milk deliveries to health food stores and a few markets. Bill has worked full-time for a dairy equipment company for over twenty years, making calls on dairy farms all over Connecticut to install and maintain equipment. Every morning and evening the couple spend about two hours milking and caring for their twenty-five Jersey cows. They also care for eight sheep, two pigs, eight piglets and their daughter's horse, all on forty acres of pasture.

Foxfire Farm raw milk has been available in health food stores throughout much of Connecticut for several years. "It's so up and down," Elisa said. "One week we might sell five hundred gallons, and the next it's fifty. You never know. Especially in the summer, it goes down. People go away, or they get busy and don't think of it. What we don't sell raw, we sell to be pasteurized. The price we get fluctuates according to the market. Last year this time it was seventeen dollars a hundredweight. This year it's ten dollars. We'd like to sell more raw milk to the stores, but the demand just isn't there, at least not in this part of the state. I think a lot of people are a little afraid. The students [twenty thousand University of Connecticut students live in Storrs, about eight miles away] don't have any money, they don't even go to the farmers' markets.

"The milk we sell just about pays for the cost of keeping the cows and running the operation. If we didn't have our day jobs, there's no way we could survive. But we love it! We're really glad we bought the place."

We talked about chickens and eggs, pigs and goats, bulls and calves, dairy cattle and milk. I learned how hard it was to market the products of a small farm in Connecticut. The state has only one USDA-inspected beef processing plant and all beef sold retail to consumers must go through that plant. On-farm sales of chickens requires processing at the nearest USDA-inspected plant—out of the state—at a cost of over one dollar a bird (to do what could be done more cleanly and at far less expense on the farm if state regulations allowed it).

While raw milk sales from licensed farms such as Foxfire are legal in Connecticut, adverse publicity and frequent warnings from the medical establishment dampen demand. Many people today have never known the taste of farm-fresh, wholesomely raised chicken, eggs, milk, butter, cheese, beef and lamb, and they have little willingness to pay a premium for quality. The result is that even with forty fertile acres they love and a willingness to work hard, Elisa and Bill can't make a living farming.

## FLACK FAMILY FARM, NEW HAMPSHIRE

Flack Family Farm is a two-hundred-seventy-acre certified organic, biodynamic Vermont farm in the northwest corner of the state. Sheep, cattle, chickens, turkeys and pigs graze in the pastures. In addition, the Flacks cultivate vegetables and medicinal herbs. Doug Flack, a trained ecologist, has worked with the land for almost thirty years. Interns, on-site university classes and farm discussion groups help connect the farm with the community.

The farm's website advertises veal, lamb, beef, pork, eggs, sauerkraut, vegetables, medicinal herbs and wool. Until recently, Flack could not advertise his raw milk and was limited to selling twenty-five quarts per day directly to customers on the farm. New regulations passed early in 2008 raised the limit to fifty quarts and specifically allow advertising. Many of the state's raw milk dairies have now put signs up at the farm's entrance, announcing the availability of fresh milk.

Doug belongs to the Vermont Grass Feeders' Association, which has a membership of over two hundred; about half the members are dairy farmers. Doug's cows feed on green pastures during warm months and hay in the winter. He is adamant in the belief that the finest milk and meat come from animals that receive little or no grain. Grain, he says—and many agree with him—profoundly changes the rumen of the animal and the quality of the milk.

He speaks of changes in Vermont dairy farming. "In the late seventies, there were about seven thousand dairy farms in Vermont. Two years ago, there were about sixteen hundred, and now I'd guess it's less than thirteen hundred. Many of those that remain have gotten larger, and many are confinement operations that feed a lot of grain.

"There are a half a dozen confinement farmers right in this town who won't drink their own milk raw. They go to the store for milk. That's how bad milk from confinement cows is. A lot of those animals are excreting Salmonella in the milk.

"Ten years ago, there were two or three thousand farms, mostly small, selling raw milk. There are still several hundred. In most parts of the state, you can find good grass-fed raw milk if you drive twenty or thirty miles. In a few out-of-the-way places, you might have to drive fifty or seventy-five. But the odd thing is that in the cities, there's none available, and people by and large don't know where to get it, because we can't sell milk off the farm.

"What's needed is a change in the regulations to allow off-farm sales of unlimited amounts of milk. On-farm sales should not require a permit or a license; I can't see the point of getting the state involved at that level. You could require farmers who want to distribute raw milk to retail outlets to have a license or permit, which would mean regular testing of the milk and inspections of the farms. That is the system that prevails in most European countries and a few states in America.

"The key to healthy raw milk is pasture feeding and a minimum of grain feeding," says Doug. "I think that in lieu of state-regulated raw milk sales, a private organization of dairy farmers would be better. We could enforce standards for membership and expel anyone violating the standards. The chances of any widespread problems occurring would be nil because of the limited number of on-farm customers any one farm would have. The public would know that membership meant quality raw milk."

## DWIGHT MILLER, PENNSYLVANIA

The lane to Dwight Miller's farm passes through some of the most fertile agricultural land in the world, the richly topsoiled farm country of Lancaster County, Pennsylvania. Miller, a Mennonite farmer, borrowed money from fellow religionists to purchase the one-hundred-thirty-acre family farm from his father in the early 1990s. He and his wife and children (six in all) have embraced new ideas about farming while remaining true to the simple lifestyle that characterizes the practice of their religion.

Dwight's father fed grain to his herd of sixty mixed-breed cows, keeping them confined to the massive nineteenth century barn or to small areas of pasture. Dwight discontinued grain feeding and instituted a system of managed grazing using portable electric fences. The cows remain outside in all but the most inclement weather. Miller's milk production dropped, but so did his feed bills He got fourteen to nineteen dollars per hundredweight for his milk from a local organic dairy that purchases only milk from grass-fed cows, which was at least fifty percent more than the rate farmers get for conventionally produced milk. Vet bills also declined and the fertility of his herd increased.

Even so, keeping up with the mortgage payments was not easy. In 1999, Miller got wind of the raw milk movement. He began to sell raw milk on the farm and at the local farmers' market, and organized deliveries to several consumer groups. Before long, he was selling his entire milk production directly to consumers, either in the form of fluid milk or as deep yellow butter, thick sweet cream, cultured cream, yogurt, kefir and cottage cheese. He also sells hard cheeses made from his milk at a local cheese factory. The large selection of products attracts many customers who are willing to pay high prices for his milk, cream and butter. Miller now averages almost fifty dollars per hundredweight for his milk.

Miller also sells eggs, chickens, turkeys, beef, veal, beef and chicken broth, pork, lard, honey and maple syrup. The chickens are housed in a portable coop that is moved to new pasture several times weekly, following the cows by several days so that the birds can feast on the bugs that proliferate on the underside of the cow paddies. Miller fattens his hogs on the whey and skim milk leftover from making butter, cream and cheese.

Since transitioning to direct sales, his income has almost tripled, allowing him to pay down his mortgage at a much faster rate than anticipated. Miller has plans to build a structure to house all his milk processing equipment (now housed in several outbuildings on his farm) under one roof, and a cave for aging cheese and hams.

Miller is one of about one hundred dairy farmers in Pennsylvania with a state-approved license to sell raw milk. Early in 2003, his inspector told him that the state was in the process of rewriting the dairy regulations, and that the new regulations would eliminate raw milk licenses and do away with raw milk sales in Pennsylvania. That did not happen; instead the number of permitted farmers increased threefold.

Nevertheless, Miller is poised to set up a cow-share or farm-share program should the state make things too difficult for permitted farmers. A number of Pennsylvania farmers have joined an organization called C.A.R.E. (Community Alliance for Responsible Ecofarming), a private club arrangement which they claim allows them to sell raw dairy and other farm products to consumer C.A.R.E. members without a permit. So far, PDA has not gone after C.A.R.E. farmers. For the moment, Miller's customers sign a statement affirming their right to purchase products directly from a farmer, without interference from government officials.

Pennsylvania law permits the sale of raw milk, but a technicality puts sales of raw butter and cream in a kind of legal limbo. The regulations stipulate that milk sold raw must be kept chilled and constantly agitated, making the production of cream and butter from raw milk impossible. Miller overcomes this hurdle by selling the milk to his customers and then contracting with them to produce butter and cream from the milk they have purchased.

RAW MILK AND THE LAW

Nearly one hundred years of concerted effort on the part of many powerful interest groups has succeeded in severely limiting the legal availability of raw milk for most Americans, particularly those living in large urban areas or any distance from dairy farms.

- Twenty-six states technically allow on-farm sales of raw milk, but nearly all place restrictions on the farmer by limiting the amount he may sell, banning advertising, imposing excessive fees or regulations, or allowing local town Boards of Health to ban sales. Two of those twenty-six states limit sales to raw goat milk (Arkansas and Mississippi). The states are Arizona, Arkansas, California, Connecticut, Idaho, Illinois, Kansas, Maine, Massachusetts, Minnesota, Mississippi, Missouri, Nebraska, Nevada, New Hampshire, New Mexico, New York, Oklahoma, Oregon, Pennsylvania, South Carolina, South Dakota, Texas, Utah, Vermont and Washington.

- Ten states have provisions allowing for some retail sales: Arizona, California, Connecticut, Idaho, Maine, New Mexico, Pennsylvania, South Carolina, Utah and Washington. In practice, however, raw milk is widely available in stores only in California, Connecticut, Pennsylvania, South Carolina and Maine. Raw milk was available in stores in Santa Fe, New Mexico until recently, when the last raw milk dairy farmer in the state retired. In Utah, only one off-farm store provides raw milk for sale, and it is owned by the dairy supplying the milk, as required by law.

- Seven states allow sales of raw milk for animal consumption only, without requiring the addition of dyes. Those seven states are Alabama, Florida, Georgia, Indiana, North Carolina, North Dakota and Tennessee. Raw milk as pet food is widely available in Florida, Georgia, Indiana and North Carolina. In Georgia and North Carolina, activist raw milk supporters were able to defeat proposed regulations to add a charcoal dye to the milk.

• Two states make all sales of raw milk illegal with the exception of raw goat milk when prescribed in writing by a licensed physician. Those states are Kentucky and Rhode Island.

• Fifteen states and the District of Columbia make all sales of raw milk illegal. Those states are Alaska, Colorado, Delaware, Hawaii, Iowa, Louisiana, Maryland, Michigan, New Jersey, Ohio, Virginia, West Virginia, Wisconsin and Wyoming.

• In at least six of these states, cow-share, herd-share or farm-share programs provide milk to participating consumer-owners. These states include Alaska, Colorado, Michigan, Ohio, Virginia and Wisconsin.

It is a remarkable fact that raw milk remains widely available; in fact, in most states, the demand for raw milk is growing rapidly. In 1986, the federal government banned all interstate shipments of raw milk, cream and butter, and, as we have seen, the FDA, the USDA, and the CDC have for decades propagated a constant barrage of misinformation about the alleged dangers and lack of benefits of raw milk. Many professional organizations condemn raw milk and call for compulsory pasteurization. And yet legislators in the majority of states throughout the country have managed to defend the right of farmers to sell a limited amount of raw milk on the farm and, in a few states, in retail stores. Taking the optimistic view, you can still get raw milk, one way or another, in all but nine of the fifty states—and in several of these raw milk is widely available in a kind of raw milk underground.

State legislators hold the key to continued availability of raw milk. Many have rural roots and grew up on raw milk; some instinctively see through government propaganda. Given accurate information about raw milk, many more could become allies in a "farm freedom" campaign to guarantee the rights of farmers to market and sell the products of their farms, including raw milk, to the public, and the right of the public to buy them without interference from government officials. Of course, federal authorities would certainly challenge any such movement in the courts, with citizens and state governments standing together to oppose the dragon of corporate power and federal bureaucratic rule that has handcuffed small farmers everywhere.

Court challenges over cow-share programs and regulatory efforts to further restrict the availability of raw milk have met heavy consumer resistance, in spite of biased media coverage that merely reports government propaganda. Some state agencies have suggested legislation to prevent even farmers and their families from drinking their own raw milk. In October 2001, the milk industry proposed an amendment to the Michigan State Dairy Code that would have prevented the consumption of raw milk by anyone. The amendment was rejected.

In Canada—where according to a recent popular television news show a quarter of a million citizens drink "underground, black market" raw milk—the law prevents farmers from giving raw milk even to family members, although there are no reports of enforcement (yet). Penalties for farmers selling or giving away raw milk include fines up to two hundred fifty thousand dollars and three years in jail.[2]

However, most countries in the world allow for choice in the matter of raw milk; official campaigns to make raw milk unavailable seem to be limited to English-speaking countries. A 1995 report from the World Health Organization stated that the sale of raw milk is permitted by national regulations in most European countries, both in stores with microbiological monitoring by public health authorities and on the farm directly to the consumer without monitoring. On-farm sales were reportedly "becoming very popular" in some countries such as Austria, France and the UK. In Italy and a few other European countries, raw milk vending machines provide raw milk on the farm and even in office buildings and schools.

The British Royal Family regularly consumes "Green Top" milk, green being the color-coded bottle cap denoting raw milk.[3] Despite this, the British government, which failed in a 1989 attempt to legislate compulsory pasteurization, announced in November of 1997 its renewed intention to outlaw all raw milk, so far without success.

America has led the charge to ban all sales of raw milk. The Centers for Disease Control (CDC), the U.S. Department of Agriculture (USDA), and the Food and Drug Administration (FDA) have all taken official positions calling for compulsory pasteurization and the criminalization of raw milk sales. Professional medical, veterinary and dairy organizations have unanimously followed suit. For the past thirty years, American medical journals have regularly argued for compulsory pasteurization. During the last twenty years, many states have restricted or outlawed sales of raw milk; health departments in many more are determined to follow. Strictures against raw milk are very much in tune with America's move since about 1980 towards demonstrably less individual freedom and increasing penalties for nonviolent offenders against government-imposed taboos.[4]

COW SHARES: OWNING A PIECE OF YOUR OWN COW

In several states where sales of raw milk are illegal, dairy farmers and consumers have formed cow-share programs—arrangements whereby consumers legally own a share of the farmer's cows, pay a monthly boarding fee and share in the milk. David Lynch of the Guidestone CSA (community supported agriculture) Farm and Center for Sustainable Living initiated the first cow-share program in 1995. Located in the foothills of the Rocky Mountains near Loveland, Colorado, Guidestone is a fully diversified one-hundred-fifty-acre organic farm, supporting a fifty-share CSA garden and a raw milk dairy. The farm is a project of The Stewardship Community (TSC), a non-profit organization formed in 1988 and dedicated to promoting environmental awareness.

The farm also offers natural beef, pork, lamb, chicken and turkey, as well as honey, herbal products and bread baked in a wood-fired brick oven on site. Of the one hundred fifty acres, one hundred twenty are in pasture and five in row crops. Guidestone is located in a valley that has been farmed organically for fifty years. The milking herd of ten Jersey and Jersey-Devon cross cows generates about seventy-five thousand dollars a year income for the farm via the cow-share program.

According to Lynch, agricultural director for TSC, "Selling directly to the consumer and bypassing the middle men allows us to get retail prices for our products. Diversity is sustainable. Monocultures are not. We've found that diversifying the things from our farm has created a year-round income for us. Most CSA gardeners receive six months of income from vegetables (in our part of the country) but with eggs, milk and meat we can sustain the farm all year."

In setting up the program, Guidestone's lawyer worked closely with the Colorado Department of Agriculture and Board of Health officials to make sure the program would not violate state laws, which prohibit any sale of raw milk to consumers. Several documents create a legally binding contract between shareholders and Guidestone. A bill of sale is used to establish ownership of shares in the dairy herd, and a boarding contract outlines the dairy's responsibility to provide a steady and safe supply of fresh raw milk. Shareholders make regular monthly payments for the boarding of their share of the herd. Another document outlines the herd health plan a veterinarian uses to monitor the management of the herd, and another detailed document defines the standards for the dairy facilities and the milk handling procedures; it guarantees a management program that is comparable to a Grade A Dairy. Guidestone provides copies of these documents to individuals and groups interested in organizing cow share programs for a small fee (used to help defray the legal costs involved in drafting the originals).

Individuals or families pay a twenty-five dollar membership fee per share; each share yields approximately one gallon of milk per week. Shares may be sold back at any time. A regular monthly boarding fee (around thirty dollars) is charged for the cost of feeding, housing and milking the cows. Guidestone now serves about one hundred fifty member families—with a long waiting list of others.

Lynch has no plans to expand the Guidestone cow share operation. "We get calls from Arizona and Utah wanting us to ship milk, which of course we can't do. But what I really want is to encourage small dairies to emerge to serve the local populace. Raw milk is best produced and supplied as a local operation, with people going to the farm and getting in touch with the men and women who are producing their food. I'd like to see a voluntary cooperative system in which raw milk dairies with cow-share programs belonged to an organization that sets and enforces membership standards."[5,6,7]

In 2005, after Colorado officials theatened to end their endorsement of cow share operations, the Colorado General Assembly passed legislation codifying the exemption of cowshare programs from the definition of sale. Today, thanks to the pioneering efforts of David Lynch, over one dozen cow-share operations provide raw milk to Colorado consumers.

## CLEARVIEW ACRES, WISCONSIN

Tim Wightman and Gleta Martin had been running a CSA garden on their Wisconsin farm, Clearview Acres, for four years when they heard about Guidestone. Wisconsin calls itself the Dairy State but the food safety standards stipulate that there will be no raw milk sales whatsoever, except to a state-approved dairy plant, whereupon all milk will be pasteurized. Wightman and Martin decided to work with the Department of Agriculture, Trade and Consumer Protection (DATCP) to set up a cow-share program, which would allow shareholders to drink their own milk.

Tim and Gleta were not satisfied with the two-page contract that DACTP suggested, finding that it did not provide enough provisions for testing and safety. Tim revised the contract to allow for greater safety provisions.[8]

The program they set up required farmers to keep extensive documentation on the transactions, but Tim and Gleta felt it would prove worthwhile. By the spring of 2001, over one hundred people had signed up, some driving one hundred twenty miles each way to get their milk. Tim and Gleta called their program Milk Direct™.

Tim and Gleta collected many stories about the effects of their milk on their clients. A retired dairy farmer had to use crutches because of severe arthritis. He had quit drinking milk twenty-five years earlier, because his doctor told him his cholesterol was too high. Within two weeks of drinking raw milk, he threw away his crutches and has suffered no problems with arthritis since. Another client told Tim and Gleta of her three-year-old grandson who'd stopped eating processed milk products because they gave him severe diarrhea. Now he was drinking two or three gallons of raw milk each week without problem.

Tim and Gleta next began sharing legal and technical advice with other farmers wanting to set up cow-share programs through the Milk Direct™ program, which included standards for testing to ensure that the highest safety standards would be met. By the spring of 2001, farmers and consumers had started several cow-share programs in other parts of Wisconsin, including one that had received approval for a large bank loan. Dairy farmers in Texas, Tennessee, the Carolinas and New Jersey had made inquiries about the program.[9]

But that spring, the Wisconsin Agriculture Department attempted to shut down the Milk Direct™ program by sending threatening letters to all the program farms in Wisconsin. None of those farms were visited to see the operations and standards in place. A legal challenge by the state was anticipated, and Tim and Gleta reported having "prominent, well-placed political attorneys at the state capital, ready to defend us."[10]

On September 24, 2001, Clearview Acres received a complaint from the state of Wisconsin stating that the sale of their raw milk posed "an imminent public health hazard." The farm was cited for nine violations and a tenth separate offense of placing advertisements.[11]

After a prehearing in October, Clearview Acres in December filed a brief requesting all charges be dropped. State officials meanwhile charged that the farm's milk had caused a local campylobacter outbreak (as described in Chapter 15), even though only few of the many confirmed cases drank Clearview Acres raw milk, and the farm's raw milk consistently tested negative for the organism. The outbreak came just after Thanksgiving. Studies have shown that some seventy-two percent of turkeys carry campylobacter, making undercooked turkey a possible cause; and many of the Clearview clients reported having eaten undone hamburger at a local restaurant. Clearview Acres planned to resume providing cow-share owners with their milk pending the results of state tests on the milk.[12]

In March 2002, the state finally released documents requested by Clearview Acres' counsel; no lab tests for campylobacter were included, in all likelihood because none had been performed. The documents indicated that DATCP had encouraged several farmers in the state to set up cow-share programs expecting someone to get sick from raw milk so they could shut the whole program down. Tim's insistence on safety protocols defeated this plan. As Tim and Gleta went ahead with their program, the state sent a spy to buy a cow share and pick up milk weekly. The released documents reveal that the milk was tested for over a year for the presence of listeria and salmonella and that DATCP complained when the tests turned out negative. Then the state tried to take away Gleta's Grade A permit, but was stymied for lack of jurisdiction. Finally, DATCP blamed Clearview Acres milk on the local campylobacter outbreak and sent the cease-and-desist order. Thus, the Wisconsin agency responsible for food safety had been caught deliberately promoting raw milk sales with improper safety protocols in an attempt to cause an outbreak of illness.

Tim and Gleta continued to defend themselves in administrative proceedings. The local press provided very positive coverage, publishing convincing arguments to counter DATCP's disinformation campaign, but the coverage in the major papers was negative. Still, by the spring of 2002, about eleven hundred people in Wisconsin were securing raw milk through cow-share programs—with no reports of food-borne illness.[13,14]

After DATCP's cease-and-desist order, cow-share owners initiated a letter-writing and media campaign. Then Clearview Acres and the other cow-share farms received official notice that such programs could continue if organized as "farm-share" rather than "cow-share." Donations from several Wisconsin cow-share owners enabled the Weston A. Price Foundation to launch a legal fund for raw milk; the fund's first check went to a lawyer for creating a limited liability corporation (LLC) for Clearview Acres and to serve as a model for the other farms in Wisconsin and in the U.S.

The Clearview Acres LLC was created to hold a Grade A milk permit. Non-voting shareholders may purchase shares in the company for the sole and explicit purpose of obtaining raw milk and raw milk products. The incorporation papers stipulate a manager whose purpose is to manage the company and monitor the Grade A status of the permit. The manager (usually the farm owner or owners) is the sole and explicit person to whom is entitled any profit.[15]

An interesting backdrop to the Wisconsin situation is the fact that the Wisconsin Statutes (Section 97.24-2-d-2, Milk and Milk Products) state "This section does not prohibit incidental sales of milk directly to consumers at the dairy farm where the milk is produced."[16] The Wisconsin DACTP has interpreted "incidental sales" to mean that only one sale is allowed to any given consumer and has used this interpretation to prohibit on-farm sales. According to the dictionaries, incidental means "having a minor role in relation to a more important thing or event; not essential." No dictionary defines "incidental" as "once."

COW-SHARES IN OTHER STATES

Cow-share programs are underway in a number of other states. For example, raw milk may be legally sold only as pet food in Indiana, prompting the initiation of several cow-share programs there. Unlike the situation in a number of other states, employees of the Indiana Agriculture Department have been supportive—with the exception of State veterinarian Bret Marsh. His efforts produced a cease-and-desist order in November 2002 against Apple Family Farms, where some fifty families owned shares in four dairy cows.

Cow-share owners initiated a letter-writing campaign to state officials, demanding their rights to their milk. Media reports consistently favored the cow-share program as a way to save small farms. The result was a retraction by the state. The Apples were required to make some semantic changes in their contract, one of which stipulated that cow owners participate in twice-yearly meetings to discuss the care and feeding of their cows, but the cow-share will continue. Efforts are also underway to change the Indiana regulations to allow on-farm sales of raw milk.[17]

Michigan has some of the most restrictive raw milk laws in the country. In 1948, Michigan became the first state to pass a compulsory pasteurization law; it is one of the fifteen states that bans farmers from selling raw milk even on the farm.

In October 2001, in a startling example of what could lie ahead in other states or nationally, the milk industry attempted to amend the Michigan State Dairy Code to make it illegal for family members and workers on dairy farms to drink raw milk. Michigan farmers and members of the Weston A. Price Foundation testified before the Michigan

Senate Committee for Farming, Agribusiness and Food Systems. Committee members were startled to learn that raw milk was allowed in other states without any problems—contrary to what they had been told by the Michigan State agriculture department—and that pasteurized milk was responsible for numerous outbreaks of food-borne illness.

Later that year, local chapter members of the Weston A. Price Foundation and dairy farmer Chuck Oliver met with elected representatives of the Michigan legislature and the Department of Agriculture in an effort to amend the dairy code in favor of citizen rights to establish cow-share programs. Regulations subsequently adopted did not specifically deal with cow-share programs, but some believe they can be interpreted to allow them. Oliver informed the state that he would initiate such a program and then, working with Lisa Wesala of the Detroit chapter of the Foundation, he did so.[18] Oliver's program now serves over one hundred families and many other Michigan farms have followed suit and set up cow-share programs.

Citizens of New Jersey, where raw milk sales are banned, must travel into Amish country in Pennsylvania to obtain raw milk. In the spring of 2002, Governor James McGreevey told the head of New Jersey's Department of Agriculture that his job is to "Preserve our farms, fight for our farmers and ensure that our agricultural industry is profitable and strong, innovative and poised for a bright future." The state once had thousands of prosperous small dairy farms, but these were extinguished after strict pasteurization laws forbidding even on-farm sales were passed in the early 1950s.

In Maryland, state regulators passed "emergency" regulations defining cow-shares as a sale. The Weston A. Price Foundation challenged the ruling in court, arguing that the change in regulations was improper and had actually changed the legal definition of the word "sale." The Foundation lost the case but appealed to the Superior Court in June, 2008. The court normally rules on appeal cases within three weeks but as of January, 2009, it still had not issued an opinion on this case.

North Carolina and Utah have passed legislation specifically banning cow shares, and in West Virginia, as in Maryland, the Department of Agriculture issued an administrative rule against the practice. In

Utah, the new regulation was part of a raw milk bill that allowed retail raw milk sales if the dairy owned at least fifty percent of the store selling the milk—a regulation that allowed one large raw milk dairy to engage in retail sales of raw milk, but not any of the smaller dairies. Washington state requires cow-share programs to have a permit and New York officials interpret current regulations as requiring a permit—although there are many cow-share programs operating under the radar in New York, without permits or inspections.

However, in Michigan, the Justice Department told the Department of Agriculture they had no jurisdiction over cow shares and in Ohio, the Department of Agriculture lost a bid to stop a cow-share program in court. Thus, precedent and concensus can be interpreted as allowing cow-shares as private arrangements guaranteed by law, unless specifically banned by a vote of the legislature.

Cow-share programs provide a solution to growing consumer demand in states where raw milk is prohibited. A farmer I spoke with lives in one of those states. He told me he quietly sells all the milk his several cows produce, and trucks in milk, cream, butter and cheese from several hundred miles away once every three weeks to satisfy the demand from the people in his area.

I asked him what sort of risk he was running. "I don't know," he said. "I know it's illegal, but I don't know what the penalties are. We're real quiet about it, real careful. We're below the authorities' radar, they don't know we're doing it. If they did, I don't know what they'd do. But if they caught me, I'd still keep doing it. I'd still sell it to people, they'd have to lock me up to stop me. I'm just that kind of person. I do what I think is right. People need this milk. They want it real bad. You should hear the stories they tell me."

Americans involved in raw milk legal issues are not constitutional scholars. Yet time and again these individuals express the belief that laws making fresh, unprocessed food—particularly raw milk—illegal constitute a violation of fundamental constitutional rights. They find it hard to believe that state officials may prohibit the right to choose foods that clearly pose little risk and provide many benefits.

## RAW MILK IN CANADA

On December 18, 2001, Canadian Television (CTV) aired a segment headlined "Black market for raw milk growing in Canada: Raw milk lovers flaunt [sic] the risks to boost an underground economy in the illegal liquid." According to the report, "A dark shadow is being cast over the food that gives us life. CTV News has uncovered a growing underground of illegal, unpasteurized milk. 'What we're providing is milk at its purest,' says one raw milk farmer, who only agreed to be interviewed if his identity is concealed.

"According to a government document, a quarter of a million Canadians drink unpasteurized milk. The farmer interviewed by CTV News says the demand is high. Some customers travel more than two hundred kilometres to buy his illegal milk. 'I would say they beg for the milk. It's not even asking. They beg for the milk.'

"Farmers that sell unpasteurized milk or give it away can face fines up to two hundred fifty thousand dollars and up to three years in jail.

"Kathleen Carpentier got her own cow because she wanted all-natural milk products. 'Raw milk is nutrient dense and like liquid gold—it's just precious,' says Carpentier. 'If people were to know and understand the virtue of raw milk, it would be an easy choice for them to choose for the nutrition of their family. It just seems absurd to me that something as basic as selling raw milk would be thought of as illegal.'

"Under the law, only the owner of the cow can drink its milk unpasteurized. Carpentier drinks the milk legally. But she also feeds it to her children. 'My children won't drink [store bought] milk any more. It just tastes too weird to them. It doesn't have the same freshness and flavour of raw milk.' Technically, giving away raw milk, even to family members, is illegal."

The leader of the raw milk movement in Canada is Michael Schmidt. He and his wife purchased Glencolton Farms in 1983 when they came to Canada from Germany. Michael has a master's degree in farming and was trained on certified organic farms in Germany. He taught biodynamic farmers throughout Germany and in Egypt, Russia and China. In Canada, Schmidt became involved in a variety of innovative organic agricultural projects.

"The cow has four teats which tradition distributes as follows," says Michael. "One for the calf, one for the other animals on the farm, one for the family that lives on the farm and one for families that live in the towns or cities." The cows at Glencolton Farms are allowed to go dry during the winter, producing no milk until their calves are born in the spring. They feed on lush green pasture from late May to early December and are fed hay and a supplement of ground weeds, sticks and herbs in the winter. This is an important biodynamic principle—that all food for farm animals originate on the farm. The pigs and fowl at Glencolton receive whey and skim milk, the by-products of cheese- and butter-making. Most of the animals live in excess of twelve years.

Soon after the Schmidts bought their farm, people came to buy their products, and many wanted raw milk. Michael developed a program called "My Cow's Milk" that was similar to cow-share programs later developed in the U.S.—consumers leased a portion of a cow. He opened a store on his farm in 1992.

In 1994 the Canadian Broadcasting Corporation made a documentary about Glencolton that the CBC claimed "would shake the entire dairy industry." It did, and sooner than the network thought; two days before the film was aired, regulators raided the farm, seized unpasteurized dairy products and subsequently charged Schmidt under the Health Protection and Promotion Act. That launched the beginning of what came to be known as the Milk War. Schmidt's jury trial took place in May of 1995.

The government presented a variety of specious arguments against raw milk. Witnesses for the defense included a physician who testified that he had never encountered any adverse effects among hundreds of patients who consumed raw milk. The doctor also described a hospital of four hundred beds hospital in Germany where raw milk is served as a treatment for many serious diseases.

After a four-month wait, the presiding judge ruled the Schmidts' raw milk a health hazard. The day before that verdict, health officials raided the Schmidts' farm again, dumping milk, butter and cheese. At Michael's request, the products were given to the pigs, so they wouldn't be wasted.

A civil trial followed the jury trial. In the interim a series of events involving damage on the farm occurred, including break-ins, destruction of equipment and animals, and surveillance with infrared cameras and listening devices. One of Schmidt's employees was actually accosted and held for several hours by sinister men who spoke German in the dialect of East Germany. Apparently certain "public relations" firms offer surveillance and harassment of rivals as a service to their clients, hiring former members of the East German secret police to get the job done.[19]

Preparations for the civil trial went badly. Because his insurance company dropped coverage of the farm, Schmidt pleaded guilty; immediately afterwards, he received notice of reinstatement.

The Schmidts fought back by launching a publicity campaign resulting in many positive articles and letters in the agricultural press. Michael proposed a two-year research project on the sale of raw milk, supervised by the government. He estimated that fifty thousand Canadians—dairy farmers and their families—still drank raw milk in Ontario. A newspaper ran the headline "Huge Raw Milk Black Market," and several editorials called for the legalization of raw milk sales.

But the Milk Marketing Board, which controls milk production in Canada, turned down Michael's proposed project. He then announced that he would continue providing raw milk and that if the police came back on his farm again, he would go on a hunger strike.

The Milk War forced the Schmidts to sell most of their cows and five hundred acres of their six-hundred-acre farm. At one point, they were down to just four cows, before beginning to rebuild their herd.

For a number of years, Schmidt continued to provide raw milk through a cow-share system, unhindered by the authorities. He also provided butter, cheese, cream, bacon, sausage, salami and bread in his once-a-week drive to Toronto.

On November 21, 2006, a raid on Glencolton Farms began phase two of the Milk War. Armed agents of the Ministry of Natural Resources presented Michael with a search warrant and, for the next seven and one-half hours, the investigators searched, questioned and confiscated. Every bottle of milk, cultured milk, quark, cream and sour cream, along with fresh cheese, ready for delivery in Toronto that morning, was confiscated, and then dumped into a local landfill site in the contaminated substances area! The farm's cheese-making and other dairy equipment were completely dismantled and carted off.

According to Schmidt, the government fabricated stories linking milk products from his farm to two cases of sick children the previous summer. He said that it was common knowledge that they had become sick from eating tainted hamburger meat. The family was unknown to Schmidt, were not members of his cow-share program and did not consume his unpasteurized milk.

Subsequently a warrant was issued for Michael's arrest, but he continued to make deliveries to Toronto. This time public opinion has been strongly in his favor. A trial has been delayed several times. When it finally occurs, Schmidt plans to act as his own attorney.

## RAW MILK IN GREAT BRITAIN

In England, the Dairy Products Hygiene Regulations of 1995 state that raw milk may be sold by the farmer on the farm premises where the animals are kept, to the ultimate consumer of the milk or to a distributor. The distributor may sell the raw milk only in the container in which he receives it, "direct to the ultimate consumer." He may sell it "from a vehicle which is lawfully used as shop premises."[20]

The Ministry of Agriculture, Fisheries & Food (MAFF) has long opposed the sale of raw milk, called "green top" in England because by custom it is capped with a green top. While the Ministry got nowhere under Mrs. Thatcher's Conservative party, the Labour party recommended a ban on the sale of green top milk for "public health reasons" just four months after securing power.

Richard Copus then joined with Sir Julian Rose to form A Campaign for Real Milk, which took its name from the successful Campaign for Real Ale that had prevented the large breweries from taking over England's national drink. Rose is a leading organic farmer and chairman of the Soil Association. The two men launched a publicity and political campaign. The turning point came when a member of the European Parliament "issued a statement saying that imports of raw milk from the continent for personal consumption could not be banned," says Copus. "The vision of consumers bringing back cartons of unpasteurized milk from France, where it is freely available in the shops, whilst English farmers were prevented from selling it, eventually won the day, but not without its costs. Testing for producer-retailers became stricter and more farmers fell by the wayside."

Today "green top" milk has become very popular. About two hundred producers in England and Wales are selling all they produce. (Raw milk was banned in Scotland over twenty years ago.) Small farmers sell it in traditional glass bottles with a green foil top—gold striped if they have a Channel Island herd. All containers in England must carry a government health warning, the only warning on any British foodstuff: "This milk has not been heat treated and may contain organisms harmful to health."[21]

## RAW MILK IN AUSTRALIA

In Australia, the national standards allow individual states to permit the sale of raw milk for human consumption, but it is legal in only two Australian states. One, South Australia, has a regulatory regime permitting sale. In the other, Queensland, only raw goat's milk can be legally sold for human consumption; a change in the regulations could allow sales of cow's milk.

One dairy farmer in Queensland recently began marketing his Jersey milk directly to health food stores as "Pet's Milk," according to attorney Bruce Bell, who defended the farmer from charges by the Queensland Dairy Authority that he was actually selling the milk for human consumption. The Authority brought charges after an inspector posing as a new health shop proprietor visited the farm and was given some milk as a sample; the milk laws in Australia define "sell" as "including giving away as a promotion."

This "evidence" was inadmissible in court, and the Dairy Authority withdrew their action the day of the court hearing, after the farmer had been forced to spend thousands of dollars on lawyer's fees. But inspectors continued to intimidate retailers carrying the farmer's "Pet's Organic Fresh Milk" product. Although there is no control under law of non-meat pet food, inspectors bought retail samples of the milk when it was close to its twelve-day-old recommended "Use-By Date" and had it tested. They then went back to the retailers and told them the milk failed to meet lawful standards, despite the fact that the national testing standard applicable to human consumption of milk they were using states "Retail samples may not be used."

The state inspectors also told retailers that the milk had caused an outbreak of cryptosporidium. In truth, one of a total of five cases had occurred in a child who drank the milk, whose four siblings were the other cases. All of the children had been exposed to pets and other vectors of infection. No one else became ill, even though the shops supplied about one thousand liters of raw milk daily to the people of Queensland. Obviously the Pet's Milk did not cause the infections, yet the Health Department issued a press release implying it did. News headlines screamed "Dangerous milk," and sales volume dropped by two-thirds—a familiar story.

Bell requested the Health Department's files under freedom of information regulations and found that over one thousand dollars in fees were required. Instead, he commenced an action in the state supreme court for judicial review and subpoenaed the documents, some of which were delivered after stalling tactics failed. Unfortunately, the judge dismissed the case, finding that the matters at hand were not of a "substantial nature affecting my [Bell's] client's interests." The court also found that the testing methods used by the Dairy Authority were valid. Interestingly, in their evidence, the Dairy Authority stated that their campaign was motivated by complaints from three named large milk processors that "our product was placed alongside theirs in the shops and selling too well for their liking."[22]

The Pet Milk dairy then adopted a new marketing plan—they sold the milk frozen as Cleopatra's Bath Milk, to be absorbed through the skin. Sales in health food shops are said to be brisk. A similar product, Aphrodites's Bath Milk, is available in shops in Melbourne.

Meanwhile, a number of cow-share programs have started up throughout Australia, especially in Queensland.

## THE WESTON A. PRICE FOUNDATION AND
## A CAMPAIGN FOR REAL MILK

Leading the activist movement to establish universal access to high quality raw milk is The Weston A. Price Foundation. Founded in 1999 to disseminate the research of nutrition pioneer Weston A. Price, the non-profit organization is dedicated to restoring nutrient-dense foods, rich in vital fat-soluble activators found exclusively in animal fats, to the American diet. The Foundation sponsors "A Campaign for Real Milk" as one of its projects. The Washington DC-based foundation publishes a quarterly journal, *Wise Traditions in Food, Farming and the Healing Arts*. Each issue includes several feature articles and a report on "A Campaign for Real Milk."

"A Campaign for Real Milk" is described on the Foundation's website[29] and literature as follows: "Back in the 1970s, a couple of blokes were sitting in an English pub, bemoaning the consolidation of the brewing industry in England and the decline of British beer and ale. A commodity that represented the soul of Britain, carefully brewed lagers from countless small-scale manufacturers, each with a distinctive color and taste, had been edged out by the insipid canned beers of a few large monopolistic breweries. What was needed, they decided, was a return to traditional brewing methods. They launched 'A Campaign for Real Ale,' which soon became the force that turned back the mega-brewers and reinstated varied and delicious ales to English tables and pubs.

"Back in the '20s, Americans could buy fresh raw whole milk, real clabber and buttermilk, luscious naturally yellow butter, fresh farm cheeses and cream in various colors and thicknesses. A supply of high quality dairy products was considered vital to American security and the economic well being of the nation.

"What's needed today is a return to humane, non-toxic, pasture-based dairying and small-scale traditional processing, in short . . . A Campaign for Real Milk!"

The first issue of *Wise Traditions*, published in the spring of 2000, listed eleven local chapters in eight states. Local chapters provide information on sources of organic or biodynamic foods, milk products from pasture-fed livestock (preferably raw) and pasture-fed eggs and livestock. By spring 2008, members had established over three hundred local chapters in all but two states, and in Canada, Latin America, Australia, New Zealand, the UK and Europe. Many of these chapters have helped consumers find raw milk and spearheaded cow-share programs.

*Wise Traditions* also features "The Shop Heard 'Round the World, Dedicated to Helping the Consumer Obtain Nutrient-Dense Foods and Accurate Nutrition Information;" advertisers list farm-fresh food, products and services. Listings in "The Shop Heard 'Round the World" have grown from two pages in the first issue to over twenty in the most recent.

THE FARM-TO-CONSUMER LEGAL DEFENSE FUND

As demand for raw milk grew, so did the need for legal support. The Weston A. Price Foundation found itself trying to meet the demand for counsel, an assignment not included in its mission statement.

The idea for the Farm-to-Consumer Legal Defense Fund actually came from a Foundation board member, Valerie Cury Joyner, a homeschooling mother who had benefitted from the protections afforded by the Home School Legal Defense Association. "We need something to defend small farmers and raw milk sales," she said. "No one messes with homeschoolers anymore because they have legal defense. Small farms need the same protection."

The Fund was launched July 4, 2007 and bankrolled by the Weston A. Price Foundation during its first year. The Fund's legal counsel, Gary Cox, was successful in obtaining the restraining order against AB 1735 in California and has taken a case to defend the right to unpermitted farm-share operations in New York.

Attorneys for the Fund provide a twenty-four hour legal hotline, and have developed a handbook on farmers' legal rights. They have helped hundreds of farmers set up cow-share programs and have solved many problems that farmers encounter—such as over-zealous inspectors—with a simple phone call to the state.

As part of its mission, the Fund works for direct sales of raw milk and other farm products without a permit; and reasonable permitting regulations for the retail sale of raw milk.

BACK TO THE LAND

In 2003, I bought thirteen acres of land, a former dairy farm, near Watertown, Connecticut, complete with a house built in 1880 and two old barns. Ever since, my partner Elly and I have begun working to make the place a farm again, with Jersey cows and other farm animals, all on pasture.

At my invitation, the Connecticut Department of Agriculture dairy inspector for our part of the state visited our farm just after we purchased it. As he toured our facilities, he helped me understand what the requirements were for a Grade A raw milk license. He couldn't have been more helpful ("I love raw milk," he commented at one point), and the same is true for several people from the state branch of the USDA office who have visited in connection with my application for a federal grant to help build fences and reestablish pastures. With their help and that of many farmers and friends aiding us with encouragement and advice, we soon were producig our own milk, meat and eggs.

The involvement of these individuals has been heartening, a welcome contrast to many of the stories that I've related in other parts of this book, and a sign, I think, that times are changing. . .

. . . for change they must. We have discussed the array of forces aligned to prevent farmers, fledgling and otherwise, from selling raw milk and other farm products to their neighbors. If the forces pushing compulsory pasteurization and other regulations that make it so difficult for farmers to sell farm products—milk, meat, fruits, vegetables and grains—have their way, the end result will be a kind of food fascism that insists on control of the entire food supply—all in the name of consumer protection of course—and every farmer in the thrall of the corporate buyer, offering him a price that cannot even cover his costs.

Fortunately, what the dairy industry has striven mightily to eradicate—wholesome milk and independent dairy farmers—is growing up like new grass on a spring morning. Every week hundreds of consumers discover that raw whole milk products from grass-fed cows represent the answer they were seeking to their health problems; and every week dozens of farmers wake up to the fact that the direct sale of raw milk, raw cheese, raw butter, raw cream (and the hogs and chickens that thrive on the by-products), is the answer they were looking for also, the way to save the family farm—and not just save the farm but make a decent living in farming. And every week, even a few enlightened administrators and politicians realize that on-farm and delivery sales of raw milk can create the kind of local wealth that will reverse the population flow away from small towns and reinvigorate our communities.

Raw milk is the key to the health crisis, the farm crisis, the economic crisis, the small town crisis, even the environmental crisis, the political crisis and the educational crisis. Every person in America can take part in this transformation, and so can you, simply by drinking your milk raw.

# Appendices

# Appendix One
## The Legal Status and Availability of Raw Milk Today

Since the first edition of this book, raw milk availability has expanded greatly throughout the United States, often through cow-share and herd-share agreements. According to the US Centers for Disease Control and Prevention's FoodNet Population Survey, in 2002 over three percent of respondents reported to have consumed unpasteurized milk in the previous seven days before the survey. A conservative estimate of raw milk consumption today puts the number of consumers at five percent of the population, or one and one-half million people.

Several states have seen huge increases in raw milk availability. For example, in 2003, only one dairy in Washington had a license to sell raw milk; today there are literally dozens of farms in Washington producing raw milk, which is sold on farm and in retail establishments. In spite of intense hostility from the Department of Agriculture, today in Virginia, consumers in almost any part of the state have access to raw milk through cow-share programs, many of which deliver the product to the door. In fact, raw milk is difficult to obtain in only nine of the fifty states: Delaware, Hawaii, Iowa, Louisiana, Nevada, New Jersey, New Mexico, North Dakota and Rhode Island. Citizens of these states must acquire raw milk from neighboring states or through quiet underground arrangements.

The information in this section is subject to change. Please consult www.realmilk.com/happening for updates and more detailed information, and www.realmilk.com/where for names of specific dairies and raw milk providers.

IN THE UNITED STATES

ALABAMA
Raw milk sales are allowed only for animal consumption. Several farms now supply raw goat and cow milk for pets.

ALASKA
Raw milk sales are illegal but state regulations are presently interpreted to permit raw milk distribution by cow-share or herd-share programs. A number of small farms are now supplying raw milk to Alaska residents through these programs.

ARIZONA
Raw milk sales are legal under a state licensing system that requires the milk to carry a warning label. After a long hiatus, raw cow and goat milk is now widely available through a number of sources.

ARKANSAS
Raw milk sales are illegal with the exception of on-farm sales directly to consumers of raw goat milk. According to the regulations, "Incidental sales of goat milk are not prohibited." Incidental sales are defined as ". . . those sales where the average monthly number of gallons sold does not exceed one hundred (100) gallons." Raw goat milk from small herds is widely available in the state.

CALIFORNIA
Raw milk sales are legal by licensed farms and may be sold both on the farm and in retail stores in every county but Humbolt (where the dairy industry has lots of clout). Currently, two producers supply raw milk to California consumers through retail stores, Claravale Dairy and Organic Pastures Dairy. Claravale Dairy, located in Panoche, provides raw milk

and cream in glass bottles to San Francisco Bay area natural foods stores. Claravale's Jersey cows receive a combination of pasture, hay and commercial feed. Organic Pastures, based in Fresno, milks over four hundred fully pasture-fed cows, providing raw milk in hard plastic containers as well as raw butter, cream, cheese, kefir and colostrums, in many natural foods stores throughout the state.

Several years ago, the Los Angeles County Board of Health banned sales in the county. Consumer advocates fought back and won a victory when the County Board of Commissioners voted to overrule the Board of Health.

In 2007, "stealth" legislation mandating a ten-coliform-per-milliliter limit in bottled raw milk threatened to eliminate raw milk in California. Alternative legislation, which proposed testing of actual pathogens rather than mostly beneficial coliforms, passed both the House of Representatives and the Senate by a large majority, only to be vetoed by the governor. However, the California Department of Food and Agriculture (CDFA) has not taken an aggressive posture in administering the coliform limit, probably in realistic expectation of an enormous consumer outcry. Thus, raw milk continues to be widely available in California retail stores; goat milk is also available through share programs directly from farmers.

COLORADO

Raw milk sales are illegal in the state, but Colorado was the home of the first cow-share program, through Guidestone CSA in Loveland. Originally state-approved, the program was threatened when the Department of Public Health and Environment announced proposed regulatory changes that would have made cow-share programs illegal. However, when state officials heard testimony about the health benefits and safety of raw milk, they stated that the current law would stand until further deliberations, and shortly thereafter, legislation was passed that legalized cow-share programs. Since then, share programs have proliferated; currently almost three dozen cow- and goat-share programs provide raw cow and goat milk to Colorado consumers. The Raw Milk Association of Colorado provides legal and lobbying services to this growing movement.

CONNECTICUT

Raw milk sales are legal at licensed farms and in retail stores. Numerous state requirements must be met to obtain a license to sell raw milk, but the required regular testing and inspection is paid for by the state and small farmers are able to operate under the system. The Environmental Committee at the state legislature is friendly toward small farmers and raw milk producers and has twice in the past ten years killed bills that would have outlawed all sales of raw milk in the state. However, legislation slated for 2009 coming before the Environment Committee would require farmers to pay for testing and would no longer allow the sale of raw milk at retail stores. Such a move would make it fiscally impossible for most Connecticut raw milk producers to stay in business.

DELAWARE

Raw milk sales are illegal.

DISTRICT OF COLUMBIA

Raw milk sales are illegal but raw milk is available through cow-share programs in nearby Virginia.

FLORIDA

Raw milk sales for human consumption are illegal; however raw milk for pet consumption is widely available directly from the farm, through co-ops and even in a few retail stores.

GEORGIA

The Georgia Dairy Act of 1980, Rules and Regulations, section 40-2-1-01(a) states: "Raw Milk and Raw Milk Products for Human Consumption: It shall be unlawful to sell, offer for sale, or otherwise dispense raw or unpasteurized milk, cream, or other milk products except raw milk cheese properly processed and aged according to Federal requirements."

Raw milk sales are thus illegal, with one exception—raw milk may be purchased from farms licensed under animal feed laws, for animal consumption only. In recent years, about a dozen farms have obtained licenses to sell raw goat or cow milk for animal consumption.

HAWAII
Raw milk sales are illegal. However, many people in rural areas throughout the islands keep goats.

IDAHO
Raw milk sales are legal with a license, but currently there are no licensed raw milk facilities in the state, and the last raw milk retailer went out of business in the early 1990s. There are numerous legal requirements to obtain a license to sell raw milk and raw milk products at the retail level. Nevertheless, limited amounts of raw goat milk and raw cow milk are available, the latter through cow-share programs.

ILLINOIS
Raw milk sales are legal if the milk is produced according to state rules and regulations and is sold on the farm. No special license is required, and there are no other requirements for the milk. According to the Illinois Grade A Pasteurized Milk and Milk Products Act, Section 8, effective January 1, 2002: "... The pasteurization requirement in this Section shall not be applicable to milk produced in accordance with Department rules and regulations if sold or distributed on the premises of the dairy farm." This clearly allows commercial producers to sell their raw milk directly to consumers on the farm. The policy of the Illinois Department of Public Health is not to apply the rules and regulations to farmers with just a few cows that sell on the farm. Currently raw milk is widely available through direct farm sales.

INDIANA
Raw milk sales are illegal with the exception of on-farm sales "for pet consumption only." A group of farmers and consumers is working on the liberalization of raw milk sales in Indiana. In the meantime, a growing number of cow- and goat-share programs provide raw milk and raw milk products to Indiana residents.

IOWA
Raw milk sales are illegal.

## KANSAS

Raw milk and raw milk product sales are legal if carried out on-farm to the "final consumer." Advertising is limited to a sign on the farm, which must state that the products are raw, unpasteurized and ungraded. Packaging or containers must be similarly marked. A growing number of small farms now sells raw milk and raw milk products directly to consumers.

## KENTUCKY

Raw milk sales are illegal with this exception: you may purchase raw goat milk with a written prescription from a licensed medical doctor. The dairy must meet grade A requirements and the doctor's statement must be kept on file for one year, with a copy sent to the state. However, raw milk is available through several cow-share programs.

## LOUISIANA

Raw milk sales are illegal. A few farmers may be providing raw milk through cow-share programs but they are keeping quiet as state officials claim that cow-share programs are illegal.

## MAINE

Raw milk sales are legal in Maine both on the farm and in retail stores. As revised in 1999, Maine law states: "The standards [for milk and milk products] must be consistent with the requirements of the official standards, known as the Pasteurized Milk Ordinance, as issued by the Secretary of the United States Department of Health and Human Services, Food and Drug Administration, except that the standards may not prohibit the sale of unpasteurized milk and milk products in the State." A permit is officially required to sell raw milk, but in practice the state allows any farmer to sell raw milk on the farm without a permit as long as the farmer does not advertise. There are dozens of sources in the state, even though agriculture department officials recently took an aggressive stance against several that were posted at www.realmilk.com.

## MARYLAND

Raw milk sales are illegal, and in 2006 the state passed "emergency" changes in the regulations to make cow-shares illegal. The Weston A. Price Foundation is currently challenging these regulations in court. Meanwhile, Maryland residents can easily obtain raw milk from nearby Pennsylvania.

## MASSACHUSETTS
Dairy farmers may obtain a license to sell raw milk, or they may sell limited quantities on the farm in nearly half of the state's towns.

Department of Food and Agriculture Commissioner Jonathan Healy stated the following in a September 2001 letter to a dairy farmer: "Massachusetts General Laws allow local town boards of health to decide on whether or not to allow the sale of raw milk, with only a requirement that such raw milk be sold on the farm where produced and that signs be present informing consumers that the milk offered for sale is raw and unpasteurized. Of the Commonwealth's 351 towns, 155 allow the sale of raw milk." The towns prohibiting sales by and large did so by passing ordinances during the 1940s and 1950s. Today, most local town boards of health are unaware of the issue. Chapter 94, Section 40 of the laws states that no license is required for a farmer to sell up to twenty quarts of milk per day directly to consumers. This means that farmers in towns approving the sale of raw milk may sell up to twenty quarts per day on the farm. Currently raw milk is widely available through on-farm sales, through co-ops and through cow-share and herd-share programs. The state does not seem to be enforcing the twenty-quart limit.

## MICHIGAN
Raw milk sales are illegal. In 2002, a legislative effort to make it illegal for the farmer himself, his family, and his farm animals to drink raw milk was defeated. This defeat opened the way for share programs and today there are numerous cow- and goat-share programs throughout the state. A 2006 attempt by the Michigan Department of Agriculture (MDA) to shut down an active cow-share program met with a huge outcry. Today the MDA has an open dialog with representatives of the Michigan raw milk movement while cow-share programs proliferate in the state.

## MINNESOTA

In Minnesota, the State Constitution states in Article XIII, Section 7: "Any person may sell or peddle the products of the farm or garden occupied and cultivated by him without obtaining a license therefor."

Minnesota statute (Section 28A.15, Subdivision 1) states that licensing requirements ". . . shall not apply to persons selling the products of the farm or garden occupied and cultivated by them."

The state Department of Agriculture, in direct violation of both the State Constitution and statutory law, attempted to stop such sales at Mom's Dairy, owned by Roger and Michael Hartman, but was defeated in court. Meanwhile, the Hartmans still sell raw dairy products on the farm and through home delivery and a number of other raw dairy farmers around the state are quietly selling raw milk, cream, butter and cheeses both on the farm and by delivery to cooperatives formed by consumers.

## MISSISSIPPI

Raw milk sales are permitted for on-farm sales of raw goat milk directly to the consumer from a farm where not more than nine goats are producing milk. No advertising is allowed. A number of farms now supply raw goat milk to Mississippi consumers.

## MISSOURI

Raw milk and raw cream sales are legal directly from the producing farmer to the consumer, both on the farm and by delivery from the farmer to the consumer. So states section 196.935 of the Missouri Revised Statutes ("an individual may purchase and have delivered to him for his own use raw milk or cream from a farm"). On-farm sources of raw milk are widely available in the state.

## MONTANA

Raw milk sales are illegal. A small number of cow-share and herd-share projects are underway.

NEBRASKA

Raw milk sales are permitted for on-farm sales directly to the consumer. The farmer may not legally advertise the sale of raw milk in any way, including telling someone on the telephone that he or she has raw milk for sale! Attempts to revise the milk laws to allow advertising and deliveries have not been successful so far.

NEVADA

Raw milk sales are technically legal in the state of Nevada but in practice, none is available. Recent FDA action has halted sales of raw milk containing colostrum across state lines. Those living near the western border can purchase raw milk in California.

NEW HAMPSHIRE

Raw milk sales are legal on farm and through delivery with a license being required for producers selling more than twenty quarts per day. A milk plant also may sell raw milk directly to the consumer. Dozens of small farms are engaged in direct sales of raw cow and goat milk.

NEW JERSEY

Raw milk sales are illegal. Efforts are underway to establish cow-share programs and even to re-establish raw milk sales in the original home of the certified raw milk movement. Meanwhile, consumers can obtain raw milk from nearby Pennsylvania.

NEW MEXICO

Raw milk and raw milk product sales are legal both on the farm and in retail stores; a state permit is required. Unfortunately, the last raw milk dairy farmer selling through retail stores retired in 2002. Currently one farm sells raw milk, south of Albuquerque.

NEW YORK

Raw milk sales are permitted on the farm if the producer has a permit. A sign at the point of sale must be posted stating, "Notice. Raw milk is sold here. Raw milk does not provide the protection of pasteurization."

Unfortunately, the farms licensed to sell raw milk tend to be a long way from the population centers of New York, namely Manhattan and surrounding areas.

The New York Department of Agriculture claims that cow-share and farm-share programs require a permit, a stance that the Farm-to-Consumer Legal Defense Fund is challenging in court.

## NORTH CAROLINA

Raw milk sales are illegal except on-farm for animal consumption, and the state has passed legislation making cow-share programs illegal. Several farms do provide raw cow and goat milk for animal consumption. Raw milk activists recently defeated a move by North Carolina officials to require a black dye in raw milk intended for animal consumption.

## NORTH DAKOTA

Raw milk sales are illegal except as pet food. The North Dakota Dairy Commission has no control over milk sold for animal consumption. A few farms are quietly selling raw milk as pet food.

## OHIO

Raw milk sales are illegal except on farms grandfathered in in 1965 as raw milk retailers. Young's dairy, the last remaining raw milk dairy, stopped selling raw milk in January 2003 when an outbreak of salmonella sickened forty-seven people, sixteen of whom worked at the dairy. The strain originated elsewhere in the state and officials could not positively attribute the problem to Young's. Nevertheless, the state put considerable pressure on the dairy (threatening to take away their Grade A license and close down the pasteurized portion of their business) which then closed down the raw milk portion of their operation. The outbreak and subsequent decision by the dairy came just a week after the Ohio Farm Bureau Federation voted to support an effort aimed at permitting more sales of raw milk.

A 2006 move by the Ohio Department of Agriculture to take away the Grade A license of a farmer engaged in a cow-share program was defeated in court. Since that time, cow-share programs have proliferated in the state, and raw milk is now widely available there.

OKLAHOMA

Raw milk sales are allowed on the farm. For years, Swan Brothers Dairy near Tulsa has sold raw milk, cream and cheese from pastured animals from their on-farm store with full cooperation from state officials. Today, dozens of farms provide raw milk through on-farm sales.

OREGON

Raw goat milk sales are legal both on-farm and retail, with no permit being required to sell on the farm if the producer has no more than nine milking goats. Raw cow milk sales are illegal except on farms with fewer than three milking cows; these farms require no license. Currently there are many cow-share programs in Oregon.

PENNSYLVANIA

Raw milk sales are legal both on the farm and in retail stores. Producers must have a permit and can only sell to stores if they have their own packaging operation with labeling and bottling machines. In 2008, over one hundred farms had permits to sell raw milk. Many other farmers are selling raw milk without permits or providing it through cow-share programs.

Although the sale of any raw dairy products other than milk and cheese aged sixty days is prohibited, raw butter and cream are widely available. Some farmers have entered into "labor contracts" with customers who want butter and cream, receiving payment for their labor in processing the customer's milk rather than for the butter and cream itself.

RHODE ISLAND

Raw milk sales are illegal with one exception: ". . . a physician may authorize an individual sale of goat milk directly from producer to consumer by written, signed prescription." It is very difficult to obtain raw milk in Rhode Island and in fact, there is very little consumer demand.

SOUTH CAROLINA

Raw milk sales by licensed producers are legal on-farm and for distribution and sale in retail stores. Raw milk is widely available in the state, and has actually been encouraged by the state's department of agriculture.

## SOUTH DAKOTA
Raw milk sales are legal on the farm and through delivery. According to the South Dakota Department of Agriculture, producers are responsible for bottling the milk and must have a milk plant license in order to be able to use bottling equipment on their farms.

## TENNESSEE
Raw milk sales are illegal except as pet food. For a period, state authorities harassed dairy farmers selling raw milk and milk products labeled as pet food but this practice seems to have died down. There are a number of cow-share programs in the state and a committee is working on changing the law to allow on-farm sales.

## TEXAS
Raw milk sales are permitted on-farm directly to the consumer by farms holding a grade A "Raw for Retail License" from the Texas Health Department. For many years, raw milk sales were limited to a few licensed goat milk dairies in the state.

For many years, White Egret Farms in Austin sold grade A raw goat milk, raw milk cheeses, goat yogurt and natural meats. In August 2000, the farm was raided by Texas Department of Health (TDH) inspectors for alleged violation of over forty health and safety regulations. Owner Lee Dexter then filed over twenty-five hundred pages of scientific literature with the Attorney General's Office demonstrating the safety and efficacy of raw goat milk and raw milk cheeses. The TDH subsequently detained the farm's products in multiple locations and "paid visits" to its customers and processors. The TDH strategy culminated in the issuance of an Emergency Order prohibiting the sale of the farm's cheeses in late 2001. The TDH also published an extremely damaging and widely distributed press release.

After hearing two days of testimony in December 2001, Judge Cathleen Parsley issued a Proposal for Decision lifting the Emergency Order.

The judge stated that the Order had "pummeled Ms. Dexter's business, and, as it turns out, with little legal justification to do so." She also stated that the Department had held the farm liable for violations against regulations that were not yet in effect, did not prohibit the activity cited, were not applicable, or did not say what the TDH interpreted them to say. She concluded that the TDH failed to show how the alleged misconduct posed a threat to human health. White Egret Farm continues to sell its products to the public.

Today many farms in Texas hold a Raw for Retail License and raw milk from both goats and cows is widely available throughout the state.

## UTAH

Sales of raw milk at the farm are legal in Utah and several dairies now sell raw milk to satisfy increasing consumer demand. A bill allowing the sale of raw milk at an off-site retail store passed both the Utah House and Senate in February, 2007. Unfortunately, this bill will not necessarily make raw milk more available to consumers, as it favors only one large dairy, belonging to a corporation that owns an off-site store. (The bill requires fifty-one percent ownership of the store, something most small dairies can't afford.) In addition, the bill outlaws cow-share programs—an ominous trend. One raw dairy farmer has reported that the dairy inspectors in Utah are strict but generally supportive.

## VERMONT

On-farm raw milk sales are legal, but until recently a farmer could sell no more than twenty-five quarts per day and was not allowed to advertise. Recent legislation raised the limit to fifty quarts and allows the farmer to post a sign at the farm gate. Raw milk is widely available throughout the state.

## VIRGINIA

Raw milk sales are illegal, but raw milk is widely available throughout the state through cow-share and herd-share agreements, many of which deliver the milk to the consumer's door.

## WASHINGTON

Only dairies with a grade A permit may sell raw milk or engage in cow-share or herd-share arrangements. Several years ago, there was only one legal source of raw milk in the state, a Benedictine Nunnery on Shaw Island. Today, raw milk is widely available through on-farm sales, in retail stores and through cow-share and herd-share agreements.

## WEST VIRGINIA

Raw milk sales are illegal, but several sources of raw goat milk are posted at www.realmilk.com.

## WISCONSIN

From the Wisconsin Statutes, Section 97.24, Milk and Milk Products: "This section does not prohibit incidental sales of milk directly to consumers at the dairy farm where the milk is produced." The state agriculture department, however, interprets "incidental" as meaning one sale, and no more, effectively blocking farmers from selling directly to consumers.

After initial approval of cow-share programs, which proved extremely popular, the Department of Agriculture, Trade and Consumer Protection (DATCP) declared that they could not be used. However, during court proceedings, the judge acknowledged that bona fide owners of a milk producer license may consume raw milk directly from the farm. With the help of the Weston A. Price Foundation, a model "farm-share" legal document was drawn up. By early 2003, over one thousand individuals were securing raw milk through the newly instituted farm-share programs. Today raw milk is widely available in the state through such arrangements.

## WYOMING

Raw milk sales are illegal but there are several cow-share programs in the state.

OTHER COUNTRIES

AUSTRALIA
National standards allow for a state to permit the sale of raw milk for human consumption, and South Australia allows sales within the framework of a regulatory regime. Regulations in Queensland and New South Wales allow for the sale of raw goat milk but not raw cow milk. In Queensland, raw cow milk is available in health food stores as Cleopatra's Bath Milk, and cow-share programs are underway in Queensland and other states.

CANADA
Federal law prohibits the sale or giving away of any raw milk, and many provincial laws reinforce this prohibition—in Ontario, farmers may be fined two hundred fifty thousand dollars and sentenced to three years in jail for selling raw milk. Although the government claims that cow-share programs are illegal, there are a number of such arrangements in Canada, especially in British Columbia.

Michael Schmidt of Glencolton Farms provides raw milk via a cow-share program to consumers in Toronto. Several raids on his farm have turned the outspoken farmer into a modern folk hero. A trial to determine the constitutionality of his cow-share program and the fate of similar programs throughout Canada will take place in 2009.

ENGLAND
In England, the Dairy Products Hygiene Regulations of 1995 state of raw milk: ". . . an occupier of a registered production holding may sell such milk at or from the farm premises where the animals from which the milk has been obtained are maintained, to: (a) the ultimate consumer for consumption other than at those farm premises; (b) a temporary guest or visitor to those farm premises as or as part of a meal or refreshment; or (c) a distributor.

A distributor may sell such milk: (a) in the containers in which he receives the milk with the fastenings of the containers unbroken; (b) from a vehicle which is lawfully used as shop premises; and (c) direct to the ultimate consumer."

Some two hundred producers sell raw milk directly to consumers in England. The royal family has always consumed raw milk, and Prince Charles has publicly defended the practice.

## EUROPE

On-farm and some retail sales of raw milk are permitted in Germany, Holland, Belgium, Switzerland, France, Italy, Denmark and Sweden. Some stores in Belgium sell frozen mare's milk. Raw milk vending machines are becoming increasingly popular. However, farmers who sell raw milk must pass much more stringent inspections than those who sell their milk for pasteurizing.

## RUSSIA

Raw milk is available in the countryside and, to a limited extent, in Moscow.

## WALES

In the spring of 2002, Welsh officials proposed a ban on the sale of raw milk. However, after considerable pressure, officials announced that sales of raw milk and cream would continue, with a voluntary change in the labeling.

# Appendix Two
## Preparation of Raw Milk Products

Here are a few simple techniques for preparing delicious raw milk products. The basic ingredients are fresh raw milk and fresh raw cream from grass-fed cows.

CLABBERED MILK OR RAW YOGURT

When fresh raw milk stands at temperatures higher than about 70 degrees F, natural fermentation takes place, resulting in separation of the milk into curds and whey within a few days. With proper timing and temperature control, a delicious food results.

You may remove some or most of the cream first by allowing the milk to stand for several hours and then skimming the cream. Then place the milk in container of glass, stainless steel or glazed pottery. To make clabbered milk, no additional ingredients are necessary; the organisms that naturally occur in the milk will cause it to ferment. To make yogurt, begin by adding a spoonful of plain yogurt as a starter and stir; the organisms in the starter will work together with those in the milk.

Fermentation will proceed most easily at temperatures over 80 degrees, but to preserve all the enzymes in the milk, do not heat over 100 degrees. Cover and place the container in a warm place—keep the milk temperature between about 85 and 100 degrees to get a tasty product that is more sweet than acidic.

You will need a room thermometer to find a place that will work best for fermentation. If the temperature on the top of your refrigerator or in a closet with the light turned on ranges between 85 and 100 degrees, put your container of milk there. Other possibilities include placing the container in hot water or rigging up a light bulb in an ice chest.

When the milk "sets up" or "jells" and looks like yogurt with cream on the top (typically within 18 to 36 hours), fermentation has turned it into clabbered milk or yogurt, and it's ready to eat or refrigerate. If it stands at the warm temperatures longer, separation into curds and whey occurs, and over time the products become bitter. A tasty product can be made, albeit more slowly, at temperatures between about 70 and 85 degrees, but if it is any cooler, the process is markedly slowed down, and the product tends to have a bitter taste.

With an endless variety of subtle variations, this is the basic way raw milk has been preserved and made into a superior, easily digested food in cultures throughout the world for many thousands of years. Kefir and buttermilk are very similar, but have a more liquid consistency than clabbered milk or yogurt. They require special cultures.

Try serving your homemade fermented milk with gently melted butter, raw cream and unheated, unprocessed honey over the top.

### QUARK, CREAM CHEESE AND WHEY

To make cream cheese and whey from your separated milk or yoghurt, place it in a colander lined with a kitchen towel set over a bowl. Cover and let the whey drain out. A thick yogurt-like product will be left in the towel-lined colander, which is called yoghurt cheese or quark. This product is delicious mixed with honey or maple syrup.

To make cream cheese, tie up the towel containing the quark into a little sack and suspend over a bowl until whey no longer drips out. The result will be a very firm cream cheese.

Fresh whey will store for many months in glass jars in the refrigerator. Whey is a most useful product for making soaked grains, lacto-fermented vegetables and healthy soft drinks. It is also an important ingredient in homemade baby formula (page 431).

### FARMER'S RAW COTTAGE CHEESE OR LEMON CHEESE

As with yoghurt, some or most of the cream may be skimmed off the top of the raw milk. For 1 gallon of milk at room temperature, mix in the strained juice of 8 lemons. Cover. Within 15 minutes or so, curds will form. Line a colander with cheesecloth or a kitchen towel, pour the liquid curd into it, cover, and allow to drip into a bowl for a few hours (or overnight for a drier, less lemon-flavored cheese). The yield is about three pints of cheese and two quarts of lemon whey.

ICE CREAM

Great raw ingredients are half of the story when it comes to making delicious ice cream; the other half is great equipment. Highly recommended: a digital automatic ice cream maker. You don't need ice; the canister in which the ice cream is made is placed in the freezer for several hours before use, and that provides the necessary low temperatures. I recommend one made by Keystone Manufacturing Company called the Deni Scoop Factory (Model 5400), which is available on the internet.

For the basic recipe you will need 1 quart raw cream. Beat 3-6 egg yolks until pale and ribbony. Add 1/4-1/2 cup natural sweetener (maple syrup, maple sugar, rapadura or raw honey), 1/2 teaspoon vanilla and 1 tablespoon of something alcoholic—it can be vodka if you do not want to interfere with the vanilla flavor, or some kind of liqueur, such as Amaretto. The alcohol lowers the freezing temperature so that the ice cream remains relatively soft when frozen. Stir the cream into this mixture and process in your ice cream maker according to instructions.

For a variation, you can add 2-3 tablespoons cocoa or carob powder, 1/2 cup chopped nuts (first sautéed in a little butter with a sweetener added), 1/2 cup desiccated coconut or about 1 cup puréed fruit. If you add fruit, you will need to reduce the amount of cream accordingly.

Healthy ice cream is one of life's true luxuries, an old hippie's revenge on the Washington cholesterol cops. Try it with a couple of shots of Jersey raw cream over the top. Makes you think about keeping a family cow.

BUTTER

A great source for learning about butter making is Joann Grohman's *Keeping a Family Cow*: "Sweet cream can be made into butter, but the flavor is less interesting than if slightly 'ripened' cream is used. Sour cream of consistent flavor can be obtained by inoculating the cream either with mesophilic starter or sour cream starter.

"An electric mixer can be used for very small quantities, using the batter beater rather than a wire whisk. [But] I have discovered that my food processor fitted with the plastic dough blade makes butter more efficiently than anything else. It rarely takes more than three minutes, usually about 90 seconds. I now simply pour a series of batches into a colander type sieve and drain and wash the butter in that. The regular metal blade also works but goes so fast you can easily lose control and over beat the butter.

"If your cream is slightly sour, on the way to becoming butter, unless quite warm, it will pass through a thickened stage about the consistency of commercial whipped topping. If you stop at this stage and save some of this mixture, it's perfect for sour cream of the sort favored for cheese cakes and baked potatoes.

"After the butter is washed, it must be pressed to remove all water. Before pressing, add one teaspoon salt for each pound of butter unless you prefer it unsalted. (Salted butter keeps better.) Press the butter thoroughly by folding and pressing, never smearing, which will develop a greasy consistency rather than the waxy consistency characteristic of nice butter. Keep going until water is no longer being squeezed out. All the buttermilk and water must be out if the butter is to keep well. Pat the butter into a butterball or any shape you like and wrap it in butter paper if available. . . Old-timers used to keep butter in a covered crock in a cool place. Depending on the weather and your techniques, it can keep several months that way. A freezer is more reliable."

RAW MILK WARMER

Place 2 cups raw milk in a jar and set the jar in simmering water. Add about 1 tablespoon natural sweetener (maple syrup, maple sugar, rapadura, raw honey or molasses) and about 2 tablespoons cocoa or carob powder. You may also add 1-2 tablespoons nutritional yeast (I recommend Frontier Brand) to make an Ovaltine-like drink. As the milk warms, stir occasionally with a whisk. Drink when warm, but not hot, to the touch.

RAW MILK TONIC

This is a wonderful recovery drink for convalescents, for athletes, and anyone wanting to stay in perfect health. Place 4-6 egg yolks, 2 tablespoons molasses and 1/2 teaspoon vanilla extract in a bowl. You may also add 2-3 tablespoons raw cream. Mix thoroughly with a whisk and then stir in 2 cups raw milk.

SMOOTHIES

In a food processor or blender place about 1 cup fruit, such as a banana, peaches or berries, 1-2 tablespoons melted coconut oil, 2-4 egg yolks and 2-4 tablespoons natural sweetener (maple syrup, maple sugar, rapadura or raw honey). Add 2-3 cups fermented raw milk such as yogurt or kefir. Blend until frothy.

RAW MILK BABY FORMULA

This is an excellent formula for babies should the mother be unable to nurse for whatever reason. Use the best quality full-fat raw milk from grass-fed cows. The lactose, *Bifodobacterium infantis*, cod liver oil, sunflower oil, coconut oil, nutritional yeast, gelatin and acerola powder may be obtained from Radiant Life (888) 593-8333. Makes a one-day suipply of 36 ounces, or six 6-ounce bottles.

> *2 cups clean raw milk from pastured cows,*
> *preferably Jersey or Guernsey cows*
> *1/4 cup homemade liquid whey (page 428)*
> *4 tablespoons lactose*
> *1/4 teaspoon* Bifodobacterium infantis
> *1/2 teaspoon high-vitamin cod liver oil*
> *(to supply 5000 IU vitamin A)*
> *1 teaspoon expeller-expressed sunflower oil*
> *1 teaspoon extra virgin olive oil*
> *2 teaspoons coconut oil*
> *2 teaspoons Frontier brand nutritional yeast flakes*
> *2 teaspoons Bernard Jensen gelatin*
> *1 7/8 cups filtered water*

*1/4 teaspoon acerola powder*

*1-2 tablespoons raw cream (if the milk comes from Holstein cows)*

Fill a measuring cup with 2 cups water and scoop out 2 tablespoons (which leaves 1 7/8 cups). Pour half the water in a pot on the stove top on medium low heat and add the gelatin and lactose. Stir until dissolved. Meanwhile, pour the milk into a large glass container (an 8-cup glass Pyrex works well) or right into a blender with measuring markers and add the remaining ingredients (oils, whey, powders, etc.) except the coconut oil. Once the water/lactose/gelatin mixture is dissolved, pour in the rest of the water to cool it off a bit. Then add the coconut oil and allow it to melt completely. Pour the dissolved water/lactose/gelatin/coconut oil mixture into the glass container or blender with milk. Blend everything for about 3 seconds.

Pour the formula into 6 glass bottles, seal with the caps and place them in the refrigerator. To serve, place a nipple on a bottle and warm in a bottle warmer. Shake well and serve to baby.

GOAT MILK BABY FORMULA

Although goat milk is rich in fat, it must be used with caution in infant feeding as it lacks folic acid and is low in vitamin $B_{12}$, both of which are essential to the growth and development of the infant. Use the recipe for Raw Milk Baby Formula given above; inclusion of nutritional yeast to provide folic acid is essential. To compensate for low levels of vitamin $B_{12}$, add 2 teaspoons frozen organic raw chicken liver, finely grated, to the batch of formula.

# Appendix Three
## A Reply to the
## U.S. Food and Drug Administration's
## Official Statement on Raw Milk

The following letter summarizes the U.S. government's official arguments against raw milk. My comments are in italics.

Dear [Addressee],

This is in reply to your e-mail message of March 11, 2003, in which you requested a statement on the Food and Drug Administration's (FDA) position on the public health concerns surrounding the sale/consumption of raw milk.

Please be advised that FDA and other federal and state health agencies have documented a long history of the risks to human health associated with the consumption of raw milk. Clinical and epidemiological studies from FDA, state health agencies, and others have established a direct causal link between gastrointestinal disease and the consumption of raw milk.

*Authorities have greatly exaggerated the "risks to human health associated with the consumption of raw milk." Even before sanitation procedures became routine in dairy barns, honest investigators have demonstrated that the risk from raw milk is very low. Any raw food may contain harmful bacteria if it is produced or stored in an unsanitary manner. Would the FDA outlaw all raw foods? And while the bacteria that might be present in raw milk and other raw foods can cause temporary gastric upset, it poses a serious danger only to those with compromised immune systems (usually the result of immunosuppressive drugs).*

The microbial flora of raw milk may include human pathogens present on the cow's udder and teats. Further, the intrinsic properties of milk, including its pH and nutrient content, make it an excellent media [sic] for the survival and growth of bacteria.

*Milk is indeed an excellent medium for the survival and growth of bacteria—good bacteria. When pathogenic bacteria are added to raw milk, the good bacteria, along with numerous other anti-microbial compounds in raw milk, help prevent their growth or in some cases even eliminate them, as shown in several published studies and in recent tests with the milk from Organic Pastures Dairy in California (see www.organicpastures.com). In addition, raw milk from healthy cows raised on fresh pasture, produced under sanitary conditions, simply does not contain pathogenic bacteria.*

On August 10, 1987, FDA published in 21 CFR Part 1240.61, a final regulation mandating the pasteurization of all milk and milk products in final package form for direct human consumption. This regulation addresses milk shipped in interstate commerce and became effective September 9, 1987.

*This ruling was made for the benefit of the dairy industry and has nothing to do with the safety of raw milk. In their argument, the FDA ignores numerous outbreaks of food-borne illness due to pasteurized milk.*

In this Federal Register notification for the final rule to 21 CFR Part 1240.61, FDA made a number of findings including the following:

* Raw milk, no matter how carefully produced, may be unsafe.

*Careful production of raw milk always ensures a safe product. The same cannot be said for pasteurized milk, most of which comes from animals in suboptimal or outright poor health and which furthermore can be contaminated post pasteurization, as happened in a 2007 outbreak of listeria from skim and 2% low-fat milk in Massachusetts, which sickened five people, killing three elderly men and an unborn child.*

* It has not been shown to be feasible to perform routine bacteriological tests on the raw milk itself to determine the presence or absence of all pathogens and thereby ensure that it is free of infectious organisms.

*It is entirely feasible for producers and inspectors to perform routine tests for bacteria in milk. Mark McAfee of Organic Pastures Dairy in California performs such tests daily and posts the results on his website (www.organicpastures.com). His bacteria counts are routinely much lower than the very low standards required for unpasteurized milk and he has never detected any pathogen in his milk. Government-sponsored testing by agencies friendly to producers of raw milk would be a boon to small farms everywhere and would help start a resurgence of America's farming communities.*

* Opportunities for the introduction and persistence of Salmonella on dairy premises are numerous and varied, and technology does not exist to eliminate Salmonella infection from dairy herds or to preclude re-introduction of Salmonella organisms. Moreover recent studies show that cattle can carry and shed *S. dublin* organisms for many years and demonstrated that *S. dublin* cannot be routinely detected in cows that are mammary gland shedders.

*These points apply to unhealthy cows in modern confinement dairies. I do not recommend consumption of raw milk from these dairies. However, the FDA fails to make this distinction, or any distinction about differences in the quality of raw milk produced under widely disparate conditions. It also fails to acknowledge that Salmonella can be contracted from drinking pasteurized milk as well; in fact, the largest outbreak of Salmonella in the nation's history that affected an estimated 150,000 to 200,000 people occurred in 1985 and was traced to 2% low-fat pasteurized milk produced by a Chicago milk plant.*

- During this rule making process, the American Academy of Pediatrics and numerous others submitted comments in support of the proposed regulation.

*For decades, the American medical establishment has argued for compulsory pasteurization of all milk, while endorsing formula feeding for babies and the untenable cholesterol theory of heart disease. It opposes all alternative, nontoxic therapies for cancer, while over half of cancer patients seek such treatment. During the early 1600s, William Harvey discovered that blood circulates in the human body; it took the medical establishment over one hundred years to accept this fact. Throughout the 1800s, untold thousands of women died shortly after childbirth of puerperal fever. Philipp Semmelweis discovered that the infectious agent was transmitted by the hands of doctors delivering babies after they had carried out work in the dissecting room. His reward: rejection and ostracism, commitment to a mental institution and suicide at the age of forty-seven. I suggest that the medical establishment's arguments against raw milk are at best erroneous, and at worst malicious. The sanctity of America's food supply and the health of our children are too precious to leave any longer entirely in the hands of a medical establishment that has again and again demonstrated a lack of insight, foresight and character.*

In deciding upon mandatory pasteurization, FDA determined that pasteurization was the only means to assure the destruction of pathogenic microorganisms that might be present.

*The FDA ignores the fact that Johnes' bacteria survive pasteurization and, if present in large enough amounts,* Listeria monocytogenes *and* E. coli O157:H7 *can also survive pasteurization. The industry's solution to this problem is ultra-pasteurization, but the FDA avoids informing the consumer of this fact. If the FDA's goal is indeed "to assure the destruction of pathogenic organisms that might be present" in the food supply, we may look forward to compulsory irradiation of all foods—to "ensure our safety," and ensure more profits for the food processing and irradiation industries.*

This decision was science-based involving epidemiological evidence. FDA and the Centers for Disease Control and Prevention (CDC) in Atlanta have documented illnesses associated with the consumption of raw milk, including "certified raw milk" and have stated that the risks of consuming raw milk far outweigh any benefits.

*Can we trust the "documented" cases published by the CDC? Careful analysis of these "documented cases" reveals that the vast majority are biased and flawed. For example, recently the CDC blamed a Wisconsin outbreak of campylobacter involving eight hundred people on raw milk. Only twenty-three of those stricken had consumed raw milk—so obviously raw milk was not the cause (see www.realmilk.com/pr_071402. html). In addition to such dubious documentations, the CDC documented nearly eleven times as many illnesses that it attributed to pasteurized milk as it did to raw milk between 1980 and 2005. And in any event, it is the consumer who should make the decision as to whether the risks of consuming raw milk outweigh the benefits, not a government agency with close ties to the dairy industry. FDA and CDC statements about a lack of any benefit from raw milk consumption make a mockery of their claim to "science-based" decisions.*

In light of research showing no meaningful difference in the nutritional value of pasteurized and unpasteurized milk, FDA and CDC have also concluded that the health risks associated with the consumption of raw milk far outweigh any benefits derived from its consumption.

*Note the adjective "meaningful." FDA and CDC dismiss the great body of scientific evidence indicating the superior nutritional benefits of raw milk as not "meaningful." The work of Pottenger and many others has proven the nutritional superiority of raw milk compared to pasteurized. These agencies apply the words "meaningful" and "science" only to information that suits their industry-influenced agenda. Contrary information is simply not "meaningful," and not "science."*

There are numerous documented outbreaks of milkborne disease involving Salmonella and Campylobacter infections directly linked to the consumption of unpasteurized milk in the past 20 years. Since the early 1980s, cases of raw milk-associated campylobacteriosis have been reported in the states of Arizona, California, Colorado, Georgia, Kansas, Maine, Montana, New Mexico, Oregon, and Pennsylvania.

*Many of these cases were assumed and not proven, while others resulted from drinking shabbily produced raw milk that was intended for pasteurization. But while even licensed raw milk has resulted in rare cases of food-borne illness, the numbers are extremely small compared to those caused by other foods—to the tune of seventy-six million cases per year. Hamburger, mayonnaise, ice cream, eggs, luncheon meats, seafood, lettuce and pasteurized milk have all caused outbreaks of food-borne illness but the FDA does not call for a removal of these items from the marketplace. The double standard is obvious. Carefully produced raw milk has an outstanding safety record. Organic Pastures Dairy sells over 5,000 quarts of raw milk weekly in California without a single documented case of illness. Local Farm has sold raw milk in Connecticut for over ten years without a single case of illness. With government cooperation, farms all over America could duplicate this success.*

An outbreak of Salmonellosis, involving 50 cases was confirmed in Ohio in 2002. Recent cases of *E. coli O157:H7*, *Listeria monocytogenes* and *Yersinia enterocolitica* infections have also been attributed to raw milk consumption.

*Regarding the Ohio case, this was the first incident of this kind at the dairy, which had been in operation for two generations and hosted hundreds of thousands of customers per year. The county health authorities concluded that they "cannot say as to whether or not pasteurization would have prevented this outbreak." The Ohio Department of Agriculture and county health authorities recommended a number of sanitation improvements, repairs and the institution of a milk quality evaluation program, but they never gave the farm a chance to institute those recommendations: instead, they issued a "temporary" stop-sale order that would remain in effect "until further notice" while simultaneously recommending the farm relinquish its license, which it did three days later. In none of the recent cases of E. coli O157:H7 dubiously attributed to raw milk were any contaminated milk samples found. The* Listeria monocytogenes *outbreaks were traced to cheeses made from raw milk that were probably contaminated during cheese production and the contamination was never traced back to the raw milk itself. The CDC has no record of recent yersinia outbreaks traced to raw milk. By contrast, at least two outbreaks of listeria have been traced to pasteurized fluid milk, killing a total of 18 people, and a large multi- state outbreak of yersinia was traced to pasteurized milk in 1982.*

In the court case Public Citizen v. Heckler, 653f. Supp. 1229 (D.D.C. 1986), the federal district court concluded that the record presents overwhelming evidence of the risks associated with the consumption of raw milk, both certified and otherwise. The court stated that the evidence FDA has accumulated concerning raw milk conclusively shows that raw and certified raw milk are unsafe and there is no longer any question of fact as to whether raw milk is unsafe.

*Had complete evidence been presented, the court could not have made such "conclusive" conclusions. Fortunately, this uninformed court decision does not apply to state laws. Raw milk is still legally available in the majority of states in the U.S.*

State health and agricultural agencies routinely use the U.S. Public Health Service/FDA Pasteurized Milk Ordinance (PMO) as the basis for the regulation of Grade A milk production and processing. The PMO has been sanctioned by the National Conference on Interstate Milk Shipments (NCIMS) and provides a national standard of uniform measures that is applied to Grade A dairy farms and milk processing facilities to assure safe milk and milk products. Section 9 of the PMO specifies that only Grade A pasteurized milk be sold to the consumer.

*These national standards have resulted in the continued degradation of the American milk supply, with the result that more and more individuals are unable to consume commercial milk without suffering health problems. A shrinking customer base is the price the dairy industry has paid for "uniform standards." Fortunately, Section 9 of the PMO does not allow the federal government to overrule state laws allowing the sale of raw milk.*

In summary, since raw milk may contain human pathogens, the consumption of raw milk products increases the risk of gastrointestinal illness due to the likelihood that it may contain infective doses of human pathogens. The only method proven to be reliable in reducing the level of human pathogens in milk and milk products is by those milk products being produced and processed under sanitary conditions and subsequently being properly pasteurized. The U.S. Food and Drug Administration, therefore, strongly advises against the consumption of raw milk.

*Note that the FDA does not claim that pasteurization will completely get rid of pathogens, only reduce them; and also that even with pasteurization, the milk must be produced under sanitary conditions. Conditions are manifestly not sanitary for the majority of milk produced in the U.S.*

*there have been many outbreaks of food-borne illness from pasteurized milk. In any event, the U.S. Constitution clearly allows every American the freedom to follow his own conscience in matters of food choice. This freedom has been severely restricted in most states and the FDA would have the federal government completely restrict it in every state with laws compelling mandatory pasteurization and forbidding even on-farm sales of raw milk. Will the U.S. government follow the Canadian model and forbid the farmer to feed even his own family raw milk from their own cow? Clearly, mandatory pasteurization is a fascist tactic, the tool of corporate- and industry-influenced government agencies that would be another step towards the enslavement of a once-free people. They cry "public safety;" what we hear is "corporate profits."*

References related to this subject may be found in the following documents:

a.  *American Journal of Public Health*, November 21, 1997
b.  *Journal of the American Medical Association*, October 1984, May 1999, March 3, 1989
c.  *Journal of Public Health Policy, Inc.*, September 1981
d.  *Morbidity and Mortality Weekly*, June 28, 2002
e.  *Journal of Food Protection*, Volume 61, Number 10, 1998
f.  *United States Department of Agriculture Fact Sheet*, July 1995

*Most of these publications are position papers that naturally reflect the FDA bias against raw milk. The* Journal of the American Medical Association *article October 1984 is the duplicitous "Health Fetish" article that completely distorts the findings of Dr. Pottenger (see www.realmilk. com/schmid_healthfetish.html). The* Morbidity and Mortality Weekly *article repeats CDC falsehoods about an outbreak of campylobacter in Wisconsin (see www.realmilk.com/pr_071402.html). Several of the incidents detailed in the* Journal of Food Protection *article involved pasteurized milk and cheese. These articles perpetuate FDA's double standard and ignore the long record of safety and benefit from carefully produced raw milk.*

We trust this information responds to your request. If you would like additional information or have any questions, please feel free to call Mr. Robert Hennes, Chief, Milk Safety Team at (301) 436-2175. If we can be of any further assistance, please feel free to contact us.

Sincerely,
Joseph R. Baca, Director, Office of Compliance
Center for Food Safety and Applied Nutrition

*I urge everyone to contact the Center for Food Safety and Applied Nutrition and insist on your right to consume raw milk produced by America's family farms. To all of you who care about raw milk and freedom, there's work to be done. In the late 1700s, the Irish statesman Edmund Burke wrote, "All that is required for evil to triumph is for good men to do nothing." Good men and women everywhere should understand that the right to choose the food we eat is basic to life, liberty and the pursuit of happiness. Vigilance is the price of freedom and if ever there was a time for vigilance and for activism, it is now.*

# Appendix Four
## Resources

THE FARM-TO-CONSUMER LEGAL DEFENSE FUND

Established in 2007, the Farm-to-Consumer Legal Defense Fund (FTCLDF) is a non-profit organization made up of farmers and consumers to provide legal defense for direct farm-to-consumer sales. As part of its mission, the Fund works for direct sales of raw milk and other farm products without a permit; and reasonable permitting regulations for the retail sale of raw milk. Attorneys for the Fund provide a twenty-four hour legal hotline, and have developed a handbook on farmers' legal rights. They have helped hundreds of farmers set up cow-share programs and have solved many problems that farmers encounter—such as overzealous inspectors—with a simple phone call to the state.

Any farmer in the business of producing raw milk for consumers should be a member of the FTCLDF. Consumers of raw milk should also join to provide strength in numbers. Yearly fees increase the funds available to provide legal defense for raw milk.

For raw milk farmers, the Fund publishes a *Raw Milk Production Handbook*, which contains practical advice on everything from purchasing cows to basic sanitation procedures.

A sister organization, the Farm-to-Consumer Foundation, allows supporters to make tax-deductible donations to this worthy cause.

## THE WESTON A. PRICE FOUNDATION

The Weston A. Price Foundation is a nonprofit, tax-exempt charity founded in 1999 to disseminate the research of nutrition pioneer Dr. Weston Price. As we have discussed, Dr. Price's research demonstrated that humans achieve perfect physical form and perfect health generation after generation only when they consume nutrient-dense whole foods and the vital fat-soluble activators found exclusively in animal fats.

The Foundation is dedicated to restoring nutrient-dense foods to the human diet through education, research and activism. It supports a number of movements that contribute to this objective including accurate nutrition instruction, organic and biodynamic farming, pasture-feeding of livestock, community supported farms, honest and informative labeling, prepared parenting and nurturing therapies. A major Foundation goal is universal access to clean raw milk from grass-fed cows.

The Foundation has approximately four hundred local chapters throughout the U.S. and overseas. A principal task for chapter leaders is to find local sources of raw milk and facilitate consumer access to raw milk by publishing resource guides, organizing co-ops and cow-share programs, and lobbying for an improved regulatory climate for raw milk. The quickest way to find raw milk in your area is to contact your nearest Weston A. Price Foundation local chapter. Local chapters, including contact numbers, are posted at westonaprice.org/localchapters/.

Members of the Foundation receive a quarterly journal that contains updates on the science, politics and legal aspects of raw milk throughout the world; members also receive action alerts by email to enlist support in maintaining and expanding access to Nature's perfect food.

## A CAMPAIGN FOR REAL MILK

A Campaign for Real Milk is a project of the Weston A. Price Foundation. It has a separate website, www.realmilk.com, which posts sources of raw milk (realmilk.com/where.html) and science-based articles on the safety and health benefits of raw milk. The Campaign also issues point-by-point responses to various government documents demonizing raw milk. Of particular interest are the following:

+ An extensive Powerpoint presentation on the safety, health, economic and legal issues associated with raw milk and raw milk products (realmilk.com/ppt/index.html). The presentation represents a compilation of all the known scientific references on the superlative safety and health benefits of raw milk. Citizens are welcome to use the Powerpoint for presentations to groups interested in the subject of raw milk.

+ A fully referenced point-by-point rebuttal to an anti-raw milk Powerpoint presentation by John Sheehan, head of the FDA's division of dairy and egg safety (realmilk.com/documents/SheehanPowerPoint Response.pdf).

+ A fully referenced point-by-point response to a document prepared by food safety lawyer William Marler. Marler cites over one hundred reports of outbreaks of illness purportedly caused by raw milk in an effort to prove that raw milk is an inherently dangerous food (realmilk.com/ResponsetoMarlerListofStudies_.pdf). The response to William Marler shows that well over ninety percent of these reports do not meet scientific standards and would not hold up in a court of law.

+ Testimony presented in Superior Court of California by Ron Hull, PhD and Ted Beals, MD, in defense of beneficial bacteria in raw milk. The testimony led to granting of a temporary restraining order against the enforcement of anti-raw milk legislation and helped preserve raw milk availability in California.

LOCAL RAW MILK GROUPS

A number of raw milk advocacy groups have been formed in various states to defend raw milk farmers and lobby for less restrictive regulations. These include the California Real Milk Association (CREMA), Rural Vermont and the National Organic Farming Association of Massachusetts (NOFA-MASS). For information on activist groups in your state, contact your nearest Weston A. Price Foundation local chapter.

NEWTRENDS PUBLISHING

In addition to the *Untold Story of Milk*, NewTrends publishes many other fine books on diet and health including the best-selling *Nourishing Traditions* and *Performance without Pain*, a guide to healing serious medical conditions using raw milk and raw milk products. NewTrends also offers DVD presentations by Sally Fallon Morell on raw milk and traditional diets. For details, visit www.newtrendspublishing. com.

# References

## Chapter 1: Milk and Civilization

1. *Holy Bible*, King James Version. Crusade Bible Publishers, Nashville, 1975.
2. Grohman, Joann S. *Keeping a Family Cow*. Coburn Press, Dixfield, Maine, 1981 (first published in 1975 as *The Cow Economy*), 272.
3. Grohman, 1.
4. Crumbine, Samuel, and Tobey, James. *The Most Nearly Perfect Food*. Williams Wilkins Co., Baltimore, Maryland, 1930, 58.
5. Browne, Lewis. *This Believing World*. 1928. In Crombine and Tobey, 58.
6. Bronowski, Jacob. *The Ascent of Man*. Little, Brown and Company, 1973, Boston, Massachusetts, 60.
7. Hartley, Robert M. *An Historical, Scientific and Practical Essay on Milk as an Article of Human Sustenance*. J. Leavitt, New York, New York, 1842, 25.
8. Crumbine and Tobey, 58-59.
9. Barton, George A. *Encyclopedia of Religion and Ethics*. 635. In Crumbine and Tobey, 57.
10. Hartley, 50-56.
11. Crumbine and Tobey, 59.
12. Hartley, 44.
13. Hartley, 41.
14. Crumbine and Tobey, 59-60.
15. Crumbine and Tobey, 78.
16. Hartley, 41-47.
17. McCollum, EV, and Simmonds, N. *The Newer Knowledge of Nutrition* (3rd edition). Macmillan, New York, New York, 1925. In Crumbine and Tobey, 9.
18. Hartley, 50-56.
19. Crumbine and Tobey, 67-71.

# Chapter 2 : Bovine Friends in Early America

1. Quoted in Grohman, Joann S. *Keeping a Family Cow*. Coburn Press, Dixfield, Maine, 1981 (first published in 1975 as *The Cow Economy*), 13.
2. Selitzer, Ralph. *The Dairy Industry in America*. Books for Industry, New York, New York, 1976, 3.
3. Hartley, Robert M. *An Historical, Scientific and Practical Essay on Milk as an Article of Human Sustenance*. J. Leavitt, New York, New York, 1842, 67-8.
4. Selitzer, 6.
5. Selitzer, 7-9.
6. Selitzer, 3-10.
7. Selitzer, 11.
8. Grohman, 4-5.
9. Selitzer, 13.

# Chapter 3 : Bad Milk: The Distillery Dairies

1. Hartley, Robert M. *An Historical, Scientific and Practical Essay on Milk as an Article of Human Sustenance*. J. Leavitt, New York, NY, 1842, 72.
2. Selitzer, Ralph. *The Dairy Industry in America*. Books for Industry, New York, New York, 1976, 30.
3. Selitzer, 123.
4. Hartley, 133-47.
5. Koch's postulates are a series of steps that should be followed to prove that a specific microbe is the causal agent of a specific infectious disease. The postulates state that the organism must always be present in the diseased tissue, it must be isolated and grown in pure culture, and the pure culture when injected into an experimental animal must induce the disease. Brock, Thomas D. *Robert Koch: A Life in Medicine and Biology*. ASM Press, Washington, DC, 1999, 179-180.
6. Selitzer, 38-9.
7. Hartley, 107, 116, 137.
8. Personal communication, Ron Hull, PhD, November 20, 2008. The milk company was Alba Cheese in Tullamarine, Australia.
9. Selitzer, 124.
10. Hartley, 173-4.
11. DDGS & Pellet Manufacture Workshop at NCI Attracts Feed Industry. www.northern-crops.com/newsinfo/newsrel/2008-4-22.html, accessed November 19, 2008.
12. Hartley, 218-19.
13. Hartley, 224.
14. Hartley, 208-17, 280-300.
15. Hartley, 232.
16. Hartley, 235-6.
17. Selitzer, 123-36.
18. *Proceedings of the First Annual Session of the American Association of Medical Milk Commissions*. The American Association of Medical Milk Commissions, 1908, 18-19.

# Chapter 4: Microbes versus Milieu

1. Nicolle, Jacques. *Louis Pasteur—The Story of His Major Discoveries*. Basic Books, Inc., Philadelphia, Pennsylvania, 1920, 148.
2. Galdston, Imago. Beyond the Germ Theory: The Roles of Deprivation and Stress in Health and Disease. *Beyond the Germ Theory*, edited by Imago Galdston. New York Academy of Medicine Books, New York, New York, 1951, 14.
3. *The Oxford Encyclopedic Dictionary*, Clarendon Press, Oxford, England, 1991.
4. Nonclercq, Marie. Antoine Bechamp, 1816 – 1908. Maloine, Paris, France, 1982, in *The Curse of Louis Pasteur* by Nancy Appleton. Choice Publishing, Santa Monica, 1999, 47.
5. Appleton, Nancy. *The Curse of Louis Pasteur*. Choice Publishing, Santa Monica, 1999, 61.
6. Appleton, 62.
7. Wade, Nicholas. Bacteria Thrive in Inner Elbow; No Harm Done. *New York Times*. May 23, 2008.
8. *Science News Online*. February 2, 2002; Vol 161, No. 5.

# Chapter 5: Certify or Pasteurize?

1. *Proceedings of the First Session of the American Medical Milk Commissions*. Cincinnati, Ohio, 1908, pp. 9, 13-14, from the Henry Leber Coit papers, MS C 35, in the History of Medicine Division, National Library of Medicine.
2. Straus, Lina Gutherz. *Disease in Milk, The Remedy Pasteurization: The Life Work of Nathan Straus*, 1917, second edition.
3. Coit, Henry. The origin, general plan, and scope of the Medical Milk Commission. *Proceedings of the First Session of the American Medical Milk Commissions*. Cincinnati, Ohio, 1908, 10-17.
4. History of the Movement to Obtain Certified Milk and the Origin and Purpose of the Medical Milk Commission. In *Clean Milk*, a Bi-Monthly Bulletin of the Medical Milk Commission of Essex County, New Jersey, volume 3, Number 5, September 1922.
5. Straus, 15.
6. Straus, 24.
7. Straus, 28.
8. Straus, 29.
9. Straus, 30.
10. Straus, 48.
11. Straus, 228.
12. Straus, 242.
13. Straus, 55-56.
14. Straus, 56.
15. Thomson, James C. Pasteurized Milk, A National Menace: A Plea for Cleanliness. *The Kingston Chronicle*. Edinburgh, Scotland, 1943.
16. Straus, 60.
17. Straus, 57.

18. Frost, William Dodge. Some Bacteriological Problems of Milk Control. *Certified Milk Magazine*. January, 1929, 6-10.
19. Straus, 69.
20. Straus, 248.
21. Straus, 208.
22. Straus, 214.
23. Straus, 269-270.
24. Straus, 272.
25. Straus, 243.
26. *The Pharmaceutical Journal and Pharmacist*. April 18, 1914, page 555.

## Chapter 6: The History of the Milk Cure

1. Crewe, JR. Raw Milk Cures Many Diseases. *Certified Milk Magazine*. January, 1929, 3-6.
2. Porter, Charles Sanford. *Milk Diet as a Remedy for Chronic Disease*. Long Beach, California, 1905.
3. Porter, 18.
4. Porter, 68.
5. Porter, 16-17.
6. Porter, 31.
7. Porter, 52.
8. Porter, 66.
9. Porter, 127-9.
10. MacFadden, Bernarr. *The Miracle of Milk: How to Use the Milk Diet Scientifically at Home*. McFadden Book Company, New York, New York, 1933.
11. Sir William Osler, MD (1849-1919), was professor of medicine at Johns Hopkins and Oxford and the preeminent physician of his time. His *Principles and Practice of Medicine* (1892) became the standard clinical textbook for English-speaking medical students. His teaching method combined clinical practice and observation with laboratory research, but medical education has unfortunately gone in a different direction, in which medical teachers are rarely engaged in medical practice.
12. Crewe, 3-6.
13. MacFadden, 83.
14. *American Journal of Public Health* 18:634, 1928.
15. Howell, Edward. *Enzyme Nutrition: The Food Enzyme Concept*. Avery, New York, New York, 1985, 100-101.

## Chapter 7: Enzymes: Essential to Life

1. *Dorland's Illustrated Medical Dictionary*. 28th Edition, WB Saunders Company, Philadelphia, Pennsylvania 1994, 562.
2. *The Oxford Encyclopedic English Dictionary*. Oxford University Press, New York, New York, 1991, 478.

3. Howell, Edward. *Food Enzymes for Health and Longevity*. Lotus Press, Twin Lakes, Wisconsin, 1994, 78. Originally published in 1946 as *The Status of Food Enzymes in Digestion and Metabolism*.
4. Troland. *Cleveland Medical Journal* 15:377, 1916, quoted in Howell 79.
5. Laird. *Medical Record* 101:535-540, 1922, quoted in Howell, 79.
6. Hotchkiss, Thomas. A Personal Memoir of Francis M. Pottenger, Jr., M.D. The Price-Pottenger Nutrition Foundation, San Diego, California, 1975.
7. Pottenger, F.M., Jr. Clinical Evidences of the Value of Raw Milk. *Certified Milk*. Jul 1938;3:17-22.
8. Pottenger, F.M., Jr. The Influence of Heat Labile Factors on Nutrition in Oral Development and Health. 42nd Annual Convention, Southern California State Dental Asssociation. 1939.
9. Pottenger, F.M., Jr. and Simonsen, D.G. Deficient Calcification Produced by Diet: Experimental and Clinical Considerations. *Transactions of the American Therapeutic Society*. 1939.
10. Personal communication, Pat Connolly, Curator, The Price-Pottenger Nutrition Foundation, San Diego, California.
11. McCarrison, Robert. *Nutrition and Health*. Faber and Faber, London, England, 1953.
12. Potter, M and others. Unpasteurized Milk—The Hazards of a Health Fetish. *The Journal of the American Medical Association*. Oct 19, 1984;252(15): 2048-2052.
13. Pottenger, FM, Jr. The Effect of Heat-Processed and Metabolized Vitamin D Milk on the Dentofacial Structures of Experimental Animals. *American Journal of Orthodontics and Oral Surgery*. Aug 1946;32(8):467-485.
14. Howell, 17.
15. Howell, 78-79.
16. Price, Weston A. *Nutrition and Physical Degeneration*. The Price-Pottenger Nutrition Foundation, San Diego, California, 1939, 59-72.
17. Howell, 20.
18. Howell, 24-28.
19. A guide to the use and preparation of fermented foods is found in Fallon, Sally. *Nourishing Traditions: The Cookbook That Challenges Politically Correct Nutrition and the Diet Dictocrats*. NewTrends Publishing, Washington, DC, 2000.
20. Cunningham, M, and Acker, D. *Animal Science and Industry*. Prentice-Hall, Upper Saddle River, New Jersey, 2001, 612.
21. Roadhouse C, and Henderson J. *The Market Milk Industry*. McGraw-Hill, New York, New York 1950, 31-32.
22. *Indian Journal of Experimental Biology* 1998;36: 808-810.
23. *British Journal of Nutrition* 2000;84(Suppl. 1):S11-S17; Zimecki and Kruzel. *Journal of Experimental and Therapeutic Oncology*. 2007;6(2):89-106; *Journal of Experimental Medicine*. 2002 Dec 02;196(11):1507-1513.
24. *Clinical Infectectious Disease*. 2008 June 15; 46(12): 1881–1883.
25. FDA News, August 22, 2004.
26. Ford JE, Law BA, Marshall VM, Reiter B. Influence of the heat treatment of human milk on some of its protective constituents. *Journal of Pediatrics*. 1977;90(1):29-35.

27. Roadhouse, 439.
28. *Pediatric Gastroenterological Nutrition.* 1986 Mar-Apr;5(2):242-7.
29. Roadhouse, 655-657.
30. Howell, 33-41.
31. Gonzalez NJ and Isaacs LL. Evaluation of Pancreatic Proteolytic Enzyme Treatment of Adenocarcinoma of the Pancreas, With Nutrition and Detoxification Support. *Nutrition and Cancer* 1999;33(2):117-124.
32. Howell, 179.
33. Howell, 180.
34. Schmid, Ron. *Traditional Foods Are Your Best Medicine.* Healing Arts Press, Rochester, Vermont, 1997, 12-16. First published in 1986, Ocean View Publications, Stratford, Connecticut. Also published as *Native Nutrition*, Healing Arts Press, 1994.
35. Price, 59-72.
36. Howell, 139.
37. Price, 59-72.
38. Thomas JJ. Biol Chem, 1928;80: 461-75. Quoted in Howell, 139-140.
39. Howell, 140.
40. Howell, 140.
41. Garber. Hygeia, 1938:16: 242. Quoted in Howell, 140.
42. Howell, 138.
43. Stefansson, Vilhjalmur. *The Fat of the Land.* The MacMillan Company, New York, New York, 1956, 34-35.
44. Urquhart. *Canadian Medical Association Journal.* 1936;34:487-501. Described in Howell, 141.
45. Vilhjalmur Stefansson. *The Fat of the Land.* MacMillan Company, 1956
46. Rabinowitch. *Canadian Medical Association Journal* 1935;34:487-501. Quoted in Howell, 141-142.
47. Rabinowitch and Smith. *J Nutrition* 1936;12:337-56. Quoted in Howell, 141-142.
48. Fallon, 30-31.

## Chapter 8: Milk in the Last Traditional Cultures

1. Hooton, Earnest A. In Price, Weston. *Nutrition and Physical Degeneration.* The Price-Pottenger Nutrition Foundation, San Diego, California, 1939, xvii-xviii.
2. Bronowski, Jacob. *The Ascent of Man.* Little, Brown and Company, Boston, Massachusetts, 1973, 47-8.
3. Pelto, Gretel and Pertti. *The Cultural Dimension of the Human Adventure.* Macmillan Publishing Company, New York, New York, 1979, 99-102.
4. Grohman, Joann. *Keeping a Family Cow.* Coburn Press, Dixfield, Maine, 1981, 2-3.
5. Price, Weston. *Nutrition and Physical Degeneration.* 137
6. Biss K and others. Some unique biologic characteristics of the Masai of East Africa. *The New England Journal of Medicine.* Apr 1, 1971;284(13):694-699.

7. Manners, John. Kenya's Running Tribe. www.umist.ac.uk/sport/2, accessed June 4, 2002.
8. Bale J and Sang J. Kenyan Running: Movement Culture. *Geography and Global Change*. Frank Cass, Portland, Oregon, 1996, 149-150.
9. Huntingford. *The Nandi of Kenya*. 21-22. In Bale and Sang, 151.
10. Bale and Sang, 151-153.
11. Abrahamson, Alan. Former Olympic Star Keino and His Wife Have Taken In More Than 100 Children and Given Them Hope. Byline Eldoret, Kenya. *The Los Angeles Times*. February 25, 2001, Section D, page 1.
12. Miller, David. Tibetan Nomads. Conservancy for Tibetan Art and Culture. www.tibetanculture.org/articles/miller.htm. Accessed March 2, 2003.
13. Pelto, 99.
14. Miller.
15. Grohman, 1-2.
16. Bronowski, 48.
17. *The Oxford Encyclopedic English Dictionary*. Oxford University Press, New York, New York, 1991, 808.
18. Mobley, George F. Lapps in a Modern World Face Timeless Realities. *Vanishing Peoples of the Earth*. National Geographic Society, 1968, 36-57.
19. www.laplandfinland.com, accessed September 14, 2002.
20. Mobley, 36.
21. Hartley, Robert M. *An Historical, Scientific and Practical Essay on Milk as an Article of Human Sustenance*. J. Leavitt, New York, NY, 1842, 62.
22. Hartley, 65.
23. Mandelbaum, David. "Nilgiri Peoples of India: An End to Old Ties," in Vanishing Peoples of the Earth. *National Geographic*. 1968, 76-91.
24. www.sdnp.delhi.nic.in/nbsap/subthemes/pastoralnomads/nbsapworkshop.html, accessed September 14, 2002.
25. www.pastoralpeoples.org/lpp/activities/alsipuradecl.htm, accessed September 14, 2002.
26. Price, Weston A. *Nutrition and Physical Degeneration*. 1939.
27. Masterjohn, Chris. On the Trail of the Elusive X Factor. *Wise Traditions in Food, Farming and the Healing Arts*, quarterly journal of the Weston A. Price Foundation. Vol 8, No 1, Spring 2007, www.westonaprice.org/basic-nutrition/vitamin-k2.html.
28. Schmid, Ron. *Traditional Foods Are Your Best Medicine*. Healing Arts Press, Rochester, Vermont, 1997, 12-16. First published in 1986, Ocean View Publications, Stratford, Connecticut. Also published as *Native Nutrition*, Healing Arts Press, 1994.
29. Price, Weston A. Field Studies on the Relation of Diet to Dental Caries Made in 1931 and 1932 in Switzerland, France, Italy, Scotland, and Islands in the North Atlantic. (Read before the Odontological Society of Western Pennsylvania, Pittsburgh, November, 1932.)
30. Price, Weston A. Why Dental Caries with Modern Civilizations? Field Studies in Primitive Loetschental Valley, Switzerland, Parts I – III. *Dental Digest*, March, 1933.
31. Price, Nutrition and Physical Degeneration, 27.

## Chapter 9: Betrayal

1. Mackaye, Milton. Undulant Fever. *Ladies Home Journal*. December 1944.
2. Harris, Harold J. Raw Milk Can Kill You. *Coronet*. May 1945.
3. Harvey, Holman. How Safe Is Your Town's Milk? *The Progressive*. July 15, 1946.
4. Harvey, Holman. How Safe Is Your Town's Milk? *The Reader's Digest*. August 1946.
5. Darlington, Jean Bullitt. Why Milk Pasteurization, Part I: Sowing the Seeds of Fear. *The Rural New Yorker*. March 15, 1947.
6. Harris, Harold J. The Raw Milk Menace. *Hygeia*. March 1941, 250. In Darlington.
7. Harris, Harold J. Brucellosis. *Journal of the American Medical Association*. 1946;131(18):1485-1493.
8. One such case was reported in *The Lancet* 1999;354-360. The case cleared up quickly with a course of antibiotics.
9. U.S. Public Health Service. Summary of Milk-Borne Disease Outbreaks, 1923-1941. In Darlington.
10. U.S. Public Health Service. Disease Outbreaks Conveyed Through Milk and Milk Products in the U.S., 1942, 1943, 1944. In Darlington.
11. Eliason, Alton. The Crime Against Raw Milk. *Wise Traditions in Food, Farming and the Healing Arts*. The Weston A. Price Foundation, Washington, DC, Summer 2000, 59-63.
12. Nestle, Marion. *Food Politics: How the Food Industry Influences Nutrition and Health*. University of California Press, Berkeley, California, 2002, 2.
13. Owen B and Braeutigam R. *The Regulation Game: Strategic Use of the Administrative Process*. Ballinger, Cambridge, Massachusetts, 1978, 7. In Nestle, 111.
14. Nestle, 112.
15. Nestle, 114.
16. Nestle, 4.
17. Wazana, A. Physicians and the pharmaceutical industry: is a gift ever just a gift? *Journal of the American Medical Association* 2000;283:373-380.
18. Blumenthal, D and others. Participation of life-science faculty in research relationships with industry. *New England Journal of Medicine* 1996; 335:1734-1739.
19. Wadman, M. Study discloses financial interests behind papers. *Nature* 1997;385:376.
20. Nestle, 117.
21. Selitzer, Ralph. *The Dairy Industry in America*. Books for Industry, New York, New York, 1976, 126.
22. Nestle, 4, 11.
23. Nestle, 12.
24. Nestle, 17.
25. Nestle, 18-19.
26. Nestle, 22.
27. Nestle, 25-26.
28. Nestle, 28.
29. Nestle, 33, 70, 79-80.

30. Nestle, 80-81.
31. Nestle, 95-96.
32. Nestle, 99-100.
33. Nestle, 97.
34. Nestle, 33, 70, 79-80.
35. Nestle, 97.
36. Nestle, 122.
37. Nestle, 148-153.
38. Nestle, 162-164.
39. Nestle, 165-66.
40. Nestle, 168.
41. ADM is the company that has spent billions of marketing dollars to bring soy foods to every health food store and supermarket in America, foods that compete with milk and other dairy products. Do you trust what ads for soy foods tell us about their alleged health benefits? If you do, I suggest you read about these products at theSoy Alert! section of the Weston A. Price Foundation website, www.westonaprice.org, and learn how the soybean industry turned the toxic waste products of vegetable oil production into America's best-selling "health food."
42. Nestle, 197.
43. Nestle, 202.
44. Nestle, 176.
45. Nestle, 199.
46. Henson, Dave. The end of agribusiness. In *The Fatal Harvest Reader*, ed. Andrew Kimbrell, Island Press, Washington, District of Columbia, 2002, 227-229.
47. Nestle, 231-233.

# Chapter 10: Cholesterol, Animal Fats, Heart Disease

1. Ravnskov, Uffe, MD, PhD. *The Cholesterol Myths*. NewTrends Publishing, Washington, DC, 2000. We are indebted to Dr. Ravnskov for many of the insights and analyses summarized in this chapter.
2. Enig, Mary, PhD. *Know Your Fats*. Bethesda Press, Silver Spring, MD, 2000.
3. Kannell, WB, Gordon T. The Framingham diet study: diet and the regulation of serum cholesterol. *The Framingham Study: An Epidemiologic Investigation of Cardiovascular Disease*. Section 24, Washington, DC, 1970.
4. Ravnskov, 30.
5. Keys, Ansel. Atherosclerosis: A problem in newer public health. *Journal of Mount Sinai Hospital* 20, 118-139, 1953; described in Ravnskov, 30.
6. WHO Monica Project: Assessing CHD mortality and morbidity. *International Journal of Epidemiology* 18, suppl. 1, S38-S45, 1989. WHO Monica Project: Risk factors. Same journal and issue: S46-S55.
7. Ravnskov, 101.
8. Ravnskov, 104.
9. Keys, Ancel. *Eating Well*. March/April 1997.

10. Castelli, W. *Archives of Internal Medicine* Jul 1992;152(7);1371-1372.
11. Ramsay and others. Dietary reduction of serum cholesterol concentration: time to think again. *British Medical Journal* 303:953-957, 1991.
12. Nichols AB and others. Daily nutritional intake and serum lipid levels. The Tecumseh study. *American Journal of Clinical Nutrition* 29:1384-1392, 1976.
13. Weidman WH and others. Nutrient intake and serum cholesterol level in normal children 6 to 16 years of age. *Pediatrics* 61:354-359, 1978.
14. Frank GC and others. Dietary studies and the relationship of diet to cardiovascular disease risk factor variables in 10-year-old children—the Bogalusa heart study. *The American Journal of Clinical Nutrition* 31:328-340, 1978.
15. Morris JN and others. Diet and plasma cholesterol in 99 bank men. *British Medical Journal* 1:571-576, 1963.
16. *Journal of the American Dietetic Association* 86:744-758, 1986.
17. Landé KE, Sperry WM. Human atherosclerosis in realtion to the cholesterol content of the blood serum. *Archives of Pathology* 22:301-312, 1936.
18. McGill HC and others. General Findings of the International Atherosclerosis Project. *Laboratory Investigations* 18:(5):498, 1968.
19. White, Paul Dudley. *Heart Disease*. New York, 1943.
20. Enig, Mary, PhD, *Trans Fatty Acids in the Food Supply: A Comprehensive Report Covering 60 Years of Research*, 2nd Edition, 1995, Enig Associates, Inc., Silver Spring, MD, 4-8.
21. Ravnskov, 30.
22. Enig, *Trans Fatty Acids in the Food Supply*, 4-8.
23. Yudkin J. Diet and coronary thrombosis. Hypothesis and Fact. *The Lancet* 2:155-162, 1957.
24. Masironi R. Dietary factors and coronary heart disease. *Bulletin of the World Health Organization* 42:103-114, 1970.
25. Guberan E. Surprising decline of cardiovascular mortality in Switzerland: 1951-1976. *Journal of Epidemiology and Community Health* 33, 114-120, 1979.
26. Ravnskov, 32.
27. Ravnskov, 42-43.
28. Ravnskov, 44.
29. Ravnskov, 46.
30. Jacobs D and others. Report of the conference on low blood cholesterol mortality associations. *Circulation* 86, 1046-1060, 1992.
31. Ravnskov, 41.
32. Moore, Thomas J. *Lifespan: What Really Affects Human Longevity*. Simon and Schuster, New York, 1991, 193-195.
33. Ravnskov, 257-269.
34. Ravnskov, 49-51.
35. Moore, 195.
36. www.msnbc.msn.com/id/25556140/, accessed November 18, 2008.
37. Ravnskov, 49-51.
38. Anderson KM and others. Cholesterol and mortality. 30 years of follow-up from the Framingham Study. *Journal of the American Medical Association* 247, 2176-2180, 1987.

39. Gotto AM and others. The cholesterol facts. A joint statement by the American Heart Association and the NHLBI. *Circulation* 81:1721-33, 1990.
40. Castelli WP and others. Cardiovascular risk factors in the elderly. *American Journal of Cardiology* 63:12H-19H, 1989.
41. Simons LA and others. Risk factors for coronary heart disease in the prospective Dubbo study of Australian elderly. *Atherosclerosis* 117:107-118, 1995.
42. Zimetbaum P and others. Plasma lipids and lipoproteins and the incidence of cardiovascular disease in the very elderly: the Bronx aging study. *Atherosclerosis* 12:416-423, 1992.
43. Krumholz HM and others. Lack of association between cholesterol and coronary heart disease mortality and morbidity and all-cause mortality in persons older than 70 years. *Journal of the American Medical Association* 272:1335-1340, 1994.
44. www.thincs.org/WAPF2003.htm. Accessed August 20, 2003.
45. Forette B and others. Cholesterol as risk factor for mortality in elderly women. *The Lancet* 1:868-870, 1989.
46. Jacobs D and others. Report of the conference on low blood cholesterol: *Circulation* 86:1046-60, 1992.
47. Dagenais GR and others. Total and coronary heart disease mortality in relation to major risk factors. *Canadian Journal of Cardiology* 6:59-65, 1990.
48. Shanoff HM and others. Studies of male survivors of myocardial infarction. *Canadian Medical Association Journal* 103:927-931, 1970; Ravnskov, 170.
49. National Research Council. *Diet and Health.* Washington D.C. 1989, National Academy Press, 166.
50. Pocock SJ and others. Concentrations of high-density lipoprotein cholesterol, triglycerides and total cholesterol in ischaemic heart disease. *British Medical Journal.* 298:998-1002, 1989.
51. Ravnskov, 85.
52. National Research Council. *Diet and Health.* Washington D.C. 1989, National Academy Press.
53. Ravnskov, 137-142.
54. Taylor CB and others. Atherosclerosis in rhesus monkeys. *Archives of Pathology* 76:404-412, 1963.
55. Stehbens WE. An appraisal of the epidemic rise of coronary heart disease and its decline. *The Lancet* I:606-611, 1987.
56. Moore, 191-192.
57. The Coronary Drug Project Research Group. Clofibrate and niacin in coronary heart disease. *Journal of the American Medical Association* 231:360-381, 1975.
58. Dorr AE and others. Colestipol hydrochloride in hypercholesterolemic patients—effect on serum cholesterol and mortality. *Journal of Chronic Disease* 31:5-14, 1978.
59. Ravnskov, 152-153.
60. *British Heart Journal* 40;1069-1118, 1978; *The Lancet* 2:379-385, 1980.
61. The Lipid Research Clinics' coronary primary prevention trial results. 1. Reduction in incidence of coronary heart disease. *Journal of the American Medical Association* 251, 351-364, 1984.
62. Ravnskov, 170.

63. *The Atlantic Monthly.* January 1990.
64. *British Medical Journal* 301, 815, 1990.
65. Ravnskov, 171-172.
66. Ravnskov, 173.
67. Ravnskov, 206-207.
68. Ravnskov, 207-208.
69. Ravnskov, 213.
70. Newman TB, Hulley SB. Carcinogenicity of lipid-lowering drugs. *Journal of the American Medical Association.* 27:55-60, 1996.
71. Sacks FM and others. The effect of pravastatin on coronary events after myocardial infarction in patients with average cholesterol levels. *New England Journal of Medicine* 335:1001-1009, 1996.
72. Ravnskov, 214-215.

## Chapter 11: Dairy Farming in the 21st Century

1. Blayney, Don P. The Changing Landscape of U.S. Milk Production. *USDA Statistical Bulletin.* Number 978, June 2002, 10. Accessed at www.ers.usda.gov, November 14, 2002.
2. Hagenbaugh B. Dairy farms evolve to survive. *USA Today.* August 7, 2003, p. B1.
3. Blayney, 8.
4. Blayney, 2.
5. Blayney, 7.
6. Pollan, Michael. The Unnatural Idea of Animal Rights. *The New York Times Magazine.* November 10, 2002, 63.
7. Pollan, 60, 63.
8. Ensminger, M.E. *Dairy Cattle Science.* Interstate Publishers, Danville, Illinois, 1993, 379.
9. Ensminger, 382, 384.
10. Ensminger, 384.
11. Ensminger, 381-382
12. Ensminger, 332.
13. Haynes, N. Bruce. *Keeping Livestock Healthy, a Veterinary Guide.* Storey Communications, Pownal, Vermont, 1985, 286-287.
14. Santos, Jose, and Overton, Michael. Diet, Feeding Practices and Housing Can Reduce Lameness in Dairy Cattle. *Progressive Dairyman and Hay Grower.* March, 2001. From 2001 Intermountain Nutrition Conference, 145-158.
15. Ruegg, Pamela. http://www.uwex.edu/milkquality/vetclinic/pdf/mastitis_control, accessed November 25, 2002.
16. Rice DN, and Bodman GR. The Somatic Cell Count and Milk Quality. Cooperative Extension, Institute of Agriculture and Natural Resources, University of Nebraska-Lincoln web site, www.ianr.unl.edu/pubs/Dairy/g1151.htm, accessed November 25, 2002.
17. Ruegg, Pamela. http://www.uwex.edu/milkquality/vetclinic/pdf/mastitis_control, accessed November 25, 2002.
18. Jones, GM. *Guidelines for using the DHI somatic cell count program.* Virginia Cooperative Extension Dairy Science Publication 1998, 404-228.

19. Schroeder, JW. Weather damaged teats mean high somatic cell count— methods of controlling mastitis. North Dakota State University Extension Service, March 1997.
20. Cherrington VA, Hansen HC, and Halverson WV. The leucocyte content of milk as correlated with bacterial count and hydrogen ion concentrations for the detection of mastitis. *Journal of Dairy Science*. 1933;(16):59-67. In Chester Roadhouse and James Henderson. *The Market Milk Industry*, second edition. McGraw-Hill, Company, New York, New York 1950, 49.
21. Ensminger, title page.
22. Jensen, SK. Quantitative secretion and maximal secretion capacity of retinol, beta-carotene and alpha-tocopherol into cows'milk. *Journal of Dairy Research*. 1999;66(4):511-22.
23. www.just-food.com/news_detail.asp?art=54999. Accessed August 22, 2003.
24. Ostrom, MR, and Buttel, FH. In Their Own Words: Wisconsin Farmers Talk about Dairying in the 1990s. *PATS Research Report No. 3*. January 1999, 1-43. Published by the Program on Agricultural Technology Studies (PATS), College of Agricultural and Life Sciences, University of Wisconsin, Madison.
25. Berry, Wendell. *The Unsettling of America*. Sierra Club Books, 1986, 1997, 234.
26. www.opensecrets.org/dairy. Accessed April 25, 2003.
27. www.oligopolywatch.com/2004/09/12.html. Accessed November 18, 2008; Zamiska, Nicholas. How Milk Got A Major Boost By Food Panel. *Wall Street Journal* (Eastern Edition). August 30, 2004.
28. www.reuters.com/article/pressRelease/idUS108905+05-Sep-2008+PRN20080905. Accessed November 18, 2008
29. *Midwest Dairy Association Update*. March 2008.
30. http://80-global.factiva.com.proxygw.wrlc.org/ (Land O'Lakes, Inc.). Accessed June 11, 2003.
31. www.mycattle.com/news/dsp_national_article.cfm?storyid=7057. Accessed August 22, 2003.
32. http://80-global.factiva.com.proxygw.wrlc.org (Foremost Farms USA, Cooperative). Accessed June 11, 2003.
33. http://80-global.factiva.com.proxygw.wrlc.org/ (Dairy Farmers of America, Inc.). Accessed June 11, 2003.
34. http://80-global.factiva.com.proxygw.wrlc.org/ (Dean Foods). Accessed June 11, 2003.

## Chapter 12: Modern Milk

1. Chen, Edwin. *PBB: An American Tragedy*. Prentice-Hall, Inc. Englewood Cliffs, New Jersey, 1979, xi-xii.
2. Chen, 4-32.
3. Chen, 38-60.
4. Chen, 91-110.
5. Nebert, Daniel, and Shertzer, Howard. *Interface: Genes and the Environment*. Issue Number 14, Spring, 1998. The Center for Environmental Genetics, University of Cincinnati, 1-2.

6.  Chen, 311-313.
7.  Ryan CA and others. Massive outbreak of antimicrobial-resistant salmonellosis traced to pasteurized milk. *Journal of the American Medical Association.* 1987;258:3269.
8.  Ryan, 3272.
9.  Ryan, 3273.
10. Ryser, Elliot. Public health concerns. In: Marth E, Steele, J, eds. *Applied Dairy Microbiology.* New York, NY, Marcel Dekker, Inc. 2001, 280.
11. Ryser, 280-281.
12. Ryser, 282-283.
13. Ryser, 283.
14. Ryser, 307-308.
15. Ryser, 308.
16. Ryser, 309-310.
17. Ryser, 311.
18. Kaneene JB, Ahl AS. Drug residues in dairy cattle industry: epidemiological evaluation of factors influencing their occurrence. *Journal of Dairy Science.* 1987;70:2176.
19. Ryser, 312.
20. Ryser, 310.
21. Epstein, Samuel S. Unlabeled milk from cows treated with biosynthetic growth hormones: a case of regulatory abdication. *International Journal of Health Services* 1996;26,(1):173.
22. Lloyd, Richard, and Forsey, Helen. *Natural Life.* Issue 63, Sept.-Oct. 1998. Internet publication, accessed at www.life.ca/nl/66/nobgh.html on December 6, 2002.
23. Lloyd and Forsey, p 66.
24. Epstein, 174.
25. Pappa, V. and others. Insulin-like growth factor-1 receptors are overexpressed and predict a low risk in human breast cancer. *Cancer Research* 1993;53:3736-3740. In Epstein, 180.
26. Epstein, 183.
27. Possible Link Between Johne's Disease and Crohn's Disease? Internet publication, accessed at www.hooah4health.com/environment/johnes.htm on July 9, 2003. This site is sponsored by the US Army Office of the Surgeon General, the US Army Center for Health Promotion and Preventive Medicine, the Army National Guard, and the Office of the Chief, Army Reserve.
28. Gutnecht, Kurt. Dire Warnings About Johne's Disease—a wake-up call for the dairy industry? *Wisconsin Agriculturist.* December 2002. Accessed at www.moomilk.com/archive/nutrition-16.htm on July 9, 2003.
29. Quoted in Gutnecht.
30. Quoted in Gutnecht.
31. Green, Emily. Is Milk Still Milk? In the name of safety, our most ancient food has been changed almost beyond recognition. *Los Angeles Times.* August 2, 2000
32. Addis, Paul. *Food and Nutrition News.* March/April 1990, 62:2:7-10.
33. Jennings IW. *Vitamins in Endocrine Metabolism.* Heineman, London, UK, 1970.
34. www.msnbc.msn.com/id/26827110/, accessed November 18, 2008.

## Chapter 13: Lactose Intolerance and Modern Milk

1.  Harrison, Gail. Primary adult lactase deficiency: a problem in anthropological genetics. *American Anthropologist* 1975;77:812-835.
2.  Jiang T and Savaiano DA. In Vitro Lactose Fermentation by Human Colonic Bacteria Is Modified by *Lactobacillus acidophilus* Supplementation. *Journal of Nutrition* 1997127:1489-1495; Tannock GW. *Normal Microflora: An Introduction to Microbes Inhabiting the Human Body.* Chapman & Hall, London, 1995, p 105.
3.  http://www.realmilk.com/documents/LactoseIntoleranceSurvey.doc, accessed January 10, 2009.
4.  Kretchmer, Norman. Lactose and Lactase. *Scientific American* 1972;227:70-78.
5.  Kretchmer, 77-78.
6.  Simoons, Frederick. Primary adult lactose intolerance and the milking habit: a problem in biologic and cultural interrelations, II. A cultural historical hypothesis. *The American Journal of Digestive Diseases* Aug 1970;15(8):695-710.
7.  Savaiano DA and others. Lactose malabsorption from yogurt, pasteurized yogurt, sweet acidophilus milk, and cultured milk in lactase-deficient individuals. *American Journal of Clinical Nutrition* Dec 1984;40:1219-1223.
8.  http://www.realmilk.com/documents/LactoseIntoleranceSurvey.doc, accessed January 10, 2009.

## Chapter 14: Homogenization and Heart Disease

1.  Selitzer, Ralph. *The Market Milk Industry.* Magazines for Industry, New York, New York, 1976, 173.
2.  Selitzer, 173-177.
3.  Selitzer, 176-177.
4.  Dawkins H, Oster K and Ross D. *The XO Factor.* Park City Press, New York, New York, 1983, 4.
5.  Selitzer, 7.
6.  Selitzer, 10.
7.  Oster K and Ross D. The Presence of Ectopic Xanthine Oxidase in Atherosclerotic Plaques and Myocardial Tissues. *Proceedings of the Society for Experimental Biology and Medicine.* 1973.
8.  Dawkins H, Oster K and Ross D. *The XO Factor.* Park City Press, New York, New York, 1983, 44.
9.  Selitzer, 46.
10. Oster K, Oster J, and Ross D. Immune Response to Bovine Xanthine Oxidase in Atherosclerotic Patients. *American Laboratory.* August, 1974, 41-47.
11. Rzucidlo S and Zikakis J. *Proceedings for the Society of Experimental Biology and Medicine* 1979; 160: 477-482.
12. Enos W and others. Coronary Disease Among United States Soldiers Killed in Action in Korea. *Journal of the American Medical Association* 152:1090-1093.

13. I am indebted to Mary Enig, PhD, for her analysis in this section. This information first appeared in *Wise Traditions*, quarterly journal of the Weston A. Price Foundation, Washington, DC, Summer 2003, 41-42.

14. Ross DJ, Sharnick SV and Oster KA. Liposomes as proposed vehicle for the persorption of bovine xanthine oxidase. *Proceedings for the Society of Experimental Biology and Medicine* 1980:163;141-145.

15. Clifford AJ, Ho CY and Swenerton H. Homogenized bovine milk xanthine oxidase: a critique of the hypothesis relating to plasmalogen depletion and cardiovascular disease. *American Journal of Clinical Nutrition*. 1983:38;327-332.

16. McCarthy RD and Long CA. Bovine milk intake and xanthine oxidase activity in blood serum. *Journal of Dairy Science* 1976:59;1059-1062.

17. Dougherty TM, Zikakis JP, Rzucidlo SJ. Serum xanthine oxidase studies on miniature pigs. *Nutrition Report International* 1977:16;241-248.

18. Ho CY, Crane RT, Clifford AJ. Studies on lymphatic absorption of and the availability of riboflavin from bovine milk xanthine oxidase. *Journal of Nutrition* 1978:108;55-60.

19. Bangham AD. Physical structure and behavior of lipids and lipid enzymes. *Advances in Lipid Research* 1963:1;65-104.

20. Ho CY and Clifford AJ. Bovine milk xanthine oxidase, blood lipids and coronary plaques in rabbits. *Journal of Nutrition* 1977:107;758-766.

21. Annand JC. Denatured Bovine Immunoglobulin Pathogenic in Atherosclerosis. *Atherosclerosis* 1986;59:347-351.

22. Annand JC. Further Evidence in the Case Against Heated Milk Protein. *Atherosclerosis* 1972;15:129-133.

23. www.foodsci.uoguelph.ca/dairyedu/homogenization.html, accessed May 28, 2002.

24. Spitsberg, VL. Invited Review: Bovine Milk Fat Globule Membrane as a Potential Nutraceutical. *Journal of Dairy Science*. 88:2289-2294, 2005; Stefferl A and others. Butyrophilin, a Milk Protein, Modulates the Encephalitogenic T Cell Response to Myelin Oligodendrocyte Glycoprotein in Experimental Autoimmune Encephalomyelitis. *Journal of Immunology* 2000, 165:2859-2865.

## Chapter 15: The Safety of Raw vs Pasteurized Milk

1    http://www.cfsan.fda.gov/~dms/rawmilqa.html#cure, accessed January 4, 2009.

2. Rogers Associates. *Fundamentals of Dairy Science*, 2nd Edition. Reinhold Publishing Co., New York, New York, 1935, 27, 281.

3. *The Drug and Cosmetic Industry* 1938:43:1.

4. *Indian Journal of Experimental Biology* 1998;36: 808-810.

5. *Indian Journal of Experimental Biology* 1998;36: 808-810; *British Journal of Nutrition* 2000;84(Suppl. 1.): S19-S25.

6. *Journal of Dairy Science* 1991;74:783-787.

7. *Indian Journal of Experimental Biology* 1998;36: 808-810; *British Journal of Nutrition* 2000;84(Suppl. 1.): S19-S25; *Life Sciences* 2000;66(25):2433-

2439; *Trends in Food Science & Technology* 16 (2005) 137-154.

8. Personal Communication, Ron Hull, PhD.

9. *British Journal of Nutrition* 2000;84(Suppl. 1):S11-S17;

10. Zimecki and Kruzel. *Journal of Expimental and Therapeutic Oncology* 2007;6(2):89-106.

11. *Journal of Experimental Medicine*, 2002 Dec 02;196(11):1507-1513.

12. *MSN-Mainichi Daily News*. April 11, 2007.

13. *FDA News*. August 22, 2004.

14. *Scientific American*. December 1995; *British Journal of Nutrition* 2000:84(Suppl. 1):S3-S10, S75-S80, S81-S89; personal communication, Ron Hull, PhD.

15. *British Journal of Nutrition* 2000:84(Suppl. 1):S3-S10, S75-S80, S81-S89

16. *British Journal of Nutrition* 2000:84(Suppl. 1):S3-S10, S39-S46; *Scientific American*. December 1995.

17. Isaacs CE. Human Milk Inactivates Pathogens Individually, Additively, and Synergistically. *Journal of Nutrition*. 2005 May;135(5):1286-8.

18. *Scientific American*. December 1995; *The Lancet* 17 Nov 1984;2(8412):1111-1113.

19. Personal communication, Ron Hull, PhD.

20. http://www.cfsan.fda.gov/~ear/milksafe/milksa44.htm, accessed January 4, 2009.

21. Zimecki M and Kruzel ML. Milk-derived proteins and peptides of potential therapeutic and nutritive value. *Journal of Experimental and Therapeutic Oncology* 2007;6(2):89-106. In *Response to the FDA*, http://realmilk.com/documents/SheehanPowerPointResponse.pdf, accessed January 4, 2009.

22. *Applied and Environmental Microbiology* 1982;44(5):1154-58; *Mikrobiyolji Bul* 1987:21(3):200-5

23. *Life Sciences* 2000;66(25):2433-9; *Indian Journal of Experimental Biology* 1998;36:808-10.

24. Mark McAfee, President, Organic Pastures Dairy, unpublished data. The tests were carried out by BSK Food & Dairy Laboratories (2002). Technicians inoculated raw colostrum and raw milk samples from Organic Pastures Dairy with three pathogens. Pathogen counts declined over time and in some cases were undetectable within a week. The laboratory concluded: "Raw colostrum and raw milk do not appear to support the growth of Salmonella, E. coli O157: H7 or Listeria monocytogenes."

25. Hutchinson DN and others. Evidence of udder excretion of Campylobacter jejuni as the cause of milk-borne campylobacter outbreak. *Journal of Hygiene* (Lond) 1985 94:205-15.

26. *Journal of Applied Microbiology*. 2003;95(3):471-8.

27. *Neonatal Network*. 2000 Oct;19(7)21-5.

28. *Journal of Hospital Infection*. 2004 Oct;58(2):146-50.

29. Personal communication, Ted Beals, MD.

30. *Advanced Experimental Medical Biology*. 2004;554:145-54.

31. *Advanced Experimental Medical Biology*. 2004;554:145-54.

32. *The Lancet*. 1984 Nov 17;2(8412):1111-1113.

33. *Central African Journal of Medicine*. 2000 Sep;46(9):247-51.

34. *European Journal of Pediatrics.* 2000 Nov;159(11):793-7.
35. *Archives of Disease in Childhood. Fetal and Neonatal Edition.* 2003 Sep;88(5):F434-5.
36. Pettifor JM and others. Mineral homeostasis in very low birth weight infants fed either own mother's milk or pooled pasteurized preterm milk. *Journal of Pediatric Gastroenterological Nutrition.* 1986 Mar-Apr;5(2):248-53.
37. Stein H and others. Pooled pasteurized breast milk and untreated own mother's milk in the feeding of very low birth weight babies: a randomized controlled trial. *Journal of Pediatric Gastroenterological Nutrition.* 1986 Mar-Apr;5(2):242-47.
38. Ford JE and others. Influence of the heat treatment of human milk on some of its protective constituents. *Journal of Pediatrics.* 1977 Jan;90(1):29-35.
39. http://www.cdc.gov/nczved/dfbmd/disease_listing/salmonellosis_gi.html, accessed January 4, 2009.
40. http://www.breastfeeding.com/advocacy/advocacy_recalls.html, accessed January 4, 2009.
41. *Morbidity & Mortality Weekly Report.* Mar 2, 2000:49(SS01);1-51.
42. Black RE and others. Epidemic Yersinia enterocolitica infection due to contaminated chocolate milk. *New England Journal of Medicine.* January 12, 1978; 298(2):76-79.
43. Segal, Marian. Invisible villains; tiny microbes are biggest food hazard. *FDA Consumer.* Jul-Aug, 1988.
44. Fleming DW and others. Pasteurized milk as a vehicle of infection in an outbreak of listeriosis. *New England Journal of Medicine.* 1985 Feb 14; 312(7):404-407.
45. Ryan CA and others. Massive outbreak of antimicrobial-resistant salmonellosis traced to pasteurized milk. *Journal of the American Medical Association,* 1987;258:3269-74. Two surveys to determine the number of persons who were actually affected yielded estimates of 168,791 and 197,581 persons, making this the largest outbreak of salmonellosis ever identified in the United States. Details of three outbreaks: 1984-AUG, 1 outbreak of S. typhimurium, ~200 cases; 1984-NOV, 1 outbreak S. typhimurium; 1985-MAR, 1 outbreak S. typhimurium, 16,284 confirmed cases
46. Centers for Disease Control and Prevention. Outbreak of Salmonella enteritidis Associated with Nationally Distributed Ice Cream Products--Minnesota, South Dakota, and Wisconsin, 1994. *Morbidity & Mortality Weekly Report.* 1994 Oct 14; 43(40); http://vm.cfsan.fda.gov/~mow/salice.html, accessed 28 May 2007
47. Robbins-Browne, R. Yersinia enterocolitica. In *Food Microbiology: fundamentals and frontiers,* (Eds) Doyle MP and others. Pp 192-215. ASM Press, Washington, D.C., USA.
48. Olsen, Sonja J and others. Multidrug-resistant Salmonella Typhimurium infection from milk contaminated after pasteurization. *Emerging Infectious Diseases* [serial on the Internet], 2004 May, available at http://www.cdc.gov/ncidod/EID/vol10no5/03-0484.htm, accessed May 28, 2007.
49. State of Colorado Laboratory Services Division 2005-2006 Annual Report, page 17, http://www.cdc.gov/foodborneoutbreaks/us_outb/fbo2005/2005_Linelist.pdf, accessed January 4, 2009.

50. Yuan, JW and others. Campylobacteriosis Outbreak Associated with Pasteurized Milk — California, May 2006. Epidemic Intelligence Service Conference 2007 (CDC), 2007 Apr 16; page 62. Available at http://www.cdc.gov/eis/conference/archives/EIS_program%20indd.pdf, accessed May 28, 2007.

51. *Associated Press*, January 8, 2008.

52. http://cspinet.org/new/pdf/outbreak_alert_2006_color.pdf, accessed January 4, 2009.

53. Tauxe RV. Emerging Foodborne Pathogens. *International Journal of Food Microbiology* 78(2002) 31-41.

54. Green, Emily. The great egg panic; new proposals rekindle the debate over eggs' safety. *The Los Angeles Times.* January 5, 2000.

55. Schlosser, Eric. *Fast Food Nation.* Houghton Mifflin Company, New York, New York, 2001, 197.

56. Schlosser, 263-264.

57. Schlosser, 197. Data from Nationwide Federal Plant Raw Ground Beef Microbiological Survey, August 1993-March 1994. United States Department of Agriculture, Food Safety and Inspection Service, Science and Technology, Microbiology Division, April 1996.

58. *Applied and Environmental Microbiology* 2001:67(12):5431-5436.

59. *Journal of Food Protection* 1999;62(7):805-7.

60. *Journal of Food Protection* 1998; 61(9):1161-1164.

61. *Applied & Environmental Microbiology.* Mar 1979; 37(3):559-566.

62. http://www.who.int/foodsafety/publications/fs_management/en/surface_decon.pdf, accessed January 9, 2009.

63. *Morbidity & Mortality Weekly Report.* Mar 2, 2000:49(SS01);1-51.

64. http://www.cfsan.fda.gov/~dms/spinacqa.html, accessed January 10, 2009.

65. http://seattletimes.nwsource.com/html/nationworld/2003524364_lettuce14.html, accessed January 10, 2009.

66. http://www.cfsan.fda.gov/~dms/spinacqa.html, accessed January 10, 2009.

67. http://www.montereycountyweekly.com/archives/2008/2008-Jun-19/e-coli-outbreaks-in-fresh-produce-coincide-with-the-push-for-volume-variety-and-yearround-supplies/1/@@index, accessed January 10, 2009.

68. *American Journal of Epidemiology.* 1983 Apr;117(4):475-83.

69. *Morbidity & Mortality Weekly Report* 2002 Jun 28;51(25):548.

70. http://www.realmilk.com/pr_071402.html, accessed January 4, 2009.

71. Mazurek J and others. A Multistate Outbreak of Salmonella enterica Serotype Typhimurium Infection Linked to Raw Milk Consumption – Ohio, 2003. *Journal of Food Protection.* 2004;67(10):2165-2170.

72. http://realmilk.com/ppt/index.html, page 21, accessed January 4, 2009.

73. Personal communication, Ted Beals, MD.

74. Thanks to Ted Beals, MD, for his expertise on raw milk testing and input into this section.

75. Dillon VM and Cook PE. Biocontrol of undesirable Microorganisms in Food. In *Natural Antimicrobial Systems and Food Preservation*, editors VM Dillon and RG Board, CAB International, UK.1994, pp255-296. Pitt WMand others. Investigation of the antimicrobial activity of raw milk against several foodbourne pathogens, *Michwissenschalf* 2000 55 (5) 249-252.

76. Personal communication, Ted Beals, MD.

77. The minimum infectious dose for various pathogens in various foods are published in the DFA "Bad Bug Book," posted at http://vm.cfsan.fda.gov/~mow/intro.html. The doses for *E. coli O157:H7* and *L. mono* are given as "unknown." Regarding the dose for *Campylobacter jejuni*, the document states, "Human feeding studies suggest that about 400-500 bacteria may cause illness in some individuals, while in others greater numbers are required."

78. Anonymous letter. *Wise Traditions in Food, Farming and the Healing Arts*, quarterly journal of the Weston A. Price Foundation. Fall, 2008, Vol9 No 3, page 6.

79. http://realmilk.com/documents/ResponsetoMarlerListofStudies.pdf, page 4, accessed January 10, 2009.

80. Taubes G. Do We Really Know What Makes Us Healthy? *New York Times Magazine*, September 16, 2007.

81 Linnan MJ and others. Epidemic listeriosis associated with Mexican-style cheese. *New England Journal of Medicine* 1988;29:319(13):823-8.

82. http://realmilk.com/documents/SheehanPowerPointResponse.pdf, p43.

83. Murthy GP and Cox S. Evaluation of APHA and AOAC Methods for Phosphatase in Cheese. *Journal of the Association of Official Analytical Chemists* 1988;71(6):1195-1199.

84. Geneix N and others. Development of a monoclonal antibody-based immunoassay for specific quantification of bovine milk alkaline phosphatase. *Journal of Dairy Research* 2007;74(3):290-5.

85. MacDonald PD and others. Outbreak of listeriosis among Mexican immigrants as a result of consumption of illicitly produced Mexican-style cheese. *Clinical Infectectious Disease.* 2005;40(5):677-82.

86. Intrepretive Summary – Listeria Monocytogenes Risk Assessment, Center for Food Safety and Applied Nutrition, FDA, USDHHS, USDA, Sept. 2003, page 17

87. http://www.fsis.usda.gov/OA/recalls/prelease/pr065-2000.htm, accessed January 11, 2009.

88. http://www.fsis.usda.gov/OA/news/2000/raeford.htm

89. http://www.cfsan.fda.gov/~ear/milksafe/milksa1.htm

90 Response to FDA powerpoint

91. http://www.foodsafety.ksu.edu/articles/384/RawMilkOutbreakTable.pdf, accessed January 11, 2009.

92. http://www.realmilk.com/documents/CDCReportSummary1998-2005.doc.

93. www.marlerblog.com

94. http://www.marlerblog.com/2008/06/articles/lawyer-oped/raw-milk-pros-review-of-the-peerreviewed-literature/, accessed Jaunary 5, 2009; http://www.marlerblog.com/2008/06/articles/lawyer-oped/raw-milk-cons-review-of-the-peerreviewed-literature/, accessed January 5, 2009.

95. http://www.about-ecoli.com/news/robeson2.htm, accessed January 10, 2009.

96. http://realmilk.com/ResponsetoMarlerListofStudies_.pdf

97. Schlosser, 219.

98. Schlosser, 202.
99. Schlosser, 219.
100. Ryser, 351-352.
101. Ryser, 348.
102. Ryser, 348.
103. Douglass, 84.
104. Ryser, 366.
105. Ryser, 366-367.
106. Werner SB and others. Association between raw milk and human Salmonella dublin infection. *British Medical Journal* 1979;2(6184):238-41.
107. Fierer, J. Invasive Salmonella dublin infections associated with drinking raw milk. *Western Journal of Medicine* 1983, 138:665-9.108.
109. Riemann HP and others. Toxoplasmosis in an infant fed unpasteurized goat milk. *Journal of Pediatrics* 1975 87:573-6.
110. Ryser, Elliot. Public health concerns. In: Marth E, Steele, J, eds. *Applied Dairy Microbiology*. New York, Marcel Dekker, Inc. 2001, 264.
111. Roadhouse C, and Henderson J. *The Market Milk Industry*. McGraw-Hill, New York, New York 1950, 60.
112. Milk Committee of the Canadian Public Health Association: Survey of Milk-Borne Diseases in Canada, 1912-1940 Incl. *Canadian Public Health Journal* Apr 1941;32(4):83-84. In Darlington, Jean Bullitt. Why Milk Pasteurization, Part I: Sowing the Seeds of Fear. *The Rural New Yorker*. March 15, 1947.
113. U.S. Public Health Service: Disease Outbreaks Conveyed Through Milk and Milk Products in the U.S., 1942, 1943, 1944. In Darlington, Jean Bullitt. "Why Milk Pasteurization, Part I: Sowing the Seeds of Fear. *The Rural New Yorker*. March 15, 1947.
114. U.S. Public Health Service: Summary of Milk-Borne Disease Outbreaks, 1923-1941. In Darlington, Jean Bullitt. Why Milk Pasteurization, Part I: Sowing the Seeds of Fear. *The Rural New Yorker*. March 15, 1947.
115. Frost, William Dodge. Some bacteriological problems of milk control. A paper delivered at the annual meeting of the American Association of Medical Milk Commissions, June, 1928.
116. Darlington, Jean Bullitt. Why Milk Pasteurization, Part I: Sowing the Seeds of Fear. *The Rural New Yorker*. March 15, 1947.
117. Tauxe RE. Emerging Foodborne Diseases: An Evolving Public Health Challenge. *Emerging Infectious Diseases* Oct-Dec 1997, Vol 3, No 4.
118. Ryser, 318.
119. Ryser, 321-322.
120. McIntyre LJ and others. Escherichia coli O157 outbreak associated with the ingestion of unpasteurized goat's milk in British Columbia. *Canadian Communicable Disease Report* 2001 28:6-8.
121. Scholosser, 195.
122. http://www.doh.wa.gov/hws/doc/EH/EH_FS.doc; http://www.cspinet.org/foodsafety/outbreak/outbreaks.php?mainsearch=&sort=states&dir=DESC&letter=l, accessed January 4, 2009.
123. http://www.fda.gov/fdac/departs/1999/199_irs.html, accessed January 11, 2009.
124. http://realmilk.com/washington-lessons-learned.html, accessed January 10, 2009.

125.http://www.aafp.org/afp/20060915/991.html, accessed January 11, 2009.
126. *Morbidity & Mortality Weekly Report* 2006 Sep26;55:1-2; http://www.cfsan.fda.gov/~dms/spinacqa.html, accessed January 5, 2009.
127. http://www.montereycountyweekly.com/archives/2008/2008-Jun-19/e-coli-outbreaks-in-fresh-produce-coincide-with-the-push-for-volume-variety-and-yearround-supplies/1/@@index, accessed January 9, 2009.
128. http://realmilk.com/ppt/index.html, slides 37-38, accessed January 10, 2009.
129. Intrepretive Summary – Listeria Monocytogenes Risk Assessment, Center for Food Safety and Applied Nutrition, FDA, USDHHS, USDA, Sept. 2003, page 17
130. http://realmilk.com/documents/SheehanPowerPointResponse.pdf, page 49, accessed January 10, 2009.
131. Bravo G. Raw Milk Safety. *Wise Traditions in Food, Farming and the Healing Arts*, quarterly journal of the Weston A. Price Foundation. Spring 2008, Vol 9, No 1, page 7.
132. Green E. The Great Egg Panic: New proposals rekindle the debate over eggs' safety. But some scientists say the fears are overblown. *Los Angeles Times.* January 5, 2000, http://articles.latimes.com/2000/jan/05/food/fo-50795, accessed January 10, 2009.
133. *Ibid.*
134. *Ibid.*
135. *Ibid.*
136 Korlath JA and others. A point-source outbreak of Campylobacteriosis associated with consumption of raw milk. *The Journal of Infectious Diseases* Sep 1985;152(3):592-596.
137. Blaser MJ and others. The influence of immunity on raw milk-associated Campylobacter infection. *The Journal of the American Medical Association* Feb 1987;257(1):43-46.
138. Jordan, Edwin Oakes. The Bacteriology of Milk and Milk Products. *Textbook of General Bacteriology*, Chapter 40, 1936.
139. Diez-Gonzalez F and others. Grain feeding and the dissemination of acid-resistant Escherichia coli from cattle. *Science.* Sep 11, 1998; 281:166-168.
140. Koopman JS and others. *American Journal of Public Health* 1984, 74:12:1371-1373.

## Chapter 16: Raw Milk and Children

1. "Feeding raw milk to your infant is abusing the child." LeLeiko N and others. Nutrition in Infancy and Childhood. In *The Mount Sinai School of Medicine Complete Book of Nutrition*. Victor Herbert Ed. St. Martin's Press, New York, New York, 1990, p 208.
2. http://www.cfsan.fda.gov/~acrobat/rawmilk3.pdf, accessed January 4, 2009.
3. *Archives of Pediatrics.* 1926 Jun; 43:380
4. *Archives of Pediatrics.* 1929; 46: 85

5. Fisher RA and Bartlett S. *Nutrition Abstracts and Reviews.* Oct 1931;1:224. In Krauss WE and others. Studies on the nutritive value of milk, II: The effect of pasteurization on some of the nutritive properties of milk. *Ohio Agricultural Experiment Station Bulletin* 519, Jan 1933,8.

6. Kramer MM and others. A comparison of raw, pasteurized, evaporated and dried milks as sources of calcium and phosphorus for the human subject. *Journal of Biological Chemistry.* 1928;79::283-290. In *Ohio Agricultural Experiment Station Bulletin* 519, January 1933, 8.

7. *The Lancet* May 8, 1937:1142.

8. Thomson, James C. Pasteurized Milk, A National Menace: A Plea for Cleanliness. *The Kingston Chronicle.* Edinburgh, Scottland, 1943, 5.

9. Erf O. *History of Randleigh Farm*, 4th Edition, Wm R. Kenan, Lockport, New York, 1942, 265.

10. Mercer JM. An experiment in milk pasteurization. *Nature's Path.* March 1941. In Bryant CP. *The Truth About Pasteurization.* Published by the National Nutrition League, Seattle, Washington, 1943.

11. Mattick EC and Golding J. *The Lancet.* Mar 22, 1931, 667.

12. Mattick EC and Golding J. *The Lancet.* Sep 19, 1936, 703-704.

13. *Jersey Bulletin* 1931 50:210-211;224-226, 237.

14. Lozoff B and others. Preschool-Aged Children with Iron Deficiency Anemia Show Altered Affect and Behavior. *Journal of Nutrition* 137:683-689, March 2007.

15. Bahrs AM and Wulzen R. *Certified Milk* 1941;16:5, 6, 8.

16. Bahrs AM and Wulzen R. Proceedings of the American Physiology Society. Chicago, Illinois. *American Journal of Physiology.* 1941. In Darlington.

17. http://realmilk.com/ppt/index.html, pp 59-60, accessed January 12, 2009.

18. Oski, Frank. *Don't Drink Your Milk.* Teach Services, Inc., Brushton, New York, 1983, 1996, 3.

19. Oski, 22.

20. Oski, 62.

21. Scott, FW. Cow milk and insulin-dependent diabetes mellitus: is there a relationship? *American Journal of Clinical Nutrition.* 1990;51: 489-491.

22. Oski, 20-21.

23. Oski, 21-22.

24. Oski, 23-24.

25. Oski, 62.

26. Oski, 62-63.

27. Oski, 63.

28. Riedler J and others. Exposure to farming in early life and development of asthma and allergy: a cross-sectonal survey. *The Lancet.* 2001 Oct 6;358(9288):1129-33.

29. Perkin MR and Strachan DP. Which aspects of the farming lifestyle explain the inverse association with childhood allergy? *Journal of Allergy and Clinical Immunology.* 2006 Jun;117(6):1374-81.

30. Waser M and others. Inverse association of farm milk consumption with asthma and allergy in rural and suburban populations across Europe. *Clinical & Experimental Allergy.* 2007 May; 35(5) 627-630.

31. Wang X, Parsons CM. Effect of raw material source, processing systems, and processing temperatures on amino acid digestibility of meat and bone meals. *Poultry Science.* 1998 Jun;77(6):834-41.
32. Hess AF. Infantile scurvy: its influence on growth. *The American Journal of Diseases of Children.* Aug 1916, 152-165.
33. Hess AF. Infantile scurvy: a study of its pathogenesis. *The American Journal of Diseases of Children* Nov 1917, 337-353.
34. Bell, RW. The effect of heat on the solubility of the calcium and phosphorus compounds in milk. *Journal of Biological Chemistry* Jun 1925;64(2):391-400.
35. Darlington, Jean Bullitt. Why Milk Pasteurization, Part II: Plowing Under the Truth. *The Rural New Yorker.* May 3, 1947, p. 4-5.
36. Ducher R and others. *Journal of Dairy Science* 1934;17: 455 . In Lewis, LR. The relation of the vitamins to obstretics. *American Journal of Obstetrics and Gynecology.* May 1935;29(5)759-765.
37. Meyer PR. *The history and analysis of certified milk.* Master's thesis, University of Georgia, 1979, 80-82.
38. Riddell WH and others. *Journal of Nutrition.* 1936;11:47-54.
39. Hess AF. Recent advances in knowledge of scurvy and the antiscorbutic vitamin. *Journal of the American Medical Association* Apr 23, 1932;98:1429-1433.
40. Woessner WW and others. The determination of ascorbic acid in commercial milks. *Journal of Nutrition* Dec 1939;18(6):619-626.
41. Overstreet, RM. *Infantile scurvy.* Northwest Medicine Jun 1938;37(6):175.
42. *Proceedings of the National Nutrition Conference for Defense* May 1941, Federal Security Agency, p. 176; U.S. Government Printing Office, 1942. In Darlington, 5.
43. Rajakumar. *Pediatrics* 2001;108(4):E76.
44. Adolfsson O. Yogurt and gut function. *American Journal of Clinical Nutrition.* 2004;80:245-56
45. Wheeler and others. *Journal of Dairy Science.* 1983;66(2):187-95.
46. Gregory. *Journal of Nutrition* 1982, 1329-1338
47. Ford JE and others. Influence of the heat treatment of human milk on some of its protective constituents. *Journal of Pediatrics.* 1977 Jan;90(1):29-35.
48. Stein H and others. Pooled pasteurized breast milk and untreated own mother's milk in the feeding of very low birth weight babies: a randomized controlled trial. *Journal of Pediatric Gastroenterological Nutrition.* 1986 Mar-Apr;5(2):242-47; Andersson Y and others. Pasteurizatin of mother's own milk reduces fat absorption and growth in preterm infants. *Acta Paediatrica* 2007;96:1445-1449.
49. Hollis and others. *Journal of Nutrition* 1981;111:1240-1248.
50. Said and others. *American Journal of Clinical Nutrition* 1989;49:690-694; Runge and Heger. *Journal of Agricultural and Food Chemistry.* 2000 Jan;48(1):47-55.
51. Grohman, Joann. *Keeping A Family Cow.* Coburn Press, Dixfield, Maine, 2001 (first published in 1975 as *The Cow Economy*), 42.
52. Carlton L and Brauninger M. Heat-Killed Bacteria's Role in Inducing an Innate Immune Response and Its Possible Link to Autism. www.redflagsweekly.com/medical_review/2003_mar13.html, accessed on March 12. 2003.

53. Carlton L and Brauninger M. Letter to Dr. Joseph Mercola in Pasteurized Milk and its Link to Autism, Part I. www.mercola.com/2003/Jul/2/pasteurized_milk.htm, accessed July 23, 2003.

## Chapter 17: The Magic of Fermented Milk

1. Rosell JM. Yogurt and kefir in their relation to health and therapeutics. Historical notes. *Canadian Medical Association Journal* 1932;26:341-345. In Hunter, Beatrice Trum. *Yogurt, Kefir & Other Milk Cultures*. Keats Publishing, New Canaan, Connecticut, 1973, 25.
2. Hunter, 25-29.
3. Rosell JM. The nature of fermented milks. Historical notes. *Canadian Medical Association Journal* 1932;26:341-345. In Hunter, Beatrice Trum. *Yogurt, Kefir & Other Milk Cultures*. Keats Publishing, New Canaan, Connecticut, 1973, 29.
4. Connolly SJ. *The Oxford Companion to Irish History*. Oxford University Press, 1998. In Fallon, 88.
5. McLauglin, Terence. *A Diet of Tripe*. David and Charles Publishers,London, UK, 1978. In Fallon, 87.
6. Georgakas, Dan. *The Methuselah Factors*. Academy Publishers, Chicago, Illinois, 1995, 15.
7. Torey JA. Some famous centenarians. *Scientific American*. Apr 1930, 304-305.
8. Schmid, Ron. *Traditional Foods Are Your Best Medicine*. Healing Arts Press, Rochester, Vermont, 1997, 12-16. First published in 1986, Ocean View Publications, Stratford, Connecticut. Also published as *Native Nutrition*. Healing Arts Press, 1994, 54-65.
9. Consumers All. *USDA Yearbook*. 1965, 414. In Hunter, 4-5.
10. Seneca, Harry and others. Bactericidal properties of yogurt. *American Practitioner and Digest of Treatment* Dec 1950;1(12)1252-1259. In Hunter, 6.
11. Tatochenko VK. Protein Advisory Group of the United Nations System, 1972;2:34; abstracted in *Dairy Council Digest* Jul-Aug 1972;43(4):22. In Hunter, 6.
12. Dupuis Y. Fermented milks and utilization of inorganic constituents. *International Dairy Federation Annual Bulletin* 1964;43(3):36-37, 39-41. In Hunter, 6.
13. Smorodina VS. Riboflavin in milk and sour milk products of southern Takzhikistan. *Izv. Aka. Nauk. Tedzh*. SSR. Otd. Biol. Nauk, 1962;1:118-122; abstracted in *Chemical Abstracts* Sep 16, 1963;59(6). In Hunter, 7.
14. Pulyatov RP and others. Vitamin B12 in mare's milk and in koumiss. *Sb. Tr. Uz. Nauchn.-Essled. Inst. Tuberkuleza*, 1961;5:186-188; abstracted in *Chemical Abstracts* Dec 9, 1963;59(12). In Hunter, 7.
15. Seneca, Harry and others. Bactericidal properties of yogurt. *American Practitioner and Digest of Treatment* Dec 1950;1(12)1252-1259. In Hunter, 6.
16. Seneca and others. In Hunter, 8.
17. Seneca and others. In Hunter, 8.
18. A WHO Team in Mongolia. *WHO Chronicle* February 1965;19(2):70. In Hunter, 9.

19. Tatochenko. In Hunter, 9.
20. Larue A. *Journal of Dairy Science* 1972;34:395; abstract in *Dairy Council Digest*. Jul-Aug 1972;43(14):22. In Hunter, 9.
21. *Let's Live*. September 1972. In Hunter, 9-10.
22. Seneca and others. In Hunter, 10.
23. Fykow A and Mayer J. *Nutrition Abstract Reviews* 1940-41;10:162; abstracted by Seneca. In Hunter, 10.
24. Bryan AH and Bryan CA. Nature's gastrointestinal antibiotics. *Drug and Cosmetic Industry* Mar 1959, pp. 308-309. In Hunter, 10-11.
25. Grenet H and others. *Bulletin of the Society of Pediatrics* 1939;37:411. In Hunter, 12.
26. *The Lancet* Feb 2, 1957. In Hunter, 14.
27. Ferrer FP and Boyd LJ. Effect of yogurt with prune whip on constipation. *American Journal of Digestive Diseases* Sep 1955;22(9):272-273. In Hunter, 14-15.
28. *Modern Nutrition*. May 1965, 5. In Hunter, 15.
29. Antibiotic interactions. *Journal of the American Medical Association*. Jul 10, 1972. In Hunter, 15.
30. Shapiro S. Control of antibiotic-induced gastrointestinal symptoms with yogurt. *Clinical Medicine* Feb 1960;7(2). In Hunter, 15.
31. Lichtenstein J. Lactobacillus acidophilus and herpetic gingivostomatitis. *Journal of Oral Therapeutics and Pharmacology* 1964;1:308. In Hunter, 15-16.
32. Seneca and others. In Hunter, 10.
33. Fallon, Sally. *Nourishing Traditions: The Cookbook That Challenges Politically Correct Nutrition and the Diet Dictocrats*. NewTrends Publishing, Washington, DC, 2000, 89-90. Nourishing Traditions includes a thorough review of the history of lacto-fermented foods and a wide variety of recipes.
34. Haemmerli UP and others. *Disease of the Month*. Year Book Medical Publication, July 1966; abstracted in Lactose Intolerance. *Dairy Council Digest* Nov-Dec 1971;42(6). In Hunter, 17.

## Chapter 18: Whole, Raw, Grass-Fed is Best

1. Weaver, John D. *Carnation: The First 75 Years, 1899-1974*. The Carnation Company, Los Angeles, California, 1974, front piece.
2. Schulberg, Jay. *The Milk Mustache Book*. Ballantine Books, New York, New York 1998.
3. http://www.peta.org/feat/caldairy/index.html, accessed January 11, 2009.
4. Horizon milk carton, 2000.
5. Pollan, Michael. The organic-industrial complex: All about the folks who brought you the organic TV dinner. *The New York Times Magazine*. May 13, 2001, 30.
6. Pollan, 32
7. www.horizonorganic.com/products/indexmilk.html, accessed January 11, 2003.

8. For example, see the production description at http://bluefireethanol.com/technology/, accessed January 15, 2009.
9. *Stockman Grass Farmer*, June 2008, page 28.
10. Anonymous communication.
11. Price, Weston A. *Nutrition and Physical Degeneration.* The Price-Pottenger Nutrition Foundation, La Mesa, California, 1945 (first published in 1939), 433.
12. Price, 444.
13. Price, 459.
14. Price, 443.
15. Masterjohn C. On the Trail of the Elusive X Factor. *Wise Traditions in Food, Farming and the Healing Arts*, quarterly journal of the Weston A. Price Foundation. Spring 2007, Vol 8, No 1, pp 14-32.
16. Geleijnse JM and others. Dietary Intake of Menaquinone Is Associated with a Reduced Risk of Coronary Heart Disease: The Rotterdam Study. *Journal of Nutrition.* 2004; 134: 3100-3105.
17. Dhiman TR, Nanad GR and others. Conjugated linoleic acid content of milk from cows fed different diets. *Journal of Dairy Science* 1999;82(10):2146-2156.
18. Dhiman TR. Cattle fed grain any time in life may have lower meat CLA. *Stockman Grass Farmer* August 2002, pp. 1, 5, 6.
19. Offer, Nick. Effects of cutting and ensiling grass and individual cow variation on levels of CLA in bovine milk. Food Systems Division, SAC, Auchincruive, Scotland. In Flack.
20. Robinson, Jo. *Why Grassfed is Best.* Vashon Island Press, Vashon, Washington, 2000, 19-20.
21. Robinson, 22.
22. http://www.hsus.org/farm/news/ournews/marks_dairy_farm_manure_spill.html, accessed January 6, 2009.
23. http://fmmac2.mm.ap.org/polk_awards_dying_to_work_html/Dyingto-Work-Calif.html, accessed January 6, 2009.
24. Rales, M. An Inconvenient Cow. *Wise Traditions in Food, Farming and the Healing Arts*, quarterly journal of the Weston A. Price Foundation. Spring 2008, Vol 9, No 1, pp 16-23.
25. http://farm.ewg.org/farm/progdetail.php?fips=06000&progcode=dairy&page=, accessed January 11, 2009.

## Chapter 19: Raw Milk Today:

1. Youatt. *Breeds of Cattle.* In Hartley, Robert M. *An Historical, Scientific and Practical Essay on Milk as an Article of Human Sustenance.* J. Leavitt, New York, New York, 1842, 65-66.
2. *Canadian TV News.* Black market for raw milk growing in Canada. December 18, 2002. www.ctv.ca, accessed January 7, 2003.
3. www.magma.ca/~ca/rawmilk/sale.htm, accessed January 7, 2003.
4. The erosion of constitutional freedoms has been ably described by Michael Pollan in his book *The Botany of Desire*. While most Americans would agree that marijuana should not be available to children and perhaps not even to

adults, the so-called "War on Drugs" has been used as an excuse to demonize a substance until recently many considered harmless.

Pollan writes that in the late 1970s, President Jimmy Carter "proposed that marijuana be decriminalized (his sons and even his drug czar smoked), and Bob Hope was telling benign jokes about doobies in prime time. Marijuana then was harmless, funny, and, it seemed to everyone, on the verge of social acceptance.

"In the years since, there has been a sea change concerning cannabis in America. By the end of the decade the plant had suddenly acquired, or been endowed with, extraordinary new powers. A couple of facts will illustrate the change: The minimum penalty for the cultivation of a kilogram of marijuana in Connecticut has, since 1988, been a mandatory five-year jail sentence. (Other states are harsher still: growing any amount of marijuana in Oklahoma qualifies a gardener for a life sentence.)"

The demonizing of marijuana has occurred concurrently with that of raw milk, and it is not unreasonable to consider the possibility that if the authorities have their way in passing proposed legislation, producers and distributors of raw milk will be incarcerated. Consumers caught illegally securing raw milk for themselves and their families could easily be forced to testify against producers. After all, while pot may make a heroin or cocaine addict out of you, according to the government, raw milk can kill you, or your innocent child. Draconian laws for raw milk violators may well follow the marijuana model, as we have already seen in Canada. Given the lessons of the past twenty years and the current political climate in the US, it would be a mistake to underestimate the determination of the American authorities to impose their will. Corporate crooks of the Enron stripe hobnob with presidents and at worst receive suspended sentences or a few months in a country-club-like minimum-security facility. Meanwhile, marijuana growers and even users spend years in state and federal prisons doing hard time. Mr. Pollan writes, "More drug arrests are for crimes involving marijuana than any other drug, nearly 700,000 in 1998, 88 percent of them for possession. Marijuana cases account for most of the asset forfeitures that law enforcement budgets have come to rely on. Marijuana is the primary focus of drug prevention efforts in the schools, drug testing in the workplace, and public service advertising about drugs."

The radical changes taking place in the legal system could as easily be applied to individuals involved with raw milk as they have been to those involved with marijuana. As noted above, Canada already has a law that can sentence a farmer to three years in jail for giving away raw milk. And the enforcers know there's nothing like a few good examples to put teeth into a law.

Pollan summarizes what the US government has done to the constitutional freedoms of all Americans in the last twenty years in the following paragraphs:

"What a dissenting Supreme Court justice in 1988 deplored as a new 'drug exception to the Constitution' has been substantially based on marijuana cases. For example, in Illinois v. Gates (1983) the Supreme Court carved broad new exceptions to the Fourth Amendment right against unreasonable searches, as well as the Sixth Amendment right to confront one's accusers. The venerable principle of *posse comitatus*, which holds that the armed forces of the United States cannot be used to police U.S. territory, has been suspended during the war against marijuana, notably by President Reagan, who deployed troops to rout out growers in northern California. The First Amendment has suffered as well: magazines aimed at pot growers have been harassed and, in one case (Sinsemilla Tips), raided and closed down [could this book be seized?]. In 1998 the federal government threatened to revoke the license of California doctors who exercised their First Amendment right to talk to patients about the medical benefits of marijuana [will doctors legally be free to recommend raw milk?]. Also that year, Congress ordered the District of Columbia not to count the votes of its citizens in a referendum on medical marijuana [a ballot referendum on raw milk could meet the same fate]. Arguably, the war against cannabis has also eroded the Sixth Amendment right to a jury trial (since drastic mandatory minimum sentences force most marijuana defendants to accept plea bargains) as well as the presumption of innocence (since asset forfeiture allows the government to seize assets without proving guilt) [might a dairy farmer caught selling or giving away raw milk have his farm seized?].

"Remove the twenty million or so Americans who use marijuana, and we are left with a 'drug abuse epidemic' involving roughly two million regular heroin and cocaine users—a public health problem, to be sure, but serious enough to justify spending $20 billion a year (or modifying the Bill of Rights)?"

The point is not to make any particular argument about the merits or detriments of marijuana (though Pollan notes that the plant was considered one of the most useful medicinal herbs in the physician's pharmacoepia until it fell from grace in the early 1900s). Rather, it is imperative to recognize the erosion of what have historically been considered basic American freedoms. Full enforcement of compulsory pasteurization laws could easily be as draconian as full enforcement of the marijuana laws has been.

These, then, are the guns that will be trained on the producers and consumers of raw milk if legislation proposed by medical authorities, the dairy industry, and federal and state public health officials becomes the law of the land.

Mr. Pollan writes regularly for the *New York Times Sunday Magazine* (three cover stories in 2001 and 2002), teaches journalism and tends to his garden in rural Connecticut. He certainly grows no marijuana, reporting that he planted a few seeds as an experiment in the early eighties, but by then "I no longer smoked at all—pot, fairly reliably, rendered me paranoid and stupid." Once a week he makes a trip to Local Farm to purchase his raw milk, fresh from Deb Tyler's grass-fed Jersey cows.

5.  Myers, Mary. CSA farm and center for sustainable living—Guidestone Alliance offers raw milk dairy. *The Stockman Grass Farmer* May 2000;57(5):17.
6.  Personal communication with David Lynch. January 29, 2003.
7.  www.guidestonefarm.com

8.  Wightman, Tim and Martin, Gleta. The MilkDirect™ program: its effects on us and our local community. *Wise Traditions in Food, Farming and the Healing Arts*, published by the Weston A. Price Foundation, Washington, DC, Spring 2001;2(1):64-65.
9.  Wightman, 64-65
10. Wightman, Tim and Martin, Gleta. The MilkDirect™ program: its effects on us and our local community. *Wise Traditions in Food, Farming and the Healing Arts*. Summer 2001;2(2):62.
11. Wightman, Tim and Martin, Gleta. Report from Wisconsin: the MilkDirect™ Program. *Wise Traditions in Food, Farming and the Healing Arts*. Fall 2001;2(3):62.
12. Fallon, Sally. Real Milk Updates—good news and bad news. *Wise Traditions in Food, Farming and the Healing Arts*. Spring 2002;3(1):63.
14. Fallon, Sally. RealMilk Updates—good news and bad news. *Wise Traditions in Food, Farming and the Healing Arts*. Spring 2002;3(1):60-61.
15. Fallon, Sally. Real milk Updates: Victory in Wisconsin. *Wise Traditions in Food, Farming and the Healing Arts* Winter 2002;3(4): 57.
16. http://www.magma.ca/~ca/rawmilk/, accessed January 28, 2003.
17. Fallon, Sally. Real milk Updates: Victory in Indiana. *Wise Traditions in Food, Farming and the Healing Arts*. Winter 2002;3(4):56.
18. Editorial. Report from Michigan. *Wise Traditions in Food, Farming and the Healing Arts*. Winter 2001;2(4):62.
19. Fallon, Sally. Real milk in Canada: The Incredible Story of Michael and Dorothea Schmidt. *Wise Traditions in Food, Farming and the Healing Arts*. Summer 2001;2(2):58-65.
20. England: Statutory Instrument, 1995, No. 1086. The Dairy Products (Hygiene) Regulations, Schedule 4, Regulations 9(2), (4) (b) and 13 (1) (b) (iv) and (vi). Accessed at www.hmso.gov.uk/si/si1995/Uksi.
21. Copus, Richard. Real Milk is Alive and Well in England. *Wise Traditions in Food, Farming and the Healing Arts*. Winter 2001;2(4):61-62.
22. Bell, Bruce and Fallon, Sally. RealMilk Updates—Good News and Bad News: Australia. *Wise Traditions in Food, Farming and the Healing Arts*. Spring 2002;3(1):61-62.

# Index

Ron Schmid has practiced as a licensed naturopathic physician in Connecticut since the early 1980s. A graduate of the Massachusetts Institute of Technology and the National College of Naturopathic Medicine, Dr. Schmid has taught at all four American accredited naturopathic medical schools. He served as the first Clinic Director and Chief Medical Officer at the University of Bridgeport College of Naturopathic Medicine in 1999 and 2000. His first book, *Traditional Foods Are Your Best Medicine*, was published in 1987 and remains in print today.

Dr. Schmid maintains an active practice, seeing patients at his Watertown, Connecticut home and providing phone consultations for clients throughout the country. He is a regular contributor to holistic health publications such as *Wise Traditions in Food, Farming and the Healing Arts*, the quarterly publication of the Weston A. Price Foundation, and serves on the Foundation's honorary board. He is also the founder and owner of a small company that makes additive-free nutritional supplements, Dr. Ron's Ultra-Pure.

Dr. Schmid's life took a dramatic turn when he contracted Lyme disease in the summer of 2002. "I learned what it was like to be really sick; for two or three weeks I could barely move," he says. "I had to ask myself what I'd been doing wrong, and make some major adjustments. I was determined not to take antibiotics, and I didn't. You might say I've taught my body to live with Lyme successfully. Raw milk has been one of the keys to my recovery."

In April of 2003, Dr. Schmid bought a thirteen-acre farm near Watertown, Connecticut, where he and his partner Ellen enjoy taking care of their two cows, their small flock of chickens and pet turkeys, their fruit trees, raspberry bushes and asparagus patch.